The Politics of German

Protestantism

The Politics of German Protestantism

The Rise of the Protestant Church Elite in Prussia, 1815-1848

Robert M. Bigler

UNIVERSITY OF CALIFORNIA PRESS

BERKELEY LOS ANGELES LONDON

University of California Press
Berkeley and Los Angeles, California
University of California Press, Ltd.
London, England
Copyright © 1972, by
The Regents of the University of California
ISBN: 0-520-01881-8
Library of Congress Catalog Card Number: 77-142055
Printed in the United States of America
Designed by Dave Comstock

To my Parents

To my Parents

Contents

Preface

Together with the army, the bureaucracy, and the royal House of the Hohenzollerns, the established Protestant church in Prussia was one of the cornerstones of traditional Prussian-German society. Although Luther did not identify secular with ecclesiastical government, under pressure by the princes he tolerated the extension of political authority into religious affairs. Consequently the "territorial church," in which the territorial ruler acted as the highest bishop (*summus episcopus*), became the normal type of the visible Protestant church in the German states.[1]

The historical role of the Protestant church in the nineteenth and twentieth centuries demonstrated the vitality of the authoritarian tradition in German Protestantism. In the political crises of 1819,

---

1. Among noteworthy studies I would like to refer the reader to the works by Schnabel, Hintze, Meinecke, Rosenberg, Conze, Shanahan, Droz, Fischer, Holborn, Ritter Craig, Krieger, Pflanze, Hamerow, Epstein, Huber, Foerster, Kupisch, Schoeps, and Kissling, and to the more recent work by Koselleck, all of which are listed in the Bibliography.

Especially relevant to this study are Franz Schnabel's *Deutsche Geschichte im neunzehnten Jahrhundert* (in particular the fourth volume, *Die religiösen Kräfte*, pp. 279–577); William O. Shanahan, *German Protestants Face the Social Question: The Conservative Phase, 1815–1871;* and Fritz Fischer's essays "Der deutsche Protestantismus und die Politik im 19. Jahrhundert," *Historische Zeitschrift,* 171 (1951), 473–518, and "Die Auswirkungen der Reformation auf das deutsche und west-europäisch-amerikanische politische Leben," in F. K. Schumann, ed., *Europa in evangelischer Sicht* (Stuttgart, 1953), pp. 37–52.

1848, 1862, 1871, 1881, and 1918, the Protestant state church of Prussia identified itself with the defense of the authoritarian system of rulership based on inherited privilege. Even during the Nazi regime the great majority of its clergy was politically obedient because "the idea of authority was stronger than the idea of freedom." [2] While this interpretation is basically correct with regard to developments after the failure of the Revolution of 1848, only in a qualified sense does it apply to the three or four decades just preceding. In his masterful account of the "religious forces" in the German states during the first half of the nineteenth century, Franz Schnabel has drawn attention to the political pluralism of German Protestantism in this period, and also the prominent French historian Jacques Droz has stressed that "ideological disunity" in the so-called pre-March period, from 1815 to 1848, was "religious before it was political or social," and that "radicalism first assumed a theological character." [3] In view of the terrible tragedies that befell Germany and the whole world in the twentieth century, a reassessment of the significance of the Protestant church and its clergy promises to throw needed new light on modern German history.

This book examines the conservative, liberal, and radical leadership of the Protestant clergy in Prussia from 1815 to the upheaval of 1848. By focusing on the political influence of the leaders of the most significant clerical factions and their allies, I hope to contribute to a better understanding of the rise of political Protestantism in modern Germany and, more particularly, of the political role which the Protestant church and its "officers" came to play in the Prussian-German sociopolitical system.

The Protestant clergy in Prussia, as it evolved during the dynamic period from 1815 to 1848, was a complex but numerically stable group numbering about 6,000. Collectively, the clergymen formed a special segment of the bureaucratized wing of the university-trained professional classes. As officially appointed and permanently employed members of the "ecclesiastical officers' corps" of the state church, they shared certain professional tasks, training prerequisites, and legal status characteristics. At the same time, they

2. Fischer, "Der deutsche Protestantismus," p. 516.
3. "Religious Aspects of the Revolutions of 1848 in Europe," in Evelyn M. Acomb and Marvin L. Brown, eds., *French Society and Culture Since the Old Regime* (New York, 1966), pp. 134–149.

differed among themselves in significant respects: in occupational function, position, and amount and sources of income; in personal ability, achievements, skills, and education; in career patterns, class origin, family tradition, and social ties; and, consequently, in their modes of living, tastes, attitudes, loyalties, beliefs, ideas, and interests. Their relations with other social, political, and economic groups and with formal governmental institutions vitally affected their views, leanings, activities, and influence. As will be shown, these complex differences contributed to the development of political factions with conflicting ideologies and interests within the ranks of the clergy.

The purpose of my study is first to show how the Protestant clergy of Prussia, politically submissive and socially docile and conformist under monarchical absolutism, was transformed under bureaucratic absolutism into a dynamic, self-willed, and highly influential professional group constituting a new political and social elite. (The term "elite," as I use it, refers to a minority of the most effective and responsive leaders of a group designated to serve a collectivity in a socially valued way.) I also hope to show how, under the conditions, incentives, and pressures in operation between 1815 and 1848, the clergy evolved into a politically conscious, articulate, and active, though theologically and ideologically disunited, group whose influence was exerted in contrasting directions. Finally, I shall attempt to explain why in 1848 the clergy of the state church presented an almost "united front" in opposing the transformation of Prussia into a constitutionally limited parliamentary regime. This period of Protestant clerical preeminence in politics was unique in Prussian-German history. It waned in the mid-1850's, never to return.

In my efforts to dissect the process of transformation and dynamic change in the state church, I have tried to indicate the relationship between the backgrounds, the religious and theological beliefs, and the aspirations, attitudes, careers, connections, and political ideas and activities of men who were not isolated individuals but leaders and characteristic representatives of groups in German society which comprised persons from all walks of life. Obviously, this approach to historical study does not imply that ideas and attitudes are simply the products of social, political, or economic conditions. Rather, it assumes that there is a complex relationship between material and nonmaterial factors in history, and that men can choose between alternatives and enjoy or suffer the consequences. Thus the Protestant leaders can be seen as participants in the political struggle whose outcome was to shape the new German Empire under Prussian leadership.

The book originated as a doctoral dissertation submitted to the University of California at Berkeley. In subsequent years it was greatly expanded in scope and completely reworked to include the results of much further research. An earlier and much shorter version of chapter i was published in *Church History*, 34 (December, 1965), as "The Rise of Political Protestantism in Nineteenth Century Germany: The Awakening of Political Consciousness and the Beginnings of Political Activity in the Protestant Clergy of Pre-March Prussia." Some of the material in chapter ii was used in the preparation of a paper on "Professors and Politics in Modern Germany: A Study of Protestant Theology Professors in Pre-March Prussia," delivered at the Sixtieth Annual Meeting of the Pacific Coast Branch of the American Historical Association, at Stanford University, California, on August 30, 1967.

My debts to individuals and institutions are many. I wish to express my special gratitude to the following.

Professors Hans Rosenberg, Eric Bellquist, Paul Seabury, and Carl Schorske of Berkeley gave me inspiration, encouragement, and invaluable guidance while I was a graduate student. Their teaching, generous advice, and incisive comments and criticisms have helped me to think more clearly about German history and German politics.

I am very grateful to Professor William B. Slottman, also of Berkeley, who read an earlier version and offered valuable suggestions.

The late Professor Klaus Epstein of Brown University read the manuscript and helped immensely to improve the quality of chapter i.

Professors Lewis W. Spitz of Stanford University and Donald G. Rohr of Brown University were extremely kind in drawing my attention to problems concerning the interrelationship between religion and politics in German history. I am very grateful for their criticism and suggestions, expressed in response to my article in *Church History*.

Professor Hans Joachim Schoeps and Dr. Hellmut Diwald at the University of Erlangen took a kind interest in my project. They invited me to participate in the Seminar für Religions- und Geistesgeschichte in 1966, helped me locate important materials, and placed at my disposal the Gerlach family archives.

Professor Karl Kupisch of the Kirchliche Hochschule, Berlin, was most helpful with essential information concerning the Protestant church. He not only drew my attention to archival material, especially in Berlin, but also made available for me the source materials of his institution.

The late Bishop Otto Dibelius of Berlin graciously allowed me the use of his substantial source collections relating to the Wittenberg Seminary. Discussions with him helped me to clarify various aspects of the traditional role of the Protestant church in Prussian-German history.

Dr. Kurt Scharf, acting bishop of Berlin in 1966, gave me access to the materials in the Archiv des Evangelischen Konsistoriums Berlin-Brandenburg and assisted me in every possible way to locate information relevant to my work. Archivist Dr. Gerhard Fischer spent many hours patiently guiding me, answering my inquiries, and helping me to find source material.

Mrs. Anna Halfmann kindly permitted me to read the original copies of several letters of Rothe, Neander, and Heubner acquired by her late husband, Bishop Halfmann of Kiel.

In Germany, the officers of the Staatsbibliothek der Stiftung Preussischer Kulturbesitz (formerly the Preussische Staatsbibliothek) in Berlin and Marburg, the Deutsche Staatsbibliothek in Berlin, the Bundesarchiv in Koblenz, the Bayrische Staatsbibliothek in Munich, the Hamburg Staats- und Universitätsbibliothek, the Bremen Staatsbibliothek, the Literatur-Archiv des Instituts für deutsche Sprache und Literatur of the Deutsche Akademie der Wissenschaften in Berlin, and the libraries of the universities of Erlangen, Marburg, Tübingen, Munich, Bonn, and Berlin have helped in every possible way with their resources. In the United States, the libraries of the University of Chicago, Harvard University, and the University of California, and of the Pacific School of Religion and the Starr King

School for the Ministry, both of Berkeley, have similarly put me in their debt.

I wish to express my sincere appreciation to Jesse M. Phillips, the editor of the manuscript for the University of California Press. His editorial skills and interest in the subject matter were essential for the successful completion of the work.

The Woodrow Wilson Foundation, the Institute of Social Science at the University of California in Berkeley, and the Faculty Research Grants Committee at Idaho State University provided generous financial support for my efforts. Professor David E. Miller, chairman of the Department of History at the University of Utah, provided secretarial assistance for the typing of the main draft of the manuscript. I am also grateful to Professor Andrew C. Tuttle, chairman of the Department of Political Science at the University of Nevada, Las Vegas, for providing additional secretarial help.

The editors of *Church History* have kindly permitted the reprinting of parts of an article which I wrote originally for that journal.

Miss Marie Cornwall has cheerfully typed and retyped the original manuscript. I am greatly indebted to Mrs. Trudy Mattson for typing the final draft and to Mrs. Helga Brown for typing the bibliography.

For the shortcomings of the book, none of the persons or institutions named above bears any responsibility. What merits it may have are due in large part to their assistance and cooperation.

Part One

Introduction

I

The Awakening of Political Consciousness and the Beginnings of Political Activity

The religious cleavage introduced by the Reformation further complicated the old dilemma of German history. Ever since the breakdown of the power of the medieval emperors, particularist forces had been able to thwart the rebuilding of a central German authority. Whereas in England, France, and Spain the advent of the modern era brought about the emergence of closely knit national states, in Germany national unity was not achieved until 1871, and while most European countries became predominantly Protestant or Catholic, Germany remained almost evenly divided between the two denominations, although it was the birthplace of the Protestant revolt.

The North German state of Brandenburg-Prussia arose from the consolidation of three separate, heterogeneous areas at the beginning of the seventeenth century: Brandenburg in the center of the North German plain, between the Elbe and Oder Rivers; East Prussia on the shore of the Baltic Sea, between Lithuania and Poland; and the districts of Cleves, Mark, and Ravensberg in the Rhine-Ruhr region of western Germany. The House of Hohenzollern, which had ruled the principality of Brandenburg since 1417, extended its rule over Cleves and the other western areas in 1614 and over East Prussia in 1618 upon the failure of heirs in collateral lines, but at first maintained a personal union only, without a common administration, common army, or uniform political institutions.

The objective of successive Hohenzollern princes was to weld the separate territories into a single, centralized state and to establish their contiguity by annexing the German and Polish territories between Brandenburg and Cleves, Mark, and Ravensberg in the west and East Prussia in the east. The consolidated but geographically still separated lands became the Kingdom of Prussia after the Hohenzollerns secured the royal crown in 1701. The European importance of this realm was shown in the Seven Years' War (1756–1763), when it won a decisive victory over the combined forces of Austria, Russia, and France. In the eighteenth and nineteenth centuries the areas which separated the central, eastern, and western parts were finally annexed. Prussia became the nucleus of the new German Empire in 1871 and continued to play a crucial role in German politics until its dissolution by the Allied Military Government in 1947.

Brandenburg and its capital, Berlin, formed the core of the Prussian state. There developed the political, military, and social institutions that were gradually extended over Cleves, East Prussia, and subsequent conquests. Brandenburg was primarily a land of big estates where landowning nobles—the Junkers—held sway over dependent serfs and stubbornly defended their local privileges, including the selection of the local clergymen (*Patronatsrecht*). East Prussia, originally the land of the crusading Teutonic Knights, was also dominated by a Junker oligarchy which did not confine itself to the ruling of its estates. In accepting the rule of the Hohenzollerns, the Junkers of Brandenburg and East Prussia acquired the privilege of staffing the army officer corps and the higher administrative offices, both of which became European bywords for efficiency, economy, and integrity.

The emergence of the Protestant Hohenzollern monarchy, and above all the successes of Prussia, impressed upon the rest of Germany a set of values, traditions, and ideals that eventually came to be accepted as being universally German. The special position of the army's officer corps, the enormous role played by the noble squirearchy of the Junkers, the supremacy of the military over the civil—all these characteristic features of later Germany bore witness to the triumph of the Prussian spirit.

The beginnings of a nationalist spirit in Germany toward the end of the eighteenth century coincided with the emergence of the Prussian state as a great power. The German national movement was confronted by the rivalry between the Protestant Hohenzollern monarchy, with its predominantly German subjects, and the empire of the Catholic Habsburgs, where non-German elements formed the majority of the population. As a result of the Napoleonic Wars, both the old imperial structure of the Holy Roman Empire and the Confederation of the Rhine, created by Napoleon, disappeared. After 1815, the German Confederation was set up, consisting of thirty-nine sovereign states loosely joined. Prussia—with its territory greatly enlarged after the defeat of Napoleon—and the Austrian Habsburg monarchy were the chief members.

Although Prussia's gradual acquisition of Silesia, West Prussia, Posen, and the Rhenish and Westphalian territories added considerable numbers of Catholics to its population, the Hohenzollern monarchy still retained its predominantly Protestant character.

From the time of the Reformation, the Protestant territorial rulers in Germany had considered themselves Christian authorities with both temporal and spiritual functions. They were protectors as well as servants of the church. A separate body, the Consistory, was set up in each state to govern the church. The ruler usually took no action in respect to the church without first consulting the Consistory; he was very deferential in his relations with this ecclesiastical body.

As the rulers became more secular in outlook during the seventeenth and, especially, eighteenth centuries, they began to use rather than serve the church. The Consistory, which had been a body of men well versed in theology who directed the affairs of the church, was gradually transformed into just another arm of the state administration; the clergymen became agents of the rulers. The mingling of secular and ecclesiastical affairs was particularly characteristic of the Prussian administration in the eighteenth century. Although the actual business of church administration was still handled by the Consistory, ecclesiastical decisions at the highest level were made in the spiritual department of the central government. Frederick II (1740-1786) dealt with the church not as a mystical-religious body, but as a subordinate branch of the bureaucratic-military government. In 1794 the Prussian law code (*Allgemeines Landrecht*) made canon law part of administrative law and treated the church as a corporation whose rights depended on the state.

In the sixteenth century, Lutheranism became the predominant faith in Brandenburg and East Prussia, and remained so, while a considerable part of the Cleves population adopted Calvinist doctrines. As the Prussian realm expanded, more Lutherans, Reformed, and other Protestants, and also Catholics and Jews, came under the rule of the Hohenzollerns. In 1613 John Sigismund, the Elector of Brandenburg, turned from the Lutheran faith to Calvinism. Thus the Hohenzollerns ceased to be of the same faith as the great majority of their subjects in Brandenburg and East Prussia. Consequently John Sigismund accompanied his adoption of the Reformed faith with the announcement that he would make no use of his right to impose it upon his subjects—*cujus regio, ejus religio*—and that all might enjoy religious freedom. This was a highly unusual example of toleration in an age of religious intolerance. From that time on, Prussia was a haven for persons fleeing oppression because of their religion. Related to the Hohenzollerns' practice of religious tolerance was their desire to increase the population and to strengthen the economy of their territories. Thus they invited Huguenots, Jews, Mennonites, Moravians, Hussites, and other religiously persecuted minorities to settle in Prussia, whose policy of religious freedom proved to be a tremendous political advantage in divided Germany. Much of the rise and success of Prussia as a great power was due to its ability to attract talent from practically all the German states and from other countries.

The Calvinist rulers of Prussia were particularly interested in lessening theological differences between the Lutheran and the Reformed Protestants. Obedience to the laws, loyalty to the state, and the inculcation of morally good attitudes toward fellow citizens were expected from all religious groups. Both the pious Frederick William I (1713-1740) and his rationalist successor, Frederick II, looked upon theological controversy as harmful and maintained strict supervision of the various denominations to prevent it. Frederick II showed great fairness toward Catholics, but did not allow papal interference with the exercise of his royal control over the Catholic church in Prussia. The assertion of exclusive sovereignty—which tolerated no independent church government alongside the government of the state—was naturally simple in the case of the Protestant denominations, over whom the highest spiritual authority was retained by the king. This authority was exercised, through the control of church appointments, to mold the teachings of the Protestant denominations. Theological differences between Lutheran and Reformed doctrines were played down, and by the end of the eighteenth century there seemed to be no serious opposition to a confessional union of the two denominations in the Prussian state.

The official duties of the Protestant clergy in Prussia were not confined to preaching, teaching, administering the sacraments, and caring for the religious and spiritual welfare of their parishioners. As agents of the government they were, in the course of time, assigned various administrative functions in the service of the dynastic state.[1] Concurrently (and notably during the periods of "one-man rule" under Frederick William I and Frederick II), the clergy came increasingly under strict state regulation of their training, appointment, and income, and of the details of their various functions, such as their conduct, dress, and mode of living.[2] Like all other groups of the *ständische Gesellschaft,* they had their clearly defined and rigorously enforced place in the hierarchic social and political order. A Protestant clergyman's main duty was to carry out the orders of the ruler faithfully and unquestioningly and thus assist him in the task of strengthening and consolidating the Prussian state. In principle, punishment for deviant behavior could be severe, and there were few who dared disobey openly. Two clergymen who criticized the harsh recruiting methods for the army under Frederick William I were immediately arrested and sent to Berlin to be deprived of ecclesiastical office. But so unusual was open opposition

1. Otto Hintze, "Die Epochen des evangelischen Kirchenregiments in Preussen," *Historische Zeitschrift,* 97 (1906), 68–69; this periodical is hereafter cited as *HZ.*

Ludwig Lehmann, *Bilder aus der Kirchengeschichte der Mark Brandenburg* (Berlin, 1924), p. 152, calls clergymen in the eighteenth century "police officials in robes" (*Polizeibeamte im Talar*).

2. Even the content and length of sermons were prescribed by the ruler. Lehmann, p. 134.

that the ruler did not insist on the dismissal of these men. Instead, they were officially reprimanded and sent to less desirable parsonages.[3]

The "enlightened" Frederick II was indifferent to religious dogma and hence inclined, even more than his pious predecessors, to emphasize the role of clergymen in public administration. Their duties as local field agents of the government included such tasks as planting trees, announcing royal decrees from the pulpit, teaching peasants how to cultivate the soil, and providing the public authorities with population statistics and information on weather conditions, crops, and floods.

Under Frederick William I and Frederick II the Protestant clergy was, in principle, completely subordinate to the personal will of these vigilant sovereigns. Written instructions to the Consistories regulated every aspect of the clerical office. All clergymen had to go to Berlin for periodic inspections, the so-called *Prediger-Revue,* where the president of the central church Consistory transmitted to them the royal orders and questioned them about conditions in their parishes.[4]

Theology professors constituted a special clerical group whose distinguished position as scholars had been recognized since the time of Luther and Melanchthon. Their functions of interpreting the doctrinal teachings of the Lutheran church, settling theological controversies, and training and examining prospective clergymen gave them a certain degree of prestige and also considerable power to influence the recruitment of church personnel. Although the absolutist rulers of Prussia in the eighteenth century had little respect for university professors generally, and often treated them with contempt,[5] theology professors benefited from the traditional Lutheran belief that the inculcation upon the laity of Christian obedience to worldly authorities was a highly important function. Under

3. *Ibid.,* p. 133.

4. J. H. F. Ulrich, ed., *Ueber den Religionszustand in den Preussischen Staaten seit der Regierungszeit Friedrichs des Grossen* (Leipzig, 1778), prints numerous letters and reports by clergymen about their work. For a discussion of their practical activities see Walter Wendland, "Die praktische Wirksamkeit Geistlicher im Zeitalter der Aufklärung," *Jahrbuch für Brandenburgische Kirchengeschichte,* 9 (1913), 24–86; the *Jahrbuch* is hereafter cited as *JBKG.*

5. The contentious attitude of Frederick II toward theology professors and other clergymen was shown, for instance, in his note on some suggestions of the Consistory: "Members of the Consistory are asses." Lehmann, p. 147.

monarchical absolutism, however, neither theology professors nor other members of the clergy were able to exert political influence in their own right as clergymen. A few exceptional individuals—such as Johann Christoph Wöllner (1732–1800), who became minister of ecclesiastical affairs and education under Frederick William II in 1788—managed to influence public policy directly, but they did so not as clergymen but usually as self-made bureaucrats who were ennobled by the king for their services. Wöllner's career seems to confirm the findings of Hans Rosenberg that only by finding their way "into the elite of wealth within the landed aristocracy" could men of non-noble background exert significant political influence in eighteenth-century Prussia.[6] Professors in other fields than theology were similarly held to be primarily useful for the achieving of obedience and efficiency.[7]

Most clergymen accepted their assigned role as loyal and diligent subjects. In accordance with the prevailing currents of opinion, they abstained from expressing views in conflict with the official norms.[8] In short, the Protestant clergy of the eighteenth century remained a thoroughly conservative group. The great stress which the Prussian rulers put on the utilitarian tasks of clergymen was reinforced in the latter half of the century by the growing influence of the teachings of theological rationalism, which emphasized moral and pedagogical responsibilities in the pursuit of "practical" and "progressive" tasks and maintained that man's rational faculty could

6. *Bureaucracy, Aristocracy, Autocracy: The Prussian Experience, 1600–1815* (Cambridge, Mass., 1958), pp. 123 f., 160 f.; hereafter cited as Rosenberg, *Bureaucracy*.

See also Robert R. Palmer, *The Age of the Democratic Revolution* (Princeton, 1959–1964), I, 405 ff. For Wöllner's actions see Klaus Epstein, *The Genesis of German Conservatism* (Princeton, 1966), pp. 142 ff., 356–368, 390 f.; hereafter cited as Epstein.

7. Adolf von Harnack, *Geschichte der Königlich Preussischen Akademie der Wissenschaften zu Berlin* (Berlin, 1900), I, 8–36; Frederick Lilge, *The Abuse of Learning: The Failure of the German University* (New York, 1948), pp. 2–3.

8. There were some conspicuous exceptions, such as the theologian Karl Friedrich Bahrdt (1741–1792) at the University of Halle, who in the course of the radicalization of the *Aufklärung* in the last decades of the eighteenth century dared to criticize aspects of the political and social system; he was jailed. Epstein, pp. 118–120; Fritz Valjavec, *Die Entstehung der Politischen Strömungen in Deutschland, 1770–1815* (Munich, 1951), pp. 25, 133, 135, 137, 144 ff.

For an explanation of the Aufklärung, as contrasted with the Anglo-French type of Enlightenment, see Epstein, pp. 32–35.

establish and secure a simple, true, and salvation-guaranteeing religion.[9] Accepting or passively following the teachings of theological rationalism, the clergy as a class upheld the conservative political outlook traditionally associated with Lutheranism.

The idea of absolute obedience to constituted authority was supplemented by affirmation of the hierarchic order of a society where each person pleased God by contentedly performing the duties of his appointed station. The lower clergy—the village pastors—lived far from comfortably, but their positions did not entirely lack status. The upper group—theology professors, superintendents, Consistory councilors, court preachers, and chief pastors of major churches— were a rather contented part of the upper bourgeoisie, with whom they harmonized in outlook, mode of life, and family responsibilities. They had few social contacts with the aristocracy, from whom they were separated by lack of blue blood and cavalier manner, but this was more an annoyance than a bitterly felt grievance. Although village pastors may have suffered from the gap between the upper clergy and themselves, from low salaries, from isolation that led to intellectual atrophy, and from their undignified situation under the system of noble patronage, they enjoyed some prestige in their communities and there was always hope that the next generation might do better. Harassed and dependent, they nevertheless tended to develop conservative and quietistic political and social views.[10]

In contrast to the lower clergy, who had little, if any, time for or interest in intellectual pursuits, members of the upper group considered themselves—and many actually were—the intellectual cream of society. This meant that they were not averse to expressing "advanced" theological opinions. These opinions proved frequently to be fully compatible with a conservative or even reactionary outlook on political and social questions, and those who expressed them, being valued (and therefore tending to value themselves) more for their worldly than their spiritual functions, became increasingly secularized in their outlook. Klaus Epstein, in his recent study, has concluded that secularism in the Protestant clergy meant a far-

9. Hans Rosenberg, "Theologischer Rationalismus und vormärzlicher Vulgär-liberalismus," *HZ*, 141 (1930), 497 ff.; hereafter cited as Rosenberg, "Theologischer Rationalismus."

10. L. Buchmueller, "Märkische Pfarrer und Pfarrhäuser im 17. und 18. Jahrhundert," *Tägliche Rundschau*, 91 (1901), 4; Christian Meyer, "Aus dem Lebensgang eines evangelischen Geistlichen im 17. und 18. Jahrhundert," *Zeitschrift für Kulturgeschichte*, 3 (1893), 16–28.

reaching acceptance of the values of the *Aufklärung* and an emphatic repudiation of mysticism, obscurantism, fanaticism, and the other "unenlightened" aspects of the Middle Ages and their alleged perpetuation in contemporary Catholicism and Pietism.[11]

The politically submissive role of the clergy was matched by their complacent belief that "enlightened" Protestantism stood in the vanguard of the world's progress. This attitude was fully compatible with a sincere horror of every kind of radicalism aimed at changing the established political and social order. Clergymen believed that the pace of progress must be set by educated, moderate, sensible men like themselves. There can be little doubt that, up to the French Revolution, the Protestant rationalist clergymen were predominantly a force for conservative reforms having "a tendency to preserve with an inclination to improve," seeking to "maximize continuity in institutions and ideas," and opposing forcible and rapid change.[12] Theological rationalism, which by the latter half of the eighteenth century had become the dominant theological current among clergymen, fitted in admirably with the concept of a rational state in which all individuals and institutions performed useful functions. Inevitably, as the administrative role of clergymen became more important, their emphasis on purely religious duties declined.[13]

Small, scattered groups of Pietists objected to the rationalists' neglect of the personal dimension of religion, and were preoccupied with sin, personal salvation, and renunciation of the world. They remained the "quiet people" (*die Stillen im Lande*).[14] For them, the

11. As Epstein points out, one must make a broad distinction between Aufklärung and Enlightenment—owing, among other factors, to the economic backwardness of Germany, resulting in a weak bourgeoisie, and to the long-standing national preoccupation with religious controversy. The Aufklärung was primarily concerned with religious questions, and its greatest figures—Lessing, Nicolai, Mendelssohn—were deeply interested in religious affairs but relatively indifferent to political and social questions. (Pp. 32–34, 57 f.) Neology, a theology compounded of traditional and enlightened views, would seem to reinforce this point.

12. *Ibid.*, pp. 8–10.

13. The clergyman Christian Krause, defending Frederick II's complete lack of interest in church services, flatly stated that the king and other government officials had more important duties than going to church. Walter Wendland, *Siebenhundert Jahre Kirchengeschichte Berlins* (Berlin and Leipzig, 1930), p. 192; hereafter cited as Wendland, *700 Jahre*.

14. For bibliographies of Pietism see Martin Schmidt and Wilhelm Janasch, eds., *Das Zeitalter des Pietismus* (Bremen, 1965), pp. 417–429, and Horst Weigelt, "Interpretations of Pietism in the Research of Contemporary German Church Historians," *Church History*, 39 (1970), 236–241. For the relationship of Pietism to the Aufklärung see Epstein, pp. 114 f.

Protestant territorial church of the eighteenth century—having been transformed into an instrument of state power—no longer sustained the intensely personal experience which was an integral part of the Lutheran religious spirit. The Pietists did not wish to break away from the church, but sought to reform it from within. Furthermore, they desired to purify the church not by wresting control of its structure from the rationalist clergymen but by changing the hearts of the congregation. Distrusting the rationalists because of their preoccupation with worldly functions, the "quiet people" clung to the old Lutheran concept of the "priesthood of all believers." Accordingly, in religious functions they emphasized the brotherhood of the "true believers" and did not draw a clear line between ordained clergymen and the laity. This blurring of lines between the ordained and the lay faithful had deep roots in the German Protestant tradition.[15]

The Pietists believed in educating the spirit through reading the Scriptures and quiet worship. They formed *collegia pietatis* (circles of piety) in order to educate the spirit. These little groups, in which laymen usually acted as leaders, read the Scriptures and participated in a kind of worship whose components of meditation, reflection, and prayer were similar to those of a Quaker meeting.

Along with the emphasis on quiet worship went a Puritan-like morality which could be as severe as that of the Massachusetts Bay Colony, but far more often was humbly abstemious rather than censorious and repressive. The philosopher Kant and the theologian Friedrich Schleiermacher (1768-1834) came from Pietist backgrounds, and their moral philosophy shows Pietist influence. Family life was very important to the Pietists, who demonstrated a tremendous loving quality in their families. Although, as in most German families, there was sternness of discipline, there was also great gentleness; moral rigor was combined with loving-kindness. The collegia pietatis were, in effect, enlarged families, devoted to Christ-like life.

There was in Pietism a streak of withdrawal which craved

Koppel S. Pinson clearly establishes the connection between Pietism and German nationalism in *Pietism as a Factor in the Rise of German Nationalism* (New York, 1934); hereafter cited as Pinson, *Pietism*.

15. See the essay "Klerus und Laien," in *Die Religion in Geschichte und Gegenwart* (1959), pp. 1661–1664; hereafter cited as *RGG*.

release from life, the great weariness. In the storms of life, the Pietists taught, the soul must keep calm and bear up as best it can. The composer Bach was saturated with this element of the Pietist spirit. Paradoxically, the Pietists also seemed to have a sense of profound engagement in the world. They did not feel that one was making his hard earthly pilgrimage alone and isolated; the pilgrimage was to be made with others.[16] Together, they hoped to change the world by leading exemplary lives of Christian virtue, not by overthrowing state or church.

The Pietists certainly had no intention of furthering the Aufklärung. Their basic preoccupation with the problems of sin and personal salvation was alien to modernity. Yet there were tendencies in Pietism which helped pave the way for the Aufklärung. The stress upon personal experience in religion made dogmatic differences appear unimportant. (The Aufklärung regarded such differences as ridiculous.) The direct contact between the Pietist and his God deemphasized the role of the officially ordained clergy. (Aufklärung thinkers often declared the clergy to be positively harmful.) The religious individualism of Pietism showed some external similarity to the "autonomous man" (idealized by the Aufklärung) who was freed from traditional corporate ties, whether secular or ecclesiastical. Because of their principles of respect for religious individuality and their situation as a barely tolerated religious minority, the Pietists were, moreover, firm champions of religious tolerance.

As time went on, the Pietists tended to lay more and more stress upon personal deportment; moralistic behavior became increasingly important. They emphasized *Sittlichkeit* (uprightness; a mixture of ethics and propriety; moral behavior in accordance with custom). Once the emphasis began to shift from a mystical personal relation with God to the moral behavior of the individual, the door was opened to philosophy and a rational morality could make headway. Eventually, Pietist uprightness could be stripped of its religiousness and become fused with a rational utilitarianism which related the good to the useful. Thus Pietism could become secular and join itself with the "enlightened" official culture. Primarily concerned with

16. See the comments by Schleiermacher in his *Soliloquies,* trans. H. L. Friess (Chicago, 1926), pp. 37, 51 f. For the mystical aspects of Pietism see Heinrich Bornkamm, *Mystik, Spiritualismus und die Anfänge des Pietismus im Luthertum* (Giessen, 1926).

grace, the Pietists valued practical conduct above theoretical dogma. Their conduct showed a strong bent toward humanitarian, charitable, and educational efforts, as in the Francke Foundation at Halle—originally founded by the Pietist theology professor August Hermann Francke (1666–1727) and subsequently enlarged with the help of pious donors in the course of the eighteenth and nineteenth centuries.

During the reign of the pious Frederick William I, Halle became the "New Jerusalem" of Pietism as a result of Francke's leadership. But the "enlightened" Frederick II, who succeeded to the throne in 1740, was indifferent to religion, and under his rule Pietism declined in the theological faculties of the universities. For almost a century after 1740 the University of Halle was dominated by theological rationalism. Because its faculty of theology trained the great majority of Protestant clergymen in Prussia until the late 1830's, generations of them were influenced by the teachings of theological rationalism. As a result, not only Pietist laymen but also the few Pietist clergymen were isolated "quiet voices" in the rationalist sea. In the last decades of the eighteenth century, when strong rationalistic, secularistic, and even irreligious tendencies became dominant in the Aufklärung, Pietism became an ingredient of the romantic movement and of emerging German nationalism, and eventually an ally of the counterrevolutionary forces opposing the "ideas of 1789." [17] In the face of the new secular trends, the Pietists began to look for support among orthodox Lutheran and aristocratic elements also threatened in the "age of the masses."

Stressing the equality of man before God, the Pietists in their collegia pietatis had already broken through traditional class barriers. At the end of the eighteenth century, however, they were still a barely tolerated minority. Outside their conventicles of "brothers and sisters in Christ"—as the few Pietist clergymen and the small groups of lay Pietists considered themselves to be—there was still very little social intercourse between nobles and non-nobles. Moreover, since the law of the Holy Roman Empire forbade the founding of new churches, and since most Pietists were satisfied to stay in the official church as long as they were allowed to cultivate their own

---

17. Pinson, *Pietism.* See also Jerry F. Dawson, *Friedrich Schleiermacher: The Evolution of a Nationalist* (Austin, Texas, 1966), hereafter cited as Dawson, *Schleiermacher.*

religious practices and associations, there was no strong movement among Pietists for separation from the organizational structure of the church.

Pietism had its origins among the upper bourgeoisie and the nobility, and especially had found early converts and patrons in the nobility of Saxony and Prussia. On the whole, these politically conservative groups retained the leadership of the movement. Separation was not in favor among them; rather, they looked to the government for protection. In the lower classes, among artisans and peasants, Pietism became more separatist, and sectarian enthusiasm and chiliasm could occasionally burst into the open. Only in Württemberg did Pietism gain and retain a large popular basis, and there, under the guidance of Swabian ministers, it lost all tendencies to separate from the official church.[18]

Although Pietism lost its foothold in the state-controlled schools and universities under Frederick II, it had a strong mainstay in the religious colony of Herrnhut in Saxony. Count Nikolaus Ludwig von Zinzendorf (1700–1760), one of the most remarkable Pietist leaders of the eighteenth century, had invited descendants of the persecuted fifteenth-century sect of the Bohemian Brethren to his estate, Herrnhut, and there, in 1722, he helped them constitute the denomination later known as the Moravian Brethren, or Herrnhuter.[19] Eventually, Herrnhut became a haven for persecuted Moravian Protestants fleeing the rule of the Catholic Habsburgs in their homeland, as well as a center for German Pietists and sectarians. Outwardly, the Herrnhut community was within the established Protestant church but Zinzendorf was essentially indifferent to confessional distinctions. He was willing to accept any Lutheran, Calvinist, Protestant sectarian, or Catholic who worshiped Christ. One of the foremost objectives of the Herrnhut life was to produce and maintain the sentiment in which the presence of God and man's relationship to Him were continually appreciated. Aside from private group meetings of laymen, the central cultic institution was the "singing

18. See the observations of Friedrich Nicolai in his *Sebaldus Nothanker* (Berlin, 1775), II, 75 ff., and *Beschreibung einer Reise durch Deutschland und die Schweiz im Jahr 1781* (Berlin, 1785), I, 603 ff.

For an early nineteenth-century account of mystical, revivalist meetings in Berlin see M. Kulke, *Gnadenführungen Gottes in dem Leben des Schulvorstehers Friedrich Samuel Dreger* (Berlin, 1860), pp. 90 ff.

19. See the article "Herrnhuter" in *RGG* (1957), pp. 1439–46.

hour," during which, in Quaker fashion, religious professions were heard and traditional or improvised hymns were sung. Moreover, the ceaseless harmony of the universe and of God and man found its expression in music which was heard everywhere at Herrnhut and at all times of the day. The community was governed by elders, and when new communities came into existence, a loose synodical organization was formed. So impressive were the dedication, moral earnestness, and Christian piety of the Moravian Brethren that eventually the widely scattered Pietistic groups and individuals began to look to them for advice and send their children to the educational institutions of the Moravians at Herrnhut, Niesky, and Barby. Schleiermacher and a number of other German idealists received their early education in schools maintained by the Brethren. Although theological rationalism was undoubtedly the dominant creed of the majority of the Protestant clergymen by the end of the eighteenth century, Pietism was still a potent force in German life. There was practically no representative of classic German idealism who was not impressed to some degree with Pietistic religion through contact with the Herrnhut community, with the Württemberg congregation, or—as in the case of Goethe—with individual Pietists.[20]

The mystical secret society of the Rosicrucian Order became a rallying center for conservative and obscurantist forces in Prussia during the reign of Frederick William II (1786–1797), who was himself a Rosicrucian. A fellow Rosicrucian, the aforementioned J. C. Wöllner, became the dominant figure in domestic affairs during most of these years. As minister of ecclesiastical affairs and education, Wöllner set out to destroy theological rationalism in the Lutheran church, the universities, and other educational institutions. He and those who shared his views wished to rescue Prussia from what they considered the chains of irreligion wrought by the agnostic Frederick II and his "enlightened" regime. Indifferent to religious dogma himself, Frederick II had insisted on religious toleration. Count Zedlitz, his minister of ecclesiastical affairs and education, had encouraged the spread of theological rationalism by appointing rationalists to positions in the universities, in the administration of the Lutheran church, and in the public schools. Wöllner and other politically conservative Rosicrucians decided that the government

20. Hajo Holborn, "Der deutsche Idealismus in sozialgeschichtlicher Beleuchtung," *HZ*, 174 (1952), 359 ff.

must protect Prussian subjects from the dangerous consequences of rationalism, which they suspected of encouraging ways of thinking subversive to the political and social order. Reversing the Prussian governmental policy of freedom for theology professors to interpret the doctrines of their religion, Wöllner in 1788 issued his Edict of Religion, which launched a campaign against rationalism by requiring clergymen to adhere strictly to the official creed in their sermons, on pain of immediate dismissal from their positions. In 1791 he established an official inquisitorial committee whose purpose was to examine professors and other clergymen as to their religious orthodoxy. Wöllner and his fellow Rosicrucians were alarmed by the French Revolution and its possible impact on Prussia, and considered it their duty to strengthen orthodox Lutheranism by destroying rationalism.[21] These efforts, however, were fiercely opposed by theology professors, high ecclesiastical officials, rank-and-file clergymen, and others adhering to rationalism, and the next king, Frederick William III (1797–1840), soon found himself compelled to allow the edict and the committee to fall quietly into desuetude—a clear indication of the strength of rationalism in the Lutheran church. Equally significant was the fact that the conservative Prussian government had felt compelled to take steps to defend traditionalist orthodoxy against the criticism of the rationalist Aufklärung. As Klaus Epstein has pointed out, the Edict of Religion and the ensuing controversy about its enforcement can be considered a "milestone in the history of German Conservatism because it became the first occasion when a conservative government felt it must argue its case before the court of public opinion." [22] As for the Protestant clergy, its essentially conservative character tended to be reinforced by the unsuccessful attempt of religious eccentrics to purge rationalists from the church and by the abandonment of the religious policy of the Rosicrucian regime of Frederick William II. Even so, although the controversy caused by the edict came at a time when the ideas of the French Revolution were forcing rationalists, Pietists, and orthodox Lutherans alike to reconsider their religious,

---

21. [G. Friedrich von Cölln], *Vertraute Briefe über die inneren Verhältnisse am preussischen Hofe seit dem Tode Friedrichs II* (Amsterdam and Köln, 1807), pp. 16 ff.; Epstein, p. 153.

22. For an excellent analysis of the edict and its consequences see Epstein, pp. 142 ff.

political, and social beliefs, it was not until the collapse of the Prussian state in 1806 and the rise of opposition to Napoleonic rule that elements of the clergy began to seize the initiative in the developing political struggle between conservative and liberal forces in state and church.[23]

The French Revolution—as a movement that transcended the borders of France—was injected into the life of the German people more immediately and more directly than into that of any other European nation. Of course, the German response, in its political aspect, was conditioned by the Revolutionary Wars and especially by Napoleon and his conquests. Its end result was the War of Liberation in 1813. German involvement with the French Revolution was predominantly concerned with the Napoleonic era. Taking the form of nationalist resistance, the struggle against the French became the fountainhead for the quickening of German national consciousness and feeling. Although political unification was still to wait for half a century, this struggle first made German intellectuals and political leaders acutely aware of the need for it.

Friction between revolutionary France and the German states, particularly Austria and Prussia, came about because of the sanctuary found by French *émigrés* on German soil and because of the abolition of the feudal and ecclesiastical jurisdictions by the revolution, which affected German holdings in Alsace. Prussia joined the first coalition against France in 1792. The Prussian armies suffered military defeats at Valmy, and the French troops who conquered the Rhineland were warmly received there by large sections of the German population. Prussia was anxious to have peace, and suspicion of Austria prevented the joint action against France that the situation demanded. In 1795 Prussia signed the separate Peace of Basel, giving France a free hand west of the Rhine and receiving in return compensations east of it. The Treaty of Campo Formio with Austria

23. R. F. Eylert, *Charakter-Züge und historische Fragmente aus dem Leben des Königs von Preussen, Friedrich Wilhelm III* (Magdeburg, 1843–1846), III, pt. 1, 69 f.; hereafter cited as Eylert.

The best treatment of the entire complex of problems created by the French Revolution in Germany is in Franz Schnabel, *Deutsche Geschichte im neunzehnten Jahrhundert,* 3d ed. (Freiburg im B., 1948–1955), Vol. I; hereafter cited as Schnabel.

For the literature of the period see the comprehensive bibliography in Koppel S. Pinson, *Modern Germany: Its History and Civilization,* 2d ed. (New York, 1966), pp. 622 f.; hereafter cited as Pinson, *Modern Germany.*

in 1797 recognized the cession of the entire left bank of the Rhine to France.

Napoleon's policy in Germany was to play off Prussia against Austria, isolating Austria and trying to throw enough crumbs to Prussia to keep her attached to France but not strong enough to dominate the rest of Germany. His policy toward the smaller states consisted of manipulating them at the expense of the larger. The destruction of the old Holy Roman Empire by Napoleon resulted in the serious weakening of Austria's position in Germany. A preliminary step was taken by the Diet of the Empire in 1803, when in a "final recess" it passed the so-called *Reichsdeputationshauptschluss,* whereby 112 estates of the Empire were wiped out, all the ecclesiastical states were dissolved except the Electorate of Mainz, the imperial knights were eliminated as independent sovereigns, and the number of free cities was reduced to six. All told, the number of sovereign states in the Empire was reduced to about thirty. The final blow came in 1806, when Napoleon forced Francis II to renounce the title of Holy Roman Emperor and become Francis I of Austria.

The first semblance of national unification in Germany was provided by Napoleon when he created the Confederation of the Rhine in 1806. Under his suzerainty Bavaria, Württemberg, Baden, Hesse-Darmstadt, and twelve smaller German states were united to form what Napoleon sometimes conceived of as a "Third Germany" to balance the states of Prussia and Austria. Subsequently the kingdom of Saxony entered the confederation, Hanover was occupied by Napoleon as part of his strategy against England, and the Rhineland was incorporated into the French Empire. In 1807, out of the states Hesse-Cassel and Brunswick, Napoleon created the kingdom of Westphalia for his brother Jerome.

Prussia's entrance into the war against Napoleon resulted in its most disastrous military defeat, at Jena on October 14, 1806, and the occupation of Berlin by Napoleon two weeks later. When this war was ended by the Peace of Tilsit in 1807, Prussia entered a period of what Germans have come to call "deep humiliation," which was at the same time a period of preparation and strengthening of economic, military, and spiritual resources for eventual liberation.

It was becoming apparent in the latter part of the eighteenth century that supervision and effective control of the increasingly complex administration of Prussia by the ruler in person would be impossible. Undoubtedly, developments from 1786 to 1812 carried forward and consummated the process of replacing the absolute monarch as the actual director of the administrative state apparatus by the most highly placed members of the administrative bureaucracy. Responding to the threat of complete dissolution of the state after Jena, the bureaucracy embarked upon a "revolution from above" to reshape the antiquated political and social structure. This "revolution" was identical with the short-lived Prussian Reform Era (1807–1819) in the course of which a few narrow but solid bridges were built over the old caste barriers. Even though the reforms opened an era of intense constitutional controversy which continued to agitate Prussian public life, there was no revolution against either absolute government or privilege as such.[24]

The War of Liberation in 1813, while bringing freedom from Napoleonic rule, relieved the rulers of Prussia from the practical necessity of making further political concessions to the middle classes, let alone the lower levels. Among the outstanding results of the substitution of bureaucratic absolutism for monarchical authority were the "strengthening of the authoritarian rule of both the bureaucratic elite and the landed aristocracy" and the mounting of a new conservative "counterrevolution from below"—the *ständische Reaktion*—by the Old Prussian Junker squirearchy. In their reactionary struggle against centralized absolutism and democratization in any form, the Junkers borrowed some of the ideas of political romanticism as expounded by Burke, Adam Müller, Friedrich von Gentz, Ludwig von Haller, and, finally, Friedrich Julius Stahl, the anti-Hegelian philosopher of Jewish background who became the most eminent Prussian conservative theorist.[25]

When, under the impact of Napoleonic statecraft and the military collapse in 1806, the Prussian Reformers began to recast the

24. Rosenberg, *Bureaucracy*, pp. 175–201; E. von Bülow-Cummerow, *Preussen: Seine Verfassung, seine Verwaltung, sein Verhältnis zu Deutschland*, 3d ed. (Berlin, 1842), pp. 187 f.

25. See the study by Hans Rosenberg, "Die 'Demokratisierung' der Rittergutsbesitzerklasse," in *Zur Geschichte und Problematik der Demokratie: Festgabe für Hans Herzfeld*, ed. Wilhelm Berges and Carl Hinrichs (Berlin, 1958), pp. 459–486. Characteristic comments of the Gerlach brothers and other members of the group are in Hans J. Schoeps, ed., *Aus den Jahren Preussischer Not und Erneuerung: Tagebücher und Briefe der Gebrüder Gerlach und ihres Kreises, 1805–1820* (Berlin, 1963), pp. 501 f., 511 f.; hereafter cited as Schoeps, *Tagebücher und Briefe der Gebrüder Gerlach.*

traditional system of government, matters of institutionalized religion were among their basic concerns. The reorganization and eventual merging of the Lutheran and Reformed denominations in an administratively and confessionally united Protestant state church, called the Evangelical Church of Prussia, marked the beginning of a new stage in the development of the Protestant clergy in Prussia. Although confessional unity of these denominations was not achieved until 1817, the Central Consistory and all the Lutheran Consistories, together with the Directory of the Reformed church and the Consistoire Supérieur of the French Reformed church, were abolished in 1808 and replaced by new provincial boards for ecclesiastical affairs and education (*Geistliche und Schuldeputationen*) under the control of a newly created section—the *Kultusabteilung*—in the Ministry of the Interior. In 1810, Ludwig Nicolovius (1767–1839), a close friend and associate of Stein, Schoen, Dohna, and other Reformers, became the director of the section. Although in 1817 the Kultusabteilung became a separate ministry—the *Kultusministerium* —under Altenstein, Nicolovius continued to direct the administrative and personnel policies of the Protestant state church until his death.[26]

More than any other government official, Nicolovius was responsible for the reorganization of the Protestant church in the Reform Era. His promotion was greatly helped by the recommendation of Count Alexander von Dohna, who assured the government that his friend Nicolovius was the best man for the task because of his firm Pietistic faith and administrative skill.[27] The pious bureaucrat Nicolovius was to play an important role in the politically significant ascendancy of a Neo-Pietist clerical faction which allied itself with a group of religiously "awakened" Old Prussian noblemen in opposition to the "ideas of 1789." As a young student in Königsberg, Nicolovius had studied theology and had been exposed to the influence of Pietistic circles whose members encouraged him to become a

26. Because the confessional union was achieved by executive order and not by mutual agreement, theological controversies continued for several decades and a number of so-called Old Lutheran congregations even separated themselves from the state church in the 1830's. Johannes B. Kissling, *Der deutsche Protestantismus, 1817–1917* (Münster i. W., 1917–1918), I, 14–20.

27. Erich Foerster, *Die Entstehung der Preussischen Landeskirche . . .* (Tübingen, 1905–1907), I, 171 ff.; hereafter cited as Foerster, *Entstehung*.

See also the excellent biography by Fritz Fischer, *Ludwig Nicolovius: Rokoko, Reform, Restauration* (Stuttgart, 1939), pp. 221 ff.; hereafter cited as Fischer, *Nicolovius*.

government official rather than an ordained clergyman of the rationalist-dominated Lutheran church. In accordance with the Pietist concept of clergymen—which acknowledged no sharp dividing line between ordained clergy and pious laymen (*Kirchenmänner*), and emphasized that every good Christian was to act as God's agent in whatever position Providence placed him—Nicolovius considered it his sacred duty to advance the "cause of God." When his dearly beloved wife, Lulu, a niece of Goethe, died in 1811, the still young Nicolovius vowed that he would never marry again and would instead devote his life to "furthering the cause of God." [28] His great opportunity arose during the Reform Era. Nicolovius's theological training, long experience as an efficient and trusted government official, and close connections with the Reformers made him, in 1810, the obvious choice to take charge of the reorganization of the administratively united Protestant church. In this post Nicolovius was also expected to prepare the clergy for its role in the task of defeating Napoleon and restoring Prussia as a great power.[29]

The memorandums that Nicolovius issued concerning the reorganization of the church provide a good insight into his ideas about the place of the church as an institution of the state. He rarely uses the term *Kirche;* usually he speaks of church institutions (*kirchliche Anstalten*) or a Protestant church system (*protestantisches Kirchenwesen*). These terms seem to refer to institutions which, along with schools, should serve the purpose of education by awakening the "religious sentiment" in the *"Publicum"* or in "the people" (*Volk*). This concept of the role of church institutions was used by Nicolovius after 1808 and especially after 1813.[30] In his view, "the church" as an institution did not exist apart from the state, and since it was the mystical body of Christ, comprising all pious Christians, men should not aim at setting up a constitution of the clergy (*Verfassung des geistlichen Standes*) or of clergymen (*Verfassung der Prediger*) within the Prussian state. A memorandum which Nicolovius sent to the king on March 29, 1810, clearly indicates that

28. Alfred Nicolovius, *Denkschrift auf Georg Heinrich Ludwig Nicolovius* (Bonn, 1841), pp. 24 ff.
Nicolovius was a close friend of Goethe and always stayed in his house when visiting Weimar. Otto Dibelius, *Das Königliche Predigerseminar zu Wittenberg, 1817–1917* (Berlin-Lichterfelde, 1917), p. 26; hereafter cited as Dibelius.
29. Fischer, *Nicolovius,* pp. 229 ff.
30. See, e.g., his letter to Hardenberg, February 2, 1811, *ibid.,* p. 248.

he did not perceive the relationship of church and state as a problem. He saw the state as honoring clergymen and giving them security and the dignity of office so that they could discharge their duty of furthering the religious spirit of the people.[31]

In Nicolovius there was the curious combination of the efficient, conscientious, and honest Prussian bureaucrat and the pious *Gefühlsmensch* who was fanatically devoted to his mission of the "furthering the cause of God"—that is, the Pietist effort to eliminate rationalism as a dangerous creed. His mystical and spiritualistic devotion did not know theology as a scholarly discipline (*Theologie der Wissenschaft*). For Nicolovius and his fellow Pietists, theology was not a critical approach to certain problems of faith, an attempt to understand, but a study of mysteries; by theological knowledge he meant insight into the "hidden wisdom" (*verborgene Weisheit*).[32] When one of his protégés, Franz Claudius, was studying theology at the newly founded University of Berlin, Nicolovius expressed serious concern that the "cold theological wind . . . and some forms of criticism" would hurt Claudius's real theology, meaning his piety, which was being exposed to new ways of looking at things.[33] These ideas of Nicolovius were shared by Baron Hans Ernst von Kottwitz (1757–1831) and members of his Berlin circle, which became a leading center of a Neo-Pietist "Awakening" in the 1810's and 1820's and was successfully promoting the alliance between "awakened" Old Prussian aristocrats and staunchly conservative clergymen.[34]

For Nicolovius, theologians were "men of the spirit, of seriousness and depth," who, instead of asking questions, told about the mysteries of religion by special reference to personal experiences. From the beginning of his career as director of the Kultusabteilung, Nicolovius hoped that he would be able to fill important positions in the reorganized Protestant church with "true believers." In a letter to the publisher Friedrich Perthes in 1810 he implored, underlining his words: "If you know of any *real* theologians . . . please

---

31. The memorandum is printed in Friedrich and Paul Goldschmidt, *Das Leben des Staatsraths Kunth,* 2d ed. (Berlin, 1888), pp. 184–186.

32. Nicolovius to Borowski, October 3, 1821, in Fischer, *Nicolovius,* pp. 374 f.

33. Nicolovius to Friedrich Perthes, July 21, 1820, *ibid.,* p. 374.

34. A significant part of the correspondence of Kottwitz with leading members of the Neo-Pietist "Awakening" is printed in F. W. Kantzenbach, ed., *Baron H. E. von Kottwitz und die Erweckungsbewegung in Schlesien, Berlin, und Pommern* (Ulm, Donau, 1963); hereafter cited as Kantzenbach, *Kottwitz.*

let me know. I am waiting for *new men.*" [35] Because the rationalist stronghold of the University of Halle had been training clergymen of rationalist views with emphasis on reason as the supreme authority in matters of religion and in life generally, Nicolovius knew that his mission to place suitably pious clergymen in positions would require helpers. Baron von Kottwitz and his circle were anxious to cooperate with Nicolovius and help him find some "real" theologians, especially for vacant positions in universities.

Nicolovius's condemnation of enlightened rationalism as the root of all evil, including the French Revolution and its subversive influence on the traditional order, was shared by many Reformers. To these men it was deeply disturbing that the great majority of Protestant clergymen in Prussia professed a creed which, in the words of Stein, "assured the poor, deceived, passion-scourged human race that it is free from original sin." [36] These words were characteristic of a way of thinking which held that "enlightened" thinking, by denying the basically sinful nature of man and the innate superiority of certain individuals and classes, had prepared the way for the French Revolution and the ensuing political, social, and economic changes. And, indeed, the teachings of the rationalists did have room for the idea that man could improve his status and develop a more just society, based on achievement and merit, by abolishing privileges based solely on the accident of birth and on tradition. In contrast, Pietism and orthodox Lutheranism tended to emphasize that the fallen and sinful nature of man was responsible for the injustice and suffering in the world, and thus, in the view of some historians, to divert man's concern from worldly to heavenly justice and make him more likely to accept the status quo as ordained by God.[37] So

35. February 19, 1810, in C. T. Perthes, ed., *Friedrich Perthes Leben* (Hamburg and Gotha, 1848–1855), II, 190; hereafter cited as *Perthes Leben*.

Perthes, of a very poor family, by hard work and honesty became a well-known and successful publisher. Through his business and his father-in-law, M. Claudius, a clergyman of literary talent, he was brought into contact with prominent figures all over Germany. Nicolovius was one of his best friends; the two carried on an extensive correspondence.

36. Letter to Heinrich von Gagern, March 3, 1831, in Georg Pertz, *Das Leben des Ministers Freiherrn vom Stein* (Berlin, 1855), VI, pt. 2, 137. For Gagern's comments see Heinrich C. E., Freiherr von Gagern, *Mein Anteil an der Politik* (Stuttgart, 1833), IV, 304 f.

37. Fritz Fischer, "Der deutsche Protestantismus und die Politik im 19. Jahrhundert," *HZ*, 171 (1951), 474 f.; Leonard Krieger, *The German Idea of Freedom: History of a Political Tradition* (Boston, 1959), pp. 5 f.

2̶6̶1̶.̶7̶ B̶4̶8̶5̶p̶

C. 1

pervasive was the influence of Lutheran theology in German Protestantism that it tended to "absorb the Calvinist spirit in the isolated Reformed communities" in the Rhineland and Westphalia.[38] This theological-philosophical disagreement between rationalistic and Lutheran-Pietistic thinking, and the consequently different approaches to religious and secular problems, became the basis for some of the developing conservative and liberal factionalism in the decades to come.

In the course of the brief Prussian Reform Era, the suspicions and fears of some Prussian government officials regarding the consequences of theological rationalism seemed to be confirmed by the fact that a number of Protestant clergymen in the Rhineland and Westphalia had joined some of the population in welcoming the French as liberators and were continuing to support their rule there.[39] At the same time, all over the country, the violent opposition of some Pietist and orthodox Lutheran clergymen to the political and social demands of the revolutionary movement[40] encouraged the Prussian government in its belief that the traditionally docile Protestant clergy could be enlisted in the efforts to overthrow Napoleon's rule. In 1806, however, soon after the battle of Jena, a number of unusually active clergymen ventured to take the initiative in delivering political sermons before large crowds gathered in churches. Friedrich Schleiermacher—who had found the Pietism of Herrnhut too narrow and limited, and was to become the greatest

---

Also: William O. Shanahan, *German Protestants Face the Social Question: The Conservative Phase, 1815–1871* (Notre Dame, Ind., 1954), pp. 43 ff., 46 ff.; hereafter cited as Shanahan.

Spitz, Grimm, Forell, and other Reformation specialists seriously question Luther's supposed neglect of "worldly" problems. See Lewis Spitz, "Impact of the Reformation on Church-State Issues," in Albert G. Huegli, ed., *Church and State under God* (St. Louis, 1964), pp. 60–112; George W. Forell, "Luther and Politics," in Forell et al., eds., *Luther and Culture* (Decorah, Iowa, 1960), pp. 3–69; Harold J. Grimm, "Luther and Education," *ibid.*, pp. 73–142.

38. Wolfgang Köllmann, *Sozialgeschichte der Stadt Barmen im 19. Jahrhundert* (Tübingen, 1960), pp. 198 f.

39. See the chapter "Volks und Zeitgeist am Rhein von 1789 bis 1813," in J. A. Boost, *Was waren die Rheinländer als Menschen und Bürger, und was ist aus ihnen geworden* (Mainz, 1819), pp. 54–78; Eylert, III, 69 f.; Joseph Hansen, ed., *Quellen zur Geschichte des Rheinlandes im Zeitalter der französischen Revolution* (Bonn, 1931–1938), II, 378, and IV, 793.

40. For characteristic attacks on the "ideas of 1789" see Gottfried Menken, *Über Glück und Sieg der Gottlosen* (Frankfurt a. M., 1795).

liberal theologian of the century—fled in 1809 from the University of Halle to serve as pastor of the Trinity Church at Berlin, and in 1810 became one of the first faculty members of the new university there. He almost immediately joined Gottfried Hanstein (1761–1821), H. T. Ribbeck (1759–1826), and other Berlin clerics, together with the fiery ecclesiastical general superintendent of East Prussia, Ernst Ludwig Borowski (1740–1831), in arousing popular resentment to French rule.[41] The war with France, the military defeat at Jena, and the humiliation of Prussia began to turn Schleiermacher into a determined and unyielding Prussian patriot, and eventually into a German nationalist and outspoken critic of the government.[42]

Before the Napoleonic Wars, political sermons had been practically unknown in the Prussian state. Under the impact of radically changed conditions, this novel kind of sermon proved to be an ingenious and highly attractive political weapon. Because of censorship, poor newspaper reporting, and the prohibition of public gatherings during the French occupation, churches were the only places where people could assemble to hear speeches in which such public issues as war and peace and alliances were discussed. Although these speeches were presented in a theological-religious context, their emotional and political implications could be understood by everyone. Schleiermacher in particular began to preach sermons which were designed not only to lift the spirit of his listeners, but also to instill a specific political point of view.[43]

So great was the distrust and fear of the central government with regard to any political initiative taken by clergymen, however, that until 1813 it tried to restrain their efforts to stir up popular enthusiasm for resistance against Napoleon.[44] The reason for this

41. Max Lenz, *Geschichte der Königlichen Friedrich-Wilhelms Universität zu Berlin* (Halle, 1910–1918), I, pt. 1, 32 ff.; hereafter cited as Lenz.

See also Hermann Granier, ed., *Berichte aus der Berliner Franzosenzeit, 1807–1809: Publicationen aus den Preussischen Staatsarchiven*, Vol. 18 (Leipzig, 1913), Documents 43, 87, and 140 on Schleiermacher; 20, 140, 268, and 288 on Hanstein; 20, 80, and 288 on Ribbeck.

42. Dawson, *Schleiermacher*, pp. 43–67, 68–121. Also R. C. Raack, "Schleiermacher's Political Thought and Activity, 1806–1813," *Church History*, 28 (1959), 374–390.

43. Heinrich Doering, *Die deutschen Kanzelredner des 18. und 19. Jahrhunderts* (Neustadt a. d. Orla, 1830), pp. 81–92; Valjavec, *op. cit.* (n. 8 above), pp. 340 f.; Eylert, I, pt. 1, 172–176.

44. Wendland, *700 Jahre*, pp. 202–206; Lenz, I, pt. 1, 514 ff.

See also Schleiermacher, letter to his wife, May 30, 1813, in Heinrich Meisner, ed.,

attitude of the government seems to have been that—in contrast to the earlier pattern of "patriotic" sermons which, in the eighteenth century, had merely glorified the person of the ruler—the sermons by Schleiermacher and others called upon ' the people" to think for themselves and to take an active part in public affairs.[45] Schleiermacher made no secret of his belief that not the will and command of the ruler, but only the efforts of the whole people could, eventually, liberate Prussia. He was particularly anxious to emphasize his conviction that not the aristocrats but the *Bürger* were the real backbone of the nation, and that the newly created *Landwehr,* a national guard recruited from the people, would defeat the enemy.[46] Even before the military collapse of Prussia in 1806, he had demanded a fundamental recasting of the nation's political life.[47]

After Jena, Schleiermacher was the more determined to become a "political person," and at this time he began his cooperation with a group of patriotic conspirators in Berlin who were organizing a popular uprising against the French. In 1808 he went to Königsberg on a political mission to establish connections with the so-called *Tugendbund,* a similar patriotic group formed for the purpose of liberating Prussia. Schleiermacher's hope for an uprising against the French suffered a serious setback when, in that same year, Napoleon discovered the anti-French activities of Stein and other Reformers and succeeded in having Stein removed from his office as chief minister.[48] The new administration was headed by Altenstein and

---

Schleiermacher als Mensch: Sein Werden und Wirken, Familien- und Freundesbriefe, 1786–1834 (Gotha, 1922–1923), II, 178; hereafter cited as Meisner, *Schleiermacher Briefe.*

45. The "patriotic" sermons printed in J. J. Stolz, *Predigten über Merkwürdigkeiten des 18. Jahrhunderts* (Altenburg and Erfurt, 1801) and C. L. Hahnzog, *Patriotische Predigten* (Halle, 1785) present a sharp contrast to the "political" sermons published in *Neues Magazin von Fest- Gelegenheits- und anderen Predigten* (Magdeburg, 1814).

46. Letter to Charlotte von Kathen, June 20, 1806, in Georg Reimer, ed., *Aus Schleiermachers Leben in Briefen,* 2d ed. (Berlin, 1860–1863), II, 63; hereafter cited as Reimer, *Schleiermacher.*
Letter to Alexander von Dohna, March 7, 1813, in Meisner, *Schleiermacher Briefe,* II, 150 f.

47. "Grundlinien einer Kritik der bisherigen Sittenlehre," in *Schleiermachers Werke,* eds. Otto Braun and Johannes Bauer (Leipzig, 1910–1913), I, 237; *Soliloquies* (see n. 16 above), pp. 51–53, 61 f.

48. Schleiermacher to his friend C. Brinckmann, May 24, 1808, in Meisner, *Schleiermacher Briefe,* II, 107, and R. C. Raack, "A New Schleiermacher Letter on

Dohna—the latter an old friend of Schleiermacher, on whom he relied heavily for political advice. In June 1809, Dohna asked Schleiermacher to take part with Baron Wilhelm von Humboldt of the Kultusabteilung in the preparation of educational reforms, including the planning of a new university in Berlin. Schleiermacher was glad to cooperate, but he soon realized that the new administration was facing the emerging opposition of the East Elbian *ständische Reaktion* to the work of the Reformers, and that he had aroused the distrust and hostility of Nicolovius and other Pietists. As he observed the dilatory course of the reform movement and the failure of the government to renew the struggle against Napoleon, he began to despair and complained bitterly to a friend about losing his faith in the "regeneration" of the state. He became even more bitter when the new administration of Baron Karl August von Hardenberg (1750–1822) after 1810 began limiting the scope of reforms to those with a preeminently financial and economic emphasis. The opposition of Nicolovius led to the shelving of Schleiermacher's plans for a constitution of a confessionally and administratively united Protestant church which would include Lutherans and Reformed Christians and be independent of state control.[49]

The War of Liberation following Napoleon's Russian campaign in 1812 brought to a climax the politically significant efforts of enterprising clergymen who, on their own initiative or in response to the wishes of the war government, sought to arouse a spirit of active citizenship. In the years 1813–1814 Prussia was fighting for its very existence. A number of enthusiastic patriots were convinced that only the active participation of the whole people, a *Volkserhebung,* could save the regime from defeat. The ruling group in Prussia was alarmed, and such prominent Junkers as the Gerlachs and their friends accused some of the "best men in the professional arms"— meaning the military Reformers Scharnhorst, Gneisenau, Boyen, Groman, and their circle—of being "democrats" who believed in the

the Conspiracy of 1808," in *Zeitschrift für Religions- und Geistesgeschichte,* 16 (1964), 209–223; the *Zeitschrift* is hereafter cited as ZRGG. See also Raack, *The Fall of Stein* (Cambridge, Mass., 1965).

49. Schleiermacher to Brinckmann, December 17, 1809, and to Stein, July 1, 1811, in Meisner, *Schleiermacher Briefe,* II, 122, 135 f.; Fischer, *Nicolovius,* p. 303.

"sovereignty of the people" and a constitutional regime. Actually, the military Reformers merely talked about the *Volk* without really approving popular sovereignty or democracy, though they did favor a constitutional government which would allow responsible citizens some share in public life.[50]

In these years of extreme emergency the government welcomed the cooperation of clergymen in "preparing the minds of the people" for the supreme effort. Some clergymen, who did not wait for instructions, began organizing the local militia, the *Landsturm*. Schleiermacher considered the Landsturm an important expression of the latent strength of the people and urged the government to take the people into its confidence. Many clergymen enlisted as soldiers in fighting units or served as military chaplains.[51] Schleiermacher and other faculty members of the University of Berlin also volunteered for military service. Unsuccessful in his attempt to serve in the army, Schleiermacher joined his fellow Berliners in voluntary military drill to prepare themselves for fighting if the need should arise. Meanwhile he continued to preach at the Trinity Church, where he directed his most memorable sermons to troops departing for the front and to their relatives, and exhorted the German people to heed the call to arms. The impact of Schleiermacher's sermons was reflected in his acknowledged position as the "first great political preacher of the Germans since Luther." [52]

Protestant clergymen all over Germany delivered hundreds of sermons in which they compared the war against Napoleon to the

50. Wilhelm von Gerlach, "Aufzeichnungen aus den Jahren 1813–1816," in Schoeps, *Tagebücher und Briefe der Gebrüder Gerlach,* p. 122; Eylert, III, pt. 1, 172 f., 175; *The Life of Friedrich Schleiermacher as Unfolded in his Autobiography and Letters,* trans. Frederica Rowan (London, 1860), II, 202 ff.

51. Schleiermacher to his wife, May 14, 1813, in Reimer, *Schleiermacher,* II, 269 f., and to Dohna, April 17, 1813, in Meisner, *Schleiermacher Briefe,* II, 153.

As early as 1808 Gneisenau had worked out a plan for an uprising against the French and had proposed that clergymen should be used as local field agents and contact men all over the country. See Erich Botzenhardt, ed., *Freiherr vom Stein: Briefwechsel, Denkschrifte, und Aufzeichnungen* (Berlin, 1930–1937), III, 453; Gerhard Ritter, *Stein: Eine politische Biographie,* 3d ed. (Stuttgart, 1958), I, 426 f. See also Friedrich Thimme's article "Zu den Erhebungsplänen der Preussischen Patrioten im Sommer 1808, Ungedruckte Denkschriften Gneisenaus und Scharnhorsts," *HZ,* 86 (1901), 78 f., 83 f.

52. Eylert, I, pt. 1, 171–175; Georg Kaufmann, *Geschichte der Universität Breslau 1811–1911* (Breslau, 1911), pp. 78 f.; Lenz, I, pt. 1, 491 ff.

Crusades and used such religious terms as redemption, rebirth, resurrection, revelation, and martyrdom to stir up enthusiasm.[53] The conscious mingling of patriotic and religious sentiments was clearly expressed in the "Call to the Clergy of the Prussian State" (*Aufruf an die Geistlichkeit des Preussischen Staats*) which Nicolovius issued in March 1813:

> It is to you . . . members of the clergy . . . that we look with the greatest confidence. . . . You can contribute greatly to the victory of our weapons . . . by awakening the patriotic spirit of every soldier and civilian.[54]

A letter of Nicolovius to the Countess Luise Stolberg in the spring of 1814 was characteristic of the sentiment, held by some, that God was directing the armies which were fighting and defeating the forces of the French Revolution represented by Napoleon:

> We are now witnessing God's miracles. . . . This is the beginning of a new era . . . of a new Jerusalem in which God Himself will be the center and source of everything.[55]

The court preacher R. F. Eylert in Potsdam, General Superintendent Borowski in Königsberg, the theology professor H. L. Heubner at the University of Wittenberg, and the pastors Hanstein, Ribbeck, and most others in Berlin and elsewhere in the country faithfully followed the instructions of the government during the war years.[56] Schleiermacher, however, represented those clergymen who, because of their biting criticism of the selfish caste-spirit (*Kastengeist*) of the nobility and the bureaucracy, earned the hostility and even hatred of the Prussian conservative traditionalists. In his new

53. See the collection of sermons in F. J. Winter, ed., *Geistliche Weckstimmen aus der Zeit der Erniedrigung und Erhebung unseres Volks* (Leipzig, 1913). For the impact of Protestant religious ideas on the development of German national consciousness see Adolf Heger, "*Evangelische Verkündigung und deutsches Nationalbewusstsein,*" in *Neue Deutsche Forschungen, Abt. Religions- und Kirchengeschichte* (Berlin, 1939), VII, 135 ff.; Richard Wittram, *Nationalismus und Säkularisation: Beiträge zur Geschichte und Problematik des Nationalgeistes* (Lüneburg, 1949); and Karl Holl, *Die Bedeutung der grossen Kriege für das religiöse und kirchliche Leben innerhalb des deutschen Protestantismus* (Tübingen, 1917).

54. Nicolovius, *op. cit.* (n. 28 above), supplement 3.

55. Printed in *Perthes Leben*, I, 271.

56. Winter, *op. cit.*, pp. 80–177.

position as professor of theology at the University of Berlin, and as pastor of the Trinity Church, Schleiermacher considered it his duty to encourage his colleagues to protest against identifying the autocratic rule of the privileged classes with the religious crusade against the French. Toward the end of the war Schleiermacher became so bold that some of his sermons were indictments of the social system of inequality and of aristocratic arrogance. To some listeners, his courageous words were "thunder and lightning" aimed at the aristocracy. By 1813–1814, Schleiermacher had become an important spokesman for those elements of society who had lost their traditional respect for the privileged classes and were now demanding a share in the conduct of public affairs.[57]

In addition to offering sharp general criticism of the "caste spirit" of traditional Prussian society, Schleiermacher ventured to denounce certain current policies and specific measures of the government. Thus, for instance, he strongly condemned the maintenance of the alliance with Napoleon after the Russian campaign.[58] As editor of the *Preussischer Korrespondent,* a newspaper founded in June 1813 as the voice of the Prussian state at war, Schleiermacher openly challenged the government's policy of deemphasizing the role of the Landsturm in the War of Liberation—a policy indicative of the increasing pressure by conservative nobles who considered the organization of a popular armed force a serious threat to their privileged position. Although outraged by Schleiermacher's highly provocative article, the government did not dare to take official action against the popular clergyman.[59]

Such bold, self-willed behavior constituted a significant departure

57. Schleiermacher, "A Nation's Duty Is a War for Freedom," in *Selected Sermons of Schleiermacher,* trans. Mary Fredrica Wilson (New York, 1890), pp. 67 f.

See also his sermon in March 1814, in Johannes Bauer, *Schleiermacher als patriotischer Prediger: Ein Beitrag zur Geschichte der nationalen Erhebung vor hundert Jahren* (Giessen, 1908), pp. 48 f.; hereafter cited as Bauer, *Schleiermacher.* See also Eylert, I, pt. 1, 172–176; Lenz, I, pt. 1, 488 f.

58. Letter to Dohna, January 2, 1813, in Meisner, *Schleiermacher Briefe,* II, 149; Dawson, *Schleiermacher,* p. 97.

59. A combination of Schleiermacher's disgust with the government and the demands of some conservative extremists to try him for high treason resulted in his resignation from the editorship. Letter to Reimer, July 24, 1813, in Meisner, *Schleiermacher Briefe,* II, 204. See also the study by Hermann Dreyhaus, "Der Preussische Correspondent von 1813–1814 und der Anteil seiner Gründer Niebuhr und Schleiermacher," *Forschungen zur brandenburgischen und preussischen Geschichte,* 22 (1909), 424–426.

from the politically submissive role clergymen had, as a rule, played in the eighteenth century. A few decades before the Napoleonic Wars it would have been impossible for clergymen to use the pulpit to advocate the making or breaking of alliances with foreign powers. Schleiermacher's sermons and writings thus advanced the claim of some clergymen to the right to form their own opinions about affairs of state and to express these opinions freely in public, even if they conflicted with official policies. By using the pulpit and the press as forums to influence "public opinion" and even as instruments to bring political pressure to bear on the government, Schleiermacher created an important precedent for the future. Thus under the less harsh regime of bureaucratic—as compared with monarchical—absolutism, Schleiermacher and other politically conscious clergymen went beyond their officially assigned role in Prussian society and asserted the rights to political participation on their own initiative. No longer only the "living consciences of the Church," [60] they saw themselves as "living consciences of society."

The radically new claim by clergymen of the right to form their own opinions about affairs of state meant that, for the first time since the Reformation, their political attitudes, affiliations, and activities could play a crucial role in the political struggle between the government and the opposition. In the course of the struggle between conservatives and liberals in the following decades the Protestant clergy developed from an essentially cultural elite into a political elite also. As both a stimulator and a prototype, Schleiermacher was primarily responsible for the emergence of the most politically oriented elements of the clergy in the period 1815–1848. In a dramatically striking contrast with the Prussian clergy's docility toward public issues throughout most of the eighteenth century, liberal, conservative, and radical clerics were leading participants in the political struggles of these years.

Most highly placed members of the ecclesiastical hierarchy still identified themselves with authoritarian traditions, but by force of circumstances they became more alert politically and more concerned with the mood of the people than they had been before the Reform Era. Thus, Heubner, a formerly "quiet" Pietist theology professor at Wittenberg, loudly admonished his listeners to obey the

60. Hajo Holborn, "The Social Basis of the German Reformation," *Church History*, 5 (1936), 337.

instructions of the government. Reminding people of their sinfulness, Heubner advised them not to demand rights but to fulfill their duties: only by remaining in the station where God had put them could they achieve happiness, not by impertinent demands and arrogance.[61] Celebrating the occasion of Napoleon's defeat, Heubner stated flatly that the people should thank God for kings and princes who had liberated them from the rule of Napoleon, the incarnation of the Devil. Only the eternal bond between throne and altar would assure future happiness.[62] Borowski joined his conservative colleagues in sternly reminding the people that they were "soldiers of the king" and that their first and foremost duty was to "obey." [63]

The combined effect of the French Revolution, the Prussian reforms, and the supreme efforts put forth in the War of Liberation had a powerful impact on many clergymen. Some, like Heubner and Borowski, seemed to be strengthened in their belief that throne and altar must oppose the revolutionary ideas of the time.[64] In an entirely different response, Schleiermacher and some lesser-known clergymen from the ranks seemed to develop and take pride in a feeling of responsibility as representatives and leaders of the public generally and of liberal forces aiming at political and social change in particular.[65] While the clergymen who openly expressed this new kind of political consciousness were a minority, they were not isolated individuals, but men whose attitudes were indicative of the ways of

61. Heinrich Leonhard Heubner, *Die gegenwärtige Zeit der Not ein göttlicher Ruf zur Besserung: am 19. Sonntag nach Trinitatis, den 24. Oktober 1813* (n.p., n.d.), pp. 2 f.

62. D. Heubner, *Die christliche Freude über unsere Befreiung: Am zweiten Sonntag nach Epiphanias, den 16. Januar 1814* (Wittenberg, 1814), p. 2.

63. Ludwig Ernst Borowski, *Die Stimme Gottes vom Himmel herab, Es soll, es soll ja geholfen werden: Predigt zur vaterländischen Festfeier beim Beginn des Befreiungskrieges, den 11. April am Palmsonntage gehalten über Jerem. 30, 7–9* (Königsberg, 1813), p. 1. For similar views see also Borowski's *Ausgewählte Predigten und Reden,* ed. K. L. Volkmann (Königsberg, 1833), pp. 26–29, 36–62, and Eylert, I, pt. 1, 214–223.

64. Eylert, I, pt. 2, 186, 215 ff.; *Über die Ereignisse unserer Zeit* (Hanover, 1819), pp. 16–18, 26–37. See also the biography of Borowski by Walter Wendland, *Ludwig Ernst von Borowski, Erzbischof der Evangelischen Kirche in Preussen* (Königsberg, 1910), especially pp. 6–14.

65. See the characteristic comments of the liberal Breslau theology professor Johann Christian Gass, *Wie sollen wir die jetzige Zeit beurtheilen?* (Breslau, 1817), pp. 6, 17, 19–21. For the views of Pastor Carl Bernhard König, a rank-and-file clergyman in Anderbeck, see his anonymously published *Wanderung durch Vaterhaus, Schule, Kriegslager und Akademie zur Kirche* (Magdeburg, 1838), pp. 18–24.

thinking and acting of scattered groups of persons from all walks of life.

In Berlin and on some of the Junker estates in the eastern parts of Prussia, Pietist pastors such as Hermes, Jänicke, and Gossner became the favorite preachers and even friends of some high-ranking aristocratic army officers, government officials, and big landowners.[66] In the Rhineland—after 1815 a Prussian province—the leader of the Wuppertal Pietists, Daniel Krummacher, welcomed the Hohenzollern regime as a blessing for the Calvinists and Lutherans of the area.[67] His colleague, Pastor Wever of Unterbarmen, admonished not only his own congregation but the whole of Europe to "thank God for the rule of such Christian princes as the gentle tsar of Russia . . . and the pious king of Prussia," who together with other kings and princes had "triumphed against the forces of revolt against God" and against Napoleon, "the incarnation of the Devil."[68] In 1816, G. F. A. Strauss, the Lutheran pastor in Elberfeld, jubilantly expressed the view that at long last all the Protestants of the Rhineland and Westphalia could live under the Protestant regime of the Hohenzollerns.[69] Even Pastor Keller of Solingen, who had praised the French Revolution and Napoleonic rule a few years before, joined the chorus of his numerous colleagues and declared in 1815: "Even superstition which is converted into deeds . . . is better than rationalism and other atheistic philosophies which make men calculating egotists."[70] It can be assumed that these voices were especially welcome to the Prussian government as it faced the problem of integrating the western provinces, where it was hoped that the small but

---

66. See F. W. Kantzenbach, *Die Erweckungsbewegung: Studien zur Geschichte ihrer Entstehung und ersten Ausbreitung in Deutschland* (Neuendettelsau, 1957), pp. 82–111; hereafter cited as Kantzenbach, *Die Erweckungsbewegung.*

67. G. D. Krummacher, *Predigt von der Wiederherstellung* (Düsseldorf, 1816), pp. 4–7. He was the uncle of the Elberfeld pastor F. W. Krummacher (one of the pious friends of the Crown Prince, later King Frederick William IV), a special target for Friedrich Engels's antireligious criticism. See Karl Kupisch, *Vom Pietismus zum Kommunismus: Historische Gestalten, Szenen und Probleme* (Berlin, 1953), pp. 11–13.

68. C. G. Wever, *Dankrede und Gebet bei Gelegenheit der Feyer des siegreichen Einzugs* (Elberfeld, 1814), pp. 11–13.

69. *Sieben Predigten* (Elberfeld, 1816), p. 3. See also his *Glockentöne: Erinnerungen eines jungen Geistlichen* (Elberfeld, 1815), pp. 6 ff.

70. Boost, *op. cit.* (n. 39 above), p. 87.

extremely conscious and economically important Protestant minority would not only be sympathetic to Prussian rule but would provide a decisive element of support.[71]

After the defeat of Napoleon, Prussia emerged as a greatly enlarged German Protestant state. The government officially acknowledged the services of clergymen in the War of Liberation and rewarded a number of them who had distinguished themselves during the wars by their loyalty.[72] Borowski, the general superintendent of East Prussia and a personal friend and adviser of Frederick William III, who had hailed clergymen as "soldiers of the king," was promoted to the posts of chief court preacher and archbishop. In 1829, he was ennobled and became a knight of the Royal Order of the Black Eagle (*Ritter des Königlichen Schwarzen Adlerordens*).[73] Friedrich Samuel Gottfried Sack (1738–1817), the chief court and cathedral preacher and chief councilor of the Berlin Consistory, became the first bishop of the reorganized state church in 1816 and a year later was the first clergyman to be awarded the Order of the Red Eagle, First Class (*Roter Adlerorden erster Klasse*).[74] Sack's promotion was "in recognition of his outstanding services in the clergy and also for raising the prestige of the Protestant church." The title of bishop denoted a rank officially equivalent to that of a provincial governor (*Oberpräsident*), and bishops had to be addressed as "Your Reverence" (*Hochwürden*). Altenstein, the minister of ecclesiastical affairs and education, stated clearly, however, that bishops of the state church were ecclesiastical bureaucrats under his department ("Sie sind dem Ministerium . . . unbedingt untergeordnet").[75]

Ruhlemann Friedrich Eylert (1770–1852), a former rationalist who had turned to Lutheran orthodoxy and denounced the French Revolution and the *Zeitgeist* as the work of the Devil, had been

71. Justus Hashagen, *Der rheinische Protestantismus und die Entwicklung der rheinischen Kultur* (Essen, 1924). See also Alexander Bergengrün, *Staatsminister August Freiherr von der Heydt* (Leipzig, 1908), pp. 62 ff.

72. Nicolovius, *op. cit.* (n. 28 above), pp. 211 ff.

73. Wendland, *op. cit.* (n. 64 above), pp. 2–4.

74. Eylert, I, pt. 2, 165. On the position and rank of bishops in the Prussian state church see Alfred Nicolovius, *Die bischöfliche Würde in Preussens evangelischer Kirche* (Königsberg, 1834), pp. 86–89; Ernst Benz, *Bischofsamt und Apostolische Succession im deutschen Protestantismus* (Stuttgart, 1953), p. 115.

75. Benz, pp. 119–122.

court preacher at Potsdam since 1806. In 1818, he was also appointed bishop.[76] Hanstein, the pastor of the Petri Church in Berlin, whose political sermons during the wars had been appreciated by the government, was awarded the Order of the Red Eagle, Second Class, and promoted to chief Consistory councilor.[77] The same order was bestowed upon P. C. Marheineke (1780–1846), professor of theology at the University of Berlin, who had served as an army captain. A great personal enemy of Schleiermacher, Marheineke annoyed his theological rival by conspicuously wearing the order on every possible occasion to demonstrate his loyalty to, and recognition by, the government.[78]

All these and other distinctions and honors were not only in recognition for services rendered in the past, but also part of the evolving general system of incentives which the government used to win over to its side the responsive members of the clergy and to ensure their active political loyalty to the established order.[79] Some of the titles and distinctions carried considerable monetary rewards, producing regular income in addition to salaries already received from ecclesiastical posts.[80] Liberally inclined theology professors— such as Schleiermacher, his colleague Leberecht De Wette (1780– 1849), and less prominent political critics of existing conditions— could not expect official encouragement, let alone special favors.

Schleiermacher had made important contributions to the establishment of the University of Berlin and to the educational reforms under Humboldt, and his wartime services to the government were distinguished, but he had been boldly critical of the regime and of its privileged classes. Accordingly, the government denied him any direct role in the planning of the administrative and confessional unification of the state church. For a number of years after 1815 it seemed that Schleiermacher might even suffer the fate of De Wette, who was dismissed from his university position in 1819, the year that marked the official end of the Prussian Reform Era.[81]

---

76. *Ibid.*, p. 123. For a summary of Eylert's political views see Walter Wendland, "Zur reaktionären Gesinnung R. F. Eylerts," *Jahrbuch für Brandenburgische Kirchengeschichte,* 9–10 (1913), 303–306.

77. Eylert, II, pt. 1, 40–42. See also, in Gottfried Hanstein, *Predigten in den Jahren 1813 und 1814 gehalten* (Magdeburg, 1819), p. 6, the "Introduction" to his "Die ernste Zeit."

78. Lenz, II, pt. 1, 152.

79. Eylert, III, pt. 1, 344 f., 357 f.

80. For examples see chap. ii, pp. 59 f.

81. Lenz, II, pt. 1, 87, 172–176.

After the downfall of Napoleon, the German rulers began to unite the Lutheran and Reformed faiths within their territorial churches. Beginning in Nassau and Prussia (1817), the example was followed in the Rhenish Palatinate (1818), Baden (1821), Rhenish Hesse (1822), and Württemberg (1827). Lutheran opposition to immediate union was too strong in Saxony, Hanover, and Bavaria.

In Prussia, the deeply religious Frederick William III took a personal interest in the confessional union, particularly in its liturgical aspects.[82] Under the influence of the Aufklärung and early Pietism, the old division between the Lutheran and Reformed confessions had waned considerably during the eighteenth century. Particularly in the Rhineland and Westphalia, where Catholics were in the majority, relations between the two Protestant denominations had grown very close. Frederick William III, who personally had strong leanings toward Lutheranism, intended to close the gap which had existed between the dynasty and the Lutheran population since 1613, when his ancestor the Elector John Sigismund adopted the Reformed faith. In 1817, at the time of the tercentenary of Luther's Ninety-five Theses, he called for a union of the two denominations. On October 31, twenty clergymen in Berlin attended a communion service in which rites and formulas were used which left it to the communicant to interpret the Lord's Supper in either the Lutheran or Reformed manner. Frederick William III and his court held a similar service in Potsdam.

The support of religion by the king, whose piety contrasted sharply with the religious indifference of Frederick II, tended to draw theology and politics together. The renewed intimacy of church, religion, and monarchy provoked a lively and varied reaction among the church parties and confessions. In contrast to Nassau, Baden, and the Palatinate, where union was brought about through synods or congregational approval, in Prussia the king imposed the merger by a new order of worship which he himself drafted. This so-called *Agende* of 1822 aroused opposition both from those who found the new forms of church services ill chosen and from those

82. Foerster, *Entstehung*, I, 199 ff.; Hermann Wangemann, *Die kirchliche Cabinetts-Politik des Königs Friedrich Wilhelm III: Insonderheit in Beziehung auf Kirchenverfassung, Agende, Union, Separatismus* (Berlin, 1884), pp. 18 ff.; Walter Wendland, *Die Religiosität und die kirchenpolitischen Grundsätze Friedrich Wilhelms des Dritten in ihrer Bedeutung für die Geschichte der kirchlichen Restauration* (Giessen, 1909), pp. 36 ff.

who resented the introduction by royal command. Frederick William
III stubbornly pressed his Agende, and although he denied that the
congregations would be forced to adopt it, the government exerted
strong pressure to make clergymen conform and deliver the assent
of their congregations.

The king's preoccupation with the liturgical side of religion reflected his military sense of order and his uncertainty in doctrinal
matters. Also he was attracted by the assurance which the old creed
breathed: his simple soul longed for uniformity of faith. He wished,
in fact, to make the Augsburg Confession the official creed, but
realized that an attempt to do so would ruin any chance for the unification of German Protestantism. Therefore he eventually contented
himself with demanding the adherence of all clergymen to the
"symbolic books" of the historic Protestant churches. What this
meant in practice, however, was not made clear—presumably because
anything more explicit would have required assent from the living
faith of the church members. Was a clergyman under obligation only
to the substance of the various creeds? Might he consider one creed
of his choice the expression of his own faith?

This curious way of promoting orthodoxy produced the long
and at times very bitter struggle known as the *Agendenstreit,* which
was finally settled by a compromise. The king permitted local practices in liturgy to be valid in addition to the general ordinance, and
conceded in each district the use of long-established liturgical forms.
Schleiermacher and his followers then withdrew their opposition to
the Agende, for everyone who accepted the union could unhesitat-
ingly comply with the new ordinance. At the tercentenary festival of
the Augsburg Confession, in 1830, the king could congratulate himself upon the fact that the liturgy had been accepted throughout the
greater part of his realm. Except for the special case of the Silesian
Old Lutherans, very few clergymen were ready at that time to
carry their opposition to the Agende so far as to jeopardize their
appointments.

While Frederick William III considered it his mission to bring
about confessional union in the state church, and devoted much of
his time and energy to its enforcement, the main concern of the
administrative bureaucracy was the political unity of the greatly enlarged Prussian state after 1815. The government believed that such
unity could be strengthened by a centrally administered and confes-

sionally united state church (*Landeskirche*) whose clergy was actively loyal to the government.[83] Thus in 1815 the provincial ecclesiastical bodies were replaced by new Consistories which became officially part of the central administrative apparatus of the state. As in the past, the new Consistories were staffed with clergymen and lay officials and were presided over by the highest provincial authorities, the Oberpräsidenten. By a cabinet order in 1816 the Consistories were authorized to initiate disciplinary action against members of the clergy and to order their dismissal. This latter power was subject only to confirmation by the central ministry in Berlin. On the other hand, proposals for injecting some degree of self-government into the reorganized Prussian state church were consistently rejected by the government. Consequently, the administration of the Protestant church was carried out, in principle, in the same manner as that of the other chief administrative departments.[84]

After 1815, general superintendencies on the model of those already existing in the eastern provinces were established throughout the Prussian kingdom.[85] The general superintendents were appointed by the government as the directors of the Consistories, with rank immediately under that of the Oberpräsidenten. They had the right of ordination and were expected to report to the government on the conduct of the members of the Consistories and all other clergymen in their provinces. In fact, they were what Schleiermacher called the "ecclesiastical prefects of the government." In order to increase their prestige, most general superintendents were eventually appointed bishops.[86] The bishops, general superintendents, superintendents, chief Consistory councilors, and other officials of the reorganized state church were now considered professional members of the ecclesiastical branch of the civil service (*geistliche Beamte*). Members of the new "ecclesiastical officers' corps" were henceforth required to wear uni-

83. T. G. von Hippel, *Beiträge zur Characteristic Friedrich Wilhelms III* (Berlin, 1841), pp. 14 ff.; Schnabel, IV, 320–326.

84. Ernst Rudolf Huber, *Deutsche Verfassungsgeschichte seit 1789* (Stuttgart, 1957–1969), I, 450–474; hereafter cited as Huber.

See also Foerster, *Entstehung*, II, 220–223.

85. J. C. W. Augusti, *Über das Amt eines Generalsuperintendenten der evangelischen Kirche, besonders in der preussischen Monarchie: Beiträge zur Geschichte und Statistik der evangelischen Kirche* (Leipzig, 1838), pp. 278 ff.; Oskar Foellmer, *Geschichte des Amtes der Generalsuperintendenten in den altpreussischen Provinzen* (Gütersloh, 1931), pp. 84 f.

86. Benz, *op. cit.* (n. 74 above), pp. 123 f.; Foerster, *Entstehung*, II, 227.

form clothing (*Amtkleidung*). Procedures for the training and employment of clergymen were standardized in all provinces and were regulated by laws which made it clear that, from the standpoint of the central administration, only the passing of examinations after a prescribed course of studies at a university would qualify candidates for ecclesiastical appointments—the traditional religious ceremony of ordination being considered merely a supplement to the examination (*ein Anhang der wissenschaftlichen Examina*)—and all appointments had to be made by the Ministry in Berlin.[87] Centralized control and the tightening up of the organizational structure of the Protestant church as a hierarchical branch of the central administration caused serious tensions, but it also provided some new possibilities for a number of clergymen, as will be seen later.

Although the holders of local rights of church patronage, including the owners of noble estates (*Rittergüter*), retained their traditional privilege of nominating candidates for the parish ministry, they lost the rights of appointment and dismissal of "their" pastors, which after 1808 the central government reserved to itself, and this reform was keenly resented by some Prussian squires as an interference with the sacrosanct Patronatsrecht. These men continued to treat local pastors as if they were their private officials.[88] Urban communities and those congregations in the central and western parts of the Prussian state which had most recently begun to look upon the local ministers as "their" representatives were also uneasy over the right to appoint and dismiss pastors regardless of the wishes of parish members.[89] Conflict between the government and particular congregations was a possibility especially in the newly acquired western provinces of the Rhineland and Westphalia, where the Protestant communities had a strong tradition of independence under a presbyterian form of church government and a system of representative bodies called synods. Generally, Protestants in these

87. Eylert, III, pt. 1, 247 f.
88. See Erich Jordan, *Die Entstehung der konservativen Partei und die preussischen Agrarverhältnisse von 1848* (Munich and Leipzig, 1914), pp. 129 ff.; hereafter cited as Jordan.
Also Eylert, III, pt. 1, 52 f.
89. In 1815, of 627 Protestant congregations, with 789 ministers, only 47 pastors were not elected by the local church bodies (*Wahlkollegia*) of the Rhineland. See Joseph Hansen, ed., *Die Rheinprovinz, 1815–1915: Hundert Jahre preussischer Herrschaft am Rhein* (Bonn, 1917), II, 216.

provinces were more advanced economically and culturally than most of those in the east. Besides a much better remuneration, pastors in Rhineland-Westphalia enjoyed what the Elberfeld pastor Friedrich Wilhelm Krummacher (1789–1864) called "a prestige unsurpassed in any part of the kingdom." Traditional mutual respect and cooperation between pastors and local business families was especially notable in the Wuppertal and Ruhr regions. Such factors made severe difficulties in controlling and administering the state church.[90]

The Prussian rulers loathed the system of "church republics" (*Kirchenrepublik*) and insisted on the authoritarian structure of state institutions on every level. Yet they were anxious to keep the sympathy and gain the cooperation of the Protestant minority in the Rhineland and Westphalia.[91] To this end, the government put emphasis on its increasingly apparent tactics of trying to win the loyalty of the politically most important members of the clergy and making them active supporters of the official order. More important than the working out of a final agreement on the incorporation of the western Protestant church into the state church was the policy which the government followed for securing the good will and cooperation of these clergymen. Assuming that few men can resist the temptation of enhanced prestige which springs from titles, honors, and official acknowledgment of abilities and importance, the government began to appoint some of the most influential pastors of the western provinces to high positions in the ecclesiastical hierarchy.[92]

Wilhelm Johann Gottfried Ross (1777–1854), the pastor of Budberg near Rheinberg and a descendant of an old Scottish noble family which had settled on the continent in the seventeenth century, was appointed superintendent of his area in 1817 and soon afterward was promoted to the post of councilor in the newly established provincial Consistory. In 1820, Ross was officially invited to take part in the discussions regarding the incorporation of the Rhenish-Westphalian Protestant communities into the state church. Not surprisingly, in

90. "Einiges über die evangelische Kirche auf der linken Rheinseite," *Allgemeine Kirchen-Zeitung,* 1829, pp. 137–151; this periodical is hereafter cited as *AKZ*.

91. Carl Immanuel Nitzsch, *Urkundenbuch der Evangelischen Union mit Erläuterungen* (Bonn, 1853), pp. 16–24; Huber, II, 272–275; F. W. Krummacher, *Eine Selbstbiographie* (Berlin, 1869), pp. 23 ff.

92. See the very revealing comments in Eylert, III, pt. 1, 357 f., and [G. de Failly], *De la Prusse et de sa domination sous les rapports politique et religieux: spécialement dans les nouvelles provinces par un inconnu* (Paris, 1842), pp. 12 ff.

1826 this distinguished clergyman joined the forces of the supporters of the government in the provincial *Landtag* and became one of their leaders. In recognition of his services, Ross was eventually appointed chief Consistory councilor and general superintendent of his province and also bishop.[93]

There were a number of less spectacular but politically significant ecclesiastical appointments of clergymen from the western provinces. K. W. Snetlage (1780–1861), pastor in Unterbarmen, became the first superintendent of the Wuppertal in 1816. Unable to resist the offer of the government to become court preacher, he moved in 1825 to Berlin, where he became an influential member of the conservative clerical forces opposing the liberals. Snetlage's close relations with court and government circles have been described by his nephew, Friedrich Engels, who during his one year of military service spent much time at his uncle's home in Berlin.[94] The Elberfeld pastor Gerhardt Friedrich Abraham Strauss (1786–1863), who had married into the prominent von der Heydt family, also became a high ecclesiastical official in the capital after 1815, serving as court and cathedral preacher, professor of theology at the University of Berlin, and chief Consistory councilor. Until the appointment of his fellow Rhenish-Westphalian, Hengstenberg, as professor of theology in the late 1820's, Strauss was considered the main pillar of Pietist influence at the University of Berlin.[95] Another clergyman in Elberfeld, the aforementioned F. W. Krummacher, whom Engels called the "most bigoted preacher" of the "Zion of obscurants," became one of the favorites of the Crown Prince and the Pietist circle around him after 1818. He, too, was eventually called to Berlin as court preacher.[96]

Bernhard Christian Ludwig Natorp (1774–1846) from Essen, Westphalia, was another clergyman whom the government attracted to its service. As councilor of ecclesiastical affairs (*Geistlicher Rat*)

93. Justus Hashagen et al., eds., *Bergische Geschichte* (Burg an der Wupper, 1958), pp. 259–262, 269; Augusti, *op. cit.* (n. 85 above), pp. 278 ff.; *RGG* (1930), IV, 2111.

94. Kupisch, *op. cit.* (n. 67 above), pp. 17 ff.

95. Strauss was appointed professor on Eylert's recommendation to Minister Altenstein. Lenz, II, pt. 1, 316.

96. Ernst Wilhelm Hengstenberg, "Vorwort," *Evangelische Kirchen-Zeitung,* 1864, p. 80; this periodical is hereafter cited as *EKZ.*

Also: Karl Marx and Friedrich Engels, "Briefe aus dem Wuppertal," in *Werke* (Berlin, 1961), I, 419 ff.

and councilor of education (*Schul- und Regierungsrat*) at Potsdam in 1809–1816, he had a crucial role in the educational reforms usually associated with the work of Wilhelm von Humboldt and J. W. Süvern. Natorp was responsible for working out the plans, principles, and structure of the elementary school system and the teachers' colleges, and became known as the "father of the Prussian teachers' college." In 1816 he was appointed chief Consistory councilor and transferred back to his native Westphalia to cooperate with the newly installed Prussian administration there. He became adviser to Johann August Sack, the new provincial governor, and to Sack's successor, and was influential in the administrative and educational incorporation of Rhineland-Westphalia into the Prussian state.[97]

The government's efforts to secure the loyalty and the cooperation of talented and influential individuals in the Rhineland and Westphalia were part of its general strategy for strengthening the greatly enlarged Prussian state in the face of the developing political opposition. The fact that most clergymen were not only willing but even anxious to enter the new administrative structure can be explained by the natural desire for economic security and its reinforcement by the continued threat of a European revolution, the turbulence among university students, and the general reaction in the German Confederation (especially after the Carlsbad Decrees).

It seems fairly obvious that the rapid rise of the Potsdam court preacher Eylert in the government after the War of Liberation was at least partly due to the government's need for his connections and his advice on how to integrate his native Westphalia with the "Prussian system." He was appointed chief court preacher, bishop, and member of the Council of State. In his famous sermon at the military chapel of Potsdam, in 1819, Eylert denounced all political opposition to the government as treason and blasphemy. This sermon can be said to have given the signal for the wave of persecution and political witch-hunts, known as the *Demagogenverfolgung,* which followed the assassination of the reactionary poet and secret government agent Kotzebue by K. L. Sand.[98] The young theology student Sand was a member of the *Burschenschaft,* or students' association,

97. Hans Joachim Schoeps, "Neues zur preussischen Geistesgeschichte des 19. Jahrhunderts," *Zeitschrift für Religions- und Geistesgeschichte,* 3–4 (1965), 282–306.
98. Eylert, III, pt. 3, 184–189; Lenz, II, pt. 1, 77 ff. For a brief biography of Eylert see *RGG* (1957), I, 843.

and an ardent follower of the fanatical Karl Follen, a radical republican student leader at Giessen.

First founded at the University of Jena in 1815, the Burschenschaft movement represented the political activation of the academic youth of Germany. Born out of the experiences of the War of Liberation, it was a reaction against the traditional student corps of the German universities. It aimed to regenerate the moral virtues of the young people of Germany, but above all it strove to break down local allegiances and to kindle a huge nationalist flame that would engulf all of Germany. Soon there were Burschenschaften in many other universities, and in 1818, the formation of the General German Students' Union (*Allgemeine Deutsche Burschenschaft*) produced groups such as the "Blacks" (or "Unconditionals"), who placed the emphasis on political action.

Sand's insane deed gave the governments of Austria and Prussia the chance to stamp out all open signs of political opposition in the German Confederation. Metternich of Austria and Frederick William III persuaded the heads of the other states of the Confederation to put into effect the so-called Carlsbad Decrees in 1819. These provided for rigid censorship and press control, and for the supervision of universities and schools in order to ferret out all subversive elements.

The dismissal of De Wette from his professorship at the University of Berlin in the same year must be attributed, in part, to the influence of Bishop Eylert, who accused him of encouraging acts of violence such as the assassination of Kotzebue. Eylert, according to his own account, urged the king to pardon the "misguided young men" of the liberal-nationalist student movement, of which Sand was a member. Maintaining that the students of the Burschenschaften "did not know what they were doing," Eylert blamed De Wette and other liberal-minded professors for the *Freiheitschwindel* which intoxicated the young. Instead of dreaming about participation in the government of their country, he told the king, people should realize their moral shortcomings and learn to control their selfish ambitions. Thus Eylert—like many other clergymen who abandoned rationalism in the course of the upheavals of the revolutionary era and the War of Liberation and turned to the orthodox Lutheran creed—now joined the Neo-Pietists in supporting "throne and altar." [99]

99. Schnabel, II, 234 ff.; Lenz, II, pt. 1, 61 ff.; Eylert, III, pt. 3, 483.

The careless wording of a letter of condolence to the mother of Sand, in which De Wette called the assassination a "nice sign of the [liberal aspiration of] the age" (ein schönes Zeichen der Zeit), was used by the government as proof of his disloyalty as a civil servant. Actually both the orthodox Lutheran Eylert and the Pietist circle of Baron von Kottwitz exerted pressure on the government to dismiss De Wette as a dangerous political liberal.[100] The ensuing protests by Schleiermacher and some other clergymen and professors outraged the rising Neo-Pietist–orthodox clerical faction, which openly identified its particular creed with the needs and interests of the state rulers long before F. J. Stahl's concept of the "Christian" nature of the Prussian state was presented in a philosophical form.

In strong contrast to the increasingly successful cooperation between leading Rhenish-Westphalian clergymen and the government, developments in Silesia led to open conflict, in which opposition to church unification was crushed by the police and military forces of the central authorities.[101] Like the Rhineland and Westphalia, Silesia was a fairly recent acquisition of the Prussian crown, and the Lutheran congregations there had a tradition of independence, having maintained it—with some assistance from Charles XII of Sweden—even under the Habsburgs. The measures taken by the government in the 1820's for complete centralization and control of the state church, confessional union, and denial of the right to elect their own pastors caused orthodox Silesian Lutherans to organize mass resistance. Ignoring the public outcry against its repressive actions, the government eventually overcame this "Old Lutheran" resistance. Until the 1840's, the right to separation from the state church and to the formation of independent congregations was denied in all the provinces.

The coordinated procedure of constructing a unified Protestant state church and a unified state administrative apparatus caused serious friction with some of the clergy of the realm. As has been noted, the government rewarded clergymen who were conspicuously active and particularly useful supporters of its policies. Conversely, those who expressed opposition were held back in their careers by the withholding of promotion, titles, honors, and other distinctions. In extreme cases, hostile "political clergymen" were removed from

100. Neander to Heubner, n.d. (probably shortly after De Wette's dismissal), in Kantzenbach, *Kottwitz*, p. 210; Lenz, II, pt. 1, 61–87; Eylert, III, pt. 3, 483–485.
101. Huber, II, 272–275.

ecclesiastical service altogether and even jailed. The assumption by many clergymen of active roles in the Napoleonic Wars undoubtedly spread and strengthened among them the belief that participation in political life on their own initiative was not only permissible but in fact a duty imposed by their office. They thus regarded themselves as spokesmen for the aspirations of the groups in society who tended to look to them for guidance and leadership.[102]

The novel idea that the political leanings and behavior might reflect personal choice and individual convictions was at first resented by court circles and the ruling bureaucrats. Faced with the growing demands of the liberal opposition for political and social changes in church and state, markedly evident after 1815, the government soon not only allowed but actually encouraged clergymen to engage in political activities—provided their influence was exerted in the approved direction. The bureaucratic rulers of Prussia were by then aware of the role clergymen could play in the molding of opinion, and, being much more directly exposed to the political and social pressures of the times than the king and the royal court, they were anxious to secure the assistance of those who would cooperate. This new awareness appeared among the clergymen themselves. Since it tended to divide them into conservatives and reformers, the emergence of their political consciousness was a development of crucial significance for pre-1848 Prussia.

At the beginning of the century, the majority of Protestant clergymen still adhered to the teachings of theological rationalism and thus regarded reason as the supreme authority in matters of religion and life in general. Liberal and democratic in outlook, they were inclined to look with indifference or even amusement upon the few isolated Pietist conventicles in Berlin and other places. In the first two decades of the century, however, a small but influential group of "awakened" Pietists—comprising aristocratic Old Prussian landowners, army officers, and jurists—developed close personal, religious, intellectual, and social contacts with members of the small minority of antirationalist clergymen. From this mingling arose a Neo-Pietist and orthodox combination which was destined to develop

---

102. See especially the Introduction in the third edition of Schleiermacher's *Über die Religion: Reden an die Gebildeten unter ihren Verächtern* (Berlin, 1821). Also R. Hinton Thomas, *Liberalism, Nationalism, and the German Intellectuals, 1822–1847* (Cambridge, England, 1952), pp. 19 f.

into a politically important religious creed and movement called the "Awakening" (*Erweckungsbewegung*).[103] Recoiling from the impact of the "ideas of 1789," the movement emphasized the traditional Lutheran and Pietist concept of man's sinful nature and his moral duty to subordinate himself to the God-given worldly order.[104] Bitterly opposed to the aspirations of the rising liberal and democratic forces pressing from below, this new Pietist elite of aristocrats and clergymen proved to be a welcome support for the conservative nobility associated with the so-called *ständische Reaktion*.[105]

This movement was, of course, related to the general religious revival that accompanied the struggle against Napoleon and became a significant aspect of the conservative Restoration in Europe after 1815. Both Catholics and Protestants were affected by the broad revival of religious faith. In Germany, religion had fortified the people for the stern tests of the War of Liberation. Moreover, the great battles that put an end to Napoleonic rule were animated by a sense of struggle against the forces of evil. Many Germans, and other Europeans as well, interpreted the downfall of Napoleon as God's historical judgment. Rationalist ideas of the natural rights of man and secularist doctrines of state power were tarnished by the excesses of the Revolutionary and Napoleonic eras.

Many of the greatest intellects in Europe, and some of the most biting pens, devoted themselves to affirming the dogmas of Christianity and old religious beliefs. Burke, whose tremendous literary attack on the ideas of the French Revolution in his *Reflections on the Revolution in France* (1790) made him the spokesman of conservatism throughout Europe, stated eloquently the case for traditionalism and reverence for established institutions. In France, Joseph de Maistre and the Vicomte de Bonald linked insistence on

---

103. Kantzenbach, *Die Erweckungsbewegung*. For the general political impact of the "Awakening" see Schnabel, IV, 379–392; Shanahan, pp. 99–110; Huber, II, 338 ff. Also: Hajo Holborn, *A History of Modern Germany* (New York, 1959–1969), II, 134–144; hereafter cited as Holborn, *Modern Germany*.

104. For a very characteristic expression of the attitude that considered man as having been corrupted by Adam's sin ("Ja durch Adams Fall ist ganz verderbt menschlich Natur und Wesen") see Kottwitz to Tholuck, December 19, 1825, in G. N. Bonwetsch, ed., *Aus Tholucks Anfängen: Briefe an und von Tholuck* (Gütersloh, 1922), p. 29; hereafter cited as Bonwetsch, *Tholuck Briefe*.

105. "Ein Wort über die Stellung der theol. Parteien in unserer Zeit," *AKZ*, 1830, pp. 505–516. See also Jacques Droz, *Les révolutions allemandes de 1848* (Paris, 1957), pp. 137–146.

the supreme need for order with support for the legitimist monarchy and the power of the Papacy. Their brilliant polemics, which seemed for a time to demolish the ideas and arguments of liberalism, spread their influence beyond France to Italy and Germany. Some of their ideas were further popularized by Lamennais, who showed the connections between religious faith and social and political order. The keynote of the thought of these men was the demand for authority—authority in both state and church—as the only bulwark against revolution and atheism. To all who had been frightened by the experience of revolution, the appeal to religion, tradition, and conservatism, to old establishments and creeds, was strong. It seemed to tap the only source of authority rich enough to withstand the disturbing notions of liberalism, democracy, and nationalism. For at least a decade after Waterloo the forces of conservatism seemed to enjoy more positive prestige than at any time since the reign of Louis XIV.

Quickened by the experiences of religious fervor during the War of Liberation, the German "Awakening" of the nineteenth century tended to channel religious experience toward a dogmatic faith.[106] In keeping with the particularist traditions of Germany, the movement showed great diversity,[107] but its historical significance lies in the fact that it united Pietism and orthodox Lutheranism with political conservatism. Eventually it provided the spiritual basis in Germany, particularly in Prussia, for that emphasis upon Christian principles in the political and social order characteristic of the period between 1815 and 1848. A blend of Pietism and orthodox Lutheranism, the "Awakening" advocated a return to Lutheranism clad in sin and grace, and opposed the rationalism which it associated with the antireligious aspects of the Aufklärung and the French Revolution. The Neo-Pietists of the "Awakening" were no longer isolated "quiet people" of the eighteenth century whispering their creed in the collegia pietatis. Believing that the "union of throne and altar" under Frederick William III had again "spiritualized" the

---

106. "One circumstance tended to predominate and therefore to inform the whole character of German Protestantism: the tendency of Pietism to reverse the course of its previous history and make common cause with the newly strengthened orthodox, confessional spirit." Shanahan, p. 58.

107. Heinrich Hermelink, *Das Christentum in der Menschheitsgeschichte von der französischen Revolution bis zur Gegenwart* (Tübingen and Stuttgart, 1951-1953), I, 219 ff.

traditional institutions of church and state, they entered into a close alliance with some neo-orthodox clergymen of the reorganized state church. The church was to be a firm cornerstone of the God-given worldly order and not an institution lending support to the subversive activities of the liberal opposition—which was aiming at the transformation of autocratic Prussia into a constitutionally limited parliamentary regime in which privileges based solely on birth would be abolished.

Realizing that the reorganized church was one of the crucial institutions of the Prussian state,[108] the conservative Pietist aristocrats began a drive to destroy the influence of rationalism in the theological faculties of the universities. By supporting the careers of a group of talented young men whose theological and political ideas, influenced by their associations with Neo-Pietist aristocrats and clergymen,[109] were opposed to the liberals' aspirations of transforming the autocratic structure of the church and state, the Junker Pietists gained highly influential allies in their struggle to maintain their political and social privileges.

While not having an organization in the sense of a political party, the liberals nevertheless kept alive the idea of a constitutionally limited regime and found channels through which to carry on their opposition to the political and social order of the Restoration.[110] The reaction which set in after 1815, and especially after 1819, made it clear to them that means for advancing their political goals would have to be found within the established limits. Since most clergymen of the reorganized state church still adhered to the theological rationalism of the eighteenth century—which held that a rational and just society should be based on achievement and merit, and denied the innate superiority of any classes or persons—the liberals expected and

108. See Werner Conze, "Staat und Gesellschaft in der frührevolutionären Epoche Deutschlands," *HZ*, 186 (1958), 31 f. See also Reinhart Koselleck, "Staat und Gesellschaft in Preussen, 1815–1848," in Werner Conze, ed., *Staat und Gesellschaft im deutschen Vormärz, 1815–1848* (Stuttgart, 1962), p. 99; hereafter cited as Conze, *Staat und Gesellschaft*.

109. See the characteristic account by August Tholuck in *Die Lehre von der Sünde und vom Versöhner, oder die wahre Weihe des Zweiflers* (Hamburg, 1823), which describes his "awakening" by Baron von Kottwitz, his "father Abraham."

110. Schnabel, vol. II (*Monarchie und Volkssouveränität*), especially "Der Kampf," pp. 215–373. See also Wolfgang Zorn, "Staat und Gesellschaft in Preussen, 1815–1848," and Werner Conze, "Das Spannungsfeld von Staat und Gesellschaft," in Conze, *Staat und Gesellschaft*, pp. 79–112, 207–270.

cultivated the support of the rank-and-file clergy. On the other hand, the conservative and reactionary forces defending the status quo also looked to the church. For the advancement of their interests, it would be desirable to eradicate rationalism in the clergy by replacing the leading rationalists and liberals in the high levels of the ecclesiastical hierarchy with orthodox Lutherans and Neo-Pietists who would train a new generation of politically reliable and active clergymen. In short, the liberals hoped to enlist the influence of liberal clergymen in the furthering of their aims, and the conservatives were determined to make the state church a bulwark for the established order.[111] Thus the Protestant church and its clergy acquired a new significance.

Let us first turn to the activities of the conservative clergy and its allies. The "awakened" Neo-Pietists of the new century—no longer the "quiet people," but an aggressive and politically conscious clerical group—eagerly made common cause with conservative aristocrats who sought religious sanction for their privileged position. Together they were animated by the battle cry of Ludwig von Gerlach, an influential ultraconservative leader and one of the chief organizers of the Conservative party during the Revolution of 1848: "We must give our consciousness of God a political form!" [112]

111. Eylert blamed "educated people" in particular for "connecting the theological controversies with the political struggle" (III, pt. 1, 346).

112. Oscar Stillich, *Die politischen Parteien in Deutschland,* Vol. I, *Die Konservativen* (Leipzig, 1908), p. 34.

See also Jakob von Gerlach, ed., *Ernst Ludwig von Gerlach: Aufzeichnungen aus seinem Leben und Wirken, 1795–1877* (Schwerin in Meckl., 1903), I, 518 f.; hereafter cited as Gerlach, *Aufzeichnungen.* Also Eylert, III, pt. 1, 247 f.; Jordan, *op. cit.* (n. 88 above), pp. 137 ff.

Part Two

The Conservatives

2

Leadership Selection in the Reorganized Protestant State Church

I

The clergy of the reorganized Protestant state church (*Evangelische Landeskirche*) of Prussia in the nineteenth century included all members of the ecclesiastical hierarchy who had completed at least three years of university study in theology, passed the prescribed examinations, and received an appointment to office. The government appointed the ecclesiastical officials of churches, hospitals, prisons, and other institutions, including homes for disabled soldiers and orphans. It also made all the more usual appointments, from those of the upper echelons—including the theology professors, general superintendents, bishops, chief Consistory councilors, court and cathedral preachers, Consistory councilors, district superintendents, and military, university, and embassy chaplains [1]—down to

1. Evangelischer Ober-Kirchenrat, Generalia, Abteilung XV, no. 3, Archiv des Evangelischen Konsistoriums Berlin-Brandenburg, Berlin. The official collective terms *Geistliche, Prediger, Geistlichkeit,* and *Geistliche Beamte* were used to refer to the clergy, together with the more conventional designations *Pastor* and *Pfarrer*.

the bottom of the hierarchy, where the village pastors continued to constitute the vast majority. Among all these clergymen, only those whose functions included the actual administration of the sacraments were ordained.[2]

Before the reorganization of the Protestant church, clergymen seldom had been given appointments to the secular bureaucracy.[3] In the nineteenth century, however, there developed the practice of appointing politically conservative clergymen to a variety of non-ecclesiastical government positions where their particular talents and skills were believed to be helpful in the task of consolidating and strengthening the political and social structure of the Prussian state. Such special appointments and functions increased the prestige of the chosen individuals and at the same time raised the status of the clergy as a group. One such appointee was Johann Peter Friedrich Ancillon (1767–1837), a descendant of French Huguenots who had settled in Berlin in the eighteenth century. He began his career as pastor of the French Reformed church in the capital. His reactionary views in opposition to the "ideas of 1789" were much appreciated at the royal court, and he became the tutor of the Crown Prince during the Napoleonic Wars. Ancillon was markedly influential in instilling much of the future King Frederick William IV's distrust toward constitutional changes.[4] His firm support of "throne and altar" and his smooth diplomatic manners endeared him to the government, which made him a member of the Council of State (Staatsrat) in 1817. Ancillon's ability at cooperating with varied reactionary groups and individuals (including Prince Metternich) in opposing liberal tendencies and movements in Prussia and other European states during the Restoration period was eventually responsible for his appointment as minister of foreign affairs in 1832.[5] Among others in government positions were Heinrich Leonhard Heubner (1780–1853) and Johann Hinrich Wichern (1808–1881). Heubner was one of the founding directors and, after 1832, the chief superintendent of the postgraduate seminary at Wittenberg. He served on the special government commission which investigated the political and social

2. *Ibid., Abteilung* V, 17, 2223 Eo.
3. The appointment of Wöllner was one of the exceptions.
4. Paul Haake, *J. P. F. Ancillon und Kronprinz Friedrich Wilhelm IV von Preussen* (Munich and Berlin, 1920), pp. 18 ff.
5. *RGG* (1956), p. 360.

aspects of the "Pomeranian Awakening" in the 1820's.[6] Wichern was the founder and first official head of the "Inner Mission," which came to represent the sterile social outlook of Prussian conservatism. He began his career as a minister at a training school for destitute youths in Hamburg in 1833. His phenomenal talents of oratory and persuasion and his general appeal to the social conscience of German Protestants in the field of organized charity impressed the government so much that he was appointed in the "Hungry Forties" to a number of royal commissions which investigated the causes of social unrest among urban workers and agrarian laborers. In addition Wichern was employed by the government in the work of reforming the Prussian penal system. As Consistory councilor and as permanent councilor (*Vortragender Rat*) in the Ministry of the Interior, he often submitted suggestions and recommendations to the government to the effect that a "patriarchal relation" between noble land-owner and peasants and between factory owner and workers was the best guarantee for a Christian solution of the "social problem." Wichern's oratorical and organizational skills were used by the government for pacifying social unrest [7]—especially among apprentices and journeymen, who were the most articulate labor elements in Prussia before 1848.[8]

Yet the successful careers of a number of clergymen could not change the fact that employment possibilities in the clergy were in a state of stagnation. In the first half of the nineteenth century the population of Prussia increased from about 10 million to well over 16 million, and the total of the Protestant church membership from about 6 million to 10 million,[9] but there was no significant increase in the numbers of the clergy. More precisely, in 1822 there were reportedly 5,714 clergymen, and in 1847 the number was

6. *Zum Gedächtnis Dr. Heinrich Leonhard Heubners, Zum Besten der Heubner-stiftung, herausgegeben von den Mitgliedern des Königl. Prediger-Seminars* (Wittenberg, 1853), pp. 21 ff.; hereafter cited as *Zum Gedächtnis Heubners.*

7. For Wichern and the "social problem" see the discussion in Shanahan, pp. 70 ff.

8. Theodore S. Hamerow, *Restoration, Revolution, Reaction: Economics and Politics in Germany, 1815-1871* (Princeton, 1958), pp. 21-37, 75-93; hereafter cited as Hamerow, *Restoration.*

Also: P. H. Noyes, *Organization and Revolution: Working Class Associations in the German Revolutions of 1848-1849* (Princeton, 1966), pp. 15-33.

9. *Jahrbuch für die Amtliche Statistik des Preussischen Staats* (Berlin, 1863), I, 34 ff.; hereafter cited as *Jahrbuch.*

5,783.[10] The large increase in population seriously strained the drastically altered social order.[11] In view of the fact that this was an age plagued with short-term economic recessions and, up to the mid-1830's, also with long-term depression, the church congregations—which had to provide the remuneration for more than 90 percent of the clergy—were unwilling to employ new assistant pastors or to build new churches.

In Berlin, some fifty to sixty clergymen served in churches, hospitals, penal institutions, and institutions for the poor. This number was considered inadequate by active church members, including the Pietists and orthodox Lutherans.[12] In an address to the city magistrates in 1845, Frederick William IV noted that the 50,000 to 60,000 inhabitants of Berlin under Frederick William I enjoyed the services of more clergymen than did the 400,000 of the 1840's. Although the king urged the building of new churches and the employment of more clergymen by the city government to serve the spiritual needs of his "beloved Berliners," the situation did not improve. In these matters, Berlin was rather typical of conditions and attitudes in both the western and the eastern provinces of the Prussian state.[13]

What Frederick William IV failed to point out was that many congregations in Prussia resented the fact that, while they remunerated their pastors, the government exercised the exclusive right of appointment, transfer, promotion, and dismissal of all clergymen through the centrally administered provincial Consistories. Only theology professors, clergymen employed in homes for disabled soldiers and in hospitals and other state institutions, along with army chaplains, provincial general superintendents, and a very few other

10. "Denkschrift betreffend die Gründung neuer ev. Pfarrstellen und Kirchensysteme in der Preussischen Monarchie," in Evangelischer Ober-Kirchenrat, *op. cit.* (n. 1 above).

11. See Werner Conze, "Vom 'Pöbel' zum 'Proletariat': Die Voraussetzungen für den Sozialismus in Deutschland," *Vierteljahrschrift für Sozial- und Wirtschaftsgeschichte*, 41 (1954), 333–364; hereafter cited as Conze, "Vom 'Pöbel' zum 'Proletariat.'"

Also: Reinhard Koselleck, "Staat und Gesellschaft in Preussen, 1815–1848," in Conze, *Staat und Gesellschaft*, pp. 97 f.

12. "Denkschrift des Ev. Ober-Kirchenrats betreffend die Vermehrung der Dotation der Evangelischen Kirche in Preussen," Archiv des Evangelischen Konsistoriums Berlin-Brandenburg, Berlin.

13. *EKZ*, 1845, p. 934; *The German Reformation of the 19th Century* [by the German correspondent of the *Continental Echo*] (London, 1846), pp. 364–365.

full-time ecclesiastical officials, were paid directly by the government. It must be remembered that although the ecclesiastical hierarchy of the state church after 1815 held many new and old functional positions, official titles, and rank distinctions—there being one archbishop, eight or nine bishops, some thirty court preachers, and varying numbers of ecclesiastical and school superintendents, Consistory councilors, chief Consistory councilors, knights of the Order of the Red Eagle, and so on—most clergymen who held such titles and positions were at the same time ministers of congregations. Most full professors of theology in the universities also were either regular ministers of congregations or active as paid part-time preachers in parish churches. The nature of the political involvement of some clergymen of this period was greatly influenced by the ambiguous character of their position as ecclesiastical officials of the government and paid employees of congregations.

The turnover of clerical personnel was very slow. All clergymen (including full professors of theology, but not assistant professors and lecturers) had tenure for lifetime and most of them stayed in office to the end of their lives. Consequently, keen competition developed among the increasing numbers of candidates for vacant positions. Taking the period 1815–1847 as a norm, there were only 120 to 150 clerical vacancies per year, and these relatively few vacancies were quickly filled by candidates from the growing ranks of the "ecclesiastical reserve army." The average number of students of theology at the universities of Halle, Berlin, Königsberg, and Bonn ranged from about 850 in the late 1810's to 1,500 in the early 1820's, and 1,600 in the 1830's, and fewer than 700 by the end of the 1840's.[14] The trend, thus, was downward after the 1830's, but until then, despite many drop-outs and transfers to other fields of study, there existed a considerable reservoir of candidates faced with the alternative of waiting for eventual openings while trying to make a living

14. See the specific data in the histories of these universities: Wilhelm Schrader, *Geschichte der Friedrichs Universität zu Halle* (Berlin, 1895), II, 568; hereafter cited as Schrader; Lenz, II, pt. 2, 493 f. Georg Kaufmann, ed., *Geschichte der Universität Breslau, 1811–1911* (Breslau, 1911), p. 66; hereafter cited as Kaufmann, *Geschichte der Universität Breslau*. Hans Prutz, *Die königliche Albertus Universität in Preussen im 19. Jahrhundert* (Königsberg, 1894), p. 202; hereafter cited as Prutz. Friedrich von Bezold, *Geschichte der rheinischen Friedrich-Wilhelm Universität von der Gründung bis zum Jahr 1870* (Bonn, 1920), p. 189; hereafter cited as Bezold.

as tutors or in other temporary occupations, or of turning to other careers.[15] It would seem odd that despite the uncertainty of eventual employment so many students (among them some very talented ones) were determined to pursue clerical careers. Moreover, in the light of such doubtful professional prospects, it appears even more puzzling that during the first half of the century the social pattern of personnel recruitment underwent noteworthy changes. The evidence available for that period clearly indicates that quite a few clergymen now came from families of handicraftsmen, higher officials, and aristocratic army officers and landowners, while in the past as a rule only clergymen's sons had entered the clergy.

The fact that many clergymen's sons in pre-March Prussia continued to follow the traditional occupation of their ancestors needs little explanation. Aside from the impact of occupational heredity in an age of highly restricted social mobility, the clerical sons had come to appreciate the advantages of the profession and hoped that, even if they had to wait some years after the conclusion of their theological training, their backgrounds and connections would eventually help them to secure a respectable position carrying with it at least a certain modicum of economic security.[16]

Although the income of clergymen in the cities and the country varied greatly, depending on the composition of their congregations and on local conditions, the fact that all clerical offices provided some degree of economic security was attractive not only to sons of clergymen but also to some young men who came from families of struggling handicraftsmen. August Tholuck, who became a prominent conservative theology professor, was the son of an impoverished goldsmith in Breslau who strove desperately to provide for his large family of eleven. The bitter memories of his childhood must have

15. In 1828, Consistory councilor Neander stated that in the administrative district of Merseburg alone there were more than ninety candidates who had been on the official list of candidates (*Predigerliste*) for nine to ten years and were continuing to inquire regularly about possible openings. Report to the Ministry of Ecclesiastical Affairs and Education, in Dibelius, pp. 17, 107 f.

16. See the characteristic comments of the pastor of Anderbeck, in the Prussian province of Saxony, in C. B. König, *Wanderung durch Vaterhaus, Schule, Kriegslager und Akademie zur Kirche* (Magdeburg, 1838), pp. 11 f. See also the information on the social histories of Protestant clergymen in Hermann Werdermann, *Der evangelische Pfarrer in Geschichte und Gegenwart* (Leipzig, 1925), pp. 34, 111, 122 f., and Paul Drews, *Der evangelische Geistliche in der deutschen Vergangenheit* (Jena, 1905), p. 70.

made the young student Tholuck appreciate the secure position and social advantages inherent in public employment in an age of depressions and recessions.[17] Leberecht Uhlich, a pastor who was among the leaders of the liberal "Friends of Light" movement in the 1840's, was the son of an impoverished tailor who, giving up his trade to become the servant of a nobleman in order to support his family, made great sacrifices to spare his son the hardships and humiliations of his own life. As a pastor of the small community of Pömmelte near Magdeburg, Uhlich appreciated the economic security of his position, which provided him with an adequate income for his own large family.[18] Although there were many parsonages which enabled clergymen to lead a fairly comfortable life, the majority of the pastors in the country and in the urban centers were absorbed in the business of providing a living for their usually large families (which continued to be the main reservoir for Germany's cultural elite, furnishing professors, natural and social scientists, lawyers, physicians, government officials, and other academically trained professionals).[19] In general, although these pastors might be dissatisfied with their low income, economic conditions among the lower clergy (in comparison with the plight of other minor government officials, such as teachers) were by no means desperate.

The chief court and cathedral preachers in Berlin and other large cities, general superintendents, bishops, and prominent theological professors were the highest-paid ecclesiastical officials. Next to them were the chief Consistory councilors, district superintendents, Consistory councilors, embassy and military chaplains, and clergymen employed in the churches of some of the wealthier urban congregations. Some clergymen held several positions, such as chief cathedral preacher, bishop, Consistory councilor, and in some cases even university professorships, and their combined salaries compared favorably with those paid in the top levels of the administrative service. F. S. G. Sack, for instance, in 1816 received 1,000 thalers as bishop, 300 thalers as chief Consistory councilor, and 1,600 thalers from his position as chief court preacher. In addition to their cash income,

17. Leopold Witte, *Das Leben D. Friedrich August Gotttreu Tholuck's* (Bielefeld and Leipzig, 1884–1886), I, 132; hereafter cited as Witte, *Tholuck.*

18. *Leberecht Uhlich: Sein Leben von ihm selbst beschrieben* (Gera, 1872), pp. 2–6; hereafter cited as Uhlich.

19. J. F. von Schulte, "Herkunft und Alter von deutschen Gelehrten aller Art," in his *Lebenserinnerungen* (Leipzig, 1909), III, 277 ff.

men like Sack and quite a few other members of the clergy usually also received payments in kind, such as free housing and a certain amount of grain and firewood, along with other benefits. G. F. A. Strauss had a total cash salary of 3,000 thalers annually (1,500 as professor of theology at the Univerity of Berlin after 1822 and 1,500 as chief court preacher). Because of his wife's wealthy family, Strauss had a considerable additional income from private sources.[20]

As a group, however, professors of theology did not receive salaries commensurate with their official status as high-ranking civil servants and the prestige they enjoyed in society. Although it had been the policy of the government since the Reform Era to provide adequate incomes for university professors, not many of them after 1815 received the cash salary of 1,500 thalers annually which Humboldt had considered necessary for professors to maintain a proper standard of living (*standesgemäss*). On the other hand, the prominent theology professors Schleiermacher, Strauss, Tholuck, Hengstenberg, Otto von Gerlach, Richard Rothe, and C. I. Nitzsch, and a few other university professors, such as the philosopher Hegel and the jurist Savigny, received salaries of 2,000 thalers or more.[21] Of these, Strauss, Tholuck, and Hengstenberg had additional sources of income through marriage into the wealthy upper classes, and Gerlach came from a well-to-do noble family. A few particularly prominent theology professors were also employed as preachers and religious instructors by church congregations or in universities and could thus add to their income. Contemporaries were aware that the salary scale of professors and other civil servants in the nineteenth century represented a considerable improvement, compared with the eighteenth century, even though among the Protestant theologians making their living as university teachers and scholars only the full professors could be considered an economically well-rewarded and fairly satisfied group. Associate or extraordinary professors, and especially the unsalaried lecturers called *Privatdozenten* (who aspired to appointments as professors), were insecure financially unless they had private incomes. On the whole, however, most clergymen, even the

---

20. Depending on the size and wealth of congregations, nonmonetary benefits varied greatly, but in many cases constituted a major form of income. Ludwig Lehmann, *Kirchengeschichte der Mark Brandenburg von 1818 bis 1932* (Berlin, 1936), p. 239; Lenz, II, pt. 1, 317, 410; Wendland, *700 Jahre*, pp. 231 ff.
21. Lenz, II, pt. 1, 409 f.

village pastors, seemed to benefit from the increasing concern of the administrative bureaucracy with raising the economic and social status of the state church and its "officers." [22]

As has been noted, within the "bureaucratized" framework of the church after 1815 most of the special pecuniary benefits, honors, and distinctions which the government bestowed upon officials tended to serve as rewards and incentives for "desirable" clergymen. Only those men whose creed, political views, leanings, associations, and activities seemed to support the men in power could expect higher appointments, promotions, special distinctions, and favors from the government. For instance, when in 1826 the young Neo-Pietist professor Tholuck, in the first year of his new position at the University of Halle, suffered one of his many nervous breakdowns, he applied for and was granted a one-year appointment as chaplain of the Prussian Legation at Rome to recover in a more pleasant environment.[23] This post was usually reserved for particular favorites of the government. Friedrich von Tippelskirch (1802–1866), an associate and close friend of Wichern, and chief editor of the influential conservative Halle newspaper *Volksblatt für Stadt und Land zur Belehrung und Unterhaltung* in 1844–1848, was chaplain in Rome from 1829 to 1835 and would willingly have stayed longer, but the government was planning to bestow the favor on someone else.[24] Hengstenberg, the leader of the most influential conservative faction in the clergy after the late 1820's, was so absorbed in the struggle against the liberals that only occasionally did he ask for and receive from the government special paid vacation trips to Karlsbad. When he went to the spa, however, he usually arranged to meet some of the most prominent upper-class families from all over Germany.[25] Tholuck, whose nervous and always agitated nature desperately needed travel and change, greatly appreciated the willingness of the government to finance his

22. Bishop Eylert and other high-ranking nonacademic members of the ecclesiastical hierarchy were particularly impressed with the fact that while Semmler, Noesselt, Knapp, Eberhard, and other outstanding professors of the 1790's had annual salaries of some 400 to 500 thalers, Schleiermacher, Strauss, Hegel, and Savigny now received more than 2,000 thalers. Eylert, III, pt. 1, 510.

23. Witte, *Tholuck*, II, 86 ff.

24. Letter to Wichern, n.d., in Martin Gerhardt, *Der junge Wichern: Jugendtagebücher Johann Hinrich Wicherns* (Hamburg, 1925), p. 47.

25. Johannes Bachmann and Theodor Schmalenbach, *Ernst Wilhelm Hengstenberg: Sein Leben und Wirken nach gedruckten und ungedruckten Quellen dargestellt* (Gütersloh, 1876–1892), II, 87; hereafter cited as Bachmann, *Hengstenberg*.

trips to meetings and conferences in England, Holland, and Switzerland. It was in recognition of his long fight against rationalism and his influence on students at the University of Halle that Tholuck was awarded the Order of the Red Eagle, First Class, in 1844.[26]

Court preachers (*Hofprediger*), owing to their personal contacts with members of the royal family, court and government circles, and other segments of the upper classes, their high incomes and access to information, and the almost hereditary nature of their positions, traditionally constituted the upper crust of the clergy. After its conversion to the Reformed faith in the seventeenth century, the royal family had particularly favored Reformed court preachers, who had been considered among the most reliable supporters of the Crown (*Stützen des Throns*).

The functions of Reformed court preachers generally consisted of caring for the spiritual and educational needs of the royal family, the Reformed members of the court aristocracy, and the usually prosperous Reformed congregations in the predominantly Lutheran Prussian monarchy. Consequently, these men enjoyed high respect in government circles. After the final reorganization and confessional union of the Lutheran and Reformed churches, court preachers continued to be among the most important high-ranking officials of the state church. Closely tied to the Crown by tradition and interest, court preachers in pre-March Prussia continued to be (along with the military chaplains) among the staunchest supporters of the established political and social order. Both in theory and in active politics, court preachers were committed to defense of the privileges which they traditionally shared with the governing classes. In defending these privileges they continued to be the ecclesiastical "shields of the Crown." [27]

In the new age of increased and more active political opposition to the status quo under bureaucratic absolutism, the court preachers were rapidly surpassed in prestige and influence by the upcoming and politically more sophisticated and alert group of theology professors, who were dealing with representatives of a much larger public. Several professors—among them, G. F. A. Strauss and Otto von

26. Witte, *Tholuck*, II, 86 ff., 146; Adolf Hausrath, *Richard Rothe und seine Freunde* (Berlin, 1902–1906), I, 187 ff.; hereafter cited as Hausrath, *Rothe*.

27. Rudolf von Thadden, *Die Brandenburg-Preussischen Hofprediger im 17. und 18. Jahrhundert* (Berlin, 1959), pp. 3 ff.

Gerlach—were appointed court preachers as well as chief Consistory councilors, with a consequent further increase in their salaries, prestige, and political influence. In view of their high official status, strategic position, and close connections with the high government circles in the capital, the court preachers might have still exerted the primary influence over the church in public affairs. But because most of them could not compete with the political skills, sensitivity, trained minds, and public appeal of the academicians, the actual leadership for the various conservative and liberal factions within the clergy was provided by theology professors (joined by some exceptionally gifted clergymen from the ranks). In contrast, however, to the court preachers, who were an ideologically and politically united and cohesive group, the theology professors held diversified political beliefs.

II

It would be absurd to suggest that all theology students who were preparing for clerical careers were motivated only by material considerations. The post-Revolutionary religious revival created a great deal of religious fervor in many individuals. There were probably quite a few men who were attracted to the clergy because of their sincere dedication to the spiritual and idealistic nature of the profession. But it cannot be denied that economic security, in an age characterized by chronic economic instability for the vast majority of the population (including many noble landowners), and respectable status—perhaps even prominence, fame, and significant public influence by attaining a high position in the church—were powerful incentives for young men from all social levels. No less than the sons of clergymen and handicraftsmen, those new elements who came from upper-class families of high officials and aristocratic army officers and landowners were attracted by the opportunities for advancement which the church could offer to its officials.

The idea of establishing one or more permanent government institutions for the unusually promising and politically most reliable candidates from the "ecclesiastical reserve army" waiting for appointments originated with Nicolovius and the Wittenberg theology professor Heubner. The pious Heubner had accepted the incorporation of parts of his native Saxony, including Wittenberg, into the Prussian state after 1815 with resignation to God's will. His main concern had always been with sin, grace, salvation, and the danger of rationalistic thinking to man's soul. Firmly believing in the Lutheran tenet of subordination to the given worldly authorities, Heubner was especially willing to cooperate with the Prussian authorities if he could continue his fight against rationalism by establishing a Neo-Pietist stronghold at Wittenberg under Prussian rule.[28]

Heubner eventually became one of the most trusted officials of his Prussian superiors in the province of Saxony. Before the dissolution of the University of Wittenberg in 1815 by the Prussian government, Heubner was an assistant professor of theology there. Born into a family of Protestant clergymen in Lauterbach, Saxony, he became an orphan at the age of three.[29] As a struggling theology student at Wittenberg, Heubner came under the influence of the Moravian Brethren. In the rationalist theological atmosphere of the university this thin, poorly clad young man from the country found strength in the mystical and highly spiritualistic Pietist creed of the Moravians. After his spiritual "awakening" Heubner considered himself a soldier of the church in its effort to cope with the world and to overcome what it considered secular perils to religion. His unquestioning, simple faith gradually hardened into an inflexible dogmatism which found little use for systematic theology and the search for answers and explanations.[30] Although Heubner was no scholar, his dedication, hard work, and meek, humble nature were appreciated by his rationalist professors. In 1805 he passed the special qualifying examinations for prospective university teachers and was appointed Privatdozent, and in 1811 he was assistant professor.

Nicolovius made the acquaintance of Heubner while working on plans to utilize the facilities of the dissolved University of Wittenberg. In cooperation with Baron Hans Ernst von Kottwitz—an "awakened" Silesian nobleman and landowner who had settled in Berlin in 1807 and was developing what became the most influential

28. Throughout his life, Heubner always reminded his fellow men that it was their religious duty to obey worldly authorities: "Seid untertan aller menschlichen Ordnung um des Herrn willen." *Blätter zur Erinnerung an das Stiftungsfest des Prediger-Seminars zu Wittenberg* (Wittenberg, 1842), pp. 27 f.; hereafter cited as *Blätter.*

For similar views of Heubner see A. Koch, *D. Heinrich Leonhard Heubner in Wittenberg: Züge und Zeugnisse aus und zu seinem Leben und Wirken* (Wittenberg, 1885), p. 40.

29. Much of the information on Heubner is derived from *Zum Gedächtnis Heubners;* Hausrath, *Rothe;* and Dibelius.

30. Letter to Kottwitz, November 19, 1817, in Kantzenbach, *Kottwitz,* pp. 133 f.

Pietist circle of the "Awakening" in the capital—and August Neander (1789–1850), a professor of theology at the University of Berlin, Nicolovius and Heubner persuaded the government to establish a postgraduate seminary at Wittenberg in 1817.[31] The celebration of the three-hundredth anniversary of the Reformation at Wittenberg highlighted the replacement of Luther's university with a new seminary under the aegis of the Pietist "Holy Three": Heubner, Kottwitz, and Nicolovius. Through the circle of the "Old Baron"—as Kottwitz was affectionately called by his friends and admirers—Heubner continued enlarging his connections with Pietist and orthodox Lutheran clergymen and theology students, and with a group of Old Prussian and other noblemen who, embracing the antirevolutionary gospel of political Romanticism, including its irrational mysticism, had "awakened" to a deeply emotional Neo-Pietistic religion. Heubner's marriage to a young noblewoman, Catherine von Brück, in 1818, further strengthened the ties between Pietist clergymen and "awakened" noblemen.[32]

Greatly disturbed by the fact that the majority of the clergy still professed the rationalist creed, the aristocrat adherents of the Neo-Pietist and orthodox combination of the "Awakening" condemned rationalism as the root of all evil, including the French Revolution and its subversive effects on the traditional order. Under the influence of this small but powerful group of politically conscious noblemen, the "Awakening" became the rallying point for the avant garde of a special segment of the conservative movement.[33] The Wittenberg Seminary was eventually to become one of the bulwarks of the nineteenth-century Neo-Pietist effort to develop the new Prussian state church into an aggressively active instrument for defending the political and social structure of Prussia against political opposition pressing from below. To the conservatives the seminary was a crucial center for preparing the new elite of the clergy to defeat the *Zeitgeist;*

31. For the tremendous influence of the "old Baron" see the valuable collection of letters and the Introduction (pp. 1–30) in Kantzenbach, *Kottwitz.* See also Kantzenbach, *Die Erweckungsbewegung,* pp. 16 ff.; Fischer, *Nicolovius,* pp. 384 ff.; and Witte, *Tholuck,* I, 125 ff.

32. Heubner to Kottwitz, November 19, 1817, in Kantzenbach, *Kottwitz,* p. 133.

33. Schnabel, II, 26 ff.; Huber, II, 338 f.; and the article "Die Erweckungsbewegung," *RGG* (1958), pp. 622–629.

See also Walter Wendland, "Studien zur Erweckungsbewegung in Berlin, 1810–1830," *JBKG,* 19 (1924), 28 ff.; hereafter cited as Wendland, "Studien."

to the political opposition it was a bulwark of superstition and reaction.[34]

The Wittenberg Seminary had the avowed purpose of training for future careers a small number—about twenty-five to thirty—of selected and especially promising candidates from the various Prussian universities. In addition to professional competence, political reliability was essential if a candidate was to receive a scholarship at Wittenberg. In accordance with the rule of seniority, the government appointed the mildly rationalist and highly respected seventy-year-old professor Carl Ludwig Nitzsch (father of the liberal theology professor Carl Immanuel Nitzsch) as the nominal head of the new institution, and his fifty-year-old professorial colleague at the former University of Wittenberg, Johann Friedrich Schleusner, as second director. From the very beginning, however, the government made it clear that the third director, Heubner, was in charge of the affairs of the seminary.[35]

The "Era Heubner" at Wittenberg did not begin with the later appointment of Heubner as superintendent and first director of the seminary in 1832. By the early 1820's Heubner had established himself as one of the chief confidants of the government, not only in Wittenberg and the province of Saxony, but in the whole realm. Convinced that his mission was to train "fighters for God against the *Zeitgeist*," Heubner considered it his duty to remain in Wittenberg. Consequently, he continued to refuse offers from the universities of Königsberg and Leipzig and from other institutions; he preferred his role of the "Pietist general and uncrowned king of Wittenberg." Up to his death in 1853, Heubner remained, like the "Old Baron," a quiet but very powerful man behind the scenes. He preferred to leave the fighting in the open political arena to Hengstenberg, Tholuck, Otto and Ludwig von Gerlach, the Old Prussian nobleman Adolf von Thadden-Trieglaff (1796–1882), and other "true believers." Heubner's incredibly extensive correspondence with Nicolovius and with the ministers of ecclesiastical affairs and education, Altenstein and J. A. F. Eichhorn, and other government officials, as

34. *Verhandlungen der Evangelischen General-Synode zu Berlin vom 2. Juni bis zum 29. August 1846: Amtlicher Abdruck* (Berlin, 1846), pp. 97 ff.; "Die heutigen Mystiker—Mystiker aus Politik," *AKZ*, 1830, 491.

35. M. Gustav Krüger, ed., *Berichte über die erste evangelische Generalsynode Preussens im Jahre 1846: Mit einem Anhange der wichtigsten Aktenstücke* (Leipzig, 1846), pp. 62 ff.; hereafter cited as Krüger, *Generalsynode*.

well as with Kottwitz, Tholuck, and other Pietists, is indicative of the tremendous influence that he exerted in the first half of the century. Shortly after the dismissal of De Wette, in 1819, the government consulted Heubner on the filling of the vacant chair of theology at the University of Berlin.[36] Eventually the Pietist protégé Hengstenberg was appointed to the position in 1828. The government recognized the effectiveness of Heubner as an opponent of the *Zeitgeist*. In 1832, Altenstein stated explicitly, "Church and State need your services," and promised every possible help and cooperation in his work. In the same year, besides becoming superintendent and first director of the seminary, Heubner was appointed district superintendent and Consistory councilor in Wittenberg.[37]

During the "Era Heubner" the Wittenberg Seminary was a school of conservative theological and political indoctrination for a highly select group, an *Elite Anstalt*. The government provided two-year scholarships to prepare these "worthy and deserving" candidates for the "struggle against the dragon's seed (*Drachensaat*) of rationalism in their future positions."[38] The establishment of a centrally organized and government-controlled training center for future clergymen had been strongly opposed, from the beginning, by Schleiermacher and De Wette at the University of Berlin, Johann Christian Gass and David Schulz at the University of Breslau, and other liberal-minded theology professors. In 1819, Schleiermacher again expressed his belief that the Wittenberg institution would almost certainly develop into a place of indoctrination where the influence of "one particular faction" (*Partei*) would make it virtually impossible for candidates to develop their minds freely, and De Wette had joined him in stressing that the indoctrination of prospective clerical leaders ought to be avoided. They and other liberal clergymen continued to insist that it was the responsibility of the government to ensure that clerical trainees should be exposed to a variety of theological interpretations so that they could develop their own beliefs and opinions. The views of these men were apparently reflections of the demand of the liberals that universities and other institutions of higher learning should be "free market-places of ideas" and not schools of indoctrination for conservative ideologies. On the other

36. *Zum Gedächtnis Heubners*, pp. 31, 40; Dibelius, p. 159.   37. Dibelius, p. 75.
38. Nicolovius to Heubner, December 1, 1821, in Hausrath, *Rothe*, I, 160. See also Dibelius, pp. 35 ff. and the chapter "Die Ära Heubner," pp. 51–144.

hand, conservative-minded clergymen supported the seminary. Heubner and Neander in particular were convinced that it was necessary to have an institution to counteract the teachings of the rationalist theology professors at the nearby University of Halle, which until the end of the 1840's continued to educate the greatest number of theology students. Neander considered it his special duty to send some of his most promising candidates to Wittenberg.[39]

Within a few years, the Wittenberg Seminary had proved to be an efficiently operating training center and had become an important channel of Pietist patronage. Dominated by Heubner and his friends, it seemed to live up to expectations by producing candidates who denounced the *Zeitgeist,* and their subsequent appointments showed the government's favoritism toward them.[40] In the course of the discussions at the General Synod in 1846, court and cathedral preacher Friedrich Ehrenberg (1776–1852) stated that the education of the candidates was conducted with "Prussian strictness" (*Preussische Straffheit*), and that life in the seminary differed little from that of soldiers in the barracks (*Kasernenleben*) except for the Pietist custom of kissing on the cheeks (*Bruderkuss*) after prayer meetings.[41]

The fact that most candidates realized that it was to their advantage to conform to the ways of thinking and behavior expected of them did not mean that actually all of them did so conform during their stay at Wittenberg or later in their careers. A conspicuous exception to theological and political indoctrination was Friedrich Eylert (1806–1866), the only son of the court and cathedral preacher and bishop R. F. Eylert. For rebelling against the dogmatic spirit of the seminary, young Eylert was expelled in 1829. Eventually he became a physician and an active political opponent of the government; in 1848 he led the attack of a group of revolutionaries against the palace

39. Foerster, *Entstehung,* I, 161, 186, 310 f., and H. E. Schmieder, *Erinnerungen aus meinem Leben* (Wittenberg, 1892), pp. 145 ff. Schmieder was a graduate of the Wittenberg Seminary who made a splendid career as the first chaplain to be appointed to the Prussian Legation at Rome (1819–1823) and later as a teacher at the famous secondary school in Schulpforta. In 1844 he was given an honorary doctoral degree by the University of Königsberg, awarded the Order of the Red Eagle, Second Class, and promoted to chief Consistory councilor. In 1853 he became the first director of the Wittenberg Seminary. He was one of the main Pietist leaders after Heubner's death. See also Dibelius, pp. 19, 32, 165.

40. See the well-documented account in Hausrath, *Rothe,* I, 159 ff.

41. Krüger, *Generalsynode,* pp. 62 f.; Dibelius, pp. 122 ff.

of the Prince of Prussia, and in 1849 went into exile.[42] A letter written in 1831 by another candidate, Julius Rupp, was characteristic of the attitude of those who seemed to follow the "party line" for the sake of their careers and security but were in reality opposed to it. Rupp's friend Hermann Hempel, studying theology at the University of Berlin, became disgusted with the influence of the Pietist faction there, led by Hengstenberg, and wanted to change to the study of philosophy. In reply to Hempel's complaints, Rupp wrote:

> Ideas are free! I laugh at his [Heubner's] jeremiads against reason even if I do not show it. I hope you are not serious about giving up the prospect of a clerical career. After the second examination your name is put on the list of eligible candidates (*Predigerliste*) [and] eventually you will receive a position in which you can engage in activities which are not paid by the government.[43]

Rupp later was a leading figure in the political opposition at his native Königsberg. Richard Rothe and Carl Immanuel Nitzsch, two outstanding theologians of the century, also turned their backs on theological orthodoxy and Pietism after several years at Wittenberg (most of the time as instructors), although they received their first academic appointments with the help of Heubner, Neander, and other Pietists.[44]

Nevertheless, many future theological leaders of the influential Pietist faction within the conservative movement spent some time at Wittenberg and continued to return for occasional visits in their later lives. Several were placed in important ecclesiastical positions by the Pietist "Holy Three." The connections of Heubner, Kottwitz, and Nicolovius with the ministry of ecclesiastical affairs and education and with a small but increasingly influential group of aristocrats and the Crown Prince enabled them to keep a close watch on clerical openings and to act swiftly and effectively.[45] Characteristic of the

---

42. *Lebenslauf der sämtlichen Mitglieder des Königlichen Prediger-Seminars zu Wittenberg* (Stuttgart, 1868), p. 46; hereafter cited as *Lebenslauf*.
Also Wendland, *700 Jahre*, p. 285.

43. *Julius Rupp: Briefe, 1831–1884*, ed. Lina Rupp (Heidelberg, 1907), pp. 2 ff.

44. Nicolovius to Heubner, November 22, 1823, in Hausrath, *Rothe*, I, 222, 323 ff.; Heubner to Kottwitz, April 8, 1820, in Kantzenbach, *Kottwitz*, p. 137.
See also Willibald Beyschlag, *Carl Immanuel Nitzsch*, 2d ed. (Berlin, 1882), pp. 46–52; hereafter cited as Beyschlag, *Nitzsch*.

45. Nicolovius to Hengstenberg, September 2, 1828, Hengstenberg papers, Box 1; Wendland, "Studien," pp. 61 ff.

aims and the efficient operation of the Pietist "machine" is Nicolovius's letter to Heubner of December 21, 1821, in which the director of the Kultusabteilung plead:

> Please help us find pious candidates who have the *right* training
> [and] ability to oppose the Zeitgeist and who can show the people
> the right way. We in the Ministry [of ecclesiastical affairs and edu-
> cation] rely on you completely.[46]

III

Significantly enough, Nicolovius and Kottwitz seemed to be particularly concerned with filling vacant positions in the theological faculties of the universities, since the incumbents would inevitably exert
a strong influence on the molding of the minds of clergymen in the
making. In a letter of February 1821, Nicolovius assured Heubner:
"We have now [and] we shall have in the future *important positions*
to fill with the *right* type of theologians, but where can we find
them? Please help us in our task." [47] Heubner, Kottwitz, and other
leading Pietist conservatives were indeed willing and anxious to
"help in the task." The fact that after 1817 some of the most important academic and other higher ecclesiastical positions came to be
filled by the young generation of the "Wittenberg circle" was evidence of the rising influence of the Pietist faction. The careers of the
theology professors August Hahn, August Tholuck, Ernst Wilhelm
Hengstenberg, Hermann Olshausen, Otto von Gerlach, Ferdinand
Guericke, August Kahnis, and some lesser-known theologians in the
1820's, 1830's, and 1840's showed how influential the leading Pietist
conservatives could be in the placement of dependable theologians
and protégés in university positions. Most of these men spent some
time at Wittenberg as in-service trainees or as frequent visitors, and
in general they remained in close contact with Heubner throughout
their careers.[48] Not only was there a conspicuous filling of academic
positions with Pietists after the late 1810's: in the eastern provinces,
some "awakened" noble church patrons also were anxious to cooperate with Nicolovius and Heubner in employing Pietist ministers.[49]

46. Hausrath, *Rothe,* I, 160; emphasis in the original.
47. *Ibid.,* I, 163; emphasis in the original. For a similar plea see Hermann Olshausen to Otto von Gerlach, May 1, 1827, Hengstenberg papers, Box 1.
48. Tholuck to Hahn, 1832, in Bonwetsch, *Tholuck Briefe,* p. 146.
49. Ludwig von Gerlach to Hengstenberg, September 11, 1836, in Gerlach family
archives, and March 7, 1837, Hengstenberg papers, Box III.

This patronage was a further incentive for job-conscious prospective clergymen to denounce rationalism and profess a Pietistic-orthodox creed. The government's highly selective distribution of promotions, distinctions, honors, and rewards among clergymen after the War of Liberation also demonstrated that in the reorganized Protestant state church there were limited but good possibilities for rapid advancement and special recognition, provided one possessed not only talent and special skills but also the "right" creed, political leanings, and connections.

As noted earlier, before 1815 the clergymen of Prussia came primarily from families in which the ministry had been the traditional occupation for generations. Very few "new men" were from families of merchants or handicraftsmen, and practically none were from the aristocracy. Consequently, the Protestant clergy had been a fairly homogeneous social group. In the reorganized state church after 1815, new possibilities for advancement in the church hierarchy were opened for men from all parts of the country and from all social classes and denominations. Professorships in particular provided important channels for social advancement. Moreover, theology was the cheapest academic field of study, and theological training could be completed in three years. Thus many students without means now sought professional careers as clergymen.[50] When Hengstenberg, the future leader of the most powerful conservative faction, was a lecturer with a small salary at the University of Berlin in 1824–1825, he had to rely on students' fees to help cover living expenses. In a letter to his father, asking for financial help, Hengstenberg stated: "Four out of five theology students here have *testimonia paupertatis*."[51] At the University of Halle the famous Francke Foundation had been providing board and room for struggling theology students since the eighteenth century. The rationalist theologians J. A. Wegscheider, Friedrich Gesenius, and A. H. Niemeyer at Halle derived much of

---

See also Hermann Theodor Wangemann, *Sieben Bücher preussischer Kirchengeschichte* (Berlin, 1859–1861), III, 67 ff.; hereafter cited as Wangemann, *Sieben Bücher*.

50. In the 1820's, the professor of law Savigny commented to a friend that in comparison with his law students most theology students were "poor wretches" (*arme Schlucker*). Lenz, I, pt. 1, 404.

51. Bachmann, *Hengstenberg*, I, 238. For similar complaints see A. Brandis to Hengstenberg, January 22 and March 3, 1824, Hengstenberg papers, Box 1.

their influence from the fact that they had the power of patronage over vacancies in the various institutions of the foundation.[52]

Although there is a lack of comprehensive statistical evidence on the social backgrounds of theology students in the period from 1815 to 1848, the records of the Wittenberg Seminary show a remarkable range. The seminary was admittedly an elite school, and the composition of its membership, although the candidates were drawn from all social classes and from all provinces, reflected the wish of the government after 1815 to attract also the aristocratic elements of Prussian society to the clergy of the state church. In sharp contrast to the previous pattern of recruitment, where sons of clergymen predominated, a summary of the statistical evidence for the Wittenberg Seminary shows significant changes in the social background of the future leaders of the clergy.[53] Only about a third of the candidates had clerical backgrounds, and about 15 percent came from families of teachers. Sons of handicraftsmen constituted about 20 percent, and roughly the same percentage came from aristocratic families—these were the sons of upper-echelon civil servants, army officers, and landowners.

Unfortunately, there is not enough evidence available for a specification of the apparently complex reasons which prompted men such as Otto von Gerlach, Ferdinand von Quast, Baron Albert Gustav von der Trenck, Franz Hugo von Bosse, Friedrich Christoph von Kathen, Johann Christian Friedrich von Winter, Baron Hermann von der Goltz, Friedrich von Bodelschwingh, Friedrich von Tippelskirch, Walter von Randeborgh, Johann Michael Christian von Hoff, Julius von der Kuhlen, and Georg von Winterfeldt,[54] along with some sons of less well-known noble families, to enter the ranks of the clergy in the nineteenth century. Actually, none of those just named was particularly talented, and only Otto von Gerlach was eventually able to rise to the positions of professor and chief Consis-

52. *EKZ*, 1830, p. 228.

53. I owe much of the following information to the help and cooperation of the late bishop of Berlin, Dr. Otto Dibelius, who was kind enough to let me use his records relating to the Wittenberg Seminary. Some statistical data relating to the social background of candidates can also be found in *Lebenslauf* and Dibelius.

54. Most of these men spent some time at Wittenberg after completing their university studies.

tory councilor. Yet clergymen from noble families could usually count on preferential treatment at least to the extent of being appointed to desirable pastoral positions which also carried considerable prestige and an assured income. For instance, Tippelskirch served as chaplain of the Prussian Legation at Rome and later was first preacher of the Charité Hospital in Berlin. By the 1840's he had secured an excellent position as chief pastor in Giebichenstein near Halle, where his duties allowed him enough time to edit the influential conservative Halle newspaper *Volksblatt für Stadt und Land*.[55] Bosse, in Calau, was the junior of two colleagues from middle-class families. Presumably his noble background was a consideration in his appointment, in 1832, as chief pastor there at the age of twenty-eight. Although it would be difficult to make a real comparison with the old Hohenzollern strategy of enticing young aristocrats into the army as officers, one can hardly escape the conclusion that the government after 1815 tended to favor the inclination of some noblemen to become clergymen. Most clergymen with noble backgrounds did not rise high in the ecclesiastical hierarchy, but in many cases their careers were eased, and quite a few clergymen with a "von" ended up in such administrative positions as district or county superintendents.[56]

On the whole, a very impressive number of prominent and high-ranking clergymen received postgraduate training at Wittenberg and were helped in their careers by the Pietist-orthodox "machine." Nicolovius, Heubner, Kottwitz, and others of their group were very quick to notice talented and hard-working candidates and tried to win them over to their side by holding out the promise of rapid advancement, especially as professors of theology. They never failed to draw the attention of the ministry of ecclesiastical affairs and education to promising young men; frequently they implored the government to enlist these candidates for the conservative cause by securing academic appointments for them. Conversely, the government would urge Heubner to watch out for exceptionally talented

55. *EKZ*, 1844, pp. 318 f.
56. C. A. König, *Die neueste Zeit in der Evangelischen Kirche* (Braunschweig, 1842), p. 39; *Tagebuch des Kandidaten Hermann Kohler* (Leipzig, 1838), pp. 14–17; Schmieder, *op. cit.* (n. 39 above), p. 169.

There was a similar "aristocratic urge toward the church" in France after 1815. Within limits, this can be said to have been a general European trend.

and reliable candidates and request him to influence them in the approved direction so that they could be appointed to high ecclesiastical positions.[57]

There can be little doubt that the government's efforts to select and train "right-thinking clergymen" proved very successful in the decades after 1815. It must be emphasized, however, that without talent on the part of the candidates the efforts would have miscarried. The high level of ability of some of the conservative Pietist and orthodox theologians demonstrated that in order to rise in the ecclesiastical hierarchy much more than piety was needed. There were many talented young men in Prussia and the other German states who competed eagerly for those positions which seemed to combine opportunities for service, dedication, and religious and ideological satisfaction with economic security and prestige and the possibility of recognition and even fame. The years from 1815 to 1848 were full of ideological, religious, political, social, and economic tensions. A dramatic population explosion and a spectacular increase in the number of university-trained men of talent seeking careers strained the structure of traditional society to the extreme.[58] Apparently, many of those who more and more were trying to realize their aspirations and hopes were aware that their ambitions might be realized in the Protestant clergy.

In 1842, on the twenty-fifth anniversary of the founding of the Wittenberg Seminary, the "Pietist General" Heubner proudly pointed out to the minister of ecclesiastical affairs and education Eichhorn and other officials of the "Christian-German" regime of Frederick William IV that the institution was fulfilling the expectations of its founders.[59] Of the Pietist "Holy Three," only Heubner was still alive to take pride in the accomplishment, but the presence of many former Wittenberg trainees and enthusiastic supporters of the Pietist-orthodox cause now occupying high positions in the church gave eloquent testimony to the effectiveness of their work. August Hahn, then professor of theology at the University of

57. Undated letters, Neander to Heubner, in the possession of Mrs. Anna Halfmann, widow of the late bishop of Kiel, D. Halfmann. Also: Heubner to Kottwitz, April 8, 1820, in Kantzenbach, *Kottwitz*, p. 137; Dibelius, pp. 190 ff.

58. See the excellent studies of these problems in Conze, *Staat und Gesellschaft*, and Reinhart Koselleck, *Preussen zwischen Reform und Revolution: Allgemeines Landrecht, Verwaltung und soziale Bewegung von 1791 bis 1848* (Stuttgart, 1967).

59. See *Blätter*, pp. 3 ff.

Breslau, was engaged in a ruthless campaign to destroy the influence of theological rationalism in Silesia. Soon he was to be appointed general superintendent of that province to complete the coordination of the separatist Old Lutheran movement. The former Wittenberg candidate J. K. Schmidtborn had recently relieved H. A. Wiesmann, another Wittenberg trainee, as general superintendent of the Rhineland province, and C. D. Borghardt was soon to become general superintendent of the province of Saxony, relieving K. Westermeyer. Bishop and Chief Court Preacher Eylert, General Superintendent Westermeyer, and other high-ranking church officials had indicated their appreciation of the institution by sending their sons there for training. In 1844 the theologian H. E. Schmieder, one of the first candidates admitted in 1817, was given an honorary doctor's degree by the University of Königsberg and rewarded with the Order of the Red Eagle, Second Class. When Heubner died, in 1853, Schmieder was appointed to the vacant post of first director and superintendent of the seminary; eventually he was also chief Consistory councilor. At the anniversary ceremonies, the stand of the government in the furious struggle then raging between the conservative Pietist-orthodox clerical leaders and the liberal Friends of Light was noted reassuringly by Eichhorn: "The government is by no means impartial, but is biased, totally biased." [60]

60. *Ibid.*, p. 72.

3

The Theology
Professors

I

From about 1815 up to 1848 the theology faculties of the universities of Halle, Berlin, Breslau, Bonn, and Königsberg, taken all together, had between thirty and thirty-two full professors, and between ten and fifteen associate professors. The number of unpaid lecturers—the Privatdozenten—in the various faculties of theology ranged from one or two to five.[1] This small group of men, representing the intellectually and politically most alert and conscious element of the Protestant clergy, played a crucial role in the struggle between the conservative and liberal forces in Prussia. In their theological and political ideas, their activities and personal influence, these university teachers also accentuated the political plurality of the clergy.

In this period German university professors in general shared an increasing social prominence and were accorded marked respect by the government and by people of all classes. Theologians enjoyed a special intellectual prestige as teacher-scholars studying and interpreting the Scriptures, and as ministers of religion administering the

1. Schrader, II, 555; Lenz, III, 490; Kaufmann, *Geschichte der Universität Breslau,* pp. 59 f.; Bezold, pp. 180 ff.

Also: Goetz von Selle, *Geschichte der Albertus Universität zu Königsberg in Preussen* (Würzburg, 1956), pp. 311 ff.; hereafter cited as Selle, *Geschichte.*

sacraments and preaching in churches. Moreover, they were top-ranking ecclesiastical officials, responsible for the training of the clergy. Those among them who assumed an active political role in the War of Liberation had become strengthened in their belief that participation in public life on their own initiative was not only permissible but was a duty which they owed to their position as spokesmen for the aspirations of those groups of society that looked to them for guidance and leaderhip.[2] No longer were theological professors "living consciences of the Church," [3] they were also "living consciences of society." Since the latter half of the eighteenth century, *Bildung*—meaning the broad formation of mind and character acquired by education—had become an increasingly important criterion for social repute in Prussian society, including even some segments of the aristocracy.[4] Certainly the educated middle classes, who now insisted on personal accomplishment as a criterion for judging the value of men, tended to look upon professors—who presumably achieved their status through superior personal achievements, not through the accident of birth—as their heroes and as living symbols of a coming liberal era.[5] The prestige of professors and also that of writers and artists was greatly enhanced by this development, and men of those vocations grew more and more articulate in matters of public concern.[6] Among the theology professors there were considerable numbers of liberals, not just isolated individuals, who came to consider it not only their "natural right," but also their duty to express their opinions and speak out on such vital matters as freedom of conscience, of the press, speech, and assembly, and for the right to self-government in church and state and the abolition of hereditary privileges. Since professors associated with

2. Schnabel, I, 445–457; Ernest K. Bramstedt, *Aristocracy and the Middle Classes in Germany: Social Types in German Literature, 1830–1900,* rev. ed. (Chicago, 1964), pp. 42, 128 f.

3. Hajo Holborn, "The Social Basis of the German Reformation," *Church History,* 5 (1936), 337.

4. Rosenberg, *Bureaucracy,* p. 182; Schnabel, I, 204–234, 455 ff.

5. Leonard Krieger, *The German Idea of Freedom: History of a Political Tradition* (Boston, 1957), pp. 305 ff.; Bramstedt, *op. cit.* (n. 2 above), pp. 128 ff. For the political role of German professors in the last third of the eighteenth century see Epstein, pp. 52 f.

6. See the very typical letter of the nobleman and chief councilor Ritter von Hillmer addressing Professor Hengstenberg as "Hochwürdiger Herr, Hochverehrter Herr Doktor!" November 27, 1827, Hengstenberg papers, Box II.

a broad public and had contact with men from various walks of life, they were usually well aware of the existence and the particular nature of political and social issues.[7]

Despite the repressive measures of the government against all manifestations of political opposition after 1815, universities in pre-March Prussia became centers of agitation. In the absence of political parties and a national assembly where major issues could be debated in public by the contending forces, universities became ideological battlegrounds where competing views and interests clashed with increasing bitterness.[8] Theology professors found it difficult to isolate themselves in the bitter struggle that agitated the government and the politically conscious public. Their positions as appointed, salaried officials of state institutions as well as respected men of learning who prided themselves on their intellectual freedom made them subject to pressures by the government and by various political interests. On the one hand, these men were members of a bureaucratic state apparatus and thus were expected by the government to be loyal to the ruling authorities—now being challenged by political forces that sought to transform autocratic Prussia into a constitutionally limited monarchy with parliamentary institutions. On the other hand, members of the rising political opposition looked to them as men of learning and sound judgment whose trained minds and sense of responsibility should enable them to take an independent stand not only on theological matters but also on issues concerning the public welfare in general. In other words, the government and the traditionally privileged classes expected political support and moral, even religious, sanction for the status quo from the theology professors. But the opposition, too, sought to strengthen its position by seeking to enlist for its causes one of the most influential and highly respected professional groups. Consequently, by virtue of their positions, functions, and prestige, theology professors came to play a significant role in public life, directly or indirectly, and regardless of whether they were personally anxious to participate in political activity or were indifferent, or even hostile, toward it. Owing, however, to their disparate interests, backgrounds, personalities, attitudes, and connec-

7. Schnabel, IV, 359–361.
8. Hans Rosenberg, "Geistige und politische Strömungen an der Universität Halle in der ersten Hälfte des 19. Jahrhunderts," *Deutsche Vierteljahrsschrift für Literaturwissenschaft und Geistesgeschichte*, 7 (1929), 560–586; hereafter cited as Rosenberg, "Geistige Strömungen."

tions, they constituted a highly diverse group which exerted politically significant influence in a number of different directions.

Much of the effective political influence of the professors was due to the fact that in training students of theology they also helped shape, consciously or unconsciously, many of the political ideas and attitudes of future clergymen, of students in other disciplines, and of other persons who, through whatever channels, happened to become acquainted with their views. Generations of clergymen and of persons in different walks of life were influenced in their ways of thinking and of approaching problems by the teaching, writings, and behavior of such famous theology professors as Schleiermacher, De Wette, Wegscheider, Gesenius, Richard Rothe, Karl Hase, Tholuck, Hengstenberg, Hahn, Olshausen, Guericke, and Marheineke.[9]

In 1815–1848—as during the Reformation—political ideas and attitudes became associated with theological creeds. The government thus no longer looked upon controversies between theology professors as mere "parsons' quarrels" (*Pfaffengezänk*) as it had done under monarchical absolutism in the seventeenth and eighteenth centuries. Since in the midst of changing political conditions after 1815 the theology professors continued to play a crucial role in clerical personnel recruitment—by training, examining, and recommending candidates for church positions—there resulted an increased attention by the government to the creed and political leanings of prospective appointees to the universities, and its policy favored men who could be expected to support the ruling authorities.

II

For a number of years after 1815 the Hegelian approach in theology, as presented especially by the professors Philip Konrad Marheineke and Wilhelm Vatke at the University of Berlin, seemed to have the support of Altenstein, the minister of ecclesiastical affairs and education. Altenstein was apparently convinced that Hegel's philosophy, although too deep for him to grasp personally,[10] provided satisfactory answers to the great historical and contemporary prob-

9. L. Uhlich, "Aus einem Briefe an D. Bretschneider," *AKZ*, 1842, p. 879. Walter Nigg, *Die Geschichte des religiösen Liberalismus: Entstehung, Blütezeit, Ausklang* (Zurich and Leipzig, 1937), pp. 132 ff.; Schnabel, IV, 501 ff.

10. Altenstein admitted that he was "never able to advance beyond the philosophical teachings of Fichte." See *Realencyklopädie für Protestantische Theologie und Kirche* (Leipzig, 1877), I, 317 f.; hereafter cited as *RE*.

lems of state and church,[11] and that it sanctioned the existing political and social order. Because the ministerial bureaucracy was greatly concerned after 1815 with the problem of ensuring the effective functioning of the Protestant church as a state institution, it welcomed the conservative position of the theological Hegelians that "the church is the truth of the state and the state is the reality of the church" (Die Kirche ist die Wahrheit des Staats, der Staat ist die Wirklichkeit der Kirche).[12] Marheineke and his conservative faction lost their favored position only when, during the 1830's and 1840's, the so-called Left Hegelians began to turn the weapon of Hegelian philosophy against religious dogma and the existing order.[13] The careers of the "Hegelian" Marheineke and the orthodox Lutheran Johann Gottfried Scheibel at the University of Breslau reflected the fact that, up to the reign of Frederick William IV, the Pietists were by no means the only group of conservative theology professors favored by the government in the course of the period from 1815 to 1847. Nevertheless, from the late 1820's on, the most active and influential of the professorial elites that supported the traditional political and social order was, undoubtedly, the "Hengstenberg faction" (Partei Hengstenberg).[14]

The careers of August Hahn (1792–1863), Hermann Olshausen (1796–1839), August Kahnis (1814–1888), Ferdinand Guericke (1803–1878), Otto von Gerlach (1801–1849), August Tholuck (1799–1877), and Ernst Wilhelm Hengstenberg (1802–1869), and others demonstrated the influence of leading Pietist conservatives in the placement of "desirable" theologians and protégés in university positions. The historical significance of this group of men, however, must be explained in the light of their backgrounds, aspirations, career patterns, connections, activities, ideas, and political influence as these related to maintaining and strengthening the vitality of the authoritarian tradition in Prussian-German history.

11. See Marheineke's lectures in the 1820's and 1830's in his *Einleitungen in die öffentlichen Vorlesungen über die Bedeutung der Hegelschen Philosophie in der Christlichen Theologie* (Berlin, 1842). For the influence of Hegel's philosophy on theological thinking in pre-March Prussia see Rudolf Haym, *Hegel und seine Zeit,* ed. Hans Rosenberg, 2d ed. (Leipzig, 1927), pp. 392–432.

12. Marheineke, *op. cit.,* p. 16.

13. Hengstenberg to Tholuck, August 22, 1830, Bonwetsch, *Tholuck Briefe,* p. 125.

14. Hengstenberg to Tholuck, July 29, 1827, *ibid.,* p. 122; Lenz, II, pt. 2, 105 ff.; Jacques Droz, *Les révolutions allemandes de 1848* (Paris, 1957), pp. 137 ff.

In 1819, Baron von Kottwitz and other Pietist conservatives prevailed upon Crown Prince Frederick William to overcome the opposition of Altenstein and have August Hahn appointed associate professor of theology at the University of Königsberg. Shortly thereafter, Hahn became a parish pastor in Königsberg and also, though then only twenty-seven years old, superintendent of the district and hence its ranking ecclesiastical official. Subsequently Hahn, the orphan son of a village teacher, married a young noblewoman, Christine von Brück, who was a sister-in-law of both Heubner and Richard Rothe. Within two years of his appointment to the university, Hahn was made full professor. In 1834, he was appointed Consistory councilor and full professor at the University of Breslau for the avowed purpose of eliminating rationalist influence there. In 1843 he reached the climax of his career when he was made general superintendent of Silesia—apparently so that he might complete the reintegration of the separatist Old Lutherans of that province, where he became known as the "ecclesiastical commissar" (*geistlicher Commissarius*), owing to his ruthless methods. Hahn was awarded the Order of the Red Eagle, Second Class, in recognition of his services.[15]

In 1821 the pious Hermann Olshausen was likewise appointed associate professor of theology at Königsberg, where until 1834 he led the battles of the Pietists against the East Prussian liberals. Although Olshausen's appointment was opposed by the faculty of theology and by most of the liberal professors, the young theologian enjoyed the confidence and help of the Crown Prince and his Pietist circle and also of some aristocratic Pietists in East Prussia who were disturbed by the growing strength of the liberal movement in Königsberg.[16] In 1827 Olshausen—the son of a village pastor in the duchy of Holstein—became a full professor and married a member of the East Prussian nobility, Agnes von Prittwitz-Gaffron.[17]

August Kahnis was the son of an impoverished tailor. One of the many "awakened" converts of Tholuck at the University of

---

15. *Homiletisches Journal*, 2 (1830), pt. 1; *RGG* (1958), III, 28.

16. In 1834 he transferred to the University of Erlangen for reasons of health. See *Allgemeines Repertorium für theologische Literatur und kirchliche Statistik*, 30 (1840), 91–94; *Berliner Allgemeine Kirchenzeitung*, 1839, p. 346.

17. Olshausen to Hengstenberg, December 22, 1827, Hengstenberg papers, Box I. See also Kottwitz to Tholuck, November 27, 1826, Bonwetsch, *Tholuck Briefe*, p. 31.

Halle in the 1830's, he was assisted by funds from the Francke Foundation in his theological studies.[18] By 1839 Kahnis had become one of the friends of the conservative history professor Heinrich Leo and was conducting regular collegia pietatis for professors and students at Wittenberg. He spent much of his energies fighting the influence of the Left Hegelians, whom he considered "the most dangerous enemies of Christian society." [19] In 1840 Kahnis decided to transfer to the University of Berlin. Upon the recommendation of the Halle Pietists Tholuck and Leo, Hengstenberg used his influence to get Kahnis an appointment as lecturer there.[20] Believing, however, that his career could be best promoted by transferring him from Berlin to another university, Hengstenberg in 1844 succeeded in placing him at the University of Breslau with the rank of associate professor. The grateful young man assured Hengstenberg of his "eternal loyalty." [21] The avowed purpose in this appointment was that Kahnis should help Hahn destroy the influence of the rationalist theology professor David Schulz,[22] who was a personal enemy of Hengstenberg. During his stay in Berlin, Kahnis was introduced by Hengstenberg to Ludwig von Gerlach, Hans Hugo von Kleist-Retzow, and other influential Pietist noblemen. In Silesia, Kahnis established similar contacts and in 1845 he married Elisabeth von Schenkendorf, the daughter of the noble county commissioner (*Landrat*) of Wulkow; he had first met his future wife at a social gathering in Hengstenberg's house in Berlin. Among the prominent Pietist landowners who came frequently to the Kahnis house were Count Ferdinand zu Stolberg-Peterswaldau, the president of the Breslau Consistory, and his wife Maria Agnes. The wives of Kahnis and Stolberg-Peterswaldau became close friends and helped cement

18. According to Kahnis, Tholuck's sermons had such a "fantastic" influence on him that after a "tremendous inner struggle" he was awakened to the "true belief." See his *Die Lehre vom Heiligen Geist* (Leipzig, 1846), pp. v f.

19. August Kahnis, *Dr. Ruge und Hegel: Ein Beitrag zur Würdigung Hegel'scher Tendenzen* (Quedlinburg, 1838), p. 3.

20. Kahnis to Hengstenberg, June 26, 1841, Georg N. Bonwetsch, ed., *Aus 40 Jahren deutscher Kirchengeschichte: Briefe an Ernst Wilhelm Hengstenberg* (Gütersloh, 1917-1919), I, 151; hereafter cited as Bonwetsch, *Briefe an Hengstenberg*.

21. Kahnis to Hengstenberg, July 2, 1844, *ibid.*, I, 151 f. Actually, Kahnis did not keep his promise; after 1848 he turned against Hengstenberg.

22. Kahnis to Hengstenberg, December 3, 1845, *ibid.*, p. 152; K. F. A. Kahnis, *Der innere Gang des deutschen Protestantismus*, 3d ed. (Leipzig, 1856), II, 195.

the religious, social, and political ties of the professorial-aristocratic Pietist elite.[23]

Ferdinand Guericke was a former student of professors Wegscheider and Gesenius, the leaders of the rationalist school at the University of Halle. He, too, became a "true believer" and was assisted by the Pietists in his career. In 1829 the influence of the Crown Prince was used to have the twenty-six-year-old Guericke appointed associate professor of theology at Halle. Actively encouraged by Heubner, Tholuck, and others, the young professor became one of the most intransigent theological enemies of his former teachers.[24] He cooperated with Tholuck and the other members of the "Hengstenberg faction" in their repeated but unsuccessful attempts to have Wegscheider and Gesenius dismissed from their positions.[25]

Otto von Gerlach,[26] the youngest of the Gerlach brothers who played such a strategic role in the history of Prussian conservatism,[27] received a particularly thorough training at Wittenberg in 1825–1827. The Pietist "machine" was especially anxious to bring about the appointment of the young nobleman to the faculty of the University of Berlin, even though Schleiermacher openly expressed doubts about his intellectual ability. Marheineke, who greatly disliked Schleiermacher personally, nevertheless also opposed the appointment, making a harsh protest which incurred the hatred of the "true believers," who referred to his opposition as "satanic wickedness" (*satanische Bosheit*).[28] Even Hengstenberg, the future leader of the Pietist-Orthodox faction associated with his name, admitted in private that Otto had neither the talent and ability nor the inclination for an academic career.[29] Minister Altenstein, who was strongly opposed to the appointment, stated flatly that the young man's talents

23. Friedrich Julius Winter, *August Kahnis: Ein theologisches Lebens- und Charakterbild* (Leipzig, 1896), pp. 17 ff.

24. See the Introduction in Guericke's *Geschichte der lutherischen Gemeinde in und um Halle* (Halle, 1835), and *RGG* (1957), II, 1904.

25. See pp. 102 ff., below.

26. See the Introduction in Otto von Gerlach's *Predigten,* ed. J. G. Seegemund (Berlin, 1850). Also *RGG* (1957), II, 1431; Lenz, II, pt. 1, 350 ff.; *EKZ,* 1849, nos. 1 and 2.

27. See chap. 4.

28. Hengstenberg to Tholuck, March 8, 1828, Bonwetsch, *Tholuck Briefe,* p. 123.

29. Hengstenberg to Tholuck, December 6, 1828, *ibid.,* p. 12.

were definitely not suited for academic life. Despite Altenstein's insistence that "mere piety" should not qualify a man for an academic position and that professors should keep high standards in the examination of candidates, the personal influence of the Crown Prince was again used by the Pietist faction to ensure that one of their men from an old noble family should begin an academic career in the capital. Consequently, Gerlach was appointed lecturer at the University of Berlin in 1829.[30]

Shortly after his appointment, Gerlach notified the ministry of ecclesiastical affairs and education that he was unable to produce a "significant scholarly work," such as was expected of an appointee. In a letter to his friend Tholuck, he admitted that Marheineke's opposition on the grounds of his lack of academic ability was fully justified.[31] A year later, Gerlach confided to Tholuck that even with his friend's constant prodding and encouragement he could not continue in the profession: "After serious consideration I judge myself to be completely incapable of fulfilling the functions of an independent university teacher. . . . In particular, I lack the ability for productive scholarship." (Nach ruhigster Prüfung kann ich mich für eine selbstständige Universitätsstelle nicht für geeignet halten. . . . Besonders geht mir alles wissenschaftlich produktive Talent ab.)[32] In fairness to Gerlach one should add that during his postgraduate training period at the Wittenberg Seminary he repeatedly implored his friends not to press him to enter the academic profession. In 1826 he complained bitterly to Tholuck of not being able to study—he was simply unable to suffer through so many hours at his desk: "I still do not know how to study . . . and I am sure of one thing, [that] in spite of all my efforts . . . I seem to get nowhere. . . . If you could only watch me for a single day at my desk, you would be convinced that I am not suited to the academic profession." [33]

Despite Otto's lack of talent, his Pietist-Orthodox sponsors—including his brother Ludwig, Heubner, Nicolovius, Kottwitz, and Hengstenberg—implored him to stay in the profession by transferring from Berlin to a provincial university. So keen was the competition for academic positions, however, and so obvious were his

30. Lenz, II, pt. 1, 350–362.
31. June 14, 1828, Bonwetsch, *Tholuck Briefe*, p. 133.
32. May 5, 1829, *ibid.*, p. 134.
33. February 13, 1826, *ibid.*, p. 128.

shortcomings, that efforts in 1832 to place him at Breslau were un-successful.[34] Finally, in 1834, Gerlach could no longer stand the demands and pressures of his position as university teacher. He requested the king to relieve him of it and to appoint him parish pastor in a church under royal patronage in the capital. Overjoyed when Frederick William III granted his request, he served as pastor of the St. Elisabeth Church until the accession of Frederick William IV, when Hengstenberg convinced him that it was his duty to rejoin the academic profession and lend support to the "Christian-German" regime of the new ruler. Hengstenberg prevailed upon the faculty of theology at the University of Berlin to award Gerlach an honorary doctor's degree, whereupon the government appointed him honorary professor. In 1842 Gerlach became the head of a commission of clergymen that visited England to study the efforts of English Christians to solve the "social problem" of the working classes. Understandably, he failed to grasp the significance and the real dimensions of that problem. He was unable to perceive that the economic and social problems of the Hungry Forties—including an unprecedented population increase, large-scale unemployment, and the misery of urban and rural workers—were not solvable within the framework of traditional Christian charity.[35] Shortly after his return, Gerlach was appointed Consistory councilor, and in 1847 he reached the top of the ecclesiastical hierarchy as cathedral and court preacher in Berlin. Up to his death, which came suddenly in 1849, Gerlach continued to advise the pious Frederick William IV on social and religious matters. He in particular was blamed by liberals for the king's refusal to reinstate Uhlich and other dismissed leaders of the Friends of Light in their former positions.[36]

The academic careers of Tholuck and Hengstenberg, the two most influential conservative political leaders of the Protestant clergy in the decades before 1848, were also conspicuously accelerated.

34. Hengstenberg to Ludwig von Gerlach, November 17, 1832, Gerlach family archives.

35. See Otto von Gerlach, *Die kirchliche Armenpflege nach dem Englischen des Dr. Chalmers* (Berlin, 1847). In fairness to Gerlach, one should add that he proved to be a respected parish pastor, sincerely concerned with the spiritual and economic welfare of his parishioners. His admirers often referred to him as the "Wesley of Berlin." Shanahan, pp. 89, 104, 220.

36. *Sie wissen was sie wollen! Eine Verteidigungsschrift in Sachen der protestantischen Freunde* (Leipzig, 1847), pp. 14 ff.

Significantly, August Tholuck was one of the first protégés of the Kottwitz circle in Berlin after 1817.[37] The son of an impoverished goldsmith in Breslau, Tholuck demonstrated in high school that in intellectual ability he was more than a match for his noble classmates.[38] His real opportunity to satisfy his almost pathological urge to be treated as an equal by aristocrats and other members of the upper classes [39] came when his ambition to advance brought him to the Prussian capital in 1817. There he almost immediately came under the influence of the "Old Baron" Kottwitz and was "awakened" to the Pietist creed. Through Kottwitz, Tholuck soon became acquainted with Ludwig von Gerlach, Adolf von Thadden, and a number of other Pietist aristocrats as well as with like-minded clergymen and theology students, and was greatly encouraged by these new friends, who assured him that his talents and newly espoused creed would secure him a successful career in the clergy.[40] Although almost all of his training had been in foreign languages, the twenty-three-year-old Tholuck became associate professor of theology at the University of Berlin in 1823. Impressed with his linguistic talents and hard work, Altenstein ignored the opposition to the appointment raised by Schleiermacher on the grounds of Tholuck's rather inadequate theological knowledge.[41] Two years later, Tholuck was appointed full professor at the University of Halle, where he immediately became the leader of the Pietist faction

37. For an excellent summary of Tholuck's personal relationship to his spiritual "father in Christ," Baron von Kottwitz, see Friedrich Wilhelm Kantzenbach, ed., *Baron H. E. von Kottwitz und die Erweckungsbewegung in Schlesien, Berlin und Pommern* (Ulm, Donau, 1963), pp. 29 and 127, and the 40 letters of Tholuck to Kottwitz there, pp. 87–126. Kantzenbach edited a considerable part of the huge correspondence of the "Old Baron," and his work includes extensive bibliographical references. For Tholuck's theology see the account in Karl Barth, *Die protestantische Theologie im 19. Jahrhundert: Ihre Vorgeschichte und Geschichte,* 2d ed. (Zurich, 1952), pp. 459–468.

38. Witte, *Tholuck,* I, 10. This biography is not a work of erudition, but it does contain a considerable part of Tholuck's personal diary, much of his correspondence, and a great deal of other source material.

39. See Tholuck's letters to some of his upper-class friends "for whose friendship he worked so hard" in Bonwetsch, *Tholuck Briefe,* pp. 43–58.

40. See Ludwig von Gerlach, "Diary, 1819–1820," in Schoeps, *Tagebücher und Briefe der Gebrüder Gerlach,* pp. 300 f. See also the undated letter of Kottwitz to Tholuck inviting the young man and his friend Hengstenberg to a dinner party of aristocratic Pietists in Berlin, Bonwetsch, *Tholuck Briefe,* p. 28, and Tholuck to Kottwitz, February 19, 1824, Kantzenbach, *op. cit.* (in n. 37 above), p. 102.

41. Tholuck to Kottwitz (n.d.), Kantzenbach, *op. cit.,* p. 87; Lenz, II, pt. 2, 58 f.

which sought to destroy the influence of the rationalist theologians there.[42]

In Berlin, Tholuck had become engaged to Adele, one of the daughters of T. A. Schmalz, a reactionary jurist and professor of law at the university,[43] but the carefully arranged betrothal did not lead to marriage, primarily because of the prospective husband's unbalanced mental state at the time. For a number of years the emotionally unstable and physically sickly Tholuck seemed destined to remain a bachelor,[44] but in 1838 he married Mathilde, one of the three daughters of Baron von Gemmingen-Steinegg, whose family had been converted from Catholicism to Protestantism. Tholuck's wife became a "true partner in a truly pious marriage," and proved to be a source of psychological and physical strength for her ailing and suffering but determined husband in his theological and political struggles.[45] Tholuck's mentally unstable character prevented him from concentrating on a systematic pursuit of political objectives in the manner of Hengstenberg, whose sober and inflexible theological orthodoxy had never experienced a sudden "awakening" in the conventicles of Kottwitz, Heubner, the Moravian Brethren, or other Pietists.[46] Nevertheless, his contributions to the "battle of ideas" in the 1830's and 1840's, and his eventual success in training a new generation of clergymen, denouncing the rationalist creed, and identifying itself with religious orthodoxy and political reaction made him one of the most influential clerical leaders of his time.[47]

42. See pp. 101 ff.

43. Schmalz, the first dean of the law faculty of the University of Berlin, became one of the most hated officials in the so-called *Demagogenverfolgung* after 1819. The term *Schmalzgesellen* became one of abuse for reactionary officials and politicians. See Lenz, II, pt. 1, 344 ff.

44. Hengstenberg to Tholuck, June 15, 1826, Bonwetsch, *Tholuck Briefe*, p. 116. In a letter to his friend Radecke, Tholuck called himself "le grand celibataire du monde" (January 18, 1827, *ibid.*, p. 51).

45. See *Mathilde Tholuck geb. Freiin von Gemmingen-Steinegg: Heimgegangen am 1. Mai, Bestattet am 10. Mai 1894* (Halle a. S., 1894). See also Witte, *Tholuck*, II, 97 f.

46. In 1825, when Tholuck was transferred from Berlin to Halle, Hengstenberg politely but firmly refused to take over the conduct of Tholuck's regular Thursday night prayer meetings in Berlin. Hengstenberg excused himself by stating that people who felt the need for such meetings could always go to the collegia pietatis of Kottwitz. Hengstenberg to Tholuck, April 18, 1825, Bonwetsch, *Tholuck Briefe*, p. 114.

47. Schnabel, IV, 448; Martin Schellbach, *Tholucks Predigt: Ihre Grundlage und ihre Bedeutung für die heutige Praxis* (Berlin, 1956), p. 15.

Coming into notice in the late 1820's, Ernst Wilhelm Hengstenberg in a few years became the grand organizer and strategist of the conservative political forces within the state church.[48] In contrast to most of his colleagues in the faculties of theology, Hengstenberg was never a parish pastor or a preacher. But as a professor of theology at the University of Berlin after 1826 and as editor, after 1827, of the *Evangelische Kirchen-Zeitung* and as such a staunch advocate of the "new orthodoxy," he became the political leader of the clerical faction which had close personal connections with those Old Prussian noblemen who were seeking to cement an alliance between Pietist clergymen and aristocrats. Closely cooperating with the Gerlach brothers, Thadden, General L. G. von Thile, Ernst von Senfft-Pilsach, and other prominent and politically active Prussian Junker conservatives, Hengstenberg was an influential figure in what came to be known as the "general staff of Prussian reaction." [49] His connections were not only with court and government circles and with theology professors of similar views, but also with Pietist squires in East Elbia, Calvinist businessmen and clergymen in his native Rhineland-Westaphalia and in the free cities of Hamburg and Bremen, and all over the country, increasing numbers of pastors, theology students, and candidates for clerical appointments. Among the leading conservative clergymen, Hengstenberg saw most clearly the political implications of theological rationalism.[50] Throughout his career he consistently sought to eliminate rationalism—both as a religious belief and as a politically subversive ideology.

Hengstenberg was the descendant of a Calvinist patrician family in Dortmund that had produced generations of merchants and clergymen since the sixteenth century. His father, a Reformed clergyman, had welcomed the union of Calvinists and Lutherans in 1817 and subsequently cooperated with Eylert and other high-ranking

48. See *RGG* (1957), III, 219 f. For a summary of Hengstenberg's thought see Emanuel Hirsch, *Geschichte der neueren evangelischen Theologie im Zusammenhang mit den allgemeinen Bewegungen des europäischen Denkens* (Gütersloh, 1954), V, 118–130. See also Otto von Ranke, "Hengstenberg," *Allgemeine Deutsche Biographie,* XI, 737–747; Lenz, II, pt. 1, 327 ff., and pt. 2, 117 ff. See, further, Anneliese Kriege, "Geschichte der *Evangelischen Kirchenzeitung* unter der Redaktion Ernst Wilhelm Hengstenbergs," (Ph.D. diss., University of Bonn, 1958); hereafter cited as Kriege, "Geschichte der *EKZ.*"

49. Huber, II, 338 ff.; Jordan, pp. 185 ff.; Shanahan, pp. 101 f., 201 f.

50. On theological rationalism and its political influence see Rosenberg, "Theologischer Rationalismus," pp. 497–541.

officials in the task of merging the Lutheran and Reformed churches.[51] In contrast to the Pietist converts, such as Tholuck, Hahn, Kahnis, the Gerlachs, and Thadden, Hengstenberg emphatically denied that he had ever changed his creed. In a letter to his father in 1825, he stated: "When I came to Berlin my religious convictions were the same as they are now."[52] But a careful scrutiny of Hengstenberg's writings before and after his decision to become a theologian and to settle in Berlin shows some very remarkable changes in his thinking.

In 1819 Hengstenberg began his studies in philosophy and Oriental languages at the University of Bonn. There, almost immediately attracted to the liberal-nationalistic ideas of the Burschenschaft, he enthusiastically followed the German nationalist Ernst Moritz Arndt. He also became acquainted with Burschenschaftler such as Hoffmann von Fallersleben and continued expressing the views of these men even after the dissolution of the Burschenschaft. For instance, when in 1820 the Duc de Berry was assassinated in France, Hengstenberg wrote to his father that they "all hoped Germany would follow the example" set by the French.[53] While his future Pietist allies were frequenting the meetings of Heubner and Kottwitz[54] and denouncing the rationalist Biblical interpretations as blasphemy, Hengstenberg in his doctoral dissertation at Bonn in 1823 was asserting that philology rather than theology provided the best approach to an improved understanding of the Scriptures.[55]

According to his biographer, Hengstenberg's one-year stay in Basel as a teacher of Oriental languages at the new Baseler Missionsgesellschaft, an institution for the training of missionaries,[56] and the news of the death of his mother were responsible for the young man's gradual turn to a "positive faith."[57] No doubt the loss of his

51. See Hermann Becker, "Zur Geschichte des Geschlechtes der Hengstenberg," in Karl Ruebel, ed., *Beiträge zur Geschichte Dortmunds und der Grafschaft Mark* (Dortmund, 1878), VII, 3-148; Eylert, III, 184 ff.; Bachmann, *Hengstenberg,* I, 46.

52. Bachmann, *Hengstenberg,* I, 168.   53. *Ibid.,* I, 34.

54. Nicolovius to Hengstenberg, September 2, 1828, Hengstenberg papers, Box I; Olshausen to Otto von Gerlach, May 1, 1827, *ibid.;* Tholuck to Hahn, 1832, Bonwetsch, *Tholuck Briefe,* p. 112.

55. Thesis no. 2, printed in Bachmann, *Hengstenberg,* I, 96.

56. Founded in 1815. Christian Friedrich Spittler (1782–1867) and Christian Gottlieb Blumhardt (1799–1838), two German Neo-Pietists of the South German religious "Awakening," helped to make it an influential center for German and Swiss Pietism. See Shanahan, pp. 63 f.

57. Bachmann, *Hengstenberg,* I, 158.

dearly loved mother must have been a profound shock to the twenty-two-year-old Hengstenberg. In the religiously "awakened" atmosphere of the missionary school he was most certainly encouraged by his colleagues to find in a "truly Christian" faith not only consolation but also strength for overcoming his depression. His stay at Basel was the beginning of his coming to notice in Pietist and orthodox circles as a "fighter for God." [58]

Hengstenberg's turn from being a religiously skeptical member of the Burschenschaft during his Bonn years to a religiously and politically ultraconservative "fighter for God" presents a complicated problem. It would be absurd to accept the accusations of his political and theological enemies that his apparent turn to religious orthodoxy was not sincere at all and was motivated solely by an opportunistic intention to embark on a successful career with the help of the upcoming Pietist faction in Prussia.[59] Yet there is the fact that Hengstenberg was refused permission by the government to present himself for the qualifying examination (*Habilitation*) as a prospective teacher in the faculty of philosophy at the University of Berlin, and was then advised by Eylert to go to Basel for some time and gain teaching experience.[60] It seems very likely that Eylert, a friend of Hengstenberg's father, hoped that the time spent at Basel would benefit the young man in two ways. First, he would be exposed to the influence of Pietistic and orthodox "true believers" there, so that he eventually could establish contacts with the increasingly influential group of "awakened" noblemen and clergymen in Prussia. Second, Eylert could meanwhile allay the suspicion aroused in some government circles over Hengstenberg's former political views and prepare the way for his academic career in Berlin. Thus Hengstenberg's turn to a "positive faith" could be interpreted as a repudiation of his previously held political ideas and connections. His new association with conservative Pietist aristocrats and clergymen could be considered evidence of his intention to join in the opposition to

58. See the revealing comments in the eulogy for Hengstenberg by F. Woelbling, *Der Gotteskämpfer: Leichenpredigt über Moses, 32, 28, vor der Beisetzung der Leiche Ernst Wilhelm Hengstenbergs weil. Doctors und Professors der Theologie an der Universität zu Berlin* (Neu-Rupping, 1869), pp. 5 ff.

59. See the characteristic bitter accusations by David Schulz in his *Das Wesen und Treiben der Berliner Evangelischen Kirchenzeitung* (Breslau, 1839), pp. 28–74; hereafter cited as Schulz, *Wesen der EKZ*.

60. Bachmann, *Hengstenberg*, I, 117.

liberal demands for political and social changes. In other words, Eylert's intention may have been to win over the obviously very talented young linguist to the conservative side by helping him to get established at the University of Berlin. As a matter of fact, Hengstenberg soon began corresponding with Professors Neander and Tholuck in Berlin, who assured him that his linguistic talents, as demonstrated in his dissertation, would be appreciated in the theological faculty of the University of Berlin.[61]

To promote his candidacy Hengstenberg asked his friend C. A. Brandis to have copies of his translations from Aristotle's *Metaphysics* sent to Eylert and Nicolovius.[62] Undoubtedly, the government's highly selective distribution of conspicuous promotions, distinctions, honors, and other rewards to clergymen after the War of Liberation had demonstrated to Hengstenberg that in the reorganized Protestant state chuch there were possibilities for rapid advancement and special recognition provided one possessed not only talent and special skills, but also the "right" creed, political leanings, and connections. For the rationalist theologian David Schulz, of the University of Breslau, Hengstenberg's turning from the "extreme liberalism" of his student years at Bonn to the role of an archconservative theology professor was "scandalous opportunism." Throughout his career, Hengstenberg was accused by Schulz of hypocrisy and of intolerance comparable to that of the Spanish Grand Inquisitors.[63]

In October 1824 Hengstenberg passed the qualifying examinations for the faculty of philosophy at the University of Berlin. Eylert and other friends were influential in securing his initial appointment there as a lecturer, and also in having him transferred in 1825 to the faculty of theology.[64] In this position he was given a regular income, an advantage not usually conferred on lecturers.[65] As a member of the Council of State and an official of the ministry of ecclesiastical affairs and education, Eylert was able to keep him informed of important discussions and plans of governmental authorities concerning his career.[66] Hengstenberg soon gained the

61. Lenz, II, pt. 1, 330 ff.

62. Brandis to Hengstenberg, May 26, 1824, Hengstenberg papers, Box I.

63. Schulz, *Wesen der EKZ,* pp. 28–74.

64. Eylert, III, 183 ff. See also Lenz, II, pt. 1, 331 ff.

65. Bachmann, *Hengstenberg,* I, 219. See also Lenz, II, p. 1, 332 ff.

66. Hengstenberg to Tholuck, March 8, 1828, Bonwetsch, *Tholuck Briefe,* p. 122; Lenz, II, pt. 1, 136.

confidence of the Pietist circle around the Crown Prince, whose influence was used to secure his appointment as associate professor of theology in 1826 and as full professor in 1828.[67] Apparently Hengstenberg's lack of training in theology did not delay his appointment, in the latter case, to the vacant chair of the dismissed liberal theologian De Wette—a promotion which seemed to indicate that the government was more deeply interested in the political views of professors than in their professional qualifications.

As a professor, Hengstenberg developed close connections and even personal friendships with Tholuck, and with the Gerlach brothers, Baron von Kottwitz, and other Pietist Junkers, who were more and more impressed with his dogmatic, inflexible, and determined character [68] and his uncompromising stand against the "evil manifestations of the *Zeitgeist*." [69] In the opinion of Ludwig von Gerlach, Hengstenberg "not only had the right creed," but "could also stand up for it"; [70] that is, he was one who could transform his dogmatic theological convictions into political deeds. In contrast to the views on the Scriptures that he expressed in his dissertation in 1823, Hengstenberg now declared that "philology, philosophy, and human reason" could not "penetrate matters of religion." [71] He thus voiced the Neo-Pietist and orthodox position, which rejected not only rationalism but also the philosophical approaches of the schools of Schleiermacher and Hegel to theological problems.[72] This dogmatic attitude, based on the letter of the Scriptures, became characteristic of the theology and politics of the "Partei Hengstenberg": they, and they alone, possessed the truth.

Like the theology professors Tholuck, Olshausen, and Otto von Gerlach, Hengstenberg suffered from ill health throughout his life. A chronic ailment of his feet caused him much suffering and occasionally brought on periods of serious depression. Tholuck, Ols-

---

67. *Ibid.*, 341, 344 ff.

68. Ludwig von Gerlach called these characteristics of Hengstenberg's personality "sein von Natur hartes und kaltes Wesen." Letter to Tholuck, July 8, 1827, Bonwetsch, *Tholuck Briefe*, p. 138.

69. Gerlach, *Aufzeichnungen*, I, 180 f.

70. Ludwig von Gerlach to Hengstenberg, May 17, 1833, Hengstenberg papers, Box II. See also Gerlach, *Aufzeichnungen*, I, 160.

71. Hengstenberg, "Habilitation," in Bachmann, *Hengstenberg*, I, 333 f.

72. Holborn, *Modern Germany*, II, 494 f.; Karl Schwarz, *Zur Geschichte der neuesten Theologie* (Leipzig, 1856), pp. 71–74; Hirsch, *op. cit.* (in n. 48 above), V, 118–130.

hausen, and Otto von Gerlach had recurring attacks of tuberculosis, which at times seriously interfered with their work.[73] But physical suffering also seemed to harden the dedication of these men to their struggle against disbelief and "the spirit of revolt . . . which demands only rights [and] acknowledges no duties." [74] Hengstenberg and Tholuck in particular regarded suffering as almost necessary for "fighters of the Lord on earth" whose mission was "to conquer or to die." [75] At the same time, Hengstenberg expressed his willingness to follow the "burdensome instructions" of his physician to improve his health. In order to "further the cause of the Lord" he accepted both suffering and the "burdensome instructions," and he urged Tholuck to follow his example.[76]

In contrast to the initially tolerant patience shown by Schleiermacher toward his new colleague,[77] Marheineke became furious when Hengstenberg published a pamphlet which denounced all theological approaches based on philosophical reasoning. In a sharply worded discussion, Marheineke warned Hengstenberg that by embracing the simple and naïve Neo-Pietist and orthodox creed he was jeopardizing his future as a theological scholar and also confusing the minds of clergymen who looked to the theology professors for guidance.[78]

In the early 1820's the Pietist "Awakening" in Pomerania and the Old Lutheran movement in Silesia seemed to threaten the unity of the state church and so alarmed the government that in 1825 it published an official warning to clergymen, reminding them of their duty to remain in the state church regardless of their particular creeds. When the *Allgemeine Kirchen-Zeitung,* the recognized organ of the theological rationalists, blamed the Pietists for separatist tendencies,[79] Hengstenberg's journalistic talents were used to clarify his faction's stand on the issue. In a pamphlet published in 1826, Hengstenberg stated flatly that the government had the right to sup-

73. Bachmann, *Hengstenberg,* I, 9. Gerlach and Olshausen died of tuberculosis.
74. *EKZ,* 1830, p. 703.
75. Hengstenberg to Tholuck, April 13, 1826, Bonwetsch, *Tholuck Briefe,* p. 115.
76. *Ibid.*   77. Lenz, II, pt. 1, 334.
78. E. W. Hengstenberg, *Einige Worte über die Notwendigkeit der Überordung des äusseren Wortes über das innere: Nebst Stellen aus Luthers Schriften* (Berlin, 1825).
Hengstenberg reported the discussion in a letter to his father (n.d.), Bachmann, *Hengstenberg,* I, 255 f.
79. "Mysticismus, Pietismus und Separatismus," *AKZ,* 1825, p. 721.

press any creed or teaching which endangered its existence, and that it was the duty of the government to further the cause of Christian teachings which gave support to "a Christian order in church and state." [80] Although he had just rejected the request of Tholuck, who was leaving for Halle, that he take over the leadership of the private prayer meetings of students at the University of Berlin, Hengstenberg declared: "If the rationalists insist on calling us true believers Pietists . . . then we consider it an honor to be referred to as Pietists." [81] But because it could not be denied that the Old Lutherans in Silesia were in fact trying to set up separate Lutheran congregations under the leadership of the Breslau theology professor J. G. Scheibel, Hengstenberg had sharp words for clergymen who refused to respect the order and discipline of the state church. By the logic of his unequivocal position on discipline, he was forced to use against Scheibel's refusal to accept the merger of the Lutheran and Reformed churches some of the same arguments that had been expressed at Breslau in 1821 by the rationalist theology professor David Schulz.[82] Although Hengstenberg did not denounce Scheibel as a bigot or obscurantist (*Finsterling*) as Schulz had done, he now considered himself an arbiter who had the right to "admonish" (*ermahnen*) even his friends.[83]

The Gerlach brothers and some of their friends were so impressed with Hengstenberg's journalistic talents that in 1827 they mobilized resources for a new clerical journal to be called the *Evangelische Kirchen-Zeitung* (*EKZ*) and to be edited by the young professor.[84] Professors August Neander and Abraham Strauss at the

---

80. In his *Einige erläuternde Bemerkungen zu der Ministerialverfügung über Mysticismus, Pietismus und Separatismus* (Berlin, 1826), p. 4. See also the strongly worded letter of Altenstein to Hengstenberg concerning the determination of the government to maintain the unity of the state church, May 31, 1827, Hengstenberg Papers, Box I.

In a letter to Tholuck, October 29, 1826, Hengstenberg complained that the government was slow in granting him the promised salary increase. He interpreted the delay as governmental pressure on him to disassociate himself from the extreme mystical manifestations of the Pomeranian Pietist separatists. Bonwetsch, *Tholuck Briefe*, p. 119.

81. Hengstenberg, *op. cit.* (in n. 80 above), p. 9.

82. David Schulz, *Unfug an heiliger Stätte, oder Entlarvung Dr. J. G. Scheibels* (Breslau, 1821), pp. 4 f.

83. Hengstenberg, *op. cit.* (in n. 80 above), p. 9.

84. Ludwig von Gerlach to Tholuck, May 20, 1827, Bonwetsch, *Tholuck Briefe*, p. 136; G. N. Bonwetsch, "Die Anfänge der Evangelischen Kirchenzeitung: Ein Beitrag zur Geschichte des religiösen und kirchlichen Lebens im 19. Jahrhundert,"

University of Berlin and Tholuck at Halle, Hahn at Leipzig, and Olshausen at Königsberg, the Wittenberg Seminary director Heubner, Professor Georg Gossner at Basel, Professor Guericke at Halle, and a number of theologians in Leipzig, Bremen, and Tübingen declared their enthusiastic support and promised to assist Hengstenberg.[85] Scheibel also assured him of cooperation, although he expressed the hope that Hengstenberg would be sympathetic to the special problems of Silesian Lutherans. Schleiermacher was skeptical, but not openly hostile, while Marheineke refused to participate in a venture which was so obviously dominated by his theological enemies. The name of Ludwig von Gerlach, who eventually contributed more articles to the *EKZ* than anyone else,[86] did not appear on the list of sponsors. Because most contributors wished to be anonymous, Hengstenberg promised absolute secrecy concerning the authorship of articles. For a while it seemed that his new position as editor would take so much of his time that his promotion to full professor might be delayed; consequently, it was assumed that he would have to be compensated for the financial loss he might suffer.[87] Actually, these fears were unfounded. Hengstenberg's editorship and his engagement to a young noblewoman proved to be important assets facilitating his promotion in 1828 and making him the acknowledged leader of the Pietist-orthodox clerical faction.

Much of Hengstenberg's influence in the following decades was due to the fact that as editor he had authority to accept or to reject articles.[88] Moreover, the letters and reports which he received from every corner of Prussia and from practically every country in Europe (and even from North America) made him one of the best-informed men in Prussia.[89] Many articles published

---

in *Geschichtliche Studien: A. Hauck zum 70. Geburtstag* (Leipzig, 1916), pp. 16–24; Hans Joachim Schoeps, "Ungedrucktes aus den Tagebüchern Ludwig von Gerlachs," *ZRGG*, 16 (1964), 70.

85. Hengstenberg papers, Box I.

86. "Anzeige und Plan einer Evangelischen Kirchen-Zeitung," *EKZ*, supplement no. 1, 1827; "Verfasser Verzeichnis der Artikel," Kriege, "Geschichte der *EKZ*," Appendix.

87. Ludwig von Gerlach to Tholuck, June 24, 1827, Bonwetsch, *Tholuck Briefe,* p. 137.

88. Characteristic of the influence of the Gerlachs is the letter of Ludwig von Gerlach to Hengstenberg on February 16, 1845, advising that the *EKZ* not publish articles by the "renegade" Pietist Richard Rothe. Hengstenberg papers, Box IV.

89. Hengstenberg received mail even from such a far-away place as Waukesha, Wisconsin. Peter Wilmsen, a Lutheran minister there, called the editor of the *EKZ* a "great leader"; letter August 2, 1852, *ibid.,* Box V.

in the *EKZ* after 1827 became part of a conservative effort against
the "liberal manifestations of the spirit of the times." [90] Hengstenberg's initial "Vorwort" editorial in the January 1828 issue became
the predecessor of regular annual summaries of the previous
year's developments in German society and outlines of the strategy,
plans, and slogans of the Pietist conservatives for the coming year.
Because of their political significance the "Vorwort" editorials were
eventually referred to as "throne speeches." [91] In these, "rationalist"
became a label which was applied alike to theological "rationalists,
deists, pantheists, and neologists," and to all political and social
tendencies that were critical of the established order.[92] Pastor Keet-
mann in Elberfeld, an old friend, wrote to Hengstenberg that the
EKZ was a "very courageous enterprise," adding: "I often pray for
you and your work . . . especially because I know that you are
inclined to further the cause of God by worldly means (Bei deiner
Neigung dem Reiche Gottes auch durch weltlichen Arm Bahn zu
machen)." [93] To charges that his faction was supporting the political
interests of the aristocracy, Hengstenberg stated unequivocally: "Our
politics consist of unconditional obedience . . . to the God-given
order." [94] Ludwig von Gerlach was usually successful in using the
influence of the Crown Prince to overcome the objections of government censors to highly controversial articles.[95]

Soon Hengstenberg was strengthening the personal and social
ties, as well as the political ones, that linked him to the Old Prussian
nobility. In 1826 he became engaged to fifteen-year-old Therese von
Quast, who came from one of the oldest Pomeranian noble families,
in Hengstenberg's words, they "loved each other in the Lord as
brother and sister do," and he was grateful to "The Lord who has

---

Eneas M. Rate, foreign secretary of the Continental Committee of the Free
Church of Scotland, also corresponded with Hengstenberg, whom he praised as an
"honored instrument for doing great service to the cause of Evangelical Christianity in Germany." Letter, November 20, 1845, *ibid.*

90. Ludwig von Gerlach wrote scores of letters to Hengstenberg, commenting on
significant articles, and at times ordered 50, 100, 200, or 500 reprints to be sent (at
his expense) to Thadden, Lancizolle, and other influential persons for distribution.

91. Heinrich Leo to Hengstenberg, January 14, 1847, *ibid.*, Box V.

92. E.g., *EKZ*, 1828, p. 353.

93. August 9, 1828, Bonwetsch, *Briefe an Hengstenberg,* p. 154.

94. *EKZ,* 1830, p. 5.

95. E.g., Gerlach to Hengstenberg, July 18, 1833, and Hengstenberg to Gerlach,
August 21, 1833, Gerlach family archives.

given her to me, a poor and tired pilgrim." [96] It is interesting to note that when Hengstenberg began to develop his contacts and friendships with Pietist circles in Berlin and other parts of the country, he adopted the pious phraseology characteristic of Heubner, Kottwitz, the Gerlach brothers, and other "awakened" Pietists.[97] Although certainly not an "awakened" Pietist himself, he adjusted remarkably well to the ways of thinking of his new friends and sponsors in the camp of "true believers." As far as his immediate academic career was concerned, the influence of pious aristocrats was successfully used to prevent his being removed from Berlin to some other university. When his future mother-in-law learned that the government was planning to transfer him to the University of Königsberg, she immediately visited Minister Altenstein. In the course of the interview the noble lady expressed the conviction of the group of Junker Pietists that Hengstenberg could best serve the government by working in the capital, and persuaded Altenstein to abandon plans for his transfer.[98]

Altenstein and other high-ranking members of the administrative bureaucracy had been concerned for some time about Hengstenberg's connections with mystical and separatist Pietist groups whose activities seemed to threaten the administrative unity and effective functioning of the state church. Altenstein himself considered Hengstenberg a potential troublemaker whose conscious mixing of religion and politics could create serious tensions in the state church. The majority of the clergy still adhered to the creed of theological rationalism; they did not want to face the possibility of being forced out of their positions by the small minority of the developing "Hengstenberg faction" which sought to impose its creed on the officials of the church. Altenstein still tended to agree with the view of many pragmatic-minded government officials who believed that the effective and peaceful functioning of the church could be assured best by tolerating various theological interpretations in the clergy.[99] Such a

96. Hengstenberg to Tholuck, June 15, 1826, and October 29, 1826, Bonwetsch, *Tholuck Briefe,* pp. 117, 119. On the Quast family and its connections with other Junker families see Hengstenberg's letters to his father, Bachmann, *Hengstenberg,* I, 281–286.

97. See the very typical letters in Bachmann, I, 155 f. and 232.

98. Hengstenberg to Tholuck, July 24, 1826, Bonwetsch, *Tholuck Briefe,* p. 117; Bachmann, *Hengstenberg,* II, 113.

99. Johannes B. Kissling, *Der deutsche Protestantismus, 1817–1917: Eine geschichtliche Darstellung* (Münster i. W., 1917–1918), I, 44 ff., 139 ff.

policy would prevent the domination of one "school" of theology and assure a healthy balance in the clerical profession. It was in accordance with this policy that Altenstein continued his efforts— repeatedly thwarted when the influence of the Crown Prince was used to keep the aggressive and devoted potential leader of the "true believers" in the capital—to send Hengstenberg to one or another of the provincial universities.[100] Even so, Altenstein was persuaded that Hengstenberg was actually using his influence to prevent the breaking away of some Pietist splinter groups from the state church. It was intimated that through his marriage and the resulting additional responsibility the young man would be even more concerned with convincing the government of his loyalty to the established order. Hengstenberg himself, becoming more certain that God had put him in a strategically important position at the University of Berlin, held that it would be a sin for him to desert the capital or to give up the editorship of the *EKZ*.[101] His promotion to full professor in 1828 was a clear indication of the increasing influence of the Pietist faction, and it greatly encouraged him in his belief that powerful individuals and groups in Prussia were promoting the "cause of God." [102]

Hengstenberg's marriage to Therese von Quast in 1829 was symbolic of the growing intimacy of relationships between high-ranking ecclesiastic officials and the Neo-Pietist and orthodox aristocratic families of East Elbia. The obviously arranged marriage gave Hengstenberg entrée not only to a large group of Prussian Junkers but also to some court circles.[103] Just as the ruling dynasties sought to strengthen their alliances by intermarriage, so too the group of pious Old Prussian aristocrats and the upper echelons of the Pietistic-orthodox Protestant clergy were now anxious to sanction theirs by matrimonial ties.

Heubner, Hahn, Olshausen, Kahnis, and Tholuck had married

---

100. Hengstenberg to Tholuck, June 6, 1828, Bonwetsch, *Tholuck Briefe,* p. 123. See also Lenz, II, pt. 1, 341 and 344.

101. Hengstenberg to Tholuck, March 8, 1828, Bonwetsch, *Tholuck Briefe,* p. 122.

102. Hengstenberg to Tholuck, October 6, 1828, *ibid.,* pp. 123 f.; Lenz, I, pt. 1, 346 f.

103. Ludwig von Gerlach to Hengstenberg, May 17, 1833, Hengstenberg papers, Box II; Hengstenberg to his father, August 4, 1826, Bachmann, *Hengstenberg,* I, 291; Kriege, "Geschichte der *EKZ,*" pp. 29-32.

young noblewomen, and Hengstenberg's marriage was a further indication of the intimate personal and social connections that were developing between "awakened" aristocrats and their clergymen protégés. Before the Neo-Pietist "Awakening" in the first two decades of the century, marriages of noblewomen to clergymen had been extremely rare and were considered mésalliances.[104] The abolition of the estates as legal classes in 1807 would hardly have changed the traditional attitude of the aristocracy toward clergymen had not social distance been reduced by virtue of the combined effects of the reorganization of the Protestant church and of the "Awakening," which brought together a number of Pietist clergymen, theology students, and "awakened" aristocrats. Moreover, the new positions, titles, distinctions, and honors which were bestowed upon favored clergymen of the state church tended to raise the status of the clergy as a group and the status of its upper levels in particular. Marriages of theology professors and noblewomen were now considered acceptable—and were even welcomed—by some aristocratic families and in court circles.[105] To praying together, eating together, and other forms of social intercourse which led to lifelong friendships between some theology professors and aristocrats,[106] marriage was now added and was naturally the most important development in the direction of social equality between the two groups. Beyond a doubt, Hengstenberg and his fellow Pietist theology professors had "arrived" in Prussian society. Their marriages, which provided them with sizable incomes, added a new dimension to their prestige, hitherto based on membership in the intellectual elite and on their high status in the ecclesiastical hierarchy. At the same time, their intimate relationships with aristocratic families made them more receptive to the ideas, attitudes, tastes, aspirations, prejudices, and interests of the traditionally privileged classes.

Hengstenberg's vociferous crusade against "rationalism" was brought to a head under the impact of conditions which in the meantime had crystallized at Halle. Since the latter half of the eighteenth

104. Hermann Werdermann, *Der evangelische Pfarrer in Geschichte und Gegenwart* (Leipzig, 1925), pp. 44–46; idem, *Die deutsche evangelische Pfarrfrau* (Wittenberg, 1935), pp. 67–68, 114–117.

105. Hengstenberg to Tholuck, July 24, 1826, Bonwetsch, *Tholuck Briefe,* p. 117; Kriege, "Geschichte der *EKZ,*" pp. 29–32.

106. Ludwig von Gerlach to Hengstenberg, May 17, 1833, Hengstenberg papers, Box II, and Kottwitz to Tholuck (n.d.), Bonwetsch, *Tholuck Briefe,* p. 28.

century theological rationalism had been dominant at the university, which to the end of the 1830's was the center for training the largest number of clergymen in Prussia.[107] When Tholuck was given an appointment there in 1826, the rationalist professors Wegscheider, Gesenius, and Niemeyer were the most influential members of the faculty of theology, training and influencing generations of clergymen. The appointment of the young Pietist, which signaled the beginning of decades of bitter theological and political struggles, was made in the face of public protests by hostile students and citizens of Halle and of strong opposition by the faculty of theology.[108] Niemeyer, the chancellor of the university and director of the Francke Foundation, had mobilized the majority of the faculty and, in an unprecedented move, requested the ministry of ecclesiastical affairs and education not to yield to the pressure of the Pietists and send Tholuck to Halle, pointing out that his presence would mean constant enmity in the university and would disrupt civic life in the town, thus interfering with the peaceful training of future clergymen. The very purpose of the appointment, however, was to destroy the dominant influence of the rationalists and liberals at Halle and to establish a politically conservative group there under the leadership of Tholuck and Guericke, and the Pietist circles around the Crown Prince prevailed.[109]

Those circles considered Tholuck's mission in Halle so important that they persuaded the Academic Senate of the University of Berlin to invite the Crown Prince, several cabinet ministers and other high officials, some high-ranking army officers, and all the faculty members of the university to an official banquet to celebrate the occasion and wish Tholuck well in his new position. In contrast to Schleiermacher, who was icily cold and almost hostile toward Tholuck during the banquet, the philosopher Hegel urged his young colleague to do his best to bring an end to the influence of rational-

107. Schrader, II, 568; Karl Weidemann, *Die Pietisten in Halle in ihrer tiefsten Erniedrigung, oder Was wollen die Pietisten in Preussen* (Merseburg, 1830), pp. 2 ff.
108. *Urkunden betreffend die neuesten Ereignisse in der Kirche* . . . (Leipzig, 1830), p. 11.
109. See the letter of the university chancellor, August Hermann Niemeyer, protesting Tholuck's appointment, in Witte, *Tholuck*, I, 419–423, and Tholuck's account of the attitude of his colleagues in a letter to Johann Heinrich Kurtz, professor of theology at the University of Dorpat, April 14, 1861, G. N. Bonwetsch, ed., *Briefe an Johann Heinrich Kurtz* (Leipzig, 1910), p. 23.

ism at Halle ("Bringen Sie dem Hallischen Rationalismus ein Per-
eat!").[110] So strong, however, was the reaction in Halle to the appointment that soon after his arrival Tholuck complained bitterly
about the open hostility of faculty and students and asked Hengstenberg, his "beloved brother in the Lord," to mobilize the support of
the Pietist faction for his struggle against the rationalist theologians.[111]
After a few months the frustrated and lonely Tholuck was so close
to a nervous breakdown that he asked the government for a leave.
In his misery, he confided to a friend that the presence of the fellow
Pietist Ferdinand Guericke, "a brother in Christ, but not a friend,"
did not provide much consolation in his loneliness.[112]

Anxious to promote Tholuck's recovery, the government suggested that he spend a year in Rome as the chaplain of the Prussian
Embassy. The milder climate of Italy and the light duties of his as-
signment in Rome did indeed enable him to recover sufficiently to
return to his duties at Halle in 1829. Tholuck's position was strengthened by Guericke's appointment to an associate professorship. Another important event was the appointment of Ludwig von Gerlach
as director of the provincial court (*Landgericht*) at Halle. In a letter
to Hengstenberg, Tholuck exclaimed happily: "I can hardly believe
this. . . . Please tell Ludwig Gerlach [that] Guericke and I [and]
Dr. de Valenti"—a Pietist physician in Halle—"and a few other true
believers . . . can hardly wait for his arrival." Otto von Gerlach
hastened to assure Tholuck that his brother Ludwig would do everything in his power to help the Halle Pietists in their struggle against
the rationalists.[113]

Immediately after his arrival in Halle, Gerlach joined Tholuck,
Guericke, de Valenti, and some others in the organization of "mission societies" (*Missionsvereine*) in the province of Saxony. The
avowed purpose of these societies was to "teach people obedience to
God . . . and to worldly masters." So great was the indignation of
some liberals against what they called the "shameless use of religion
by the 'sons of darkness'" (*Finsterlinge*, a term now applied to the
Pietists by their political enemies), that they called upon the public

110. Entry in Tholuck's diary, March 13, 1826, Witte, *Tholuck*, I, 449 f.
111. Letter, May 24, 1827, Hengstenberg papers, Box I.
112. Letter to Carl Radecke, January 18, 1827, Bonwetsch, *Tholuck Briefe*, p. 51.
113. May 1829, Bachmann, *Hengstenberg*, II, 180; May 5, 1829, Bonwetsch,
Tholuck Briefe, p. 134.

not to tolerate meetings of "mission societies" in church buildings. Some actual disturbances and the threat of further violence posed by the meetings soon led the provincial authorities to advise the organizers of the societies to confine their gatherings to private homes.[114]

By 1830 Hengstenberg and Ludwig von Gerlach had decided that they could no longer tolerate the influence of the rationalists over the patronage positions in the large educational complex of the Francke Foundation. The government of Frederick William III was giving the foundation large amounts of money, substantial additional sums were coming from pious donors in England and the United States, and almost a third of the 800-odd theology students at Halle were more or less dependent on it. Hengstenberg and his Pietist friends were determined that "the contemporary spirit of [rationalist] unbelief reigning at Halle should be replaced by the spirit of August Hermann Francke, the pious founder of the foundation."[115] On the advice of Hengstenberg and at the "request" of his "respected and beloved friend" Ludwig von Gerlach, Guericke secured copies of notes taken by students in the lectures of Wegscheider and Gesenius and gave them to Gerlach, with the purpose of exposing the rationalist professors in an article in the *EKZ*. Some of the published comments of the rationalist theologians were highly critical of the literal interpretation of the Scriptures and tended to discredit belief in certain dogmas. In the article Hengstenberg and Gerlach concluded that Wegscheider and Gesenius were undermining not only the traditional foundations of the Protestant church but also the existing political and social order, and demanded that they be dismissed from their positions. Gerlach later admitted that by publishing the article he wanted to "characterize" Wegscheider and Gesenius and to give the *EKZ* a "more positive tendency" which would leave no doubt of its "unequivocal stand" in the struggle against "unbelief . . . which encourages disrespect for heavenly and worldly order."[116]

The public denunciation of theology professors on the basis of lecture notes caused unprecedented excitement and indignation not only in academic circles but also in the politically conscious public.

114. *Bericht über die Umtriebe der Frömmler in Halle* (Altenburg, 1830), pp. 3–7.
115. Schrader, II, 166.
116. Gerlach, *Aufzeichnungen*, I, 180 f. See also the article and Hengstenberg's editorial comments in *EKZ*, 1830, pp. 38–40, 45–47, 309, and 1832, p. 2.

The Hengstenberg faction was accused of using religion and theology to "support the political interests and pretentions of people who seek religious sanction for their privileges [and] wish to suppress freedom of conscience and expression." Tholuck and Guericke in particular were denounced as the conscious tools of the Hengstenberg faction in its effort toward "transforming Halle from a first-class institution of learning into a center of Pietistic activity." [117] Professor Neander, who had previously supported the Hengstenberg faction, publicly disassociated himself from the *EKZ* in a statement accusing the group of having adopted the principle that the end justifies the means. Hengstenberg answered the charge by stating flatly that it was "sinful for a Christian student to be loyal to a rationalist teacher." [118]

Immediately after the publication of the article large gatherings of people in Halle expressed their indignation by throwing stones through the windows of Tholuck, Guericke, and Gerlach, who were afraid to leave their homes and asked for police protection. Public opinion was further incited by the refusal of the police to allow a torchlight procession of students to honor Wegscheider and Gesenius, who had read the article to students in their classrooms to protest the methods of the Hengstenberg faction. Although Tholuck had warned Hengstenberg that publication of the article would "foment the hatred" of their enemies and make his work among students extremely difficult, Hengstenberg was convinced that the time had come to "carry the fight from the lecture hall to the Protestant Church . . . from the field of scholarship into public life." Under the pressure of Hengstenberg, Guericke, and Gerlach, Tholuck was compelled to identify himself with the campaign against his colleagues even though his stand further antagonized the majority of the professors and students and the population of Halle.[119]

In the course of an official investigation of the charges brought against Wegscheider and Gesenius, Hengstenberg had to reveal Ludwig von Gerlach as the author of the article. Actually the liberals

---

117. Freimund Lichtfreund [pseud.], *Berichte über die Umtriebe der Frömmler in Halle, oder Welch' Zeit ist es im Preussischen Staate?* (Altenburg, 1830), pp. 9 f. Also: "Über die neueste religiöse Parteiung in Preussen," *AKZ*, 1830, pp. 441–448.

118. August Neander, *Erklärung über meine Theilnahme an der Evangelischen Kirchen-Zeitung und die Gründe mich von derselben ganz loszusagen* (Berlin, 1830), pp. 4–8; Schwarz, *op. cit.* (in n. 72 above), p. 97.

119. *EKZ*, 1830, pp. 317 f.; Bonwetsch, *Briefe an Hengstenberg*, II, 85.

had for some time been accusing Gerlach of being the official promoter of the Pietist scheme to get control of the Francke Foundation. It was also asserted that Tholuck had encouraged Gerlach to denounce the rationalist professors to pave the way for realizing his ambition to become director of the foundation.[120]

Frederick William III was particularly shocked that the liberal theologians "seemed to accept absolutely no limits to their academic freedom," and ordered a thorough investigation of the case. Subsequently Minister Altenstein appointed councilor Delbrück, a jurist of the Magdeburg Consistory, to lead the inquiry at Halle and to ascertain the "actual limits of the freedom [of professors] to teach . . . and to interpret theological truths." [121] Altenstein was under severe pressure—from the king and the cabinet, from the Pietist circle around the Crown Prince, and most of all from Hengstenberg's faction—to restrict the academic freedom of professors. At the same time he was alarmed by the spread of public demonstrations over the country and the threat of physical violence by the aroused liberal opposition, which identified itself with the defense of academic freedom. Thus the political pressures of the time transformed a supposedly theological controversy between clerical factions led by theology professors into a political battle between liberals and conservatives. Both major political groups took the opportunity to state their positions publicly and to make propaganda for their views. Consequently, the case also helped to bring about a clarification of political goals and revealed some of the methods employed by the various interest groups.[122]

In contrast to Neander and some others who dissociated themselves from the questionable tactics of the new Pietist-orthodox combination of clergymen and aristocrats, the "Old Baron" Kottwitz reaffirmed his strong support of the Hengstenberg faction. Previously he and his pious associates had always denied belonging to any particular faction. But now Kottwitz was unequivocal in his endorsement of the goals, strategy, and methods of the militant clerical group led by Hengstenberg: "I would rather fall with Hengstenberg than stand with Neander. . . . I would rather be blamed for

---

120. Gerlach, *Aufzeichnungen*, I, 181.   121. *Ibid.*

122. See the article "Ein Wort über die Stellung der theologischen Parteien in unserer Zeit," *AKZ*, 1830, pp. 505–516.

being harsh and dogmatic than praised for being wise and tender-hearted." [123] Pastor F. W. Krummacher, one of the leading clergy-men in Rhineland-Westphalia, also assured Hengstenberg of the support of the "true believers" and declared that Hengstenberg was performing a crucial role in the "struggle for the kingdom of God (*Reich Gottes*) on earth." According to Krummacher and his friends, the *EKZ* was a decisive weapon, no matter what Professor Neander thought about it.[124]

The fact that no attempt was made to arrange a meeting of the professors to discuss the theological issues involved clearly indicated that the main concern of the government was with the political reaction to the Halle affair. The final report of Altenstein to the king on August 8, 1830, maintained that the charges of the *EKZ* concerning the subversive nature of the lectures of Wegscheider and Gesenius were unfounded, and expressed disapproval of Hengstenberg's unethical journalism. "One of the most glorious achievements of Your Majesty's reign in the last twenty years has been the reorganization of the Protestant church," the Minister stated, and though he went on to praise the effective functioning of the system of general superintendencies, he did not hesitate to express his anxiety over the danger which the Pietist conventicles posed to the unity of the state church. Obviously, Altenstein's main concern in the matter was for the continued efficient functioning of the ecclesiastical apparatus, which he saw threatened by the tactics of a group of Pietist and orthodox extremists who sought to dominate the entire clergy.[125] His position that "a state organ should not interfere in theological controversies" drew a sharp rebuke from the king, whose cabinet order of September 23, 1830, stated: "I consider the influence of theology professors [who] do not feel bound by the dogmas of the Protestant church [as] eternal truths [to be] extremely dangerous for the state. . . . While I do not intend to remove them from their academic chairs, [I expect] you to make sure in the future [that] only theologians who accept the dogmas of our Evangelical Church [will] be

123. Kottwitz to an unidentified friend (n.d.). The content indicates that the letter was written at the time of the Halle denunciation. Bonwetsch, *Briefe an Hengstenberg*, I, 165.

124. F. W. Krummacher to Hengstenberg, April 6, 1830, *ibid.*, I, 167.

125. *Fortgesetzte Urkunden betreffend die neuesten Ereignisse in der Kirche . . .* (Leipzig, 1831), pp. 37 f.

appointed to new academic positions." In other words, Frederick William III refused to dismiss Gesenius and Wegscheider, but ordered that henceforth only men of the theological orthodoxy of Hengstenberg, Tholuck, Hahn, or Otto von Gerlach were to be considered.[126] The legal sovereign of Prussia seemed to be influenced more by the views of court Pietists and the Hengstenberg faction than by those of Altenstein.[127] Baron von Kottwitz, in fact, tried to mobilize support for replacing Altenstein with Wilhelm von Gerlach—the oldest brother of Otto, Ludwig, and Leopold—as minister of ecclesiastical affairs and education, but the ministerial bureaucracy was so violently opposed to the suggestion that the plan had to be abandoned.[128]

Although the political liberals considered it a victory that the rationalist professors retained their positions,[129] the fact remained that the government was from now on officially committed to a policy of investigating the ideas and convictions of candidates for theological professorships and would reject those among them who refused to endorse certain theological dogmas which until 1830 had not been considered binding. Hengstenberg, Tholuck, Guericke, and other conservative theology professors were more than ever convinced that their action of "setting the church in movement" had been right and "for the cause of the Lord."[130] Hengstenberg did not deny that he and his followers had no intention of respecting the intellectual freedom of academicians in their teaching. He stated bluntly: "Every plant—not merely the teaching (*Lehre*), but the whole person—which hath not been planted by the heavenly Father shall be rooted up."[131] Conversely, the Neo-Pietist and orthodox clique had been

126. Bachmann, *Hengstenberg*, II, 231 f. Also in Gerlach, *Aufzeichnungen*, I, 188.

127. When, in the course of a conversation with Frederick William III, the philologist and diplomat Wilhelm von Humboldt referred to Wegscheider and Gesenius as famous men, the king replied sharply: "It is not good when such people are famous." Hengstenberg to Ludwig von Gerlach, October 3, 1833, Gerlach family archives.

128. Otto von Gerlach to his brother Ludwig, July 13, 1832, *ibid.*

129. Hengstenberg to Ludwig von Gerlach, July 27, 1832, *ibid.;* Karl Rosenkranz, "An die Herren DD. Daniel von Coelln und David Schulz: Ein Sendschreiben von Dr. Fr. Schleiermacher," *Jahrbuch für wissenschaftliche Kritik,* 1831, pp. 388 ff.

130. *EKZ,* 1831, pp. 33 and 301. See also the letter of Ludwig von Gerlach to Hengstenberg reporting about Tholuck's slow but steady success in winning adherents to the Pietist cause, June 20, 1833, Gerlach family archives.

131. Hengstenberg to Ludwig von Gerlach, July 27, 1832, *ibid.* Quoting Matt. 15:13.

planted by the heavenly Father and was to be protected and developed. Part of the significance of the Halle affair was its finally establishing Hengstenberg as the acknowledged leader of the conservative political elements in the universities and the state church.[132]

The wide publicity springing from Hengstenberg's aggressive agitation in the case strongly contributed to making his faction the vanguard of a growing political group opposed to political and social reforms. The Hengstenberg faction considered the July 1830 Revolution in France to be "a clear demonstration of the connection between liberalism and unbelief"—a pernicious alliance that demanded "rights and freedom" but neglected the fact that "no freedom can exist when the mob (*Pöbel*) rebels against established rights and authority." By stating unequivocally that the "only basis for the rule of governments is their divine origin," and that "there can be no father, no master, no authority . . . which is not by the grace of God,"[133] Hengstenberg rejected the contention that "in the nineteenth century governments can no longer base their rule on blind obedience and blind faith . . . when even soldiers will no longer obey blindly."[134] Leopold von Gerlach (1790–1861), the second oldest of the four Gerlach brothers, echoed Hengstenberg's denunciation of the bourgeois monarchy of Louis Philippe by stating that the new "tyranny of the mobs" threatened to be worse than Bonaparte's had been. Thus the July Revolution further hardened the position of the conservative forces. Hengstenberg, Tholuck, and other theology professors of like mind were disgusted by what they considered the impertinent behavior of German liberals who kept pointing to the success of popular forces in Paris. Holding that such encouragement of the "mob" to rebel was sinful, they warned their country of the wrath of God, should Germans follow the French example by demanding constitutional changes. Hengstenberg was convinced that he and his faction were engaged in what he called "building the

132. See the sarcastic "Danksagungschreiben an den Herausgeber der Evangelischen Kirchenzeitung, Herrn Professor D. Hengstenberg," *AKZ*, 1831, pp. 45–47. The anonymous writer thanked Hengstenberg for setting himself up as the leader of the "Dunkelmänner" and thus having demonstrated the basic division between conservatives and liberals.

133. *EKZ*, 1830, pp. 236, 703, and Ludwig von Gerlach to Hengstenberg, August 16, 1833, Gerlach family archives.

134. Leopold Krug, *An meine deutschen Mitbürger* (Leipzig, 1830), p. 405.

kingdom of God on Earth," and that "political disturbances [would] seriously hinder" their work.[135] Thus even more strongly than before, it was the "duty of the church to reinforce the eternal foundations of governments" by continuous and active participation in political life and, most particularly, by fighting "religious rationalism" —"a form of disbelief clearly connected with liberalism and revolt against the God-given order." [136]

After the Halle affair had broken the backbone of theological rationalism in the universities, Hengstenberg began to express the view that the use of the Hegelian philosophy by the so-called Young Hegelians could present an even more dangerous challenge to the established political and social order. In a letter to Tholuck, Hengstenberg stated explicitly: "The Hegelian philosophy will in the near future develop into a much more diabolical force than the declining rationalism. . . . It is our holy duty to watch out and to attack immediately." [137] That Hengstenberg was right in sensing a serious challenge became apparent when David Friedrich Strauss, a Young Hegelian, published his *Life of Jesus* in 1835 and thus set into motion a long series of bitter theological and political struggles between liberals and conservatives.

Until the founding of the *Neue Preussische Zeitung* (popularly known as the *Kreuz-Zeitung*) in 1848, Hengstenberg's *EKZ* was one of the two most influential journals in Prussia. (The other was the conservative *Berliner Politische Wochenblatt,* founded in 1831.) There can be little doubt that in the course of the 1830's and 1840's the *EKZ* became one of the most important weapons in the "battle of ideas." The Junker Pietists supported "their" Hengstenberg in his campaign against the *Zeitgeist* and gave him their unqualified support. Particularly anxious to keep the royal court informed of his work, Hengstenberg personally saw to it that every member of the royal family received the *EKZ* regularly. Ludwig von Gerlach always made sure that Nicolovius, Eichhorn (later the minister of ecclesiastical affairs and education under Frederick William IV), and other high government officials sympathetic to the theological

135. Leopold von Gerlach to his brother Ludwig, April 4, 1833, Gerlach family archives, and Hengstenberg to Tholuck, August 22, 1830, Bonwetsch, *Tholuck Briefe,* p. 125.

136. *EKZ,* 1830, p. 688, and 1831, p. 36.

137. Hengstenberg to Tholuck, August 22, 1830, Bonwetsch, *Tholuck Briefe,* p. 125.

and political views represented by the *EKZ* received the journal. The pious Nicolovius and Eichhorn assured Hengstenberg that they appreciated his work and that they always read the *EKZ* with great interest. The young editor realized that in view of the highly controversial political character of the *EKZ* he needed not only the protection of heavenly powers but also the support of powerful individuals. Hengstenberg could always count on the support of the Crown Prince and the aristocratic Pietist circle around him, and he expected them to protect him against his numerous political enemies. In the face of bitter attacks on his theological and political views, Hengstenberg regularly urged his close followers to support him, saying typically in a letter to Tholuck, "Remind the brethren that in my exposed position I need their help and protection." [138] While insisting that it was the proper role and duty of the church to reinforce what he called "the eternal foundation of all states" by "instilling obedience and respect for worldly authorities," he always emphasized that in his ruthless struggles against the liberals he was actually trying to save the souls of misled people by removing obstacles to their salvation.[139] Not surprisingly, the liberals considered Hengstenberg one of the most dangerous *Dunkelmänner* of the century and compared him to the Grand Inquisitors who tried to save the souls of their victims by burning them at the stake.[140]

The Neo-Pietist and orthodox emphasis on absolute obedience to government also met with resistance which was mounted by some clergymen of the Old Lutheran school when they were confronted with the establishment of the confessionally and institutionally united state church. The stronghold of this so-called Old Lutheran opposition was in Silesia, and its leader was Johann Gottfried Scheibel (1783–1843), a professor of theology at the University of Breslau and the first pastor of the St. Elisabeth congregation in that city.[141]

138. June 21, 1827, *ibid.,* p. 121. Ludwig von Gerlach repeatedly reassured Hengstenberg of the support of the Pietist Junkers. See letters to Hengstenberg, August 11, 1829, and June 5, 1836, Gerlach family archives.

139. *EKZ,* 1832, p. 20.

140. Schulz, *Wesen der EKZ,* pp. 14 ff.; Schwarz, *op. cit.* (in n. 72 above), pp. 65–98.

141. For a very detailed history of the Old Lutheran movement see his *Actenmässige Geschichte der neuesten Unternehmung einer Union . . .* (Leipzig, 1834); hereafter cited as Scheibel, *Actenmässige Geschichte.* Despite its obvious bias, Scheibel's massive work is valuable for its carefully compiled material on the bitter

Scheibel was the descendant of several generations of Lutheran clergymen and teachers in Breslau. His background of religious orthodoxy and his association with some Pietist circles while studying theology at the University of Halle made him a determined foe of rationalism. In 1818 Scheibel was promoted from associate to full professor, primarily because of his loyalty to the government during the War of Liberation, and it was the government's expectation that he would continue to be an active supporter of its ecclesiastical policy.[142] Until the appointment of Hahn in 1834, theological rationalism—represented by such outstanding scholars as David Schulz and Daniel von Coelln—dominated the faculty of theology at Breslau. Scheibel's poor performance as a theological scholar and teacher did not present a serious challenge to the rationalist influence in academic circles. His colleague David Schulz publicly ridiculed his confused, emotional, and mystical creed and even questioned his qualifications for an academic chair. The influence of Scheibel in the 1820's and early 1830's grew out of his violent opposition to the arbitrary union of the Lutheran and Reformed confessions, his refusal to use the new prescribed liturgy in the church service, and the evolving political implications of his defiance of government orders.[143]

Scheibel's opposition to the state church was originally based on his Lutheran hatred of the "pagan Calvinists" whom he considered the actual perpetrators of the union. By the late 1830's, Scheibel's theological opposition to the state church had become so violent that it shocked both the government and the Hengstenberg faction, which until then had considered him an important asset in the struggle against the influence of rationalism among Silesian clergymen.[144] The political significance of Scheibel's position derives from the fact that his orthodox Lutheran views on the sacraments and liturgy were opposed to the confessional merger with the Calvinists, while his hostility to the autocratic structure and operation of the state church drove him to the acceptance and propagation of some radical notions of church government. By the late 1820's Scheibel had become con-

struggles of the Old Lutherans and the Prussian authorities. See also Huber, II, 272–275, and Holborn, *Modern Germany*, II, 490.

142. See Wangemann, *Sieben Bücher*, I, 121 ff.
See also Schulz, *op. cit.* (in n. 82 above), pp. 4 ff.
143. Kaufmann, *Geschichte der Universität Breslau*, pp. 175 ff.
144. *EKZ*, 1830, pp. 352, 404.

vinced that "true" Lutheranism meant that the assemblies of parish members (called presbyteries in the western provinces) had the right to elect their ministers and could also determine the actual teachings of the church.[145] Congregations, according to Scheibel, were the owners of local church property and the government had no right to interfere with its use. No individual or municipality had the right of patronage over parish ministries and their congregations. No clergyman should be paid by the government, and there must be no ecclesiastical hierarchy based on titles and rank. Clearly, although Scheibel despised rationalism in all its manifestations and had been among the founding members of the *EKZ,* these notions grew out of his resistance to the arbitrary merger of the two Protestant denominations. His propagation of them made him the most popular clergyman of the 1820's and early 1830's among Silesian orthodox Lutherans. Alone among the provinces, Silesia refused to accept the confessional union and the common liturgy, although officially its clergy belonged to the state church.

Thanks to Scheibel's connections with Heubner, Hengstenberg, Tholuck, and other politically reliable clergymen, and the government's desire to win support for the Protestant state church in Silesia, which had been a province of the Catholic Habsburg Empire, the so-called Old Lutherans—led by Scheibel and some other clergymen—were allowed to use the pre-union Lutheran liturgy until 1830. At least, their ministers were not actually prevented from administering the sacraments according to Lutheran rites. In 1827 Frederick William III, greatly concerned, published a pamphlet in which he appealed to the Silesian Lutherans to give up their "spiritual separation." [146] Altenstein and some other high officials were less troubled by "spiritual separation" than by alarming reports that the Old Lutheran resistance was being used by elements of the political opposition who allegedly were trying to overthrow the "order and subordination . . . necessary for society." Bishop Eylert insisted that the case did not call simply for religious toleration, which had been and continued to be the traditional policy of Prussian governments, but rather that separation was associated with an explosive political issue

---

145. Wangemann, *Sieben Bücher,* I, 158–161; Huber, II, 272 ff.
146. *Luther in Beziehung auf die preussische Kirchenagende* (Berlin, 1827), p. 2. The pamphlet was published anonymously.

of extreme seriousness. Apparently Eylert's views reflected the government policy of crushing any political faction which incited the population to resist official orders. When such high-ranking officials as the general superintendent and the district president in Silesia were openly threatened and abused by the public and were forced to leave church meetings to save their lives, the government declared that "the matter was no longer one of theological differences but one of open rebellion against the authorities." Scheibel was accused by the Hengstenberg faction of allowing political agitators to infiltrate the Old Lutheran movement and thus providing them with the opportunity to incite the population "against the government and against law and order." [147]

By 1830 there was no doubt that the resistance of Scheibel and other conservative Old Lutherans to the union was indeed being exploited by some liberals for their own political purposes. Welcoming the opportunity of agitation against the conservative government, these liberals tried to identify Scheibel's resistance to the union with their struggle for freedom of association, speech, and religious creed. Although Scheibel emphatically stated that he and other Old Lutherans were "seriously disturbed by the efforts of the political opposition . . . to confuse the minds of the people . . . by identifying their subversive demands with [the] defense of the true Lutheran religion," he could not deny that he and his colleagues had unwittingly set into motion political forces in Silesia to which they were opposed.[148]

Alarmed by the political consequences of Old Lutheran separatism, the government threatened to dismiss Scheibel and any other clergymen who refused to celebrate the three-hundredth anniversary of the Augsburg Confession according to the prescribed rites of the state church. Hermann Olshausen, who himself was the target of bitter attacks by Königsberg liberals for his connections with the pietistic-mystical "Muckers," accused Scheibel of being the "pawn of revolutionary forces" which were "refusing to obey the municipal and provincial authorities in Silesia" and "challenging the authority of the government." He added: "By your opposition to the govern-

147. Eylert, III, pt. 1, 128–133; Hermann Olshausen, *Was ist von den neuesten kirchlichen Ereignissen in Schlesien zu halten* (Königsberg, 1833), p. 14.

148. *EKZ*, 1830, pp. 377 ff.; Otto Wehrhan, *Vertheidigung der lutherischen Sache gegen Dr. Olshausen* (Meissen, 1835), pp. 14–19.

ment you in fact sanctify the impertinent demands of the liberals and of the mob *ad majorem Dei gloriam.*" [149]

When Scheibel was suspended from his positions as professor and pastor in June 1830, more than two thousand persons in Breslau and nearby communities expressed their wish to leave the state church and to form a separate Lutheran church which would be organized on the basis of self-government. Henrik Steffens, professor of physics and natural philosophy, and G. P. E. Huschke, professor of law, both at the University of Breslau, joined Scheibel in setting up a six-teen-member executive committee for a newly formed separatist con-gregation in Breslau. Aside from the three professors and a provincial law court councilor, most members of the committee were artisans (among others a carpenter, two shoemakers, a tailor, and a gardener) who could hardly be classified as belonging to the "mob" so despised by the Hengstenberg faction. Despite numerous petitions to the gov-ernment and to the king personally, the right of separation from the state church was denied to the Silesian Lutherans, and in 1832 Scheibel and a number of other clergymen were dismissed from their posi-tions. Because the government began to arrest and imprison dis-missed clergymen who tried to continue clerical functions, Scheibel left Breslau for Dresden, in Saxony, where he was allowed to serve as the minister of a Lutheran congregation.

Although Scheibel went into exile and other clergymen who de-fied the government were jailed, the political ferment which had been touched off by Silesian resistance to the state church continued after 1832. In 1833 August Hahn was appointed professor of theology at the University of Breslau and councilor of the Silesian Consistory; eventually he was made general superintendent of the province. In a few years Hahn became one of the most hated men in Prussia. It was known that he had ordered the use of military force, resulting in serious injuries to a number of persons, to break up meetings of Old Lutheran congregations, and that he had confiscated the prop-erty of congregation members and forced them to accept officially appointed clergymen in the place of those who were jailed. [150] Even

---

149. Olshausen, *op. cit.* (in n. 147 above), pp. 12 f., and *EKZ,* 1830, pp. 377 ff. For a typical instance of the many attacks on Scheibel see Georg Diestel, *Wie das Evangelium entstellt wird in unserer Zeit* (Königsberg, 1830), pp. 4 ff.

150. J. G. Scheibel, *Mitteilungen über die neueste Geschichte der Lutherischen Kirche* (Altona, 1837–1838), II, 26 ff. Also: Hermann Theodor Wangemann, *Drei*

so, the Hengstenberg faction not only approved of the repressive measures against the population but actually encouraged Hahn to purge the state church in Silesia of its dissident elements. By 1843 Tholuck could congratulate Hahn on the successful *Gleichschaltung* of Silesia, stating: "I do not doubt that your work has meant a great blessing for the province." [151]

Hengstenberg and Tholuck expressed personal sympathy for the misfortunes of Scheibel and the imprisoned Silesian clergymen, but the main concern of the Hengstenberg faction was with the consequences of the split between the "party of Old Lutherans" and the "camp of the true believers." Hengstenberg in particular blamed Scheibel and the Silesian clergymen associated with him for disobeying government instructions and thus providing an opportunity for the "political-revolutionary movement of the time" to establish a foothold in the church. In reply to several attacks in the *EKZ,* Huschke defended the Old Lutherans and declared that the leaders of the Lutherans in Breslau had never intended to transplant the principles of political freedom and equality to the church. He could not deny, however, that what he called the "revolutionary movement" had taken advantage of the Old Lutherans' resistance to the government.[152] What Huschke did not say was that Scheibel's plans for a separate Lutheran church called for a degree of self-government which could not but attract the attention of politically alert elements eager to change the autocratic system of government in church and state. Minister Altenstein and other high ranking officials were so alarmed by what they called the demands for a "democratic church constitution" (*kirchlich-demokratische Verfassung*) that they deemed it necessary to crush the Old Lutheran movement. Bishop Eylert pointed out in a meeting of the Council of State in 1834 that Scheibel's battle cry, "our first duty is to obey God and not men," not only questioned the divine origin of government but actually incited

---

preussische Dragonaden wider die lutherische Kirche (Berlin, 1884), pp. 6 ff.; idem, *Die kirchliche Cabinetts-Politik des Königs Friedrich Wilhelm III* (Berlin, 1884), pp. 327 ff.

151. Letter, December 7, 1843, Bonwetsch, *Tholuck Briefe,* p. 147. See also Hahn to Tholuck, April 5, 1837, *ibid.*

152. In J. G. Scheibel, ed., *Theologisches Votum eines Juristen in Sachen der Königlich-Preussischen Hof- und Dom Agende* (Nuremberg, 1832), pp. 6 ff., and his *Geschichte der lutherischen Gemeinde in Breslau vom Nov. 1830 bis zum Februar 1832* (Nuremberg, 1832), pp. 18–26.

rebellion.[153] Thus Scheibel ended his career in Prussia as a man branded a subversive political figure, persecuted and driven out of the country by the government, despised by the rationalists, abandoned by the Hengstenberg faction, and remembered by many in Silesia as a martyr who had fought for self-government in the church and suffered for the cause of freedom of creed, speech, and assembly. The bitterly disappointed Scheibel declared publicly that Hengstenberg, Tholuck, Olshausen, and other members of the Hengstenberg faction had been "false friends in sheep's clothing." The tremendous reaction in Prussia and abroad to the suppression of the Old Lutherans finally forced the Prussian government in 1834 to permit them to emigrate to the United States, where many of them settled in upstate New York.[154]

In 1833 the theology professor Guericke at the University of Halle left the state church and became an enthusiastic supporter of Scheibel's creed in the province of Saxony. This was another bitter blow to the Hengstenberg faction, in which he had been prominent through his ceaseless attacks on the rationalists.[155] In 1835 Guericke was dismissed as associate professor. Until his reinstatement, in 1840, he was completely isolated in his attempts at caring for the spiritual needs of the few Old Lutherans in the Halle area. The failure of Guericke to attract a larger following indicated that the Old Lutheran movement was essentially a native Silesian product which could not easily be transplanted to other parts of the country. Also it suggested that the Prussian government's position on religious freedom and obedience to worldly authorities had general support in the traditional Lutheran notion that there can be no freedom which conflicts with one's duty to the state. This position was given characteristic expression in the words of Frederick William III to Bishop Eylert: "I do not like to hear about [the Old Lutherans]. It is a very unpleasant thing. . . . We do have freedom of religion and freedom of conscience in Prussia. But freedom is not licentiousness (*Zügel-*

153. Eylert, III, pt. 1, 128, and Walter Wendland, *Die Religiosität und die kirchenpolitischen Grundsätze Friedrich Wilhelms des Dritten in ihrer Bedeutung für die Geschichte der kirchlichen Restauration* (Giessen, 1909), p. 119.

154. Schulz, *Wesen der EKZ*, p. 3, and J. G. Scheibel, *Luthers Agende und die neue Preussische* (Leipzig, 1836), pp. 3–8. See also the reports of Old Lutherans in the United States in the collection *Briefe aus und über Amerika* (Dresden, 1845).

155. Ludwig von Gerlach to Hengstenberg, September 12, 1833, Gerlach family archives.

losigkeit) which disrupts order and refuses obedience." In sum, he concluded, "True freedom consists of obedience to the law." [156]

In 1839 David Schulz bitterly attacked the Hengstenberg faction, which he accused of trying to turn clergymen of the state church into "police agents," who could "no longer think and act as free Protestants" if they became the "mere executive arm of the government in the Protestant church." Although Schulz and his rationalist colleagues at the University of Breslau had opposed Scheibel for his confused and at times very mystical orthodox Lutheran creed, they objected violently to the suppression of the Old Lutherans and accused the Hengstenberg faction of political opportunism in sacrificing some of its most active men to keep the favor of the government.[157] What Schulz failed to point out was that, especially since the July Revolution, the faction leaders had acted against the increasing political pressures in a very uniform and logical manner. The consistency of their political behavior was demonstrated by the very fact that they disassociated themselves from men such as Scheibel and Guericke when the ideas and actions of these men were no longer in line with the political maxims and ends of the Hengstenberg faction. Not even ties of personal friendship could prevent a break, once the principal political objectives of the Neo-Pietist–orthodox leaders were threatened. For Hengstenberg and his conservative faction there was no contradiction between the toleration and actual protection of the "Pomeranian Awakening," in which some Pietist aristocrats refused to observe church services conducted by rationalist ministers, and the violent attacks in the *EKZ* on the Old Lutherans in Silesia. The Old Lutherans had to be crushed not because the Hengstenberg faction objected to their rejection of the common liturgy, but because the political opposition was taking advantage of the Old Lutherans' discontent and its eruption into mass disturbances. In short, the political implications of the Old Lutheran controversy tended to support the demand of the liberals for political freedom and a representative government, while the "Pomeranian Awakening" was used by the Pietist Junkers to support their claims to patrimonial rights on the noble estates.

Although Guericke's defection was a great loss to the Hengstenberg faction, developments at the University of Halle in the 1830's

156. Eylert, III, pt. 2, 194.
157. Schulz, *Wesen der EKZ,* p. 43, and *EKZ,* 1839, p. 987.

and 1840's showed the effectiveness of August Tholuck as a conservative clerical leader. The *EKZ* denunciation had failed to remove Wegscheider and Gesenius from their positions in 1830, but it did signal the beginning of a new era in which the University of Halle became one of the major ideological battlegrounds. Philosophical, theological, and literary controversies reflected the vigorous intellectual life of the city generally and of the university in particular.[158] The University of Halle could not compete with the rapidly expanding University of Berlin in respect to government support, facilities, and the scholarly caliber of most of its professors, but it was distinguished by the variety, political alertness, and articulateness of the numerous philosophical and theological factions. All of the various shades of contemporary theological creeds were represented at Halle: rationalists, Pietists, orthodox believers, and moderate theologians of conciliation, among others.[159]

August Tholuck was in the center of the "battle of ideas" which agitated the politically conscious minds of academicians and writers at Halle in the 1830's and 1840's. He exerted a great influence not so much as a scholar but rather as a leader capable of winning adherents to a creed which rejected not only the teachings of the rationalists but also those of the left-wing followers of Hegel.[160] When in 1835 David Friedrich Strauss published his *Life of Jesus* (which by applying the Hegelian dialectic sought to destroy the credibility of the Gospels as historical evidence), the right-wing Hegelians—led by professors Marheineke and Vatke at the University of Berlin—saw their whole theological world collapse. Marheineke admitted in one of his lectures, "We are in bad shape now. . . . . We shall not recover from this blow." [161] Tholuck, who had the blessing of Hegel in 1826 for his antirationalist "mission" in Halle, was now in complete agreement with Hengstenberg and

158. Hans Rosenberg has stated that "at no other German university was the dissension among the various warring factions so sharply marked" in the 1830's and 1840's as at Halle. *Rudolf Haym und die Anfänge des klassischen Liberalismus* (Munich and Berlin, 1933), p. 12.

159. Rosenberg, "Geistige Strömungen," p. 560.

160. See Tholuck's sermons concerning the political and social issues of the 1840's in his *Vier Predigten über die Bewegungen der Zeit: Gehalten im akademischen Gottesdienste der Universität Halle im Sommer 1845* (Halle, 1845).

161. See Marheineke's lectures on Hegel's philosophy of religion, delivered in 1835–1836, in his *Zur Kritik der Schelling'schen Offenbarungs-Philosophie* (Berlin, 1845), pp. 31 ff.

Ludwig von Gerlach that Strauss's work was a typical product of the subversive influence of the speculative philosophy of Hegel on theology and a clear expression of the dangerous *Zeitgeist*.[162] While Hengstenberg actually welcomed the publication of the *Life of Jesus* as a milestone which finally separated the "true believers" from the "unbelievers," [163] Tholuck in Halle was particularly exposed to the sharp attacks from Young Hegelians who were engaged in a systematic campaign aimed at the demolition of the traditional dogmas of Christianity. They assailed Tholuck, Guericke, Ludwig von Gerlach, and others of similar hue for their supernaturalistic theology and its application to the defense of the status quo.[164] Confronted with the superior scholarship or dialectical skill of Strauss, Arnold Ruge, Bruno Bauer, Ludwig Feuerbach, and like-minded philosophers and publicists, Tholuck concentrated his efforts on strengthening his faction's position in the faculty, which was teaching, preaching, and training generations of future clergymen. He urged the faculty to reject the rational-critical approach to theology, which he blamed for the "rebellious spirit of the times . . . respecting no God in heaven and no rulers on earth." [165]

The radical and uncompromising campaign of the Young Hegelians alarmed the government so much that in 1840 Johann Albrecht Friedrich Eichhorn (1779–1856), the new minister of ecclesiastical affairs and education, declared to a group of young theologians at the Wittenberg Seminary that the new regime of Frederick William IV was by no means neutral in the theological controversies of the various factions.[166] In fact, Eichhorn assured them that the government definitely favored those clergymen who identified themselves with its struggle against the political opposition.[167] In a series of lectures in 1835–1836 and again in 1841–1842,

---

162. Gerlach, *Aufzeichnungen*, I, 230.   163. *EKZ*, 1835, p. 43.

164. In scores of articles published in the *Hallische Jahrbücher*, of which Ruge was editor from 1837 to 1841.

165. In his *Die Glaubwürdigkeit der evangelischen Geschichte: Zugleich eine Kritik des Lebens Jesu von Strauss* (Halle, 1837), p. 19. For the great influence of Tholuck on students see Schnabel, IV, 358–383.

166. Unlike Altenstein, Eichhorn was very sympathetic to the Pietists in general and to Hengstenberg in particular. Eichhorn to Hengstenberg, July 26, 1847, Hengstenberg papers, Box V.

167. For the effect of Eichhorn's speech on clergymen and other civil servants see the anonymous *Zur Beurtheilung des Ministeriums Eichhorn von einem Mitgliede desselben* (Berlin, 1849), pp. 10–29. The pamphlet probably was written by privy councillor Gerd Eilers.

Professor Marheineke, who continued to be the leading representative of the conservatively inclined Right or Old Hegelians, tried desperately to prove that, despite the Left or Young Hegelian aberration, Hegel's philosophy still provided the best intellectual weapon for sanctioning the existing order in state and church.[168] Yet in the face of the demonstrated skill of the Young Hegelians and their followers in turning the Hegelian dialectic against the "anachronistic" and "illogical" Prussian political and social system, the government of Frederick William IV was now more inclined to act in accord with the idea that the speculative philosophy of Hegel was "the greatest evil for humanity" and that its influence should be destroyed.[169]

Hegelians of both Right and Left suffered by the changed outlook of the ministry of education and ecclesiastical affairs. The growing influence of Hengstenberg in the faculty of theology at the University of Berlin isolated Marheineke and prevented the promotion of Vatke to full professor. Bruno Bauer, whose career had been furthered by Altenstein in the 1830's, was dismissed from his position as lecturer at the University of Bonn in 1842 because he denied the historical authenticity of the Gospels and attacked the Hengstenberg faction for identifying the Protestant church with the interests of the privileged classes.[170] Bauer's statement, "Hegel has been a greater revolutionary than all his [radical] students," [171] was echoed by Tholuck, who was shocked that in the 1840's "some of the most talented theology students" were "refusing to accept the truly pious creed" and "no longer turning to rationalism [but] instead—*horribile dictu*—to atheism." By then, he said, even he and Wegscheider, his old enemy, occasionally found themselves "on the same side of the fence [in] opposing the forces of unbelief," which had "no respect for the Scriptures . . . or for anything based on tradition." [172]

By the 1840's rationalism and Hegelianism in the theological faculties no longer presented serious threats to the Hengstenberg faction's dominant influence over the clergy. At Halle, Tholuck's

168. Marheineke, *op. cit.* (in n. 161 above), pp. 44 ff.

169. Karl Friedrich Schubarth, *Über die Unvereinbarkeit der Hegelschen Staatslehre mit dem obersten Lebens- und Entwicklungsprinzip des Preussischen Staats* (Leipzig, 1839), p. 30.

170. Bauer had stated his opinion in a pamphlet, *Herr Dr. Hengstenberg: Kritische Briefe über den Gegensatz des Gesetzes und des Evangeliums* (Berlin, 1839).

171. In his pamphlet *Die Posaune des Jüngsten Gerichts über Hegel den Atheisten und Antichristen* (Leipzig, 1841), p. 82.

172. Letter to Kurtz, July, 1842, Bonwetsch, *op. cit.* (in n. 109 above), p. 21.

position was strengthened by the appointment of Julius Müller in 1839 and the reappointment of Guericke in 1840.[173] When Gesenius and Wegscheider died, in 1842 and 1849 respectively, Tholuck's influence in the faculty and on students grew more formidable and tended to become decisive. By 1845, Tholuck could report to Hahn that the university was enjoying the blessings of God and that this was because "the majority of the 450 theology students follow the right way." While attendance of students at the lectures of the rationalists Wegscheider, Fritsche, and Niemeyer was "practically nil," Tholuck could boast not only that were his lectures attended by hundreds of students, but that more than a hundred were taking part in the weekly prayer meetings conducted in his home.[174] At the University of Berlin, Hengstenberg's position in the faculty of theology was practically unchallenged, and no new appointment was made without his approval. Marheineke died in 1845, and Hegelian theology as represented by Vatke was then completely isolated, Hengstenberg having made it known that attendance at Vatke's classes lessened the chances of students for future clerical appointments. Because most students heeded the warning, the influence of Vatke declined even though he continued to be highly respected as a scholar.[175] Otto von Gerlach and G. F. A. Strauss, theology professors as well as court preachers, were among the staunchest supporters of Hengstenberg. The other faculty members tended to follow a moderate course and, consequently, avoided taking a strong stand. As academic teachers and scholars, they propagated a theology of conciliation (*Vermittlungstheologie*), and similarly, in their approach to public affairs, displayed an attitude of cautious moderation.[176] Obviously they were men who did not want to become seriously involved in partisan strife.

The government was greatly concerned about the growing influence of the liberal movement in Königsberg and the fact that a theology professor in the university there, Caesar von Lengerke

173. Schrader, II, 249 ff.

174. Tholuck to Hahn, June 28, 1845, Bonwetsch, *Tholuck Briefe,* p. 148. It should be added, however, that as late as 1841 the agitation of the Left Hegelians influenced considerable numbers of students to sign a petition asking for the appointment of David Friedrich Strauss to the faculty of theology. Schrader, II, 251.

175. Lenz, I, pt. 2, 280; Karl Bauer, *Adolf Hausrath und seine Zeit* (Heidelberg, 1933), I, 77.

176. Lenz, II, pt. 2, 108 ff.

(1803–1855), publicly supported Johann Jacoby, the leader of the democratic-liberal movement in East Prussia and the author of the *Four Questions Answered by an East Prussian*. This pamphlet, published at Königsberg in 1841, expressed demands for representative institutions in Prussia and aroused the admiration of the liberals and the ire of the conservatives.[177] Thus Christoph H. Haevernick (1811–1845), a Hengstenberg protégé, was appointed associate professor of theology at Königsberg in 1841.[178] Although Haevernick's appointment resulted in a series of political demonstrations and subsequent reprisals by the government, Minister Eichhorn and Frederick William IV were determined to assure the dominance of political conservatives in the faculty of theology. Consequently, Lengerke was transferred to the faculty of philosophy in 1843.[179]

After the deaths of Johann Christian Gass, in 1831, and Daniel von Coelln, in 1833, the main representative of rationalist theology at the University of Breslau was David Schulz, who was unable to counter the growing influence of the pious professors Hahn, Boehmer, Kahnis, Gaupp, and Oehler, whose loyalty to the ruling authorities was beyond doubt.[180] The appointment of Hahn as general superintendent and director of the Consistory of Silesia in 1843 symbolized the fact that the upper echelons of the ecclesiastical hierarchy in the province had been purged of politically unreliable elements, even though Hahn had to admit that among the rank-and-file clergy rationalist influence was still deeply rooted.[181]

In contrast to the other universities, the Protestant theology faculty of the University of Bonn had been dominated by advocates of the "middle way" since its founding in 1818. The appointment of the theologians Lücke, Sack, Augusti, Gieseler, and C. I. Nitzsch

177. Ferdinand Falkson, *Die liberale Bewegung in Königsberg, 1840–1848* (Breslau, 1888), pp. 35 ff.

178. Haevernick to Hengstenberg, March 26, 1841, Bonwetsch, *Briefe an Hengstenberg*, p. 87. In the letter Haevernick expressed his gratitude for Hengstenberg's support in securing the position. See also Prutz, pp. 143 f.

179. See Haevernick's letter of July 24, 1842, asking Hengstenberg to use his influence to remove Lengerke. Bonwetsch, *Briefe an Hengstenberg*, pp. 88 f. As a student at Halle Haevernick supplied the lecture notes which were used by Gerlach and Hengstenberg to denounce Gesenius and Wegscheider. Franz Burdach, *Rückblick auf mein Leben* (Leipzig, 1848), pp. 454–456.

180. All these theology professors were appointed in the 1830's and 1840's. See Kaufmann, *Geschichte der Universität Breslau*, II, 185 ff.

181. August Hahn, *Predigten und Reden unter den Bewegungen in Kirche und Staat seit dem Jahre 1830* (Breslau, 1852), pp. 28 f.

reflected the wish of the government to have men of a conciliatory and cooperative spirit in the Rhineland and Westphalia and thus facilitate the incorporation of those areas into the Prussian state after 1815. Although in their theological views these professors reflected some of the liberal ideas of Schleiermacher, they were careful not to commit themselves to the support of demands which challenged the basic social and political structure of the Prussian state, even though they personally might have favored some changes.[182]

The activities of the increasingly influential and intolerant leaders of the Hengstenberg faction and the government's pursuit of an anti-liberal personnel policy—favoring the recruitment and advancement of conservative and, in some cases, conciliatory clergymen —resulted in some unforeseen consequences. On the one hand, scores of highly talented students—among whom were Rudolf Haym, Ludwig Feuerbach, Bruno Bauer, and Gottfried Kinkel—abandoned academic careers in theology, either voluntarily or under pressure. On the other hand, statistical evidence indicates that in the 1840's there was a general, dramatic decline in the number of students of theology. The University of Halle, which in 1828 had some 900 theology students, had not even an average of 400 in the 1840's.[183] At the University of Berlin the number declined from 641 in 1830 to 214 in 1847.[184] While the number of theology students at the University of Breslau had averaged about 100 from the late 1810's until the late 1830's, the enrollment declined to about 40 in 1842.[185] Königsberg, where the average was almost 100 students of theology before 1840, had only 67 in 1844.[186] To complete the picture, the University of Bonn, in the predominantly Catholic Rhineland, had suffered from a lack of adequate numbers of Protestant students of theology since its establishment. In the two decades after 1818 the student body attached to the faculty of theology averaged only about 50 or 60 men, and in the 1840's the faculty had serious difficulties in attracting enough applicants to maintain even that number. By 1846 there were only 38 students enrolled in the classes, and the faculty was alarmed by the signs of a declining interest in the clerical profession.[187]

182. Bezold, *Geschichte,* pp. 180 ff.   184. Lenz, II, pt. 2, 105.
183. Schrader, II, 568.   185. Kaufmann, I, 66.
186. Prutz, *op. cit.* (in n. 178 above), p. 202.
187. Bezold, pp. 189, 381. Large numbers of Rhenish-Westphalian Protestants

The waning of student interest in clerical careers seems to have been due to several causes. The economic hardships of the Hungry Forties may have prevented many young men from entering the universities as students; enrollment in other faculties also declined for several years. Significantly enough, however, the statistical evidence relating to the subsequent, really prosperous decades does not show any increase in the number of theology students at a time when enrollment in other faculties rose rapidly.[188] Clearly, therefore, the 1840's marked the beginning of a long-term trend of stabilization in the numbers of prospective clergymen which, in part, may be explained by the growing realization of the limited openings in the clerical profession and the crystallization of career opportunities in other fields. The increasing influence of patronage and the intransigence of the conservative crusaders within the ecclesiastical hierarchy also may have influenced many independent minds to seek careers in other fields where their freedom of conscience and of thought and its expression would not be restricted by the government's insistence upon conformity. The relatively numerous dismissals and voluntary withdrawals from the clergy in the 1840's attest to the fact that the Prussian state church was no longer an institution that had room for clergymen whose general views, political convictions, and activities were openly hostile to the will of the government.

The cooperation of Hengstenberg, Eylert, and other dogmatic, orthodox Protestants with the Neo-Pietists of the "Awakening" had the result of hardening the traditionally quiet and tolerant attitudes of Pietism. Hengstenberg symbolized the nature and character of the Neo-Pietist and orthodox alliance, which not only aimed at capturing the hearts of individuals (as the old Pietism had done) but also sought to control the church by ruthlessly eliminating theological opponents. While he himself had never experienced a deeply emotional "awakening" like his Pietist friends, Hengstenberg inspired great confidence in the "true believers," who looked to him as one of the outstanding "fighters for the cause of God." His own views of a rigid, orthodox Bible Christianity, tolerating no criticism of the letter of the Scriptures, blended in perfectly with the develop-

---

seemed to prefer theological study at Halle and Berlin because of the strict regulations (such as the requirement of communion certificates for examinations) rigidly enforced at Bonn. *Ibid.*, p. 188.

188. Schrader, II, 568; Lenz, III, pt. 1, 496; Kaufmann, p. 66; Prutz, p. 202.

ing dogmatism of nineteenth-century Neo-Pietism [189] and the political and social views of the "Awakening." The cold and unemotional Hengstenberg was responsible for directing much of the emotional, religious, and spiritual energies of the "true believers" into political channels opposing political and social changes. He can also be credited with exerting influence on Pietistic groups to remain within the organizational framework of the state church. Hengstenberg accomplished this purpose by emphasizing his conviction that the church itself had become "spiritualized" and was a fighting instrument of God. He succeeded in combining certain aspects of Lutheran and Calvinist Protestantism by emphasizing obedience to worldly authorities and acceptance of the political and social status quo, and by making the church an active instrument against the rational-critical *Zeitgeist*.

By the 1840's the militant group of clerical and aristocratic conservatives led by Hengstenberg had developed into the vanguard of a highly significant political faction intensely opposed to the liberals. A new generation of pious and obedient "ecclesiastical officers," trained by Hengstenberg, Tholuck, Hahn, and other professors of orthodox and Pietist beliefs, was in the process of filling in the ranks of the clergy. When the leaders of the so-called Friends of Light and German Catholic movements in the 1840's voiced demands for abolishing the autocratic structure of church and state and organized popular mass support for the purpose of establishing a people's church (*Volkskirche*), the Hengstenberg faction was infuriated. The *EKZ* charged that the liberal clerical leaders were "exciting the masses to overthrow the Protestant Church," "challenging every divine and worldly authority," and "trying to intimidate the government agencies with masses of people." [190] On the eve of the Revolution of 1848, the "Partei Hengstenberg" represented one of the most determined, ideologically and politically united factions in Prussia defending the traditional political and social order against the attacks of the political opposition.

189. See Hartmut Lehmann, "Friedrich von Bodelschwingh und das Sedanfest: Ein Beitrag zum nationalen Denken der politisch aktiven Richtung im deutschen Pietismus des 19. Jahrhunderts," *HZ*, 202 (1966), 542–573.

190. "Über die Versammlung der soi-disant protestantischen Freunde zu Koethen den 15. Mai 1845," *EKZ*, 1845, p. 550, and 1846, p. 28.

4

The Pietist Aristocrats

Some of the most active and influential political leaders of the Protestant clergy in pre-March Prussia came from a group of religiously "awakened" Old Prussian noble army officers, high government officials, and big landowners. They felt compelled to take an active part in the affairs of the church by devoting much of their energies to their role as militant "lay clergymen," or Kirchen-männer. These new and highly active leadership elements allied themselves with the theology professors of the Hengstenberg faction, several court preachers, and some Pietist members of the professional clergy to form the avant garde of a special group within the conservative movement.[1]

Such Old Prussian noble families as the Gerlachs, Marwitzes, Finckensteins, Thaddens, and Senffts had resisted stubbornly the reforms of Stein and Hardenberg and had done everything they could to render the reforms ineffective. Karl Friedrich Leopold von Gerlach (1757–1813), whose sons Leopold and Ludwig were among the most influential architects of Prussian conservatism in the nineteenth century, was a highly determined opponent of the Reformers. Together with other resentful noblemen, he denounced the work of Stein and Hardenberg as "revolutionary" and "subversive," seeing it as a mortal threat to the traditional order. His sons had close friends among the Marwitz and Finckenstein families, and were greatly influenced by their association with some of the most active

1. Schnabel, IV, 383–388; Shanahan, pp. 99–130; Huber, II, 338 ff.

125

elements of the *ständische Reaktion,* in whose opinion it was better to lose three battles of Auerstädt than to tolerate the Stein-Hardenberg legislation. The ferocious opposition of these nobles to the reforms was not forgotten by Leopold von Gerlach, who blamed the agrarian reforms in particular for the Revolution of 1848 when he stated: "The agrarian laws [of the Reform Era] had revolutionized the country [and] respect for property had come to an end. The effects [of the Reforms] and the resulting confused ideas about rights and property . . . can be blamed for the lawlessness of our days." [2]

Peasant emancipation, the abolition of serfdom and of some services and obligations to which peasants hitherto had been subject, the granting of property rights to certain categories of landed peasant tenants, the introduction of limited self-government in the towns and of freedom to buy and sell noble estates (*Rittergüter*)— these and other reform measures were resisted to the utmost by a number of noble landowners. The prolonged agrarian crisis during and after the Napoleonic Wars threatened the material basis of their traditional aristocratic position, and it seemed that the ruin of many individual members of this powerful *Junkertum* would endanger the dominant position of their class in Prussian society. [3]

After the disastrous performance of the Prussian armies at Jena and Auerstädt in 1806, a number of agitated and confused Old Prussian noblemen gathered in Berlin and founded a society called the "Christian-German Dining Club" (*Christlich-Deutsche Tischgesellschaft*). Confronted with external and internal dangers to their political and social preeminence, in their meetings they put emphasis on "patriotism" and liberation from French rule, on duty to king, Christianity, and the fatherland, and on the "defense of ancient rights." They sang patriotic songs, read poetry, and longed for

2. In *Denkwürdigkeiten aus dem Leben Leopold von Gerlachs;* hereafter cited as Gerlach, *Denkwürdigkeiten.* I, 156, 165.
See also the letters of Alexander von der Marwitz to Leopold von Gerlach, August 19, 1812, and November 2, 1813, in Schoeps, *Tagebücher und Briefe der Gebrüder Gerlach,* pp. 85 ff., 501 f., and 511 f.
3. Hans Rosenberg, "Die 'Demokratisierung' der Rittergutsbesitzerklasse," in *Zur Geschichte und Problematik der Demokratie: Festgabe für Hans Herzfeld,* ed. W. Berges and C. Hinrichs (Berlin, 1958), pp. 461–465; Jordan, pp. 87–96, 129 ff.; Magnus, Freiherr von Bassewitz, *Die Kurmark Brandenburg im Zusammenhang mit den Schicksalen des Gesammtstaats Preussen während der Jahre 1809 und 1810* (Leipzig, 1906), pp. 16 ff.

"better times." The writers Achim von Arnim and Heinrich von Kleist, and some other members of the group (including Leopold von Gerlach) eagerly embraced Romanticism and its appreciation of the mystical and irrational in human life. There was, as yet, little emphasis on religion as such.[4]

The group did not meet during the War of Liberation, but by 1816 they began meeting again and were joined by others of like mind. This romantic-conservative club took the name "Maikäferei" (the "May chafers"—an allusion to their meeting place at an inn called after the innkeeper May).[5] There were several similar groups meeting at different inns, but the Maikäferei was the most important because of the intellectual quality and social preeminence of its members, who included Leopold and Ludwig von Gerlach, together with their older brother Wilhelm (1789–1834), Carl von Voss-Buch (1795–1877), Friedrich Karl von Bülow (1789–1853), Carl von Rappard (1794–1852), Count Cajus von Stolberg (1797–1874), Count Albrecht von Alvensleben-Erxleben (1794–1855), Karl von Lancizolle (1796–1871), and Clemens von Brentano (1778–1842). The club had been founded on the initiative of Brentano. The number of members changed from time to time, but usually about twelve persons attended the meetings. Adolf von Thadden and Ernst von Senfft-Pilsach (1785–1882) did not attend meetings, but developed close friendships with the Gerlach brothers and other club members. According to Ludwig von Gerlach, the Prussian conservative element dominated in the Maikäferei, and the club was dedicated to fighting the ideas and effects of the French Revolution in the name of legitimacy and Christianity. Leopold von Gerlach and several other members eventually became the most influential figures in the "Camarilla," or "ministère occulte," comprising the "small but mighty" aristocratic circle of advisers under Frederick William IV.[6]

The Gerlach brothers, Thadden, Lancizolle, and several other

---

4. Rudolf Steig, *Heinrich von Kleists Berliner Kämpfe* (Berlin, 1901), pp. 21 ff.; Josef Nadler, *Die Berliner Romantik, 1800–1814* (Berlin, 1921), pp. 16 ff.; E. Rudorff, *Aus den Tagen der Romantik* (Leipzig, 1938), pp. 28 ff.

5. Gerlach, *Aufzeichnungen,* I, 94 ff.; Hans Joachim Schoeps, *Das andere Preussen: Konservative Gestalten und Probleme im Zeitalter Friedrich Wilhelms IV* (Stuttgart, 1952), pp. 15 f.; Schoeps, *Tagebücher und Briefe,* pp. 172 ff.

6. Ludwig von Gerlach, diary, April 1, 1816, Schoeps, *Tagebücher und Briefe,* p. 182; Gerlach, *Aufzeichnungen,* I, 95, and II, 67; Friedrich Wiegand, "Der Verein der Maikäfer in Berlin," *Deutsche Rundschau,* 160 (1914), 280.

Maikäfer began visiting the services of J. G. Hermes (1740-1818) in the small St. Getraud Church (popularly known as the *Spittelkirche*). The pious "old Hermes" was a highly respected Pietist clergyman who, together with Johannes Jänicke (1748-1827) at the Bethlehem Church of the Moravian Brethren, attracted a number of aristocrats and young students. Previously the Gerlachs and some of their friends had frequented the services of Schleiermacher, but by 1816 they found his sophisticated and philosophical sermons "cold and empty" and felt much more at home in the mystical-religious atmosphere of the Pietist gatherings conducted by Hermes and Jänicke.[7]

On May 28, 1816, Carl von Savigny, a jurist and professor of law at the University of Berlin, received the first of several letters from the young physician Johann Nepomuk Ringseis about the religious revival in Catholic South Germany. Writing from Munich, this former Berlin student friend of Savigny told about his wonderful religious experiences in the congregation of the "awakened" Catholic priest Johannes Gossner. The enthusiastic physician painted a fantastic picture of the Catholic "Awakening" which had been started by Gossner and his fellow priests, Boos and Lindl. Clemens von Brentano, a Catholic Maikäfer, copied the letters by hand and distributed them among his friends in Berlin. The reports of Ringseis caused a tremendous excitement among the members of the Maikäferei, who considered the letters a direct intervention from Heaven for the purpose of moving them to dedicate their lives to the "cause of God." Thadden, then a young officer and instructor at the War Academy in Berlin, the law student Lancizolle, and some other friends decided to go to South Germany in order to gain first-hand experience of the work of the new "apostles of Christ."[8]

Deeply impressed with the religious revival in South Germany, Thadden and Lancizolle returned to Berlin in November 1816 and told their friends about the "inspirations" they had received in the company of Gossner, Boos, and Lindl. The Gerlach brothers and

---

7. Ludwig von Gerlach, diary, March 24, 1816, Schoeps, *Tagebücher und Briefe,* p. 181; Wendland, "Studien," pp. 43 ff.

8. Fürstin Eleonore Reuss, *Adolf von Thadden-Trieglaff,* 2d ed. (Berlin, 1894), pp. 15 ff.; hereafter cited as Reuss, *Thadden;* F. W. Kantzenbach, "Die katholische Erweckungsbewegung," in his *Die Erweckungsbewegung,* pp. 27-47.

other noblemen were encouraged to develop a "truly pious belief," and soon they too were "awakened." The return of Thadden and Lancizolle actually marked the transformation of the Maikäfer and their friends into a new circle that soon developed close contacts with the "true believers" around the "Old Baron" Kottwitz and other North German Pietistic groups. Thus a new element of religious mysticism which had originated in the Catholic South was infused into the Protestant North German "Awakening." [9]

A general movement of religious "awakening" swept through Europe in the early nineteenth century like a storm. There was also a great revivalist movement in the United States. On the European continent this "awakening" affected particularly Germany, Switzerland, and France. In England it was connected with a greater emphasis on doctrine and formal liturgy. It was not restricted to any single social class, although on the continent it was very strongly represented among the landed aristocracy, especially the Prussian Junkers. It was also prevalent among the small peasants in southwestern Germany and among some middle-class people in the urban areas of the country. Often it was connected with Romantic reactions against the effects of rationalist Enlightenment, which seemed to have created the feeling of a vacuum in spiritual life. Into this empty space there entered an intense revivalist movement stressing conversion and filled with a warm spirit of vital piety.

Contrary to the account of Friedrich Meinecke, the "pietistic element" had not been conspicuous in the Maikäferei. It was only from the time of Thadden's return from South Germany that the Gerlachs and other noble Maikäfer began to be motivated by an intense religious zeal which led them to dedicate their lives to the "cause of God." [10] In contrast to the "Christian-German Dining Club" and the Maikäferei, the members of the new circle no longer met at inns, but

9. Thadden to Ludwig von Gerlach, August 15, 1819, Gerlach family archives; Alfred von Martin, "Der preussische Altkonservatismus und der politische Katholizismus in ihren gegenseitigen Beziehungen," *Deutsche Vierteljahrschrift für Literaturwissenschaft und Geistesgeschichte,* 7 (1919), 508; Kantzenbach, "Ausstrahlungen der bayrischen Erweckungsbewegung auf Thüringen und Pommern, *Zeitschrift für Ostforschung,* 5 (1956), 257 ff. The article "Erweckungsbewegung" in *RGG* (1957), I, 623–626, summarizes the various religious movements associated with the "Awakening" and has an excellent bibliography.

10. Ludwig von Gerlach, diary, January 2, 1818, Schoeps, *Tagebücher und Briefe,* pp. 267 f.; Gerlach, *Aufzeichnungen,* I, 94–96; Friedrich Meinecke, "Bismarcks Eintritt in den christlich-germanischen Kreis," *HZ,* 54 (1903), 56 ff.

gathered every Friday evening in private homes and regularly attended the church services and prayer meetings of Jänicke. Intensely preoccupied with problems of sin, salvation, and religious "awakening," these men were no longer interested in the Maikäferei, which by 1819 had slowly faded away. The final dissolution of the club marked the beginning of the ascendancy of Neo-Pietist religion in the thought and behavior of these Old Prussian Junkers, who remained a closely knit group until the end of the 1850's.[11]

The small churches of Hermes and Jänicke attracted many other religiously "awakened" noblemen and members of the upper classes. Contemporary observers in Berlin were amazed to see elegantly dressed ladies and gentlemen, army officers in splendid uniforms, as well as university professors, students, and other members of the intellectual elite enter the dimly lit St. Getraud and Bethlehem churches. Many who formerly attended Schleiermacher's services had now lost interest in his sophisticated, philosophical sermons and had come to prefer the mystical and highly emotional religious atmosphere that was evoked by such Pietist preachers as Hermes and Jänicke. Even Schleiermacher's wife went to the St. Getraud Church almost every Sunday, and the great theologian himself could be seen occasionally in the quiet little church in serious contemplation. The government and the faculty of theology at the University of Berlin were greatly impressed with the simple piety of the "old Hermes" and his successful efforts to "spiritualize" the reorganized state church. By retaining the religious fervor and emotional energies generated by the Neo-Pietist "Awakening" within the framework of the state institution, Hermes and other clergymen like him performed a significant service to the government. In recognition of his services, Hermes was awarded an honorary doctorate in theology by the University of Berlin in 1817. In making the award, the university declared that in the field of theology not only scholarship but also the piety of the individual was considered essential.[12]

The process of awakening to "truly pious belief" took different

11. Senfft to Ludwig von Gerlach, December 6, 1819, Schoeps, *Tagebücher und Briefe*, p. 313. For the influence of Thadden on Ludwig von Gerlach see Thadden to Ludwig, Good Friday, 1818, and Ludwig's diary, February 27, 1819, *ibid.*, pp. 305, 593–595. The correspondence between the two men in 1818–1820 shows clearly the dominant Pietistic element in their thinking.

12. Kantzenbach, *Die Erweckungsbewegung*, pp. 82–93, and Lenz, II, pt. 1, 286 ff.

forms in individual converts. Some, like Ludwig von Gerlach, Thadden, and the young theology student Tholuck, underwent brief periods of very intense religious-emotional experiences, while others became gradually "awakened" in the course of weeks and months. The roots of this Neo-Pietist "Awakening" went back to the collegia pietatis of the seventeenth and eighteenth centuries and their strong emphasis on the role of laymen as "tools of God." The old Pietist stress on the priesthood of all believers was now carried on by pious Junkers—especially in Berlin and the eastern parts of Prussia—who began to conduct private religious meetings, many times without the participation of ordained clergymen. The role of the lay clergy, known from earlier Pietist conventicles, acquired a new meaning when conservative noblemen and high government officials, along with their protégés among theology professors and students, underwent "awakening" and came to consider it their duty to "translate the word of God into action." Formerly "quiet voices" grew louder when the Pietists realized that influential men from some of the most eminent Junker families considered them "brothers in Christ" and fellow soldiers in the fight against rationalism and the "ideas of 1789." Pietistic clergymen began to exhibit a great deal of intolerance and self-righteousness, and to warn people not to attend the services of rationalist clergymen. Jänicke in particular was persistent in asserting that it was sinful to listen to the sermons of the "heretic" Schleiermacher, whose complex theological notions and ideas were branded by him as being even more dangerous than those of the rationalists.[13]

Between Schleiermacher and Jänicke there was indeed a tremendous intellectual gulf, but actually both men emphasized the importance of feeling in religion. Pietists had long insisted that religion was primarily a mystery, a matter of feeling; it could not be "grasped," and knowledge and experience did not help one to "understand" religion. Simple piety and unquestioning belief were considered more important than the search for truth. Jänicke and other Pietists distrusted Schleiermacher's *Gefühlsreligion* because

13. Ludwig von Gerlach, diary, 1819–1820, Schoeps, *Tagebücher und Briefe,* pp. 299–314.

For a very revealing account of the sudden and dramatic "awakening" of the young Frankfurt patrician and future politician M. A. v. Bethmann-Hollweg see Fritz Fischer, *Moritz August von Bethmann-Hollweg und der Protestantismus* (Berlin, 1938), pp. 59 ff.

they rightly understood it as a continuous search for eternal truths instead of a simple acceptance of the orthodox dogmas of the church and an emotional reliance on the inscrutable will of God. Thadden and the Gerlachs had originally been attracted to the Gefühlsreligion, and Thadden acknowledged his debt to the great theologian when he said: "Schleiermacher made me turn away from the world of animals to the world of human beings." [14] In other words, Thadden and the Gerlachs could not deny the influence of Schleiermacher on their religious thinking. It was apparent, however, that the political views of the liberal theologian would eventually antagonize the reactionary Junkers. The developing religious beliefs of these men tended to reinforce their conviction that the privileged position of the aristocracy was ordained by God and that any attempt to change it would be sinful. Thus they began to turn to the formerly isolated "quiet voices" when they realized that their own feelings concerning the acceptance of the traditional political and social order were shared by the Pietists.

The few Pietist clergymen in Berlin and other places now became the "contact men" between the new and the old "true believers." The old collegia pietatis which had survived into the nineteenth century began cooperating with the new pietistic groups of "awakened" noblemen and theologians. Strongly influenced by the Romanticism of the early nineteenth century, Thadden, the Gerlachs, and their friends found in the small churches of a Hermes or a Jänicke the mystical atmosphere of a "spiritual community" (*innere Geistesgemeinschaft*) which relaxed their agitated minds and assured them that their claims to preeminence in church and state were based on supernatural foundations. In the meetings conducted by Kottwitz the Pietist Junkers became acquainted with Nicolovius, Neander, and a number of Pietistic theology students, including Tholuck. Soon contacts were established with the Wittenberg circle of Heubner. Thadden met Jette von Oertzen, one of the three beautiful daughters of a wealthy Junker family, in the collegia pietatis of Kottwitz, and in 1820 the two were married by Jänicke in the Bethlehem Church of the Moravian Brethren. Ludwig von Gerlach married Auguste von Oertzen in 1825, and Ernst von Senfft-

---

14. Reuss, *Thadden*, p. 5, and Christian Tischhauser, *Geschichte der evangelischen Kirche Deutschlands in der ersten Hälfte des 19. Jahrhunderts* (Basel, 1900), pp. 339, 453.

Pilsach became the husband of Ida, the eldest of the three sisters. The fact that the three men became brothers-in-law further strengthened their friendship, and Ludwig von Gerlach always admitted that his ideas were greatly influenced by the archconservatives Thadden and Senfft.[15]

Although its original inspiration came from the South German religious revival, the young nobles' religion became identified with that of a small but devoted group of Pietist clergymen who had been isolated from the majority of the rationalist clergy for almost a century and who had always considered themselves the "true clergy." Pietist clergymen and laymen welcomed the opportunity to cooperate with the "awakened" noble Kirchenmänner who promised to "spiritualize" the church by helping to train the new generation of pious clergymen who would eventually replace the rationalists. From about 1815 to the early 1820's the young theology student and later clergyman Johann Georg Seegemund was the spiritual leader of a select noble group of former Maikäfer and their friends immersed in religious problems. Seegemund was a man of many talents whose seemingly wholehearted devotion to religion bordered on mysticism, and whose passionate and temperamental character combined literary talents with unusual powers of persuasion. There was no doubt about his intellectual superiority to most members of the group, in whom he aroused an interest amounting to fascination. Seegemund had been a student under Schleiermacher for several years. He told his noble friends that the "pantheistic theology" of the famous professor and clergyman had actually made him turn away from religion, and that for a time, until his "awakening" by the Moravian Brethren during the War of Liberation, he had not prayed.[16] After passing his theological qualifying examinations in 1818, Seegemund received a call from his friend Count Anton von Stolberg (who eventually became minister of the royal household under Frederick William IV) to become pastor in Wernigerode. There he embarked upon what seemed to be a promising career. The Gerlach brothers visited the young clergyman frequently and were tremen-

---

15. Schoeps, *Tagebücher und Briefe*, pp. 311 f., and Karl Friedrich Ledderhose, *Johann Jänicke* (Berlin, 1863), pp. 29.

16. Gerlach, *Aufzeichnungen*, I, 125 ff. The dates for Seegemund are unknown. All the following information is derived from Wendland, "Studien," pp. 32 ff.; Fischer, *op. cit.* (in n. 13 above), pp. 73 f.; Schoeps, *Tagebücher und Briefe*, pp. 35 f.

dously impressed by the firmness of his religious convictions. They told Seegemund of their occasional doubts on some aspects of religion, making it clear that these had their origin not in "rational" analysis but in the emotional fluctuations of their religious feelings. Agitated and deeply disturbed, the Gerlachs saw their whole newly found faith threatened, and implored Seegemund to help them overcome their doubts so that they could be certain about the right path. At one of the meetings in Wernigerode, Seegemund was successful in removing the last hesitations in the minds of the Gerlachs. From that time, they were convinced that theirs was the "cause of God." In the words of Ludwig von Gerlach, they had finally found "certainty . . . certainty in God." From the early 1820's on, the Gerlachs were totally convinced that their "mission" to make the Church a fighting instrument against the pernicious influence of the "ideas of 1789" was commanded by God, that they were doing His work, and that their enemies were the enemies of God. In the person of Seegemund the Pietist nobles found a man of humble background whose religious beliefs strengthened their identification of traditional noble privileges with the God-given order now being challenged by the political opposition. Despite his occasional immoral behavior, such as the seduction of one of his parishioner's daughters, Seegemund continued to be respected as a friend and authority by the Gerlachs, Thadden, and other noble members of the "Awakening." Eventually he married the sister of Karl von Lancizolle and thus came to be officially accepted as a social equal in the aristocracy.

The turn to Pietistic religiosity was developing parallel with the groping for the "right" political ideas. Particularly welcome to the young nobles were the theories of the staunchly conservative Swiss-German jurist Karl Ludwig von Haller, which were bitterly opposed to the political teachings and ways of thinking of the Enlightenment. The Gerlach brothers, Thadden, Senfft-Pilsach, Count Anton von Stolberg (the brother of Cajus), Count Carl von der Groeben, General Ludwig Gustav von Thile, and some other noblemen of like mind comprised a group which mixed Pietism with the defense of traditional privileges. In the 1820's the group began to enjoy the confidence and support of the Crown Prince, the future Frederick William IV (1840–1861).[17]

17. Ludwig von Gerlach, diary, Schoeps, *Tagebücher und Briefe,* pp. 209–266, and Gerlach, *Aufzeichnungen,* I, 101 ff. See also Friedrich Meinecke, "Haller und

Some of this group remained in Berlin while others returned to their estates or accepted government positions elsewhere in the country. All of them became highly prominent men who exerted considerable influence in Prussian society and the state church until the end of Frederick William IV's reign. In 1823 Ludwig von Gerlach was appointed councilor at the provincial high court (*Oberlandesgericht*) in Naumburg on the Saale, and in 1829 he was promoted to the post of director of the Saxon provincial and city court (*Land- und Stadtgericht*) at Halle. In 1835, he succeeded his deceased brother Wilhelm in the position of vice-president of the high court at Frankfurt on the Oder. During the years 1842–1844 he served as chief councilor (*Oberjustizrat*) in the Ministry of Justice at Berlin and as a member of the Council of State. From 1844 until 1874 he was the first president of the high court at Magdeburg. Although his influence declined in the late 1860's and he became isolated from other conservatives during the 1870's, Ludwig von Gerlach was undoubtedly one of the most prominent and influential Prussian conservatives, especially during the pre-March period.

A prolific writer, a cofounder and an active leader of the Conservative party, Ludwig was a potent enemy of the "ideas of 1789." He wrote hundreds of articles for the *Evangelische Kirchen-Zeitung* and the *Neue Preussische Zeitung,* rallying the forces of reaction in church and state. His brother Leopold, who had a distinguished career as an army officer, became the adjutant-general and a close friend of Frederick William IV and as such one of the most influential members of the "Camarilla." [18] Otto, the youngest brother, became an ordained member of the clergy. The three Gerlachs, Thadden, Senfft-Pilsach, and a handful of others were the most active aristocratic church leaders of the extreme right during the first half of the nineteenth century. Thadden and Senfft-Pilsach settled on their estates in Pomerania after 1823, and as wealthy and powerful landowners they took significant parts in local and national politics. In the 1840's, Senfft-Pilsach became the provincial governor of Pomerania. Thadden was an active member of the General Synod

---

der Kreis Friedrich Wilhelms IV," in his *Weltbürgertum und Nationalstaat,* 3d ed. (Munich and Berlin, 1915), pp. 218–272, and Shanahan, pp. 99 ff.

18. The memoirs of Leopold and Ludwig von Gerlach are not only mines of information for students of German history but also provide the reader with a very characteristic picture of Prussian-German conservative ways of thinking.

of 1846 and the United Diet of 1847. Together with the Gerlachs, the young Otto von Bismarck, and Hans Hugo von Kleist-Retzow (a Pomeranian Pietist whose family was related by marriage to Bismarck), Thadden was prominent in the leadership of the conservative counterrevolution in 1848–1849.[19]

Count Carl von Voss-Buch was a wealthy landowner, the adjutant for civilian affairs and close friend of the Crown Prince, and the main financial supporter of the journals *Berliner Politisches Wochenblatt* and *Neue Preussische Zeitung,* founded in 1831 and 1848 respectively by a group of conservatives including his son-in-law, General Joseph Maria von Radowitz. As a member of the Council of State and president of the Brandenburg Consistory, Voss-Buch was in a position to exert an extreme-right influence in both church and state. Count Albrecht von Alvensleben-Erxleben was appointed to the Council of State in 1833 and was sent on several diplomatic missions abroad. From 1835 to 1842 he was minister of finance. In the last years of his life he was also a member of the Prussian upper house (*Herrenhaus*). General von Thile, another pious Junker, occupied the position of chief minister of the royal cabinet (*Geheimer Staats- und Kabinettsminister*) in 1841–1849. Karl von Lancizolle became professor of law at the University of Berlin in 1823, and in 1852 was appointed director of the Royal Archives in Berlin.[20] In addition to these particularly active Kirchenmänner, scores of other Pietist noblemen held high governmental posts and considered themselves responsible for the defense of the traditional political and social order.

From the late 1820's on, it was apparent that the noble Pietist elite wielded powerful influence in Prussian governmental circles. Besides bringing Nicolovius over to their side, they managed to enlist the support of such high-ranking civil servants as Councilor K. Reinhart of the High Tribunal, Councilor L. Semmler of the Ministry of Finance, Chief Councilor Gustav LeCoq in the Foreign Office, and his brother Adolf, a legal councilor. Adolf LeCoq was a jurist with a strong practical sense. He was convinced that to counteract

19. Friedrich Meinecke, "Bismarcks Eintritt in den christlich-germanischen Kreis," *HZ,* 90 (1903), 56 ff., and Erich Jordan, *Die Entstehung der konservativen Partei und die preussischen Agrarverhältnisse von 1848* (Munich and Leipzig, 1914), pp. 132 ff.; hereafter cited as Jordan.

20. Schoeps, *Tagebücher und Briefe,* pp. 18 ff.; Gerlach, *Aufzeichnungen,* I, 159; Shanahan, pp. 115, 196.

the influence of the rationalist journals, in particular that of the widely read *Allgemeine Kirchen-Zeitung,* the Pietists needed a central church organ of their own. Recognizing the talents of Hengstenberg, LeCoq and the Gerlachs helped provide the means for starting the *Evangelische Kirchen-Zeitung,* the prospectus for which was drawn up by Adolf LeCoq personally.[21]

The "awakened" noble Pietists enlisted the support of Hengstenberg and of Tholuck, Hahn, and other young theologians associated with the Hengstenberg faction. They were also successful in gaining the cooperation of the scattered and initially small but extremely devoted group of Pietist rank-and-file clergymen. The Pietist aristocrats also cooperated closely with the theology professors of the Hengstenberg faction, who were confident that they could train a new generation of ministers to replace eventually the rationalist majority. Keenly aware that the state church was a crucial institution in the political struggle between the existing order and its opponents, these nobles mobilized their connections and resources to further the training, appointment, and promotion of clergymen whose creed was akin to their own. Since their connections included the royal court, Old Prussian noblemen, and high civil servants, the Neo-Pietist "Awakening" acquired a political cast which made it definitely an instrument of reaction.

In Crown Prince Frederick William the Pietist nobles found a helpful protector and ally in their drive to buttress the group's influence over the church. In the case of Frederick William, there was no occasion for a religious "awakening." The group merely reinforced his religious Romanticism and his distrust of rationalism and rationalist clergymen. As a boy of fifteen he had written to his tutor, Ancillon: "I know of no one whose religious beliefs rest on a more secure basis than mine . . . for I have experienced God and His works . . . from the time I was a child."[22] He was, however, highly unstable emotionally, and he and his wife, the Crown Princess Elisabeth, were surrounded by a circle of friends who were preoccupied with religious problems. They reassured each other in the belief that it was their duty to maintain themselves in the positions in which God had placed them, and thus were convinced that their

21. Kriege, *Geschichte der EKZ,* pp. 36 f.
22. Paul Haake, *J. P. F. Ancillon und Kronprinz Friedrich Wilhelm IV* (Munich and Berlin, 1921), p. 6.

privileged position in government and society rested on divine authority. The Crown Princess was a close friend of the Countess of Reden, whose castle in Thuringia was frequented by pious aristocrats from all over Germany. Members of the royal family, including the future king and his wife, often spent several days as guests of the countess, who usually invited well-known clergymen of the "Awakening," such as Gossner, to preach in the chapel of the castle.[23] The developing political notions and ideas of Frederick William were greatly influenced by his association with these mystical-religious Pietists.

In 1822 the Crown Prince became chairman of the Council of State, and in the following years his position enabled him to make a few minor political decisions. On the whole, however, Frederick William III reserved for himself the making of the more important decisions. Although irked by his obvious political impotence, the Crown Prince and his friends knew that it was only a matter of time until they became the ruling element in the Prussian state. Long before his accession to the throne, in 1840, it was widely known that the future king was actively furthering the cause of the Pietists. Young officers who hoped for promotion flocked to the discussions of Holy Scripture conducted by General "Bible" Thile to demonstrate their loyalty and devotion to "throne and altar." [24]

There was one field of activity where the influence of the Crown Prince already was decisive: he successfully secured appointments of "desirable" clergymen to high positions and thus played an active role in the process by which the ideological balance within the Protestant clergy was being changed. In 1828 the appointment of Hengstenberg, a man whose training had been in philosophy and Oriental languages, as a full professor of theology at the age of twenty-six, was a striking demonstration of the effectiveness of the

23. Fürstin Eleonore Reuss, *A Pietist of the Napoleonic Wars and After: The Life of Countess von Reden* (London, 1905), pp. 284 ff. The Crown Prince was influential in bringing Gossner to Berlin, where he became pastor of the Bethlehem Church. Heinrich von Treitschke, *Deutsche Geschichte im neunzehnten Jahrhundert* (Leipzig, 1874–1879), IV, 495; hereafter cited as Treitschke, *Deutsche Geschichte*.

24. Louise von der Marwitz, ed., *Vom Leben am preussischen Hofe, 1815–1852: Aufzeichnungen von Caroline v. Rochow geb. v. d. Marwitz und Marie de la Motte-Fouqué* (Berlin, 1908), pp. 127, 220, and Arnold Ruge, *Preussen und die Reaktion* (Leipzig, 1838), pp. 11 ff.

Pietist machine.[25] In addition to placing some of their protégés in academic and other high ecclesiastical positions, the Pietists succeeded in filling vacant pastoral posts with clergymen of their choice, particularly in the capital and on noble estates in the eastern parts of the country.[26] The Neo-Pietists of the nineteenth century were no longer the "quiet voices" but loud "true believers" demanding the purging of rationalists. By the late 1820's they were certain that the future belonged to them, and that rationalism among the clergy of the recently "spiritualized" Prussian state church would be destroyed forever.

In less than two decades there developed a radical change in the theological-ideological outlook of clergymen in Berlin. Before the Napoleonic Wars there had been only two or three Pietist clergymen in the capital. By the end of the 1820's, the process of filling vacant pastoral positions in the churches of Berlin was well under way, and the victory of the Pietist faction there was assured.[27] Outside the capital the rationalist rank-and-file majority of clergymen resisted stubbornly the attempts to impose the Pietist creed on them. But not until the 1840's did rationalist pastors finally join in the "Friends of Light" movement to protect their right to freedom of conscience and its expression. The aspirations of the liberals for reforms in church and state clashed inevitably with the ideas and activities in the Pietist-conservative alliance aiming at religious and political domination. The liberal forces viewed with alarm the collaboration of Pietist clergymen with the conservative Junkers from East Elbia, and identified the "Awakening" with political reaction.

From confused "patriotic" Romanticism to religious "awakening" and from the simple, unsophisticated, and unquestioning creed of a few Pietist clergymen to the justification of class privileges by religious sanction which compelled them to ceaseless political activity: this was the course of development for the Neo-Pietist leaders who wished to "translate the word of God into political action." In contrast to the "quiet people" of the old Pietism, who had

25. Hengstenberg to Ludwig von Gerlach, November 17, 1832, and Leopold to Hengstenberg, August 19, 1836, Gerlach family archives; Hengstenberg to Tholuck, October 6, 1828, and June 6, 1828, Bonwetsch, *Tholuck Briefe*, p. 123.

26. Thadden to Ludwig von Gerlach, June 5, 1841, Gerlach family archives; Hermann Metger, *Der Rationalismus und der Separatismus an der Ostsee* (Stolpe, 1833), pp. 7 ff.; Wangemann, *Sieben Bücher*, III, 71 ff.

27. Wendland, "Studien," pp. 74 ff.

isolated themselves from worldly affairs, the Neo-Pietist leaders of the clergy were eager to play an active role in public life. They were inspired by what Ludwig von Gerlach called a "loving urge to attack and to conquer" (liebender Aggressions- und Eroberungs-strieb). To serve the "cause of God" they had to enter the political arena and seek to destroy the *Zeitgeist* which was corrupting the world. Opponents had to be either "awakened" or eliminated.[28] Students were encouraged to denounce their rationalist professors; pious Junkers and theologians vied with each other in serving the "cause."

In the 1820's and early 1830's Thadden, Senfft-Pilsach, the three Below brothers (Gustav, Karl, and Heinrich), and a number of other Pomeranian estate owners avoided the church services of local pastors who refused to preach the Pietist creed. Until the rationalist clergymen were replaced in Thadden's vicinity in the 1830's, his home at Trieglaff served as a place where the Pietist nobles conducted services in which they themselves preached, prayed, and sang hymns. The Below brothers even administered the sacraments for a number of years to members of their families and to some of their peasants until the government used force to prevent such occurrences.[29]

The "Pomeranian Awakening" of the 1820's and 1830's was instigated by Thadden, Senfft-Pilsach, the Below brothers and other Junker Pietists who encouraged their peasants to boycott rationalist pastors and to organize devotional meetings in private homes, barns, and in the open, where peasants and landlords often fell on their knees and prayed together.[30] Because the prayer meetings of the Below brothers tended to emphasize the highly emotional, and even hysterical, aspects of the "Awakening," they had to be supervised by government officials. Such meetings usually took place in the late evening. An "inspired one" would give his message or prayer. Some other "true believer" might read excerpts from the journal *Nach-*

---

28. Gerlach, *Aufzeichnungen,* I, 117; *EKZ,* 1832, p. 20.

29. *AKZ,* 1833, pp. 198 f.; Hermann Wangemann, *Geistiges Regen und Ringen am Ostseestrand: Ein kirchengeschichtliches Lebensbild der ersten Hälfte des 19. Jahrhunderts* (Berlin, 1861), pp. 174 ff.

30. Thadden to Ludwig von Gerlach, May 23, 1820, Gerlach family archives; F. Wiegand, "Eine Schwärmerbewegung in Hinterpommern vor 100 Jahren," *Deutsche Rundschau,* 189 (1921), 323–336; Hellmuth Heyden, *Kirchengeschichte Pommerns* (Cologne, 1957), II, 181 ff.; Schnabel, IV, 384.

richten aus dem Reiche Gottes ("News from the Kingdom of God"), published by the Basler Christentumsgesellschaft, a Swiss society dedicated to the furthering of the Christian religion all over the world.[31] A single candle provided barely enough light for reading. On some occasions illiterate peasants would deliver speeches in the form of prayers. These long, passionate, and at times hysterical prayers made a great impression both on the noble landlord and on the peasant who claimed to have seen the heavens open and Christ Himself sitting upon His throne. As the candle was slowly going out, one could hear people moaning and weeping in the darkness. Nobles and peasants were "brothers and sisters" before God, and alike they suffered for their sins; but also they experienced heavenly joys. With their happiness was coupled the feeling of being different from other people. They were convinced that nobody outside the circle of "true believers" could experience bliss as they did. This feeling of moral superiority to "nonbelievers" was one of the main characteristics of the "Awakening." As for the political and social significance of the Pomeranian movement, the praying together of peasant and lord tended to sanctify the traditional patriarchal relationship between the "master" and his "subjects." The Pietist noble master was the father of his peasant children, and he felt himself to be responsible for their spiritual and material welfare.

Hans Hugo von Kleist-Retzow (1814–1892) was the uncle of Bismarck's wife and an influential figure among the Prussian religious conservatives. He grew up in the Pietist atmosphere of the "Pomeranian Awakening" and as a student of law in Berlin he was a frequent visitor at the home of Baron von Kottwitz, with whom he spent many hours discussing ways whereby the "French ideas of the *Zeitgeist*" could be opposed.[32] Upon completing his studies, Kleist-Retzow entered the Prussian civil service, where he had a phenomenal career. In 1844 he became district president (*Landrat*) in Belgard; in 1848 he was one of the leaders of the conservative counterrevolution, president of the "Junkerparlament" (an assembly of the landed nobility during the Revolution of

31. *RGG* (1957), II, 1729 f.
32. Hermann von Petersdorf, *Kleist-Retzow: Ein Lebensbild* (Stuttgart and Berlin, 1907), pp. 56–58, 84. See also Otto Pfanze, *Bismarck and the Development of Germany: The Period of Unification 1815–1871* (Princeton, 1963), pp. 333 f., and the many references in Shanahan and Jordan.

1848 in Berlin), and a prominent member of the Wittenberg *Kirchentag,* a general assembly of Protestant clergymen and laity organized against the Revolution of 1848. Kleist-Retzow later became a member of the Prussian upper house and of the Reichstag in the German Empire, and reached the height of his career as *Oberpräsident* of the Rhine Province and privy councilor (*Wirklicher Geheimrat*). Drawing his religious and ideological inspirations from the "Pomeranian Awakening" and his close associations with Kottwitz, Thadden, and the Gerlachs, Kleist-Retzow was a typical Pietist Junker whose religious, political, and social ideas encouraged German Protestants to believe that factories should be managed in the same spirit of Biblical patriarchy as their noble estates.[33]

When in the early 1840's the young Otto von Bismarck (1815–1898) found himself frustrated in his career and considered life "shallow and fruitless," he was drawn to the Pietistic circle of Moritz von Blanckenburg, a Pomeranian neighbor. Marie, daughter of Adolf von Thadden, was then engaged to Blanckenburg and was later his wife. Through Marie, Bismarck was introduced to Johanna von Puttkamer, his future wife. The Blanckenburgs and Johanna worked hard for Bismarck's conversion, and the death of Marie in 1846 was a deep personal tragedy for the young man. In December of that year he declared both his conversion and his love for Johanna, and asked for the hand of his chosen one.[34] Prayer and devotion became an intimate part of Bismarck's existence throughout his life. In contrast to his Pietist friends, however, he did not find in religion a doctrinal basis for his politics.

During the "Pomeranian Awakening," in the late 1820's, the government began to receive reports by local officials that whole villages were refusing to attend regular church services and that pious church patrons, who openly discouraged their peasants from going to church, were demanding that rationalist pastors be replaced with "true believers." Riots and threats of violence against clergymen were reported from various parts of Pomerania.[35] Naturally, the Prussian authorities were greatly alarmed by this mass unrest and disorder. The Protestant church was a state institution and its

---

33. Shanahan, pp. 118 ff., and Jordan, pp. 137 ff.

34. The letter is printed in *Fürst Bismarcks Briefe an seine Braut und Gattin,* ed. Herbert Bismarck (Stuttgart, 1900), pp. 1–5.

35. Wangemann, *op. cit.* (in n. 29 above), pp. 18 ff.

clergymen, whatever their creed, were lawfully appointed servants of the state who were to be respected and whose services were to be attended by the congregations. Noble patrons of congregations were supposed to cooperate with their pastors, certainly not to incite their peasants against them. Several government commissions were appointed in the late 1820's and early 1830's to investigate the causes and the exact nature of the "Pomeranian Awakening" and to settle the conflict between the authorities and the landlords and peasants.

Hengstenberg, the Gerlachs, and Tholuck were particularly concerned with the problem, in that the local conflicts in Pomerania threatened the Pietist "united front" and antagonized the ministerial bureaucracy, which was responsible for the smooth and efficient conduct of public administration. Through the influence of Kottwitz and with the help of the Crown Prince, Heubner of the Wittenberg Seminary became a permanent member of the commissions and visited Pomerania several times.[36] Although the central government was more concerned with the fact that the whole movement seemed to work in the direction of asserting the local authority of estate owners over their peasants—a development which the Berlin authorities disliked—the final report of Heubner in 1834 merely emphasized the religious aspects of the conflict and requested the government to transfer the rationalist pastors and to replace them with "true believers" who would be welcomed as "brothers" by both patrons and peasants. It was obvious that Heubner's seminary could immediately accommodate the government by recommending some of its candidates for the positions in Pomerania and thus help to settle the conflict.[37] In fact, by the 1840's the conflict in Pomerania was ended. The stubborn insistence of the Junkers on their right of "presenting" new pastors for appointment and the realization by most clergymen that the acceptance of the Pietist creed assured not only the good will of the patrons and their peasants but also official approval by the government resulted in harmonious cooperation between landlords and pastors. The government, anxious to secure the support of the powerful squirearchy in

36. *Zum Gedächtnis Heubners,* Appendix, "Die Mission von Dr. L. Heubner nach Pommern."

37. Thadden to Ludwig von Gerlach, December 12, 1825, and February 9, 1828, Gerlach family archives.

the struggle against the political opposition forces, openly acknowledged the Junker position by recognizing the patronage rights of
the squires and by appointing Senfft-Pilsach *Oberpräsident* of
Pomerania in 1842. Karl von Rappard, a friend of Thadden, was
happy to state "While twenty years ago . . . one had to travel over
thirty miles to find a pious pastor to baptize Mariechen Thadden
. . . now, in 1841, practically all pastors in Pomerania are true
believers." [38]

In 1829 Thadden organized the first of the annual gatherings
that, held for many years at his home, became famous as the
"Trieglaff conferences." Current public issues were discussed, information was exchanged, and plans were made for the coming
years. With the help of other Junkers he provided transportation,
board, and room for pastors who, in growing numbers, came from
all parts of Prussia and from other German states. During the
1840's, from one hundred to two hundred attended each year. Also
regularly or frequently present were the estate owners Thadden,
Senfft-Pilsach, Moritz von Blanckenburg, Kleist-Retzow, Heinrich
von Puttkamer (the father-in-law of Bismarck), the Gerlachs, the
local district president Schenkendorf-Wulkow, together with the
theology professors Heubner, Tholuck, and Hahn, and other
clerical leaders. When the repercussions of the Halle affair prevented Ludwig von Gerlach from attending the conference in
1831, his brother-in-law Thadden wrote assuringly to him: "[We
all appreciate] your courageous stand in the Halle dispute. We
thank you from the bottom of our hearts. For us, the [revolutionary]
events in Paris are not as important as the struggle against rationalism at Halle." [39] In other words, the East Elbian elements of the
ständische Reaktion rallied in defense of their pious creed and their
noble privileges, which they saw threatened by the "ideas of 1789"
and "the harlot reason." Kottwitz, the great promoter of Pietist
theologians, always reminded his friends that even the word
Hochschule was blasphemy because nothing could be *hoch* before
God. [40]

38. Reuss, *Thadden*, p. 53. See also Thadden to Ludwig von Gerlach, October 28,
1841, Gerlach family archives, and Wangemann, *Sieben Bücher*, III, 66–95.

39. Thadden to Ludwig von Gerlach, 1831, Reuss, *Thadden*, p. 45. On February
11, 1832, Thadden again apprised Gerlach of the pious Junkers' gratitude for his
"leading the struggle against the rationalists." Gerlach family archives.

40. [August Tholuck], *Die Lehre von der Sünde und vom Versöhner: Oder die
wahre Weihe des Zweiflers* (Hamburg, 1823), p. 18.

According to the Pietists, man had been corrupted by original sin, and consequently reason was not a reliable guide: faith, and faith alone, was to be trusted, both in religious and in worldly matters. The Pietist Junker was convinced that God had placed him in his position as master over his subjects (the *Herrenverhältnis*), and that it was his duty and part of his service to God to stay there. No worldly power, no liberal *Zeitgeist* could change the relationship. The "true believer" could not be selfish; he was dedicated to the "cause of God." His life was a service to God; worldly pleasures, such as the theater, dancing, drinking, and smoking, were not for him.[41] Ceaseless activities occupied his mind and body for twenty-four hours a day. Life for him was a constant struggle against what he considered the forces of evil on earth. Theodor Fontane, one of the most subtle interpreters of nineteenth-century German society, wrote: "Life for him [the Pietist] was a serious matter, [and] to live meant to fight. He was not to my liking. But I respected him." [42] Pietists were activists in the true sense of the word, and it was easy for people to recognize them in all walks of life. Leberecht Uhlich, one of the leaders of the liberal Friends of Light in the 1840's, stated in his memoirs that because he was usually hard-working and very conscientious as a young pastor some people believed him to be a Pietist: "Those of my colleagues who were not Pietists did nothing more than they were officially required to do." [43] Feeling that they were the "tools of God" on earth, the Pietists worked as missionaries on the home front. To release their constant tension, they had to make themselves conspicuous in the world by their active lives. When their behavior excited anger and hostility among their political as well as their theological opponents, they were all the more confident that they were progressing on the right path.

In an article for the *EKZ*, Ludwig von Gerlach attacked the disrespect for traditional rights shown by the liberals and argued that the Pietists, who defended "ancient rights . . . based on tradition . . . and sanctified by God," were therefore seeking a better

41. See the very revealing comments of Tholuck in his *Wider die Theaterlust* (Berlin, 1827), pp. 4, 7, and 11.
42. Theodor Fontane, *Gesammelte Werke* (Berlin, 1920), III, 276. See also Ernest K. Bramstedt, *Aristocracy and the Middle Classes in Germany,* rev. ed. (Chicago, 1964), pp. 141 f., 256 ff., 338, and 340.
43. *Sein Leben,* p. 18.

kind of political freedom than were the liberals.[44] Indeed, he went on, the honoring of the rights of others was the precondition for political freedom: one could not expect a defense of political freedom by impertinent elements which questioned the traditional order and demanded equality with the "higher estates." [45] Gerlach made perfectly clear the conviction of the Pietist elite that political power must always belong to the noble masters in Prussia. In the demands of the opposition for political and social rights he saw insolence (*Anmassung*), presumptuousness (*Unbescheidenheit*), jealousy, and other moral shortcomings. Hence from the point of view of religion and morality, the demands of the nonprivileged classes for political equality with the higher estates originated in the filth of human passions (*aus dem Kote menschlicher Leidenschaften*), and accordingly were wrong and sinful.[46] Thus morality and religion were to serve the interests of the Old Prussian ruling class.

The "awakened" Prussian noblemen who had turned from Romanticism to Pietism were convinced that defense of the "cause of God" went hand-in-hand with the defense of their noble privileges. With a perfectly good conscience, they equated the two. Religion and politics were completely fused by the Pietist leaders.[47] At the same time, the theological and political opponents of the Pietist Junkers publicly accused them of using religion as a mere ideological smoke screen. The liberals called them "secret Jesuits of the Protestant Church who want to rule by superstition," and accused them of such moral deficiencies as excessive love of power, greed, and selfishness. In a typical attack, it was asserted that noble landowners were using religion as a means to bolster their threatened political and social preeminence, to suppress people, and to justify their claims to arbitrary rule (ihre irdischen Zwecke wollen sie mit

44. 1830, p. 687.
45. *Ibid.*, p. 688. See also Ludwig von Gerlach to Hengstenberg, March 17, 1848, Hengstenberg papers, Box 5.
46. *EKZ,* 1830, p. 688.
47. See Alfred von Martin's article, "Autorität und Freiheit in der Gedankenwelt Ludwig von Gerlachs: Ein Beitrag zur Geschichte der religiös-kirchlichen und politischen Ansichten des Altkonservatismus," *Archiv für Kulturgeschichte,* 20 (1930), 155–182, and his essay, "Weltanschauliche Motive im altkonservativen Denken," in Paul Wentzge, ed., *Deutscher Staat und deutsche Parteien* (Munich and Berlin, 1922), pp. 342–384.

Hülfe der Religion erreichen, durch sie sollen die Völker im Zaum gehalten und nach Willkür geleitet werden.) [48] Such theological and political attacks on the religious foundations of worldly rule continued in the 1830's, and reached their climax in the Friends of Light and German-Catholic movements of the 1840's and the Revolution of 1848.

Thadden and other squires were greatly disturbed by the fact that since the 1770's many noble estates (*Rittergüter*) had been slipping out of the hands of old Junker families.[49] Thadden warned his fellow noblemen that selling a Rittergut was a sin and a betrayal of the trust of God because a noble estate represented much more than a mere source of income. Just as the value of the royal crown could not be expressed in material terms alone, so the true value of a Rittergut could not be expressed in purely economic terms. To possess a Rittergut meant to rule; but not everyone could or should rule. It was characteristic of the social-patriarchal approach of the Pietist Junkers that they wanted to be the benevolent fathers of their peasants, whom they expected to be obedient children: this was a relationship ordained by God, and no human power should change it. "Loving Christian service to [non-noble] fellow men" required that the squires "insist on [their] position as rulers" (seinem Nächsten in wahrer Liebe dienen . . . in dem man sich in der siegreichen Gewohnheit des Herschens behauptet).[50] Just as the king was a big landed proprietor (*Gutsbesitzer*), so each large landowner was a small king and always a master. So declared Thadden, adding: "Even when the fur cap is his crown, the walkingstick his scepter, and the potato his orb, the master always rules. Whoever denies this is a Jacobin!" [51]

In the political ferment of the 1840's, the Pietistic Junkers were

48. "Die heutigen Mystiker—Mystiker aus Politik," *AKZ*, 1830, pp. 489–493.

49. Thadden to Ludwig von Gerlach, October 22, 1833, and March 19, 1840, Gerlach family archives; Rosenberg, *op. cit.* (in n. 3 above), pp. 461–465; Jordan, pp. 129 ff.

50. Adolf von Thadden-Trieglaff, *Der Schacher mit Rittergütern: Vorgetragen in der General-Versammlung der Pommerschen ökonomischen Gesellschaft am 10. Mai 1842, zu Coeslin, 1844* (n.p., n.d.), p. 3. The Junkers were particularly concerned with the indebtedness of noble estate owners to Jews. See Thadden to Ludwig von Gerlach, October 22, 1833, Gerlach family archives.

51. Adolf von Thadden-Trieglaff, *Über Menschenschau unter Landwirten: Rede gehalten am 21. April 1839 zu Regenwalde* (Berlin, 1842), p. 6.

among the most determined supporters of the "Christian-German" government of Frederick William IV in its rejection of demands for representative government and the abolition of aristocratic privileges. Thadden, Senfft-Pilsach, Kleist-Retzow, and other Pomeranian nobles, in close cooperation with the Hangstenberg faction, insisted that their struggle was for "the rule of the Lord on earth" and against the forces of evil associated with the liberal *Zeitgeist*.[52] They looked to the pious king as the "first among equals" and expected him to support their claims to preeminence. In their struggle against centralized administration in the Prussian state and the liberal "ideas of 1789," these Junkers were fighting a two-front war. Eventually, they were fortunate to borrow some of the ideas of Friedrich Julius Stahl, a Jewish convert to Christianity from Bavaria who eventually settled in Berlin and became, especially after 1848, the champion of Protestant religious orthodoxy against the liberal *Zeitgeist*. Stahl's ideas concerning a paternalistic and absolute monarchical-Christian state were to provide the ideological tools in the fight against liberalism, constitutionalism, and revolutionary nationalism. Due to Stahl's influence, the reactionary and Romantic conservatism of the East Elbian Pietists was brought closer to an understanding of the modern state. By overcoming the narrow limits of Ludwig von Haller's feudal and private conceptions of the law, Stahl eventually enabled the conservatives to fight the liberals with ideological weapons which could reach a larger audience.[53]

Religion embattled against revolution had long absorbed the attention of Frederick William IV, who ascended the throne in 1840 at the age of forty-five years. His remarks at the coronation— "I and my house, we wish to serve God"—reaffirmed his denunciation of revolution when he was consecrated as crown prince in 1813. His convictions had only deepened under the influence of his pious friends, and his reign was characterized by his regard of the state as a moral instrument serving Christian necessity. Essentially, his policy as king was a declaration of war upon what he considered the anti-Christian tendencies loosed by the French Revolution and the rational intellect.

52. Thadden to Ludwig von Gerlach, September, 1841, Gerlach family archives, and Kleist-Retzow to Hengstenberg, October 13, 1845, Bonwetsch, *Briefe an Hengstenberg*, I, 161 f.

53. For the influence of Stahl on the development of nineteenth-century German conservatism see Shanahan, pp. 100, 244 f., 300 f., 310.

Frederick William IV believed in the existence of a mysterious illumination by which God's grace was bestowed upon kings as distinct from other mortals. He was convinced that he understood his era and that he could endow his beloved people with more true freedom than any written constitution could bring. All the peaceful blessings which his subjects were to expect under a "Christian-German" commonwealth were to issue from the wisdom of the Crown. Resembling that of an Old Testament patriarch was his view of his dignified office; he looked upon kingship as a paternal authority specially instituted by God for the education of his subjects. Everything that happened in the state was related to the person of the monarch. When he chided his people, he would say menacingly: "Both Solomon and Sirach recommend that naughty children shall be chastised in due season." [54] More artistic than practical, Frederick William disliked bureaucratism and the routine, orderly aspects of the governmental machinery. He had an equal loathing for the inexorable regularity of state business and for the harshness of political struggle. He never failed to draw a breath of relief when he could retire from the commonplace world into the recesses of his own rich individuality. His happiest moments were those when he could express in inspired language the flow of his thoughts and feelings.

The king was no man of the sword. Sensitivity to what was aesthetic and refined eventually caused him to hold himself aloof from the army, although at the same time this least military-minded Hohenzollern cultivated the friendship of army officers. He dreamed of a united Germany, a Christian commonwealth, a new embodiment of the Holy Roman Empire, whose center would once again be a unified "Christian-German *Reich.*" No war could ever accomplish this: only a genuine meeting of hearts and pious cooperation would make the dream a reality. He was deeply affected by pious

---

54. Treitschke, *Deutsche Geschichte,* V, 11. See also the following studies of Frederick William IV: Friedrich Meinecke, "Friedrich Wilhelm IV und Deutschland," in his *Preussen und Deutschland im 19. und 20. Jahrhundert* (Munich and Berlin, 1918), pp. 206 f.; Hermann von Petersdorf, *König Friedrich Wilhelm der Vierte* (Stuttgart, 1901); Ernst Lewalter, *Friedrich Wilhelm IV: Das Schicksal eines Geistes* (Berlin, 1938); Ewald Schaper, *Die geistespolitischen Voraussetzungen der Kirchenpolitik Friedrich Wilhelms IV von Preussen* (Stuttgart, 1938); and Georg Kaufmann, "Ranke und die Beurteilung Friedrich Wilhelms IV," *HZ,* 88 (1902), 436–473.

Romanticism and its veneration of the Christian-German Middle Ages; he wanted to rule with the consent of the people; but this consent must find medieval expression, and society must be a hierarchy consisting of happy peasants, honest townsmen, pious clergy, faithful nobles, the prince among his vassals and subjects. His political ideas were those of a Romantic at odds with his age.

Frederick William IV was incapable of resolving the problems of his time. He was intoxicated with universality to such a degree that he quickly became bored with the concentration and exactness required by his official duties. One of his many plans was the totally impractical scheme to reconstitute the Protestant state church of Prussia on the basis of an "apostolic episcopate." The plan envisaged about 350 bishoprics of approximately the same size as the existing superintendents' areas. The bishops were to be consecrated by the laying on of hands in an apostolic manner, so that the first Prussian bishops would have to be consecrated by those of England or Sweden, and would then be able to transmit the episcopal power. Superior to the bishops there were to be about thirteen metropolitans, occupying the old episcopal seats of Evangelical Prussia and presiding over "chapters" which were to assume the powers of the existing Consistories. Highest of all would be the prince archbishop of Magdeburg, the primate of Germany, whose supreme chapter would replace the ministry of ecclesiastical affairs and education. All that was left for the monarch was a formal protectorate, and the right of confirming the decisions of the great territorial synods. So glaring was the impracticability of this plan that Frederick William himself regarded it as one of his many "midsummer night's dreams." [55]

The pious monarch's mind, just as much as his physique, recalled the poet's imaginary figure of Hamlet. He was full of beautiful and lofty ideas. Also he seemed to be unstable in his decisions, or indecisive; but this aspect of his character was more apparent than real. Natures of such many-sided sensitiveness are as a rule much dependent upon the support of others, and obviously Frederick William shared many of the ideas of the Pietist nobles, even seeming at times to be almost completely under their influence; yet it was no secret that one of his closest friends and advisers was General Joseph Maria von Radowitz, a Catholic of Hungarian ancestry who had

55. Schnabel, IV, 535–539.

entered the service of the Prussian army in 1823. The "Romantic on the throne" was not really dominated by any individual or group. He simply sought the advice of like-minded individuals. With careless serenity, with perfect unconcern, he made his way through life. He believed himself endowed, thanks to what he believed was the sacredness of his royal office, with the power of taking the most comprehensive views. It amused him at times to veil his intentions in a mysterious but pregnant obscurity, to throw petty mortals into confusion by the use of nebulous words. Though he lacked far-reaching energy of will and practical understanding, he remained an autocrat in the fullest sense of the term. His decisions were determined by religious beliefs and ready-made doctrines, and these could not be overcome by considerations of political expediency.

The political temper of the late 1830's and the 1840's manifested itself in thousands of meetings, conferences, and feverish activity by the politically conscious segments of Prussian society. These years witnessed the mobilization of the conservative clergy by their leaders to oppose the demands of the liberal Friends of Light for freedom from theological dogmas and for a reorganization of the state church based on representation and self-government of congregations. In addition to the Trieglaff conferences, hundreds of meetings were organized by the Pietists all over the country.

In 1846, Frederick William IV finally decided to call the first Prussian General Synod. This assembly of notables consisted of thirty-seven clergymen and thirty-eight laymen who were summoned to discuss the clerical oath, the binding nature of the historic Christian creeds on clergymen, and proposals to bring about some changes in the organizational structure of the church. For years, these issues had been hotly debated by the liberals and the conservatives. Now the function of the synod was to "express some views" on these matters. In the course of discussions, the majority agreed that candidates for the ministry should swear allegiance to a creed which excluded mention of the more controversial dogmas, such as the Virgin Birth and the Resurrection of the Body. The majority also agreed that a system of presbyteries and synods should be introduced throughout the country in order to strengthen the principle of representation in the state church.

Ludwig von Gerlach and Thadden joined with Hengstenberg, Stahl, Heubner, and Friedrich Abraham Strauss to form the extreme-right wing, which demanded that clergymen who refused to accept the dogmas expressed in the Apostles' Creed should be expelled from the clergy. Thadden sharply attacked Carl Immanuel Nitzsch and other moderate, liberally inclined theologians, whom he accused of "compromising with the enemy" and "trying to smuggle into the Protestant church some of the liberal principles of the Friends of Light, [who wished] to use the system of ballots to decide by majority vote the tenets of the Protestant faith." In reply to the charge by the popular liberal journal *Allgemeine Kirchen-Zeitung,* published at Darmstadt in Hesse, that "the small party of the Pietists [had] a vested interest in a church hierarchy which always leads to caesaro-papism," [56] Thadden presented himself as the spokesman for the "patriotic (*vaterländische*) clergy" and declared that he was "more qualified to speak on its behalf than anyone else," adding: "Together with my numerous theologian friends, I see the danger of a hierarchy based on numbers . . . mere numbers of so-called congregations . . . a hierarchy which wants to rule without serving." Echoing the insistence of Hengstenberg's archconservative *EKZ,* that clergymen must obey the divine authority of the state, Thadden asserted: "By serving the state, clergymen rule their congregations. As servants of the state, they must also rule . . . whether they wish to do so or not" (als Staatsdiener müssen sie herschen, mögen sie wollen oder nicht.) [57] This doctrine of the self-appointed clerical leaders on the proper role of clergymen was diametrically opposed to that of clergymen with liberal leanings who insisted that pastors should serve and represent their congregations. The faction of conciliation led by Nitzsch found itself attacked by the Pietist right and the Friends of Light left.[58] Thadden defended the refusal of his faction to compromise by quoting Shakespeare: "'Ay' and 'no' too was no good divinity." [59]

The fact that after two and a half months of negotiations and debates Frederick William dissolved the General Synod and refused to consider its recommendations demonstrated the influence of the Pietist leaders, whose "main strategy [was] aimed at the breaking

56. *AKZ,* 1846, pp. 942 ff.

57. Krüger, *Generalsynode,* pp. 136 ff.; *EKZ,* 1846, pp. 838 f.

58. *EKZ,* 1846, pp. 839. Also: Leberecht Uhlich, *Siebzehn Sätze in Bezug auf die Verpflichtungsformel protestantischer Geistlichen: Ausgegangen von der Synode in Berlin* (Wolfenbüttel, 1846), pp. 4 ff.; hereafter cited as Uhlich, *Siebzehn Sätze.*

59. *King Lear,* act 4, sc. 6, cited in Reuss, *Thadden,* p. 79.

up of the assembly . . . and preventing him from accepting any of its recommendations." [60] Afterward the king conveyed his thanks to Leopold von Gerlach, for the latter's advice not to consider any proposals which would allow the ordination of clergymen without specific acceptance of the dogmas contained in the Apostles' Creed.[61] The further fact that within two years, practically all clerical leaders of the Friends of Light were dismissed from their positions showed clearly that clergymen who insisted on a right to individual freedom of creed within the state church, and to the expression of it, had to suffer the consequences.

The behavior of the Pietist leaders was based on their conviction that no assemblies and no majority decisions had authority in respect to dogmas which they considered fundamental for their claims to privilege and preeminence. The complexity of views, interpretations, and proposals of the General Synod concerning the creed, organization, discipline, and personnel of the clergy merely reinforced the conviction of the Pietist nobles that the "multitude" had no right to make decisions on such vital matters. In response to the charge of the liberals that binding dogmas would result in the loss of some of the most able clergymen from the church, Thadden merely stated in the dicussions of the synod the Biblical saying: "Des Volks ist noch zu viel!" [62] In short, Thadden declared his faction's responsibility for the purging of the Friends of Light leaders from the clergy. Together with the clerical Hengstenberg faction, the pious nobles were outraged by the demands of the Friends of Light for "free congregations . . . and a 'democratic' church government." They sensed a profound danger in the development of a "church republic" (Kirchenrepublik) consisting of self-governing congregations and freely elected clergymen. The EKZ accused the liberals of subverting church and state, and began a concerted series of attacks against what it called "the theology of the majority." [63] Thadden acknowledged in the meetings of the synod that his group was "only a very small faction" (nur eine kleine Partei), but at the same time he assured the Pietists that their influence was already powerful and was steadily growing. He left no doubt that under the

---

60. Gerlach, *Aufzeichnungen*, I, 452.
61. Gerlach, *Denkwürdigkeiten*, I, 112.
62. Reuss, *Thadden*, p. 80.
63. "Demokratische Verfassungsgelüste," *EKZ*, 1847, p. 3; "Theologie der Majorität," *ibid.*, p. 326.

"Christian-German" regime of the pious Frederick William IV the "small but mighty" faction would become the leading element in Prussia.[64] Stressing the cohesion and unity of his faction, Thadden openly admitted that they were in fact narrow-minded and perhaps not so well educated or so interesting as their enemies. What really mattered, however, was unity of purpose and esprit de corps, not popular appeal. Thadden and his fellow Pietists knew that they could not match the flamboyance of Uhlich, Rupp, Ronge, Baltzer, Dulon, and other popular heroes of the Friends of Light and German-Catholic movements. But in view of the demonstrated disunity and even bitter rivalry of their theological and political enemies, the Pietists could rightly boast of their firm "united front" in opposition to the liberal *Zeitgeist*. Defending the autocratic structure of the state church against what he called the danger of "developing a church of mobs" (*Pöbelskirche*),[65] Ludwig von Gerlach seemed to be in complete agreement with Bindewald, an influential bureaucrat in the ministry of ecclesiastical affairs and education, who expressed the official opinion of the government when he sarcastically remarked that a Protestant church organized and controlled by the congregations would certainly result in such chaos that soon it would have to be placed under the control of the Ministry of War.[66]

On the eve of the Revolution of 1848, the Pietist nobles stood ranged in close alliance with the theology professors led by Hengstenberg and with Pietist rank-and-file clergymen, members of the royal court, and many high civil servants. At home, their privileged positions as owners of Rittergüter and patrons of local parishes enabled them to exert considerable pressure on great numbers of village pastors, who consequently affirmed loyalty to the traditional order against the challenge of the political opposition and the liberal clerical leaders.[67] At the royal court, the influence of the Junker Pietists on the head of state seemed to be so great that even the king's brother William, the Prince of Prussia, accused General Leopold

64. Krüger, *Generalsynode*, p. 136; Hermann Wagener, *Die kleine aber mächtige Partei* (Berlin, 1885).

65. *EKZ*, 1846, p. 716.

66. Quoted in Johann Hinrich Wichern, *Gesammelte Schriften*, ed. Friedrich Mahling (Hamburg, 1901), I, 384.

67. See the scores of declarations signed by hundreds of clergymen, especially from the Old Prussian provinces, in the *EKZ* in the 1840's.

von Gerlach and his circle of actually determining royal decisions.[68]

The initially defensive alliance of Pietist clergymen and "awakened" Old Prussian noblemen against rationalism and the *Zeitgeist* was certainly not an expedient rationally arrived at, nor was it accepted by the Junkers and the Pietist clergymen as a distasteful necessity. There is no reason to doubt the sincerity and religious devotion of the East Elbian squires and of Hermes, Jänicke, Tholuck, and other "true believers." Nevertheless, the German Neo-Pietist "Awakening" of the nineteenth century was influenced and dramatically transformed into a politically significant movement by the "awakened" Pietist elite of Junkers. Their preconceived ideas and attitudes concerning the political and social order transformed the initially inner-directed religious movement of a few, isolated Pietist clergymen and laymen into an aggressive, outer-directed political movement claiming divine sanction. By enlisting the religious, and even spiritual, influence and emotional fervor of such talented men as Hengstenberg, Tholuck, Heubner, and others from the non-noble elements of society, the pious squires reinforced their reactionary struggle against the "ideas of 1789." Reciprocally, the new dimensions of Neo-Pietism enabled the initially frustrated and deeply disturbed Junkertum to regain its confidence and enlist the support of some of the most talented and ambitious members of the clergy and other public officials for their side. Eventually, these nobles convinced themselves and their allies that their "cause" was the "cause of God," and that their preeminence in state and society rested on divine foundations. Unlike the Pietists of the seventeenth and eighteenth centuries, the Neo-Pietists of the nineteenth century were no "quiet people" who believed in religious toleration. Nor did they think that they could change the sinful world by merely leading exemplary lives of Christian virtue. The Gerlachs, Thadden, Senfft-Pilsach, and other Pietist nobles wanted to destroy their theological and political enemies, whom they considered rebels against the divine order.

The militant "Camarilla" of 1848 which was headed by Leopold von Gerlach had little resemblance to the collegia pietatis of the old Pietism. Although the elite of pious Junkers was by no means the only conservative political group, it was the dominant element in the Prussian conservative movement of the pre-March period.

68. Gerlach, *Aufzeichnungen,* I, 458.

Part Three

The Liberals

5

The Theology Professors

The measures of the Prussian government after 1815 made it extremely difficult for the liberals to express their opposition to autocratic government openly. The Carlsbad Decrees, enacted by the alarmed member states of the German Confederation after the assassination of the reactionary poet and journalist August von Kotzebue by the young student Karl Ludwig Sand in 1819, provided for rigid censorship and repressive police measures against political opponents and were also aimed at eliminating universities as centers of political agitation. The student associations, or Burschenschaften, were disbanded and their members prosecuted and jailed; surveillance and severe censorship assured that universities would not become centers of opposition to the established order. The German Confederation became "an instrument of permanent conspiracy by the separate governments against their subjects."[1]

One cannot speak of a liberal "movement" in the genuine sense of the word in Germany before the 1840's. Nevertheless, even before industrial developments began to affect the traditional social structure and a popular force developed to challenge the status quo, numerous intellectuals and progressive bureaucrats sought channels through which opposition to the government could be expressed.[2]

1. Willibald Beyschlag, *Aus meinem Leben: Erinnerungen und Erfahrungen der jüngeren Jahre,* 2d ed. (Halle, 1896), I, 30.

2. Leonard Krieger, *The German Idea of Freedom: The History of a Political Tradition* (Boston, 1957), pp. 273 ff., hereafter cited as Krieger, *The German Idea of Freedom.*

There were also some theology professors who were opposed to the binding dogmas, uniform liturgy, and autocratic structure of the reorganized Protestant state church. Like its political and economic counterparts, theological liberalism emphasized the freedom of the individual from dogma, his right to free development and realization of his talents and capabilities. In accordance with its emphasis on individual rights and responsibilities, theological liberalism also tended to favor the principles of self-government and representation in the church. In this sense, political, economic, and theological liberalism in nineteenth-century Germany had the same roots.[3]

The liberal theology professors held greatly varied notions, opinions, and approaches. At the same time, they tended to favor one or another particular theological school of thought.[4] Schleiermacher's theology, for instance, inspired Carl Immanuel Nitzsch (1787–1868), Richard Rothe (1799–1867), Friedrich Lücke (1791–1855), Karl Heinrich Sack (1789–1875), and a number of other moderately liberal theology professors and ministers in the decades before 1848. Unlike Hengstenberg in his leadership of the conservatives, however, Schleiermacher never organized a clerical faction dedicated to the principles of theological liberalism. Nor did the rationalist professors of theology in the various universities develop a group consciousness and esprit de corps matching the unity of purpose, cooperation, and effective drive of the Pietist faction. Consequently the liberals could not impose their theological and political views on the Protestant clergy.

Except for Richard Rothe, whose father was a high government official in Breslau, the most prominent liberally-inclined theology professors came from families of clergymen.[5] At the time of their appointment, they obviously enjoyed the favor of a government that respected and acknowledged their professional qualifications. Schleiermacher was one of the first faculty members to be appointed to the new University of Berlin (founded in 1810), and Nitzsch,

---

Also: R. Hinton Thomas, *Liberalism, Nationalism and the German Intellectuals, 1822–1847* (Cambridge, England, 1951), pp. 6 ff.; hereafter cited as Thomas, *Liberalism*.

3. Schnabel, IV, 490 ff.

4. Walter Nigg, *Die Geschichte des religiösen Liberalismus* (Zurich and Leipzig, 1937), pp. 132 ff.

5. Schleiermacher and Sack were descendants of generations of Reformed court preachers; Nitzsch's father was a professor of theology; Lücke's father was a pastor.

Lücke, and Sack had also been among the first faculty appointees at the new University of Bonn (1818). Rothe, instructor and eventually professor of theology at the Wittenberg Seminary during the years 1828–1837, had been a special favorite of the government since his student days in Berlin and Wittenberg, and the Pietists had been particularly anxious to keep the very promising young scholar in the service of the Prussian state. Wegscheider and Gesenius at the University of Halle, David Schulz and Johann Christian Gass at the University of Breslau, and some other rationalist theology professors had been appointed before 1815 and were well-established theological scholars by the 1820's.[6]

That the government was not willing to tolerate open criticism of the established order by theology professors was shown by its refusal after 1815 to allow Schleiermacher an active part in the organization of the administratively and confessionally united church, and by the dismissal of De Wette in 1819.[7] In 1822 Schleiermacher came very close to being dismissed from his position, when the special investigating committee of the German Confederation discovered several letters of Schleiermacher to his brother-in-law, the German nationalist Ernst Moritz Arndt, while searching the latter's home. In the letters, written in the years after the enactment of the Carlsbad Decrees, Schleiermacher expressed his abhorrence for government censorship and the secret police and condemned the suppression of the Burschenschaften in such strong terms that several government officials demanded his immediate dismissal. Fortunately for Schleiermacher, Altenstein was then minister of ecclesiastical affairs and education and was convinced that the dismissal of the famous theologian would make him a popular martyr and that the liberals would make political capital of the incident. Consequently he handled the investigation in such a dilatory manner that after a few years the case was dropped.[8]

Altenstein's fears concerning Schleiermacher's political influence rested on the fact that the professor was vehemently opposed to the government's efforts to impose a common liturgy and a

6. Lenz, I, pt. 1, 32 ff.; Bezold, pp. 32–36; Hausrath, *Rothe*, I, 106 f.; Schrader, II, 47 ff.; Kaufmann, *Geschichte der Universität Breslau*, pp. 175 ff.

7. Foerster, *Entstehung*, II, 131 ff.; Schnabel, IV, 335 f.

8. Reinhart Koselleck, *Preussen zwischen Reform und Revolution: Allgemeines Landrecht, Verwaltung, und soziale Bewegung von 1791 bis 1848* (Stuttgart, 1967), pp. 406 f.; Lenz, II, pt. 1, 84 ff. and 172 ff.

common set of dogmas upon the reorganized Protestant state church after 1817. Moreover, Schleiermacher held that the union of Lutheran and Reformed Protestants should not have been imposed by the government from above: only assemblies or synods of representatives, freely elected by the congregations, should have the right to decide on such vital matters.[9] Schleiermacher was among the many liberals who suffered bitter disillusionment when the Prussian government, after the downfall of Napoleon, failed to realize their hopes for a constitution and an independent, free church. He had taken a significant part in political activities during the War of Liberation, but he considered the "general state of affairs" after 1815 "too deplorable for an honest man to wish to participate in public life." Characteristic of the general disillusionment of the liberal-minded theologians with the government's abandonment of their plans for a church constitution and self-government of congregations was Schleiermacher's statement that the time might come when religious conviction would force them to leave the autocratic church.[10] He nevertheless continued to raise his voice in matters concerning the Protestant church and exerted considerable influence up to his death in 1834.

Because the church was one of the crucial state institutions, its affairs were intimately connected with some of the most important political problems of the time. Schleiermacher was particularly distressed by the rising Pietist faction led by Hengstenberg and his "awakened" Junker allies. In 1821, when friends persuaded him to publish a third edition of his famous *Speeches on Religion to the Educated among its Detractors,* he bluntly stated in the new Introduction that "now it would be more opportune to address speeches to the multitude of superstitious and super-pious (*Frömmelnde*) slaves of the letter." In other words, it was no longer the skepticism of the educated that gravely threatened religion. Schleiermacher saw the dogmatic and intolerant Neo-Pietists as much more dangerous to true Christianity than the "enlightened" educated people had ever been. Consequently he attacked the intolerance of the new "true believers" and their hatred of those who disagreed with them. He also expressed concern about the tendency of the so-called "Christian

9. Schnabel, IV, 334 ff.
10. Schleiermacher to Charlotte von Kathen, April 9, 1824, in Reimer, *Schleiermacher,* II, 383 f.

circles" to designate everything and everybody as black or white. In concluding his observations Schleiermacher stated that "whatever benefits such a religious awakening may bring to some individuals, in the end society as a whole suffers." [11] For Schleiermacher and other liberal professors very few things were "black or white" in theology and in life generally. Schleiermacher particularly insisted on tolerance of varying theological interpretations.

Although after 1815 the government forbade political activity by Schleiermacher, its censors did not refuse permission, despite misgivings, for the publication of some of his writings on church matters. There were many clergymen who dared to express support for his views. In 1824, in a pamphlet, *On the Liturgical Right of the Protestant Princes,* he explicitly denied the right of the king of Prussia as *summus episcopus* to impose a liturgy on the Protestant church, and asserted that only assemblies of clergymen and their congregations had the right to decide on matters of faith and liturgy.[12] In the course of the *Agendenstreit* over the uniform order of worship,[13] Schleiermacher's opposition to the centralized and autocratic structure of the church further alienated the government.

In the Rhineland, C. I. Nitzsch was greatly impressed with the system of presbyteries and synods there. After his appointment as professor of theology at the University of Bonn in 1822, the former instructor at the Wittenberg Seminary adjusted with remarkable facility to his new environment. Although a Saxon by birth, in a few years he earned the respect and sincere admiration of Rhenish Protestants, who began to refer to him as the "Schleiermacher of the Rhineland." [14] Nitzsch became convinced that direct negotiations between the government and representatives of such assemblies of notables as the provincial synods would soon reduce the tension between the government and those who were opposed to the autocratic structure of the church. He did not realize at the time that the government's toleration of the old Rhenish Protestant system

11. *Über die Religion: Reden an die Gebildeten unter ihren Verächtern,* 3d ed. (Berlin, 1821), pp. xiii–xiv, 246.

12. *Über das liturgische Recht evangelischer Landesfürsten: Ein theologisches Bedenken von Pacificus Sincerus* (Berlin, 1824), pp. 3 ff. It was known that "Pacificus Sincerus," the author of the pamphlet, was Schleiermacher. See also Schnabel, IV, 335 ff.

13. See the article "Agendenstreit" in *RGG,* 1957, I, 34 ff.

14. Beyschlag, *Nitzsch,* pp. 182 ff.

of presbyteries and synods after 1815 was part of the official policy of retaining the sympathy of Protestants in the recently acquired Rhineland. Consequently he strongly urged the government to use the Rhenish system as a model for establishing similar representative church bodies for the whole country. Such an arrangement, argued Nitzsch, would allow the reorganized state church to become one of the most viable institutions in Prussia and thus would strengthen the cohesion of the monarchy.[15] Apparently the liberal-minded theologian was much impressed by the traditional system of self-government in the Rhenish-Westphalian Protestant church. He became a firm believer in the right of congregations to select their own clergymen and hoped that eventually the other parts of Prussia would also develop representative church bodies. Nitzsch was particularly enthusiastic about the spirit of cooperation between the congregations and their elected clergymen.

Because significant segments of the Catholic majority in Rhineland-Westphalia were hostile to Prussian rule, it became essential for the government to gain and maintain the support and cooperation of the small but economically and culturally very advanced Protestant minority, who had developed a strong sense of pride in their traditional custom of choosing their local ministers by the elected members of the presbyteries.[16] Hence there was no question of abolishing the system of presbyteries and synods, but the government insisted on making official appointment of the nominees of congregations. In contrast to Pomerania and other eastern provinces, where conflict had developed over the assumption by the government of the traditional right of appointment, in the western provinces the problem was to maintain that right for the government while allowing the congregations to continue their role in the selection of local clergymen. Eventually a compromise was worked out whereby the right of official appointment was reserved to the central government and the right of selection and nomination was conceded to the Pietist Junker landlords in East Elbia and to

15. C. I. Nitzsch, *Theologisches Votum über die neue Hofkirchenagende und deren weitere Einführung* (Bonn, 1824), pp. 4 ff.

16. On the problems which developed in Rhineland-Westphalia after 1815 see the source collection in Joseph Hansen, ed., *Die Rheinprovinz, 1815–1915: Hundert Jahre preussischer Herrschaft am Rhein* (Bonn, 1917). See also Justus Hashagen, *Der rheinische Protestantismus und die Entwicklung der rheinischen Kultur* (Essen, 1924).

the representative presbyteries in the western provinces. Thus the historical forces operating in the eastern and western parts of the kingdom tended to assert themselves in Prussia after 1815 and to reflect basic differences in the religious and sociopolitical conditions of east and west.

Schleiermacher, Nitzsch, and several other liberal-minded theology professors urged the government to establish synods, a system of representative church bodies. They indicated that the tensions between the central government and those who believed that the church should be a self-governing free institution could be removed if assemblies of clergymen could initiate discussions with the government. Schleiermacher in particular favored the organization of a general church assembly for the whole country—a general synod—which would be empowered to make decisions relating to the internal affairs of the church and its relations with the secular authorities. But adoption of this proposal would have meant recognition by the government of the right of assemblies to participate in the government of the church and, consequently, the transformation of the church into what Marheineke and other conservatives called "an independent republic within the kingdom of Prussia." [17]

The government became alarmed when Schleiermacher and other liberals began to demand not only a free representative system of church government without secular controls but also a constitution for the church. In a memorandum Schleiermacher reminded Altenstein that clergymen had a unique position among civil servants by virtue of their relationship to their parishioners. The bold professor stated flatly in 1826 that the position of clergymen rested primarily on their service to the members of their congregations and not to the government, and that accordingly they should feel no need for subservience (*Unterwürfigkeit*) to the government. Altenstein was strongly opposed to what he called Schleiermacher's plans for a "church republic," and the government repeatedly threatened to remove the liberal clergyman from his academic position; however, the great prestige and influence of Schleiermacher prevented the carrying out of these threats.[18] The Agendentreit, although precipitated by Frederick William III's introduction of a

17. P. K. Marheineke, *Über die wahre Stille des liturgischen Rechts* (Berlin, 1825), p. 4.
18. Foerster, *Entstehung*, II, 235.

uniform order of worship in 1822, was essentially a political battle between the government and some liberal clergymen who favored the transformation of the state church into a self-governing institution. Already in 1817 Schleiermacher had expressed the view that just as there was a need for a constitution in the church, a free state also ought to have a constitution which reflected the will of its citizens. Since then, he had become even more convinced that a free church could only function in a free state and that the government had no right to impose decisions on clergymen without having consulted representative church assemblies of elders.[19]

The Prussian government refused to consider Schleiermacher's proposals for a Protestant church based on self-government in which congregations and clergymen would decide on matters of doctrine, liturgy, and organization. Indeed, the government could not negotiate with spokesmen of any particular synods or other church bodies. To do so would mean yielding to the liberals' demands for representative institutions and a constitution. Frederick William and the administrative bureaucracy continued to be violently opposed to any system of representative assemblies elected by church members, correctly believing that such an arrangement would result in further demands for a representative political system.[20] Schleiermacher continued to express the view that the church must have a constitution to assure its independent development, but because of the government's determined efforts to stamp out the political opposition he began to use more caution concerning demands for reforms, realizing that by concentrating on church affairs he could still exert a great deal of influence.[21]

While the government was determined to resist the demands for self-rule in the church, it was eventually willing to allow certain changes in the uniform liturgy. Modified regulations in 1829 allowed some measure of freedom in religious ceremonies and procedures. With the significant exception of the Old Lutherans, the new Agende was soon accepted by the overwhelming majority of the Protestant clergy. Apparently, for the time being the government

19. Schnabel, IV, 335 f.
20. Eylert, III, pt. 1, 364 f.; Foerster, *Entstehung*, II, 236.
21. See his *Gespräch zweier selbstüberlegender evangelischen Christen über die Schrift Luther in Bezug auf die neue preussische Agende: Ein letztes Wort oder ein erstes* (Berlin, 1827), pp. 2 ff.

was fairly successful in diverting the attention of the rank-and-file clergy from representative institutions and in convincing them that despite numerous regulations they still had a great deal of freedom. As for the aging Schleiermacher, he began to tire of his efforts for the sake of what seemed to be a lost cause. Nitzsch also seemed to realize that he could accomplish much more by concentrating his efforts on strengthening the already functioning church synods in the western provinces than by engaging in a perpetual struggle to establish new ones for the whole country. David Schulz, the rationalist theology professor at the University of Breslau, accused Schleiermacher, Nitzsch, and other conciliatory theologians (*Vermittlungstheologen*) of compromising their principles "for the sake of peace and convenience . . . and thus in fact betraying their congregations, which had looked to them as their leaders." [22] Even more bitter were the attacks of Scheibel, the Old Lutheran theology professor, who called upon the congregations to "repudiate" clergymen who had "deserted their flocks" and "become mere tools of the government." [23]

Schleiermacher, clearly, did not command an organized and determined following like the Hengstenberg faction or the Old Lutheran leaders in Silesia. He was also growing weaker, as his old physical ailments recurred more often. Unlike Hengstenberg and Tholuck, who considered physical suffering an almost necessary form of service for the Pietist "cause," the aging Schleiermacher saw illness as a warning to accept his limitations. In his last years he realized that much time would be needed to bring about the changes in church and state. He had grown very tired of the bitter controversies with the government, and he expressed concern over the effects of those controversies on the confessional unity of the church. As the 1820's ended and the new decade began, the formerly so antagonistic theologian was consulted several times in connection with the separatist Old Lutheran movement in Silesia.[24] In January of 1831 his old enemy, Bishop Eylert, was instructed by Frederick William III to visit him and assure him of the good will of the government. According to Eylert, he was also instructed to offer

---

22. In his *Vollgültige Stimmen gegen die evangelischen Theologen und Juristen unserer Tage welche die weltlichen Fürsten wider Willen zu Päpsten machen oder es selbst werden wollen* (Leipzig, 1830), p. 7.

23. Scheibel, *Actenmässige Geschichte,* I, 37 ff.   24. Lenz, II, pt. 1, 449.

Schleiermacher the positions of general superintendent and bishop of Silesia. Although greatly touched by what seemed to be a significant gesture of reconciliation on the part of the government, the aging scholar told Eylert that because of his deep involvement in and love for the academic profession he could not accept the offer. The conversation convinced Eylert that Schleiermacher had mellowed a great deal and was no longer hostile to the government.[25] It would seem that the death of his only son, Nathanael, had a part in Schleiermacher's assent to the humble proposition that the development of a free and viable Protestant church would require a very long time. The same fighter who had denounced the government of Frederick William III for subjecting the church to the supervision of "ecclesiastical prefects of the state" (*geistliche Prefekten des Staats*) now expressed his appreciation for the privately submitted offer to the Silesian posts. In view of Eylert's obviously biased recording of events in his memoirs, one does not have to accept the account of the conversation exactly as he gave it, but the fact still remains that in his last years Schleiermacher assisted the government and refrained from attacks on the autocratic structure of church and state.

Schleiermacher, Nitzsch, Lücke, Sack, and other moderates acknowledged the right of the rationalist theologians to express their views freely, and condemned the unethical journalism of the Hengstenberg faction in the Halle denunciation. Yet they were alarmed by what they called the "demonstrated cynical disbelief" of the rationalist theologians. Schleiermacher in particular was disturbed by the "baneful influence" of their interpretations of the Scriptures on future clergymen. He therefore openly attacked David Schulz and Daniel von Coelln, the outstanding rationalist theologians at the University of Breslau. For their part, the rationalists expressed bitter disappointment with the "theologians of conciliation," describing them as wolves in sheep's clothing who had failed to take a clear and unequivocal stand against the Hengstenberg faction. The conflict between the rationalists and conciliatory or moderate liberals came to a head when Schleiermacher and some like-minded theology professors stated that they considered the "danger of disbelief growing out of rationalism" just as harmful for the church as the intol-

25. Eylert, I, pt. 1, 176.

erant fanaticism of the Pietists.[26] Schulz and Coelln asserted that the moderates had betrayed the cause of intellectual freedom in the universities by their demands that rationalist influence be checked.[27] Although Ludwig von Gerlach continued to condemn what he considered the "soft" attitude of the moderates toward the rationalists,[28] it was obvious from the many comments in the *EKZ* that the Hengstenberg faction was glad to see its theological and political opponents engaged in mutual recrimination.

In his last years Schleiermacher was deeply disturbed both by the growing influence of the Hengstenberg faction and by what he called the "un-Christian implications of rationalism." In a letter to Lücke in 1830 he expressed the dilemma of the liberals by posing the painful question: "Should history's verdict mean that Christianity would be identified with [the Pietists'] barbarism and scientific inquiry with [the rationalists'] disbelief?" ("Soll der Knoten der Geschichte so auseinandergehen . . . das Christentum mit der Barbarei und die Wissenschaft mit dem Unglauben?") [29] Not too many years before, Schleiermacher had sharply criticized Professor Marheineke and other Protestant clergymen for accepting and wearing such distinctions as the Order of the Red Eagle, which he regarded as signs of subservience to the government. And as a consequence of his attacks on the government in the 1810's and 1820's Schleiermacher had repeatedly been threatened with dismissal. Now, grown tired of being a political outcast for so many years, he was happy that the government appreciated his services.[30]

On April 6, 1831, Schleiermacher published in the official *Allgemeine Preussische Staatszeitung* a denial of certain statements about

---

26. Schleiermacher, *An die Herren D. D. Daniel von Coelln und David Schulz: Ein Sendschreiben* (Berlin, 1830), p. 1.

27. Daniel von Coelln and David Schulz, *Über die theologische Lehrfreiheit auf den evangelischen Universitäten und deren Beschränkung durch symbolische Bücher* (Breslau, 1831), pp. 2 f., and *Zwei Antwortschreiben an Herrn Friedrich Schleiermacher* (Leipzig, 1831), p. 3.

28. Letter to Hengstenberg, February 28, 1830, Hengstenberg papers, Box I.

29. Schleiermacher to Lücke, an open letter printed in *Theologische Studien: Eine Zeitschrift für das gesammte Gebiet der Theologie in Verbindung mit D. Gieseler, D. Luecke und D. Nitzsch*, 1830, p. 490. In addition to publishing the letter, the journal expressed the position of the moderate theologians, led by Nitzsch, who opposed both rationalism and Pietism and sought Schleiermacher's support.

30. Schleiermacher to Frederick William III (n.d.), Reimer, *Schleiermacher*, II, 444.

him in the French journal *Messager des Chambres*. To the contention of the *Messager* that he was a leading member of the political opposition in Prussia, Schleiermacher flatly asserted: "I belong to no party of the left." Prussia, he added, had made "great progress since the Peace of Tilsit . . . without revolution, without representative assemblies, and even without freedom of the press." These statements were factually correct, but certainly evasive of his commitment in previous years to the liberal cause. In an apparent effort to prove his loyalty to the government, he declared: "I shall always be on the side of the king"—thus completely repudiating his former opposition.[31] It was understandable that Schleiermacher did not want foreigners to praise him as the liberal foe of the Prussian government when he was actually trying to cooperate with it. But it was not necessary for him to deny that the government had forbidden him for a time to preach. Schleiermacher told the editor of the *Messager* that not government prohibition but the orders of his physician during a period of illness had prevented him from preaching—an obvious distortion of the truth. Apparently the professor had come to the conclusion that only through cooperation with the government could progress be achieved. Consequently, he must have been trying to forget the time when he had bitterly opposed its policies. He knew that any reassertion of his former demands for the transformation of autocratic Prussia would seriously jeopardize the respect newly won from the ruling authorities. He did not seem to feel the strength necessary for a continuation of the old battles at a time when the liberal conciliatory position was obviously threatened by both the Pietist right and the left-wing tendencies of the rationalists. Schleiermacher reminded the *Messager* and its readers that the terms right, left, right center, and left center did not apply to the political situation in Prussia, and expressed particularly his objection to being identified with the revolutionary theories attributed to the left.

Schleiermacher was correct in stating that in 1831 there were still no clear-cut political party groupings in his country similar to those of France. Unlike France, where by the 1830's opinion had already crystallized around certain ideological and material interests as represented in the Chamber of Deputies, the political life of Prussia

31. For the statement see *ibid.,* pp. 445–447.

was still characterized by the lack of a party system. Because there was no national assembly, the aspirations of the various interest groups were expressed in the activities of numerous theological, professional, literary, and other factions. Yet a definite acceleration of political life had occurred, and undoubtedly the bitterness, deep hostility, and ruthless methods of the Hengstenberg faction toward every element in the country opposed to the established order had contributed greatly to this development. In 1831 Schleiermacher could deny the existence of a "party of the left . . . with revolutionary theories," and could declare: "The people have always been with the king, and the king has always beeen with the people." A year later, however, he expressed alarm over the possibility that the Germans would follow the example of other European nations by resorting to violence in order to realize their political aspirations. Thus Schleiermacher was approaching the end of his career with the sad realization that in "departing from this life [he would] leave Germany in such unsettled conditions" as made his hopes for peaceful and orderly changes in church and state highly improbable.[32] The "unsettled conditions" of which Schleiermacher complained in 1832 really meant that in the 1830's public and theological issues definitely began to shape church parties. It was clear that ecclesiastical and theological issues could not be separated from the great public questions. This circumstance, together with the religious disposition of Frederick William III, made the church an arena of political controversy.

Richard Rothe—the brother-in-law of the Wittenberg Seminary director, Heubner, and one of the great hopes of the Pietist faction in the 1820's—also underwent remarkable intellectual changes in his later years. Under the influence of the writings of Schleiermacher, Nitzsch, and, especially, the liberal theology professors Karl Hase, of the University of Jena, and Carl Daub, of the University of Heidelberg, Rothe had become convinced by the 1830's that the Pietists' "moral superiority [was] based on the false premise that they alone possessed the truth." Repelled equally by the dogmatic intolerance of the Pietists and the cold, calculated reasoning of the rationalists in religious matters, Rothe claimed that "in the bitter factional strife between the 'true believers' and the so-called rationalists" he was

32. Schleiermacher to his wife, September 5, 1832, *ibid.,* p. 470.

able to maintain a neutral and independent stand.[33] Together with Nitzsch, Lücke, Sack, and other moderates, Rothe abhorred the "politics" of the Hengstenberg faction.[34] He particularly welcomed the fact that even Professor Neander, the old promoter of Pietism at the University of Berlin, had become so disgusted with the faction's ruthless and unethical methods that after the Halle denunciation he publicly disassociated himself from them. In a bitter statement Neander accused the *EKZ* of advocating "spiritual despotism" and the establishment of a new Inquisition.[35] When Hengstenberg declared in the *EKZ*, "a uniform creed must be the cornerstone of the church . . . and clergymen who reject the dogmas of the Protestant faith are free to exercise their freedom of teaching only *outside* the church,"[36] Neander, Rothe, Nitzsch and other moderate theologians issued a pamphlet denouncing "that faction which seeks government support . . . by asserting that there is a connection between political 'demagogism' and 'disbelief.'"[37] Thus the former supporter of the Hengstenberg faction now turned against it; he had joined Rothe, Nitzsch, and other moderate theologians in attacking the dogmatic and intolerant views expressed in the *EKZ*. In contrast to some Pietists who wanted to "translate the word of God into action," Rothe insisted on keeping his own activities apart from any political movement, expressing horror at the fact that "wherever one looks, one sees factions and political struggle." Nitzsch also was distressed by the bitter struggles of the political factions in the church; he spent much of his energy in opposing the extremists of the left and right.[38]

By 1834 Rothe was refusing to read the newspapers and had come to the conclusion that he should leave his position at the Wittenberg Seminary and seek employment at a university where he would not be disturbed by political pressures, which he could no

33. Rothe to Baron von Bunsen, 1831, Hausrath, *Rothe,* I, 339.

34. *Ibid.,* I, 340 f.; Beyschlag, *Nitzsch,* pp. 140 ff.; Lenz, II, pt. 2, 338 f.

35. "Erklärung über meine Teilnahme an der Evangelischen Kirchen-Zeitung und die Gründe mich von derselben loszusagen," in *EKZ,* 1830, p. 137.

36. *Ibid.,* p. 209; emphasis in original.

37. "Antwort auf die Gegenerklärung der Redaction der Evangelischen Kirchen-Zeitung Nr. 18. und 19," in *Dr. Neanders Erklärung über seine Teilnahme an der Evangelischen Kirchenzeitung nebst rechtfertigender Erörterung der ersteren* (Berlin, 1830), p. 2.

38. Rothe to Baron von Bunsen, 1832 and 1833, Hausrath, *Rothe,* I, 339, 376; Beyschlag, *Nitzsch,* p. 246.

longer tolerate. Heubner and the whole "Wittenberg circle" had for years been trying to convince this mild-mannered and scholarly young colleague that he should join the ranks of the Neo-Pietist *ecclesia militans*. But Rothe had never really adjusted to the narrow horizons of the seminary, and had always felt uncomfortable in the dogmatic and at times truly mystical atmosphere of Wittenberg. In 1837, finding the political and social pressures exerted upon him unbearable, he decided to leave his native Prussia and accepted a position at the University of Heidelberg,[39] where (except for five years at the University of Bonn, 1849–1854) he spent the rest of his life. To the grief of his former associates, Rothe eventually became prominent as a liberal clergyman in Baden, participating actively in the church assemblies of his adopted country. Ludwig von Gerlach insisted that the *EKZ* refuse to publish articles by the "renegade" Rothe in order to prevent the spreading of his ideas.[40] The "Old Baron" Kottwitz, however, kept hoping that Rothe would eventually return to the ranks of the "true believers" and implored Heubner not to give up the lost sheep.[41]

By the early 1840's the Hengstenberg faction had been highly successful in its drive to replace or to isolate the rationalist theology professors at the universities of Berlin, Halle, and Breslau. Because the political opposition seemed to be particularly strong in Königsberg,[42] and because the theology professor Caesar von Lengerke publicly supported the liberals there, the faction determined to use its influence to purge the faculty of theology of liberal elements. In 1841 the Hengstenberg protégé Christoph H. Haevernick (who as a student had provided the lecture notes for denouncing Wegscheider and Gesenius in the *EKZ*)[43] was appointed associate professor of theology. He immediately began a campaign to establish the dominance of political conservatives in the university.[44] Now he expressed alarm over what he considered the "arrogant impertinence" of the

39. Hausrath, *Rothe*, I, 340.

40. Letter to Hengstenberg, February 16, 1846, Hengstenberg papers, Box IV.

41. Kottwitz to Heubner, November 23, 1847, Hausrath, *Rothe*, II, 21.

42. Ferdinand Falkson, *Die liberale Bewegung in Königsberg, 1840–1848* (Breslau, 1888), pp. 35 ff.

43. Treitschke, *Deutsche Geschichte*, III, 405, and V, 171; Franz Burdach, *Rückblick auf mein Leben* (Leipzig, 1848), p. 454.

44. See Haevernick's letter to Hengstenberg thanking him for the influence of the conservative faction in promoting the appointment, March 26, 1841, Bonwetsch, *Briefe an Hengstenberg*, p. 88.

liberals in the whole community. Haevernick particularly blamed Johann Jacoby and other liberal leaders with Jewish backgrounds for the "baneful influence of the *Zeitgeist*" among the people of Königsberg.[45] Jacoby had just published his celebrated pamphlet, *Four Questions Answered by an East Prussian,* in which he stated some of the demands of the political opposition for constitutional rights. The government of Frederick William IV was particularly outraged by Jacoby's insistence that one should no longer request but demand rights.[46] Hengstenberg received scores of letters from Haevernick, urging him to help remove such politically dangerous men as Lengerke from academic positions. Haevernick complained bitterly of continuous attacks by the liberals and asserted that the public demonstrations against him were the result of Lengerke's association with the "most vulgar Jacobin rabble."[47] Lengerke enjoyed tremendous popularity among students and in the community at large, and apparently the government was so concerned over the possibility of large-scale demonstrations and other disturbances that it would not consider dismissing him, but in 1843 it transferred him from the faculty of theology to that of philosophy. This move brought about the conservative domination of the faculty of theology at Königsberg.[48]

In contrast to the intense factional struggles between theology professors at Halle, Breslau, and Königsberg, the faculty of theology at the University of Bonn was characterized until 1839 by peaceful cooperation. Nitzsch, Sack, and other theologians of conciliation at Bonn rejected both Pietism and rationalism as presenting views that were too dogmatic and deterministic. At the same time, they insisted that the government should maintain a tolerant and neutral attitude in theological controversies as it had done before the Neo-Pietist "Awakening."[49] Although these moderate, conciliatory theology professors had not been born in the Rhineland, in the course of years they developed a great respect and appreciation for the long tradition and effective working of the presbyterian form of church government in the Protestant communities of the western parts of

45. Letter to Hengstenberg, July 7, 1842, *ibid.,* p. 89.
46. Treitschke, *Deutsche Geschichte,* V, 140.
47. Letters to Hengstenberg, July 24, 1842, and September 3, 1842, Bonwetsch, *Briefe an Hengstenberg,* pp. 90–94.
48. Prutz, pp. 143 f.
49. Bezold, pp. 321 ff.; Schnabel, IV, 496.

the kingdom. They hoped that eventually the Prussian state church could develop into a less tightly organized institution and one in which each congregation would have a degree of self-government. Nitzsch in particular expressed optimism that eventually the government would realize the advantages of a cooperative but independent church. He implored Berlin to allow the election of the members and officials of synods in every province, and to organize a representative general synod for the whole country.[50] Nitzsch and his like-minded colleagues abhorred the ruthless tactics of the Pietists. But they believed in compromising on almost every issue, and hoped that in the long run moderation and conciliation between what they considered the extremes of Pietism and rationalism would be more beneficial than inflexibility.[51]

Nitzsch, an ardent supporter of the union of the Lutheran and Reformed churches, played the leading role in the negotiations between the government and prominent Rhenish clergymen which preceded the "Agreement of 1835," wherein were set forth the final details of the incorporation of the western Protestant church into the Prussian state church.[52] By that time the Saxon Nitzsch had become the most influential Rhenish clergyman. His appointment in 1835 to the positions of vice-president of the provincial synod and Consistory councilor clearly demonstrated that he had won not only the confidence and respect of Rhenish Protestants, but also official recognition by the government, which by then hoped that the moderate theology professors would counteract the radical theological and political criticism of the Young Hegelians.[53]

Although the Agreement of 1835 was considered a compromise, it expressly subjected the presbyteries and synods in the western parts of Prussia to the control of the central administration as represented by the provincial general superintendent, the numerous district superintendents, the provincial Consistory, and the provincial governor. The moderates were pleased, however, with the fact that the Rhenish presbyteries and synods were allowed to continue to function effectively. They believed that these church bodies were

50. Bezold, pp. 187 ff.; Otto Ritschl, *Die evangelisch-theologische Fakultät zu Bonn in dem ersten Jahrhundert ihrer Geschichte* (Bonn, 1919), pp. 46 ff. See also Huber, II, 270 ff.

51. Schnabel, IV, 498.   52. See Huber, II, 271.

53. Beyschlag, *Nitzsch,* pp. 216 ff.; Hashagen, *op. cit.* (n. 16), pp. 97 ff.

meanwhile serving as models for the other parts of the country, and hoped that eventually the whole Protestant church would become a self-governing institution.[54] While the government did not encourage such expectations, it welcomed the increasing hostility of the moderates to the Young Hegelians. Using Hegel's philosophy as an arsenal of intellectual weapons, David Friedrich Strauss, Arnold Ruge, Bruo Bauer, and Ludwig Feuerbach not only were attacking the dogmatic foundations of religion generally, but also were turning the Hegelian dialectic against what they called the "anachronistic" and "illogical" Prussian political and social system.[55] Strauss in his *Life of Jesus* (published in 1835–1836) sought to destroy the credibility of the Gospels as historical evidence. Ruge, the acknowledged leader of philosophical-political journalism in the late 1830's and early 1840's, carried on the fight for the emancipation of the middle classes in the *Hallische Jahrbücher,* of which he was coeditor in 1837–1841. Ruge enlisted the collaboration of most of the leading liberal thinkers and publicists of Germany, whose articles in this journal profoundly influenced the temper of the times.[56]

The moderate theologians of conciliation were shocked by the radicalism of the Young Hegelians who declared openly that emancipation from religion was the sine qua non of political and social reforms. Such radical Young Hegelians as Karl Marx, the brothers Bruno and Edgar Bauer, Arnold Ruge, and Max Stirner developed their opposition to the existing order "on the shoulders of their colleagues D. F. Strauss and Ludwig Feuerbach, whose break was

54. C. I. Nitzsch, "Die drei letzten Jahrzehnte: Eine kirchengeschichtliche Betrachtung," *Monatsschrift für die evangelische Kirche von Rheinland und Westfalen,* 1842, pp. 4 ff.

55. For the tremendous influence of Hegel's philosophy on the ideological struggles of the 1830's and 1840's see Hans Rosenberg's essay "Zur Geschichte der Hegelauffassung," in Rudolf Haym, *Hegel und seine Zeit: Vorlesungen über Entstehung und Entwickelung, Wesen und Wert der Hegel'schen Philosophie,* ed. Hans Rosenberg (Leipzig, 1927), pp. 510 ff., and Haym's lectures on Hegel's philosophy of religion, *ibid.,* pp. 392 ff. For a discussion of the Young Hegelians' turn to political reality see Julius Löwenstein, *Hegels Staatsidee: Ihr Doppelgesicht und ihr Einfluss im 19. Jahrhundert* (Berlin, 1927), pp. 80 ff.

56. For Arnold Ruge and the influence of the *Hallische Jahrbücher* see Hans Rosenberg, "Arnold Ruge und die Hallischen Jahrbücher," *Archiv für Kulturgeschichte,* 20 (1930), 281–308. See also Rudolf Haym, *Aus meinem Leben: Erinnerungen* (Berlin, 1902), pp. 104 ff.; hereafter cited as Haym, *Erinnerungen.*

Also: Walter Neher, *Arnold Ruge als Politiker und politischer Schriftsteller* (Heidelberg, 1933), pp. 36 ff.

essentially with religious orthodoxy and its ethical implications." [57] The Young Hegelians reacted violently to the increasing association of the regime of Frederick William IV with their theological and philosophical antagonists. The publication of Strauss's *Life of Jesus* had set into motion an avalanche of theological, philosophical, and political criticism which reached its climax in the 1840's. Thus the Young Hegelians' unprecedented attacks on the religious foundations of the Prussian state contributed significantly to the clarification of the goals and interests of the various political factions. [58] In view of the steady development of a secularized conception of the monarchy since 1740, the idea of a romantic-religious regime seemed outrageously reactionary and outmoded not only to the Young Hegelians but also to other critics of the government. At the same time, the widespread political repercussions of the Young Hegelians' attacks on traditional Christianity were clear indications of the Pietist-conservative success in identifying the Prussian monarchy with a "state-oriented Christianity."

Nitzsch did not deny the right of Strauss and other Young Hegelians to engage in Biblical criticism. But the moderates in effect agreed with the Hengstenberg faction that anyone who taught that the significant events of Jesus' life belonged to the realm of myth rather than history should not occupy an ecclesiastical office. [59] Faced with the uncompromising attacks of the Young Hegelians on the traditional foundations of Christianity, the "Schleiermacher of the Rhineland" and his moderate theology professor colleagues found themselves on the same side as Hengstenberg, Tholuck, the Gerlachs, and the rationalists Wegscheider and Schulz. They were alarmed when they saw that in the hands of Strauss's disciples theological criticism was becoming indistinguishable from philosophical materialism. Ludwig von Gerlach—eager to demonstrate to the moderates that they had to support the conservatives in the face

57. Krieger, *The German Idea of Freedom*, pp. 297 f.

58. See Ruge's letter to David Friedrich Strauss on March 16, 1839, in *Arnold Ruges Briefwechsel und Tagebuchblätter aus den Jahren 1825–1880*, ed. Paul Nerrlich (Berlin, 1886), I, 165, and the studies of Gustav Mayer, "Die Junghegelianer und der preussische Staat," *HZ*, 121 (1920), 429–436, and "Die Anfänge des politischen Radikalismus im vormärzlichen Preussen," *Zeitschrift für Politik*, 6 (1913), 1–112.

59. C. I. Nitzsch, *Bemerkungen über den Standpunkt der Schrift Das Leben Jesu* (Bonn, 1836), pp. 2–4.

of the common enemy—urged Hengstenberg to use the *EKZ* for attacking the Young Hegelians by printing an extensive discussion of the dangerous impact of Strauss's teachings on the church and other institutions in Prussia and other German states.[60] Subsequently, Hengstenberg's journal published scores of articles and editorials denouncing the Young Hegelians.

Nitzsch, Sack, Gieseler, and some other advocates of the "theological middle way" wished to qualify the existing structure of the state church by extending to the rest of Prussia the presbyterial form of government and the system of synods (as these functioned in the western provinces). They were careful, however, to avoid committing themselves to the support of demands which challenged the basic political and social structure of state and church.[61] When in 1839 the government wanted to transfer Bruno Bauer from Berlin to the University of Bonn, Nitzsch and his colleagues protested strongly, pointing out in an official memorandum to the government that Bauer, as a Hegelian, would seriously disturb the friendly cooperation which prevailed in the faculty, and requesting that Minister Altenstein appoint someone whose theological views were in harmony with their own. Even so, the government insisted on its right of appointment without considering the wishes of the faculty, and Bauer was transferred to Bonn—apparently the ailing Altenstein preferred to have the very talented but increasingly troublesome young scholar away from the capital. To make matters worse, Bauer bitterly resented what he considered his "deportation" from Berlin to the Rhineland, and did all he could to antagonize his new colleagues.[62]

Bauer had been a highly promising student under Marheineke at the University of Berlin and had taught there as a lecturer since 1834. Altenstein was particularly impressed by his talents and hoped to put them to work in strengthening the conservative cause. The expectation of Bauer's usefulness seemed to be confirmed by his plan to bring about an alliance of Right Hegelians with the Hengstenberg faction. In 1837 the ambitious young man expressed his deep

60. Letter, Christmas Day, 1836, Gerlach family archives.
61. Nitzsch summed up the position of the liberal moderates in his article "Verständigungen über die christliche Kirchenverfassung: Insbesondere über das Amt des Ältesten," *Monatsschrift für die evangelische Kirche von Rheinland und Westfalen,* 1842, pp. 18–24.
62. Quoted in Bezold, p. 372.

hostility to the theological views represented in Strauss's *Life of Jesus* and warned of their destructive influence on clergymen.[63] But presently he was associating with Karl Marx and other Young Hegelians, whose use of the dialectic method so impressed him that he changed many of his ideas. By 1839 the former conservative Right Hegelian lecturer was attacking the Hengstenberg faction for identifying the Protestant church with the interests of the privileged classes. Reversing his previous theological and political views, Bauer now criticized Strauss for "failing to utilize the critical method" and urged the Young Hegelians to "remove the stupidities of the past" completely.[64]

The identification of the new regime of Frederick William IV with the Pietist faction and the refusal of the Bonn professors to recommend him for promotion to a professorship embittered Bauer beyond description. In 1840 the frustrated lecturer began to publish devastating attacks on the authenticity of the Scriptures and on conservative and moderately liberal clergymen, whom he accused of hypocrisy and of deliberately promoting falsehoods.[65] In 1843 Bauer's scandalized colleagues at the University of Bonn addressed another official memorandum of the faculty of theology to the minister of ecclesiastical affairs and education—this time to Eichhorn, who had succeeded Altenstein. The alarmed professors urged the dismissal of the "Robespierre of theology" who had ridiculed the personnel, creed, and office of the professional clergy. Nitzsch and his colleagues insisted that Bauer, in view of his abusive attacks on the clergy, should be barred permanently from a theological career.[66]

The official dismissal of Bauer from the ranks of university theologians later in that year was an open demonstration of the influence of the Pietist faction in the new regime.[67] It also indicated that the views of the theological radicals had so alarmed the liberal

63. "Das Leben Jesu von D. F. Strauss," *Zeitschrift für spekulative Theologie,* 2 (1837), 86.
64. *Herr Dr. Hengstenberg: Kritische Briefe über den Gegensatz des Gesetzes und des Evangeliums* (Berlin, 1839), pp. 4 ff.
65. See his *Kritik der evangelischen Geschichte des Johannes* (Leipzig, 1840) and *Kritik der evangelischen Geschichte der Synoptiker* (Leipzig, 1841).
66. Bezold, p. 374.
67. Already in 1836 Leopold von Gerlach had reported to Hengstenberg that the Crown Prince was exerting pressure on Altenstein to cancel plans for the appointment of Bauer. August 19, 1836, Gerlach family archives.

moderates as to move Nitzsch and other theologians of conciliation to join in the campaign of the conservative Hengstenberg faction to purge the clergy of radicals. In 1842, Moritz August von Bethmann-Hollweg (1795–1877), who had been professor of law at Bonn since 1829, was appointed government inspector (*Regierungsbevollmächtigter*) of the university. This also was an obvious indication of a certain rapprochement between the liberally inclined moderates and the Pietists. Under the increasing theological, political, social, and economic pressures of the 1840's, which threatened to undermine the traditional bases of the Prussian state, the conservatives were agreeable to a certain degree of cooperation with the moderates. Bethmann-Hollweg had been "awakened" in the Pietist circles of Berlin in 1816, and eventually he became a good friend of the Gerlachs, Tholuck, and other "true believers." [68] At Bonn, Bethmann-Hollweg also made close friendships with Nitzsch, Sack, and other moderate theologians. Under the influence of his new friends in the Rhineland, the deeply religious law professor also developed an understanding and appreciation of such local church institutions as presbyteries and synods, and eventually became a prominent leader of the Protestant church. Bethmann participated actively in the deliberations of the provincial synods. Year after year, he sought to convince the Rhinelanders that cooperation with the government was the best guarantee for the well-being and growth of the Rhenish Protestant church and of the whole province. This cautious, moderately conservative law professor (who in 1848 became one of the founders of the Conservative party) exerted a tremendous influence on the moderate theology professors and other Protestant clergymen. Faced with the uncompromising radicalism of the Young Hegelians, Nitzsch and his colleagues actually welcomed the opportunity of cooperation with the government.

Bruno Bauer, by deliberately provoking his academic colleagues to take a stand against his theological and philosophical views, brought about his dismissal. The final turn of the "Robespierre of theology" to an extreme political radicalism shocked even Arnold Ruge and the other journalists associated with the *Hallische Jahrbücher*.[69]

68. See Fritz Fischer, *Moritz August von Bethmann-Hollweg und der Protestantismus* (Berlin, 1938), pp. 32 ff.

69. Ruge, *op. cit.* (n. 58 above), I, 242 ff., 281, 286, 290 f.

The career of Gottfried Kinkel (1815–1882), although it developed along lines very different from Bauer's, also demonstrated the increasing cooperation of the moderates with the government in terminating the academic appointments of promising scholars who held nonconformist theological views. Kinkel, a pastor's son from Oberkassel, joined the faculty of theology at the nearby University of Bonn as a lecturer in 1837.[70] Nitzsch and his colleagues were extremely pleased with the young theologian, who had artistic and literary gifts and seemed destined for a fine academic career. In 1840, however, Kinkel scandalized them by breaking his engagement to a Protestant girl and marrying a Catholic divorcée. Through his wife, Kinkel became acquainted with a new circle of friends who questioned some of the traditional tenets of religion. For having expressed doubts of the validity of certain dogmas of Christianity, he was refused promotion to professor in 1842. Thus Kinkel was considered unworthy of holding a theological professorship despite his demonstrated scholarly achievements. Bitterly disappointed, he accused his colleagues of a "vengeance" which proved that Bauer had been right when he attacked theologians as hypocrites who would not "tolerate independent minds in their ranks." [71]

The Kinkel case showed that by 1842 the moderates had departed significantly from demanding "toleration of all opposing views" and "intellectual freedom and scientific analysis" in the field of theology. Because of his varied talents, Kinkel was able to secure an appointment as professor of art and German literature at the University of Bonn in 1845, but he never forgot the attitude of his former clergymen colleagues. Like the less fortunate Bauer, who was unable to obtain an academic position, he was influenced in his political ideas and activities during the Revolution of 1848 by his hatred of the state church and its clergy. Kinkel and Carl Schurz (the future secretary of the interior during the Hayes administration in the United States) were the two most active revolutionary leaders of the democratic left in Bonn.[72]

70. *Gottfried Kinkels Selbstbiographie, 1838–1848,* ed. Rudolf Sander (Bonn, 1931), pp. 42 ff.; Martin Bollert, *Gottfried Kinkels Kämpfe um Beruf und Weltanschauung bis zur Revolution* (Bonn, 1913), pp. 16 ff.; Bezold, pp. 321 f.

71. Letter to Georg Krafft, April 10, 1842, in Bollert, *op. cit.,* p. 91.

72. See Martin Braubach, *Die Universität Bonn und die deutsche Revolution von 1848–1849* (Bonn, 1948), pp. 47 ff.; Hermann Kersken, "Stadt und Universität Bonn in den Revolutionsjahren 1848–49" (Ph.D. thesis, University of Bonn, 1931), pp.

One of the objectives of the religious-conservative regime of Frederick William IV was to ensure that theological professorships should not be occupied by men openly hostile to the government. After all, professors were employees of the state and were paid by it. Clergymen who actively supported the administration in its struggle against the political opposition were favored and their careers promoted. Conservative domination of the theological faculties at the universities of Berlin, Halle, Breslau, and Königsberg was finally assured in the early 1840's. Even the moderate "theologians of conciliation" at the University of Bonn, who in 1830 had defended the right of Wegscheider and Gesenius to freedom of teaching, changed their views. They refused to admit to their ranks men of outstanding talent, such as Bruno Bauer and Gottfried Kinkel, whose theological-philosophical views conflicted with the traditional interpretations of the Christian religion.

The phenomenal success of the Friends of Light, a group of rationalist clergymen organized by Pastor Uhlich in 1841 (see chap. vi), alarmed not only the conservatives but also the moderates, who were equally shocked to see some rank-and-file clerics emerging as popular leaders and using open mass pressure in their struggle to assure complete intellectual freedom for clergymen and to transform the state church into a "peoples' church" (*Volkskirche*). The moderates shared the horror of the Pietists when theological rationalism (to which the Young Hegelians had previously denied any kind of dynamism) [73] was transformed from an outmoded academic creed into a weapon for political mass action.[74] Mobilization of mass support by a handful of rationalist pastors for the purpose of compelling the government to grant clergymen of the state church complete freedom in theological matters, and demands for and actual attempts at the organizing of the Protestant church as a democratic institution—these developments in the 1840's were repugnant to moderates and conservatives alike.

Especially after the dismissal of Pastor G. A. Wislicenus, one

---

58 ff.; Wilhelm Schulte, *Volk und Staat: Westfalen im Vormärz und in der Revolution 1848–49* (Münster, 1954), pp. 187 ff.

73. R. E. Prutz, "Theologie oder Politik? Staat oder Kirche?" in his *Kleine Schriften zur Politik und Literatur* (Merseburg, 1847), II, 41 ff.; hereafter cited as Prutz, "Theologie oder Politik?"

74. Rosenberg, "Theologischer Rationalismus," pp. 538 ff.

of the Friends of Light, from his position at Halle in April 1846, the problems of clerical conduct in political life and complete freedom of creed for clergymen assumed crucial importance. When Frederick William IV convened the first General Synod of the Protestant state church on June 2, 1846, one of the primary tasks of the appointed body of thirty-seven clergymen and thirty-eight laymen was to agree on the wording of a binding statement (*Verpflichtungsformel*) which would make the acceptance of certain tenets of the Christian faith mandatory for all clergymen. The other most important item on the agenda was the discussion of proposals to introduce a system of presbyteries and synods in all Prussian provinces.[75] Although the Friends of Light were not represented in the General Synod, they and their followers addressed numerous manifestoes and recommendations to its members. In particular, synod members were advised that the concept of evolutionary progress in the interpretation of the Scriptures should be accepted by the Protestant church. Uhlich and some other leaders of the Friends of Light still believed in 1846 that the popularity of their rationalist creed entitled them to urge the moderate theology professors to draft a statement of belief satisfactory to the rationalist position.[76] The Pietists, on the other hand, demanded that clergymen who refused to accept the dogmas expressed in the Apostles' Creed should be expelled from the clergy. Nitzsch in particular was attacked by the Hengstenberg faction for trying to exclude from the binding statement such dogmas as the Virgin Birth and the Resurrection of the Body.[77]

After weeks of discussion, the majority of the synod, under the leadership of Nitzsch, approved a formula which amounted to a simplification of the Apostles' Creed. They also adopted the draft of a proposed church constitution which would preserve the system of centrally controlled consistories and provide for presbyteries in the congregations.[78] Soon after the majority had voted for these measures, Nitzsch's following found itself attacked by both the Hengstenberg faction and the Friends of Light. The *EKZ* was

75. Krüger, *Generalsynode*, pp. 28 ff., and Huber, II, 280 f., The official *Verhandlungen der evangelischen General-Synode zu Berlin vom 2. Juni bis zum 29. August 1846: Amtlicher Abdruck* (Berlin, 1846) is incomplete and unreliable.
76. Uhlich, *Siebzehn Sätze*, pp. 12 ff.   78. Krüger, *Generalsynode*, Appendix III.
77. *EKZ*, 1846, p. 725.

appalled by what it called the "spirit of conciliation [which had] surrendered to majority rule," as advocated by the Friends of Light, and reiterated the contention of the Pietist faction that "theological problems could never be decided by majority votes." [79] On the other hand, Uhlich and his followers accused the moderates of "replacing the *Apostolicum* with a *Nitzschenum* whose binding dogmas would impose the same chains on the conscience of clergymen . . . and would make them slaves of the letter." [80]

On August 29 the king dismissed the General Synod. His refusal to consider any of its recommendations gave little encouragement to liberal hopes concerning the work of a united diet, to be convened in the spring of 1847 as a general assembly of all provincial diets. The Pietists were triumphant. Ludwig von Gerlach admitted that their main strategy had been to achieve "the breaking up of the assembly . . . and to prevent [Frederick William IV] from accepting any of its recommendations." [81] The pious Junkers were convinced that no assemblies and no majority decisions had the authority to make decisions affecting the foundations for their claims to privilege and preeminence. The moderates, on the other hand, had labored under the leadership of Nitzsch to preserve the existing consistorial structure of the state church. They hoped that their acceptance of autocratic rule would influence the king and thus the government to allow the organization of presbyteries and synods all over Prussia. Anxious to exclude the theological-philosophical radicals from the Protestant clergy, the moderates had demonstrated their characteristic willingness to compromise with the conservatives when they voted for a binding creedal statement that was completely unacceptable to the Friends of Light. Even among the majority, serious doubts and disagreements had been expressed about practically every item of the proposed statement. Moreover, the Pietist conservatives were not at all appeased by the concessions of the moderates. The "true believers" remained opposed to the idea that clergymen and congregations had any right to discuss and change what the conservatives held to be the fundamental principles of their religion. Thus, for instance, declaring that "service in the army is the best way to learn obedience," [82] they rejected strongly the view, put forth by some synod members,

79. *EKZ*, 1846, p. 653.
80. Uhlich, *Siebzehn Sätze*, pp. 14 f.
81. Gerlach, *Aufzeichnungen*, I, 452.
82. Krüger, *Generalsynode*, p. 49.

that theological students should be exempted from military duty. Repeatedly they emphasized that the foremost duty of clergymen was to obey and to accept the official creed.

The moderates were deeply disappointed when they saw that all their efforts toward working out a compromise with the Pietists had been in vain. The failure of the General Synod confirmed the fact that the enigmatically indecisive head of the Prussian state church merely wanted to know the opinions of this select body of clerical and lay notables. When it came to making use of some, at least, of the recommendations of the synod, the king reserved the right of action (in this case, inaction) for himself. Commenting dismally on the outcome of the synod, Richard Rothe (then teaching at Heidelberg) expressed the sentiments of his former Prussian colleagues: "May God enlighten Frederick William IV, so that he may not be misled by the adverse shape of the *Zeitgeist* into misunderstanding the spirit of the time" (Gott erleuchte Friedrich Wilhelm IV, dass er sich nicht durch die widrige Gestalt des Zeitgeistes verleiten lasse, den Geist der Zeit zu verkennen).[83]

The moderates, by the stand they took in the discussions at the General Synod and by their final recommendations, which were accepted by the majority, made it clear that the liberally inclined theology professors of the 1840's firmly supported the existing political and social order. They had been instrumental in terminating the academic careers of Bruno Bauer and Gottfried Kinkel, and had also accepted without demur the dismissal of a number of the leaders of the Friends of Light from the clergy. Obviously, Nitzsch and those theology professors who shared his views were strongly opposed to complete theological freedom for clergymen. The preference of these moderates for assemblies of notables, called presbyteries and synods, did not mean that they were in favor of a democratically organized Protestant state church. In a public speech in 1847 Nitzsch declared unequivocally that he did not wish to see the masses "take control of the Protestant church by majority votes." He and his colleagues were opposed to the efforts of the Friends of Light to organize a "people's church" (*Volkskirche*); such an institution, they feared, would soon develop into a "church of the mobs" (*Pöbelskirche*). Clergymen should never become "agents of the masses"

83. Hausrath, *Rothe*, II, 71.

and be "obliged to carry out their ever changing wishes." [84] Thus the moderates were more concerned with maintaining the status quo in the face of the demands of the Friends of Light than with bringing about changes. Because of their opposition to the principle of democracy in church and state, the moderate liberals could be enlisted by the government in the struggle against its political foes.

The vigorous rivalry of ideas among clergymen in pre-March Prussia indicated the capacity of the Protestant church for autonomous theological development. The discussions and final recommendations of the General Synod of 1846 showed the resilience of ecclesiastical society in dealing with the crucial theological and political issues of the period. It would have been inconceivable for the moderately liberal supporters of the theology of conciliation to embrace ecclesiastical and political democracy. But on the other hand the majority of the assembly could not agree with the position of the Hengstenberg faction that the foremost duty of clergymen was to obey. Attacked by the extreme left and right wings of the clergy, the moderate majority was determined to protect itself and the church from both extremes and to assure the continuous growth and development of the ecclesiastical establishment.

The theologians of conciliation could not compromise with the extreme left because its demands for complete theological freedom and majority rule appeared to lead to religious and institutional anarchy. Caught between two extreme factions, the moderates chose to reject that one which at the time seemed to represent the more serious challenge to the traditional values and interests of the church and its professional clergy.

84. Speech of Nitzsch at the meeting of the Gustav Adolph Association in Elberfeld, printed in *Verhandlungen der Provinzial-Versammlung des Hauptvereins der Gustav Adolph Stiftung in der Rheinprovinz* (Elberfeld, 1847), pp. 26 ff.

6

The Friends of Light

In 1840 Frederick William IV became the legal head of the Prussian state. Along with the passing of Frederick William III fate seemed to decree that some other high offices of state should be similarly vacated. Altenstein predeceased the monarch by a few weeks, and Nicolovius by a few months. Before the close of the year there also occurred the death of Friedrich August von Stägemann, a close friend and confidential secretary of the late king. There seemed to be room everywhere for fresh energies. But during the past quarter of a century Germany's life had run an astonishingly rapid course, and owing to the prolonged reign the natural succession of the generations had been disordered. The new men who came to the top were no longer young. Most of them, like their royal patron, had grown up among the impressions of the War of Liberation, the years of reform and reaction, and the period of religious awakening.

To the impatient generation of the Young Hegelians the religious-romantic "Christian-German" regime of Frederick William IV was even more detestable than the prosaic and dry government of his father. Hengstenberg and the Pietist group around the new king were openly jubilant when Eichhorn took over the vacated ministry of ecclesiastical affairs and education. Eichhorn's statement that the new government was "by no means neutral" but "biased, totally biased" in the theological controversies of the time greatly alarmed the opponents of the clerical conservatives. There seemed to be every indication that under Frederick William IV the "true believers" were more determined than ever to eliminate rationalist and Young Hegelian influence from the church.

Since the publication of David Friedrich Strauss's *Life of Jesus* in 1835, the left-wing followers of Hegel, known as the Young Hegelians, had been attacking the Hengstenberg faction and the religious-romantic "Christian-German" cult of the Pietists. After 1840 these attacks increased in bitterness and vehemence. Young Hegelians such as Bruno and Edgar Bauer, Max Stirner, Arnold Ruge, and Karl Marx came to political opposition on the shoulders of their colleagues David Friedrich Strauss and Ludwig Feuerbach, whose break was essentially with religious orthodoxy and its ethical implications, and they turned their attention to political liberalism and radicalism only when the regime of Frederick William IV openly associated itself with their theological and philosophical antagonists.[1]

The famous principle of Hegel that "what is real is rational and what is rational is real" could be interpreted in two different ways. A static construction served as a justification for all existing institutions. This was the view taken by the right-wing Hegelians who defended the rationality of the status quo by the reality of its existence. The pious romantic-conservatives and their allies, however, were not interested in the rational justification of ancient institutions and privileges. And when left-wing Young Hegelians used the dynamic explanation of Hegel's principle to denounce all "reality" of today as the "irrational" of tomorrow, Hegelianism was declared a dangerous and subversive philosophy by the religious conservatives.

The Young Hegelians used the dialectic method, as developed by Hegel, as their chief weapon. Strict censorship of all printed works and the generally dominant idealistic and spiritualistic German tradition accounted for the fact that the Young Hegelians' initial attack came in the field of religion. It was directed against ultramontane Catholicism, against Lutheran orthodoxy and Neo-Pietism (of which Hengstenberg and the *EKZ* were the chief spokesmen), and against the "Christian-German" cult of the noble Junkers.

Strauss's *Life of Jesus* applied the Hegelian dialectic to the study

---

1. The argument for this view is put forth very cogently in Krieger's *The German Idea of Freedom,* pp. 297 f.

of the New Testament and tried to destroy the credibility of the Gospels as historical evidence. Strauss asserted that the events described in the Gospels were not historical facts but rather "myths" which were the result of the myth-making consciousness of the early Christian community, which was brought up in the traditions of the Old Testament. Jesus was merely the personification of an idea, and therefore all the miraculous elements in the New Testament story were eliminated from the life depicted by Strauss. There was such a tremendous uproar about the book that Strauss was himself frightened by its impact; in the subsequent editions and in his other theological writings he modified his conclusions. Bruno Bauer, however, went even further than Strauss in his religious radicalism and denied both the divinity and the historicity of the founder of the Christian religion.

In 1841 Ludwig Feuerbach, the profoundest thinker among the Young Hegelians, delivered the main attack on traditional Christianity. In *The Essence of Christianity* he went back to the English and French materialists of the eighteenth century and tried to demonstrate that nothing existed outside man and nature. He coined the famous expression, "A man is what he eats." According to Feuerbach, the essence of religion is found in man and in man's desire for happiness: gods are but the projections of man's thoughts and ideals. In short, it was not God who created man but man who created the gods. Anthropology should replace theology, and supernatural religion should be replaced by a religion of love between human beings.

Feuerbach and other Young Hegelians wanted to clear the intellectual atmosphere of pre-March Germany of what they considered the excessively dogmatic and nebulous spirituality that was the product of the speculative philosophy of Hegel, Neo-Pietism, the dogmatic orthodoxy of Hengstenberg, and the union of Christianity and Teutonism in the Prussian state of Frederick William IV. Feuerbach had a tremendous influence on the "true socialist" circle of Moses Hess and Karl Grün and on the founders of "scientific socialism," Karl Marx and Friedrich Engels.

In the columns of the *Hallische Jahrbücher,* edited by Arnold Ruge and Theodor Echtermeyer in 1837–1841, the Young Hegelians declared war on Pietism in religion and reaction in politics. They saw the clear relationship between liberalism and the rationalism of the Enlightenment, and pointed out the intimate connection between political reaction and literary romanticism. Ruge espoused the cause of democratic republicanism and in his article "Self-Criticism of Liberalism" subjected German liberalism to a most realistic and critical analysis. Pointing out that German liberalism had been purely theoretical and abstract, assuming more the position of a spectator on the side lines than that of an active participant, he called for the transformation of liberalism into democracy. Deploring the nonpolitical character of the Germans, Ruge indicated that politics did affect Germans but only in the same way that the weather affected them. In both instances they had nothing to do with producing it: when Germans wanted good politics, as when they wanted good weather, they gazed upward silently and with implicit faith. Liberty, declared Ruge, expressing a frequent dictum of the Young Hegelians, could not be granted as a gift.[2] In chiding the liberal elements of German society for lack of interest in pragmatic politics, the Young Hegelians were mindful of the political consciousness and pragmatic activities of the Hengstenberg faction, which by 1840 had come near to domination of the Prussian state church.

Under the regime of Frederick William IV the Hengstenberg faction controlled the admission of new men to the Protestant clergy and made clerical appointments not so much on ability as on conformity to the officially favored creed. Rationalism and Hegelianism in the university faculties of theology no longer presented serious threats to the "true believers," since by that time the liberally inclined theology professors had also become strong opponents of the rationalist and Hegelian approaches. Most theological candidates who were now placed in ecclesiastical positions were men who had been trained by Hengstenberg, Tholuck, Hahn, and other conservative professors. Only candidates who accepted the Apostolicum as prescribed in the Agende passed their qualifying examinations.[3] So slow, however, was the turnover of clerical personnel that during the 1840's most of the rank-and-file clergy were still men who had

2. "Selbstkritik des Liberalismus," in his *Gesammelte Schriften* (Mannheim, 1846), III, 98 ff. The article was originally published in the *Deutsche Jahrbücher* in 1841.

3. Lenz, II, pt. 2, 280 f.; Walter Nigg, *Die Geschichte des religiösen Liberalismus* (Zurich and Leipzig, 1937), pp. 143 f.; Schnabel, IV, 491 f.

been trained by Wegscheider, Gesenius, and other rationalist theologians. Their creed emphasized that all human problems, including morals and religion, could be understood by plain common sense (*der gesunde Menschenverstand*).[4]

Most rationalist pastors had little understanding of deep theological and philosophical problems. To them rationalism was not a learned doctrinal system (*Lehrgebäude*) but a direction (*Richtung*), a practical approach to life infused with an element of *Gemütlichkeit*.[5] Concerned with problems which influenced their everyday life, these men usually had little interest in the "battles of ideas" being fought by the new generation of literary men and the Young Hegelians, for whom "journals were fortresses."[6] But such politically alert men as Carl Bernhard König (1797–1847), a pastor in Anderbeck near Magdeburg, held that "fruitless" theological controversies should be left to theology professors, who despite their learnedness and knowledge could never, from their study rooms and lecture halls, direct the lives of the common people: "They do not know, and cannot know, the people as we do."[7] König's views were characteristic of a small group of politically conscious rationalist clergymen who were becoming impatient with the theological and philosophical controversies of the 1830's, and who believed that they "knew the problems and aspirations of the people."[8]

Unlike most of the rank and file, these men devoted much of their time and energy to the study and private discussion of con-

4. The publisher Friedrich Perthes who was one of the best informed men in the decades after 1815, stated that the preponderant majority of clergymen before 1848 still adhered to the rationalist creed. *Perthes Leben*, III, 161. See also Heinrich Pröhle, "Protestantische Freunde und freie Gemeinden in der Provinz Sachsen," in his *Feldgarben: Beiträge zur Kirchengeschichte, Literaturgeschichte und Culturgeschichte* (Leipzig, 1859), p. 16; hereafter cited as Pröhle, "Protestantische Freunde."

5. This characteristic attitude is summarized by Carl Bernhard König in his *Der rechte Standpunkt: Ein ruhiges Wort in Sachen der protestantischen Freunde zu Köthen gegen die Verunglimpfungen derselben durch die sogenannte evangelische Kirchen-Zeitung und ihren Anhang, Motto: Vorwärts! Nicht Luther, nicht Papst, Evangelische Freiheit!* (Magdeburg, n.d.), p. 5; hereafter cited as König, *Der rechte Standpunkt*. This was the first of a series of pamphlets under the general title of *Der rechte Standpunkt*.

See also Rudolf Haym, "Die protestantischen Freunde in Halle," *Jahrbücher der Gegenwart*, 4 (1846), 812; hereafter cited as Haym, "Protestantische Freunde."

6. Heinrich Heine's words, cited in Rosenberg, "Geistige Strömungen," p. 563.

7. König, *Der rechte Standpunkt*, III, *Vorwärts! Ohne Kampf kein Sieg!* (Magdeburg, n.d.), p. viii.

8. *Ibid.*, p. vii.

temporary political problems. Some of them were impatiently await-
ing the opportunity to seize the initiative and to "proceed from
words to deeds." Although they had been disturbed by the growing
strength of the Pietist faction for some time, until the reign of
Frederick William IV these politically alert pastors did not feel
threatened in their positions or creed.[9] Most of the theological controversies had taken place at the universities, between theology
professors, and on the Junker estates in the eastern parts of Prussia.
Pastors in the central and western sections of the country had been
relatively free to interpret the prescribed liturgy in a liberal manner.
Many of them omitted the Apostolicum, the official creed, in the
church services or simply left out parts of it. This conduct reflected
the prevailing rationalist thinking and behavior of the middle
classes in the first half of the nineteenth century.[10]

In contrast to the dogmatic and intolerant stand that Neo-
Pietism had developed during the "Awakening," rationalism had
been greatly influenced by the moralistic German Aufklärung of the
eighteenth century, which fused state rationalism and Pietist ethics.
Unlike the later "true believers" of the Hengstenberg faction, the
Pietists of the eighteenth century had sought to reform the church
not by enforcing a binding, official creed and gaining control of its
hierarchical structure, but by changing the hearts of the congregations. The moralistic Aufklärung, in shifting the basis of religion
from the mystical personal relation of Pietism with God to the
moral behavior of the individual, had been influential in maintaining the comfortable faith of middle-class Germans. Their *Sittlichkeit*—virtuous behavior and uprightness in accordance with custom
—had developed together with theological rationalism. Thus many
of the gentle, sweet, and tolerant aspects of Pietism had become
essential ingredients of German rationalism and seemed to be missing among the Neo-Pietists of the Hengstenberg faction. In this
sense, the tolerant "live and let live" attitudes of the rationalist
clergymen in the 1840's had a great deal in common with the practi-

9. See the article by C. G. Fubel, a pastor in Domnitz near Halle, "Die protestantischen Freunde," *Jahrbücher der Gegenwart,* 3 (1845), 854 f.; hereafter cited
as Fubel, "Protestantische Freunde."
10. [C. B. König], *Wanderung durch Vaterhaus, Schule, Kriegslager, und Akademie zur Kirche: Mitteilungen aus dem bewegten Leben eines evangelischen Geistlichen* (Magdeburg, 1832), pp. 28 ff., and Fubel, "Protestantische Freunde," p. 866.

cal Aufklärung and thus with eighteenth-century Pietism. In contrast, the Neo-Pietists had introduced new elements of dogmatism, exclusiveness, and domination into the "Awakening" of the nineteenth century.[11]

The accession of Frederick William IV in 1840 brought increasing pressure by the government on clergymen to declare their unqualified acceptance of the official creed. Rudolf Haym, in many ways characteristic of the theological candidates of the early 1840's who changed to other studies (in his case to philosophy and philology),[12] complained bitterly about the "program of religious meddling (Religionsmacherei) initiated from above." He observed the immediate hostile reaction of clergymen and laymen to the threat against freedom of creed especially in the province of Saxony, the original home of the Reformation.[13] The shrewd journalist K. E. Jarcke expressed the prevalent mood in informed circles under the new regime when he wrote: "Religion is now the center of politics and it will become even more so in the near future." [14] Haym noted that although most people had only very general and vague notions "concerning the anticipated blessings of a constitutional government," they had enjoyed religious freedom for a long time, and "any restrictions on their freedom of creed were considered intolerable attacks upon the inalienable rights of the individual." [15] As some of the politically conscious leaders of the developing liberal movement realized, the German people lacked political experience and tended to think of social problems in religious terms. It was for this reason that the political struggle over constitutionality and civil liberties had to begin in the religious sphere.

11. See the comments of the rationalist pastor Leberecht Uhlich concerning the religious attitudes of the middle classes in his Bekenntnisse von Uhlich: Mit Bezug auf die prot. Freunde und auf erfahrene Angriffe, 2d ed. (Leipzig, 1845), pp. 7 f. In contrast to the rural lower classes, who remained deeply attached to traditional religion and to the state church, the urban proletariat became gradually alienated from the teachings of the church. See Shanahan, pp. 345 ff.

12. Hans Rosenberg, Rudolf Haym und die Anfänge des klassischen Liberalismus (Munich and Berlin, 1933), pp. 14 ff. Rudolf Haym, Aus meinem Leben: Erinnerungen (Berlin, 1902), pp. 160 ff.; hereafter cited as Haym, Erinnerungen.

13. Rudolf Haym, Das Leben Max Dunckers (Berlin, 1891), p. 66.

14. The report is printed in Karl Glossy, ed., Literarische Geheimberichte aus dem Vormärz: Jahrbuch der Grillparzer Gesellschaft (Vienna, 1912), and cited in Rosenberg, "Theologischer Rationalismus," p. 531.

15. Haym, op. cit. (n. 13 above), p. 66.

In the 1840's those groups that wanted to eradicate the influence of rationalists in the Protestant clergy were referred to by the opposition as Pietists and "the pious" (*Frömmelnde*). For the church liberals in particular, Neo-Pietism was associated with "superstition, darkness, ignorance, hierarchical despotism, and intolerance." [16] The Hengstenberg faction was determined to take advantage of the fact that the new king was their friendly protector and ally, and that Eichhorn, the minister of ecclesiastical affairs and education, openly associated the new government with the Pietists. Having eliminated rationalist influence in the theological faculties of universities, the "true believers" wanted now to destroy the old "dragon's seed [of rationalism] manifesting itself among pastors as free-thinking liberalism and *Zeitgeist*." [17] Apparently the Pietists, in view of the very slow turnover in the clergy, did not want to wait until the rationalist pastors would be replaced gradually by pious candidates. The *EKZ* was outraged that more than a decade after the Agende of 1829, many rationalist clergymen openly violated its provisions by omitting the official creed from the church service or by reading only parts of it. Quite correctly, Hengstenberg and his colleagues concluded that by these acts pastors and congregations were expressing defiance of the regulations of the government.[18]

The "Sintenis affair" of 1840 in the province of Saxony demonstrated the seriousness of the threat of a *Gleichschaltung* to rationalist pastors. Alarmed by the possibility of losing their positions if they persisted in exercising what they considered a rightful freedom of creed, they were aroused to seek ways to keep both. Wilhelm Franz Sintenis (1794–1859) was pastor of the Church of the Holy Spirit in Magdeburg. In an article published in the local paper on February 7, 1840, he denounced the public worship of the crucifix as idolatry. Subsequently he was censured by the provincial Consistory for publicly denying the divinity of Christ.[19] General Superintendent and Bishop Johann Heinrich Bernhard Dräseke (1774–1849), the theology professors Tholuck and Heubner, and some other members of the provincial Consistory demanded that Sintenis

---

16. König, *Der rechte Standpunkt, II, Motto: Vorwärts! Ohne Kampf kein Sieg!* (Magdeburg, 1844), p. 24.

17. Karl Weiss to Hengstenberg, September 20, 1840, Bonwetsch, *Briefe an Hengstenberg*, II, 132. Weiss was a pastor in Königsberg.

18. *EKZ*, 1840, p. 78.   19. *Magdeburger Zeitung*, February 7, 1840, p. 2.

be dismissed from his position, but the accused pastor hotly denied that the rationalist creed was incompatible with his clerical office. His congregation and the city council of Magdeburg (the official patron of his church) strongly supported him and appealed the case to Minister Eichhorn in Berlin. The council informed the government in an official memorandum that feeling was running high in Magdeburg and that the dismissal of the popular pastor would certainly result in mass protests by the excited population. Because the leaders of the ministerial bureaucracy were anxious to avoid public unrest, Eichhorn instructed Dräseke to censure Sintenis but not to take disciplinary action against him, because the "unexpected and fantastic reaction" to the affair was threatening to cause "serious troubles . . . not only in Magdeburg but also in other parts of the country." [20]

For censuring Sintenis, Dräseke was exposed to bitter attacks all over Germany and was accused in innumerable pamphlets of trying to set up an Inquisition in the nineteenth century.[21] He was humiliated as well by Eichhorn's instructing him to discontinue the proceedings against the pastor. When Dräseke resigned as general superintendent, the Hengstenberg faction deplored this outcome, but had cause for triumph when he was soon replaced in that post by a militant Pietist pastor, J. F. Möller.[22] The fact that the influence of Möller, Tholuck, and Heubner was decisive in the provincial Consistory meant that increasing pressure would be brought upon clergymen to perform their duties strictly in accordance with the regulations of the Agende of 1829. Although the government considered the controversy in Magdeburg as officially closed, the *EKZ* announced: "In fact, it is more accurate to say that in Magdeburg and in the whole country we are actually intensifying the greatest controversy that has agitated the nineteenth century." The journal added: "The struggle will not be ended until the evil consequences of rationalism, liberal *Zeitgeist*, the spirit of revolt, and free-thinking

20. *Urkunden über das Verfahren des Königlichen Consistorii zu Magdeburg gegen den Pastor Sintenis: Mitgeteilt von einem Freunde der Wahrheit* (Leipzig, 1840), pp. 4 ff. See also Gerlach, *Aufzeichnungen*, I, 267.

21. Especially characteristic of these accusations were the attacks made in the anonymous pamphlet *Der Bischof Dräseke und sein achtjähriges Wirken im Preussischen Staate von G. von C.* (Magdeburg, 1840), pp. 3–9.

22. *EKZ,* 1840, p. 62, and W. F. Sintenis, *Fr. Möllers Wirken: Eine Denkschrift an das Kultusministerium* (Magdeburg, 1849), pp. 3–6.

godlessness (*Freigeisterei*), are destroyed." [23] This was an open declaration of war to the rationalist rank and file. Having purged the university theological faculties of rationalist and Hegelian influence, the Hengstenberg faction was now determined to use its influence to compel rationalist pastors to accept the dogmas expressed in the Apostolicum or to face the possibility of losing their positions.

Leberecht Uhlich (1799–1872), Carl Bernhard König, Sintenis, and some other rationalist pastors in the province of Saxony reacted very sharply and immediately to the threat of what they called the attempt to purge the Protestant clergy of its "free elements." Their views were reflected in an anonymous pamphlet, issued at Leipzig in 1842, which stated that the liberal pastors had decided to be "ready for battle" and to fight against "binding dogmas, the dead letter, and other works of dust." [24] In taking such risks, these pastors presumably could count on the support of their congregations. In Saxony not only urban but also many rural congregations had the privilege of "nominating" the men whom they wanted as their pastors, and their choice was customarily accepted by the Consistory, the official appointing agency. Since the congregations provided the funds for the remuneration of pastors, these men could be expected to voice some of the aspirations and indicate the ways of thinking of the parishioners.[25] (Where parsonages were under noble patronage, as was especially the case in the East Elbian parts of Prussia, pastors were selected and "presented" for appointment by the individual patrons, who also had some power to determine their remuneration, although the funds were provided by the congregations.) [26]

Uhlich had been engaged in organizing meetings of teachers, pastors, town officials, minor civil servants, craftsmen, and farmers all over Saxony since 1840. The regular monthly conferences at the inn in Gnadau—the so-called Gnadau *Bürgerversammlungen*—

23. *EKZ*, 1840, p. 78.

24. *Was soll daraus werden? Was wird daraus werden? Gutachten in Sachen des Lichts und der Finsternis* (Leipzig, 1842), p. 4.

25. Haym, "Protestantische Freunde," pp. 800 ff. See also Walter Breywisch, "Uhlich und die Bewegung der Lichtfreunde," in *Sachsen und Anhalt: Jahrbuch der Hist. Komm. für die Provinz Sachsen und für Anhalt,* II (Magdeburg, 1926), 161 ff.; hereafter cited as Breywisch, "Uhlich."

26. See Wangemann, *Sieben Bücher,* III, 147 ff.

became particularly well known. By 1841 the meetings were attracting more than a hundred participants, and it was decided that the large restaurant of the new railroad station at Schönebeck near Magdeburg would be a better place to assemble. Although the proceedings were quite orderly, the Hengstenberg faction saw an immediate danger in the public discussion of such topics as "the proper aims of education," "reason and progress," "the meaning of religious freedom," and "what citizens expect from their governments." The clerical conservatives were scandalized when they learned that Uhlich and some other rationalist clergymen claimed that the "awakened spirit of humanity" was no longer willing to be led in tutelage.[27] Also disturbing were reports that described Uhlich as an unofficial "boss" (*Chef*) who usually presided over and conducted the meetings in a parliamentary fashion. By the middle of 1841 Uhlich had become a public figure, noted for his excellent oratorical talents and his appeal to the masses, and was being called "the Saxon O'Connell." [28]

Enthusiastic over the popularity of the Gnadau meetings, the practical-minded Uhlich now decided to appeal to the rationalist pastors who had become alarmed about the danger of losing their positions. Many formerly complacent pastors were now perturbed by the prospect of having to choose between intellectual freedom and the possibility of losing their positions. In proposing the organization of a society of clergymen opposed to binding dogmas, Uhlich hoped that they would develop a sense of group consciousness and unity of purpose which had been missing in the previous decades.[29] Apparently he also judged that the increasing attacks of the *EKZ* on other pastors who were participating in the Gnadau meetings and the denunciations of them as "Jacobins who threaten

27. *EKZ*, 1840, p. 463, and *Bekenntnisse von Uhlich: Mit Bezug auf die prot. Freunde und auf erfahrene Angriffe*, 2d ed. (Leipzig, 1845), pp. 3 ff.

28. *Sie wissen was sie wollen! Eine Verteidigungsschrift in Sachen der protestantischen Freunde* (Leipzig, 1846), p. 4.

For the impact of the "Irish question" and for Daniel O'Connell as a popular hero in the German states see Karl Holl, "Die Irische Frage in der Ära Daniel O'Connells und ihre Beurteilung in der politischen Publizistik des deutschen Vormärz" (Ph.D. diss., University of Mainz, 1958).

29. Letter to K. G. Bretschneider, president of the Consistory in Saxe-Coburg-Gotha, 1841, in K. G. Bretschneider, *Aus meinem Leben: Eine Selbstbiographie* (Gotha, 1852), p. 284.

peace and order"[30] would result in a closing of rationalist ranks. Further, since the Gnadau conferences were often harassed by the authorities, a new organization of rationalist clergymen might provide better possibilities for the discussion of public issues. In a circular letter to a number of his friends and colleagues, Uhlich gave warning that the "Sintenis affair" was only the beginning of a Pietist campaign aimed at purging the clergy of its rationalist elements. Declaring, "Our age and our present situation demand more than just battles of ideas," he called for the formation of an organization in which rationalist pastors could "get together" and "proceed to action." Uhlich stated unequivocally that the primary purpose of the organization would be to "defend the Protestant freedom of conviction and the right to fight for one's views."[31]

Uhlich, Sintenis, König, and about a dozen other rationalist pastors, together with the theology professors Wegscheider and Niemeyer from the University of Halle, met at Gnadau on June 29, 1841, and founded a society called the "Protestant Friends" (*Protestantische Freunde*). Because of their emphasis on reason as the guiding light in all human affairs, including religion, this group of clergymen was soon known as the "Friends of Light" (*Lichtfreunde*).[32] Although Wegscheider and Niemeyer participated in the meetings of the group,[33] it was obvious that the leaders were

30. *EKZ*, 1840, pp. 463 and 484.

31. Leberecht Uhlich, *Die protestantischen Freunde: Sendschreiben an die Christen des deutschen Volkes* (Dessau, 1843), p. 5. This view was expressed also by König in *Der rechte Standpunkt, V, Vorwärts! Ohne Kampf kein Sieg!* (Magdeburg, n.d.), pp. 8 f.

32. Uhlich and the other leaders of the organization preferred to call themselves the Protestant Friends. "Die protestantischen Freunde: Ein Brief," *AKZ*, 1841, pp. 1539–46. See also the article "Lichtfreunde" in *RGG*, IV (1958), 359–361, and the literature cited there.

For a general history of the Friends of Light as a dissenting religious sect see Ferdinand Kampe, *Geschichte der religiösen Bewegung der neueren Zeit* (Leipzig, 1852–1860). The religious nature of the Friends of Light as one of "two movements of religious dissent," the other being that of the German-Catholics, is emphasized in Catherine M. Holden, "A Decade of Dissent in Germany: An Historical Study of the Society of Protestant Friends and the German-Catholic Church, 1840–1848" (Ph.D. diss., Yale University, 1954).

33. Gesenius was seriously ill; he died in 1842. Characteristic of the bitterness which existed between the Pietists and the rationalists was the comment of Tholuck, written in English in his diary, on the occasion of Gesenius's death: "The death of Gesenius an occurrence which makes me feel as if some demonical influence above me was taken away." Quoted in Witte, *Tholuck*, I, 430. (Besides German,

Uhlich, König, Sintenis, and two other pastors, Eduard Baltzer (1814–1887) and Gustav Adolf Wislicenus (1803–1875). Rudolf Dulon (1807–1870), the pastor of Flessau in the old Prussian province of Altmark, also cooperated with the leaders of the society for some time; he became the second preacher of the German Reformed Church in Magdeburg in 1843 and was a radical democratic politician in the pre-March period. Uhlich soon realized that in order to make the society of the Friends of Light a popular movement, membership should not be restricted to clergymen. He encouraged his colleagues to welcome persons from all walks of life in the meetings. Thus from the beginning the leaders of the society made it clear that they intended to enlist popular support for their cause. At a conference in Halle on September 28, the leaders announced to a gathering of more than sixty clergymen and laymen that membership was open to all like-minded persons who were in favor of freedom of conscience and opposed to the autocratic form of church government. Uhlich particularly welcomed politically conscious laymen as a "vigorous element" and hoped to attract more merchants, physicians, teachers, publishers, and other members of the middle classes to the movement.[34]

The fact that by the end of 1841 the Gnadau conferences were replaced by regular biannual general conventions of the society indicated that Uhlich and the other leaders were succeeding in their drive to mobilize both clergymen and other segments of society. The esprit de corps of the liberal clerical leaders was greatly strengthened by the increasing numbers of people who streamed to their meetings and who seemed to welcome the opportunity of demonstrating their sympathy with the goals of the Friends of Light. Encouraged by the popular response, König repeatedly urged Uhlich to make contact with sympathizers all over Prussia and other German states for the purpose of establishing branches of their organization.[35] Within a year of the founding of the movement, a considerable number of similar groups had been organized. In May 1842 the Leipzig meeting was attended by more than two hundred

Tholuck wrote his diary in several foreign languages, including English and Arabic, but never achieved real competence in any of them despite much practice.)

34. Letter to Bretschneider, 1841, in Bretschneider, *op. cit.* (n. 29 above), p. 287. See also *AKZ*, 1841, p. 1532.

35. König, *Der rechte Standpunkt*, V, 6 f.

persons. Uhlich was proud to report to the rationalist theologian K. G. Bretschneider that he was receiving innumerable letters from all over Germany expressing interest in joining the "struggle for freedom of conscience and expression."[36] The handful of rationalist pastors from the Prussian province of Saxony were now not only the organizers of a clerical faction but also the leaders of a political movement.

While Uhlich was certainly the best known of the Friends of Light and apparently the most successful organizer among them, his colleagues König, Sintenis, Baltzer, Wislicenus, and Dulon were also men whose interests, talents, and skills were suited for political leadership roles; and while all these men had different personal backgrounds and career patterns, they had much in common as representative political leaders and shared certain ideas and convictions in regard to their clerical profession and to public affairs.

The leaders of the society were former students of the rationalist theology professors Wegscheider, Gesenius, and Niemeyer at the University of Halle. Several of them had been helped by the benefits provided by the Francke institutions there. They occupied good pastoral positions which gave them economic security and plenty of spare time. Uhlich, for instance, had been the pastor of Pömmelte since 1827, and his position was considered one of the best parsonages in the area; it enabled him to support a large family (he had seven children). He was satisfied with his income, and his relations with the congregation rested on mutual respect and cooperation, making him one of the most popular persons in the whole community.[37] König was also satisfied with his position in Anderbeck. He attributed the publication of his numerous pamphlets to the fact that he found writing the best outlet for his surplus energies.[38] Dulon, as second preacher of the Reformed congregation at Magdeburg, was provided with a spacious house for his family of eleven, and his salary of 1,600 thalers compared favorably with that of some university professors.[39]

While Baltzer, König, Sintenis, and Wislicenus came from families of pastors, Uhlich's father was an impoverished tailor. Du-

---

36. "Aus einem Briefe an D. Bretschneider," *AKZ*, 1842, pp. 873 f.
37. Uhlich, pp. 17 ff.   38. König, *op. cit.* (n. 10 above), p. 119.
39. Heinrich Tidemann, "Pastor Rudolf Dulon: Ein Beitrag zur Geschichte der Märzrevolution in Bremen," *Bremisches Jahrbuch*, 33 (1931), 415 ff.

lon was the descendant of an old French-Swiss noble family that settled in Prussia under Frederick William I and had been providing civil servants since that time. Dulon's father was in charge of the post office at Stendal, and several of his brothers won distinction as army officers and as manufacturers in the German Empire.[40] An excitable youth, Dulon went into the clergy primarily because of the influence of a rationalist pastor and teacher, K. T. Gieseke, later his friend and brother-in-law, who had first discovered his oratorical talents. Gieseke encouraged the almost pathological urge of Dulon to shine in the public eye, and devoted much care to training him for the future role of a great preacher. In later years Dulon acknowledged the influence of Gieseke by stating, "What I am, I am because of him." [41]

All the leaders of the Friends of Light turned their attention to political life early in their careers and developed a deep hatred for the autocratic Prussian government and the privileged classes. When Uhlich's father became the servant of a noble family, the Uhlichs experienced personally the tensions which characterized relations between the aristocracy and the nonprivileged classes of the period.[42] König's resentful attitude had its origins in the disillusionment which he and other veterans of the War of Liberation experienced after 1815. Referring to the "political witch-hunt" (*Demagogenverfolgung*) after 1819, the censorship, the "police meddling in the personal affairs" of his family and friends, the "arbitrary actions of the higher and lower officials of the various government agencies," the "arbitrary nature" of the confessional union, and the "employment of brutal military force in the persecution of the Old Lutherans," he stated: "These were the events which awakened in me the love for *political* freedom from which a love of *religious* freedom followed in a logical manner." [43] In contrast to Bauer, Kinkel, Feuerbach, David Friedrich Strauss, and other theologians who had turned to politics only "when the Prussian state of Frederick William IV associated itself with their clerical and philosophical an-

40. Paul von Dülong, *Wanderungen und Heimkehr einer deutschen Familie: Geschichte der Familie von Dülong (d'Oulon, Doulon, Dulon, Dulong)* (Görlitz, 1915), pp. 17 ff.

41. Rudolf Dulon, *Gruss und Handschlag* (Hamburg, 1853), p. ii.

42. Uhlich, pp. 1–3.

43. König, *Der rechte Standpunkt*, VI (Altenburg, 1845), pp. viii–ix; emphasis in original.

tagonists," [44] the leaders of the Friends of Light had been interested in political issues for a long time, and their theological views had been influenced by their politics from the beginning of their clerical careers.[45]

As a student Wislicenus had been a leader of the Secret League (*Geheimer Bund*) of the officially dissolved Halle Burschenschaft.[46] The Wislicenus family had a long tradition of resisting autocratic rule. As Protestants they suffered for their religious beliefs under the Habsburgs in their native Hungary in the seventeenth century. In 1674 they were expelled from the lands under Habsburg rule; eventually they settled in Saxony. Gustav Adolf Wislicenus was one of eight children. When he was only six years old, his father died; at eleven, he also lost his mother. He then lived at the home of an uncle in Merseburg during the War of Liberation. Neglected by his uncle and disliked by his aunt, the boy spent most of his time at school and roaming the streets. He became a bitter and introverted youth, happier with books than in the company of people. It was a great relief to him when in 1818 he was accepted by the Francke orphanage at Halle. Although he was much more interested in the political activities of the nationalistic student union, young Wislicenus considered himself fortunate to become a student of theology under the famous professors Wegscheider and Gesenius.

With more than nine hundred students, eight hundred of whom were studying theology, the University of Halle was at the height of its popularity in the early 1820's. Although Wislicenus shocked his roommates by declaring that as far as he was concerned religion consisted of simple moral behavior (*Sittlichkeit*), he saw no possibility other than a clerical office for a future career. Under the influence of the Secret League of the former Burschenschaft, Wis-

---

44. Krieger, *The German Idea of Freedom*, p. 298.

45. This conclusion modifies the opinion of Leonard Krieger, who states that they were "concerned in the first instance with the recasting of dogma according to the simple and reasonable principles of a commonsense natural law and began to apply these principles against established authority in the secular state only when monarchical governments supported the pietism prevalent in the established churches." *Ibid.*

46. Most of the information on Wislicenus is derived from Haym, "Protestantische Freunde"; C. Thierbach, *Gustav Adolf Wislicenus: Ein Lebensbild aus der Geschichte der freien religiösen Bewungung, Zu seinem 100 jährigen Geburtstag* (Leipzig, 1904)—hereafter cited as Thierbach, *Wislicenus;* and A. T. Woeniger, *Wislicenus und seine Gegner* (Leipzig, 1845)—hereafter cited as Woeniger, *Wislicenus.*

licenus became an enthusiastic German nationalist. Firmly believing that it was their duty to continue the work of the student unions for a united Germany, the members of the Secret League were determined to resist the Prussian government in its efforts to stamp out nationalistic agitation. Whenever arrested, they denied their membership in the forbidden organization, acting on their maxim that "The oath sworn before Delbrück [the government superintendent of the university] is not binding." [47]

Wislicenus and his fellow students received from Wegscheider the teaching that there was no contradiction between their personal theological beliefs and the obligation to adhere to the official creed. Like many other rationalist professors, Wegscheider taught his students that professional members of the clergy were civil servants and as such had to accept the official creed and regulations of the state church: as individuals clergymen were free to have their own beliefs, but as officials they had to obey the authorities. He urged future pastors to preach from the pulpit for the purpose of instilling moral behavior into their parishioners and not to expound complex theological ideas: "Before the altar and in the pulpit the clergyman is bound by the official creed and regulations." [48] Thus the pervasive influence of the "Lutheran heritage" and the Pietistic-moralistic Aufklärung were perpetuated in the thinking of nineteenth-century rationalist theologians. Through them, the curious combination of "inner freedom" and official activity continued to exert its influence on German behavior. By the 1840's, however, unprecedented pressures and tensions, and the new theological and political ideas of the time, had created a situation in which many of the younger generation of rationalist clergymen were prepared to manifest their "inner freedom." The leaders of the Friends of Light expressed the attitude of this group when they challenged the right of the government to enforce the compliance of its ecclesiastical "officers" with official norms.

In 1825, being found guilty on the charge of being a member of the Secret League, Wislicenus was sentenced to twelve years in prison, but in 1829 he was pardoned. Although seemingly repentant, he had not changed his ideas of opposition to the autocratic government. Four years in the fortress of Magdeburg had added to his

47. Thierbach, *Wislicenus*, p. 14.   48. Woeniger, *Wislicenus*, p. 4.

youthful enthusiasm for political freedom a quiet and grim determination to dedicate his life to the realization of the goals of the nationalist movement. But Wislicenus had become engaged in 1823, and he was anxious to have a position so that he could marry his devoted and patient sweetheart. The fact that he now avoided involvement in political controversies led the authorities to assume that he had changed his views. Consequently he was allowed to complete his theological studies at the University of Berlin. In 1830 he moved to Merseburg and passed his first examination, *pro licentia concionandi,* which entitled him to teach. Through the help of friends the quiet, unassuming, and still young Wislicenus secured a position in a private school, where much of his free time was spent in reading. The works of Ludwig Börne, Heinrich Heine, Karl Gutzkow, and other writers of the Young Germany group further reinforced his hatred of the regime and of its privileged classes. Having passed the second examination, *pro ministerio,* in 1833, Wislicenus was fortunate to be appointed pastor at Klein-Eichstätt in May 1834. Finally he had economic security and a modest income of about five hundred thalers which enabled him to marry and have a family. He appears also to have been respected by his parishioners for his devotion to the welfare of the community. In his spare time Wislicenus now read with enthusiasm the writings of the Young Hegelians. Under the influence of David Friedrich Strauss he became convinced that the church had to be reformed.[49]

To Wislicenus religion was a deeply personal affair, the foundation of the individual's moral behavior. He blamed the state church and the Pietists for using religious dogmas to stifle independent thinking, and held that in a free church and in a free society religion should not be used by ecclesiastical and secular authorities as a brake to defer the hopes and aspirations of people for a better life on earth. Like many other rationalist pastors, Wislicenus did not consider the officially prescribed creed binding; he simply ignored the Apostolicum. By the end of the 1830's he had become convinced that it was a matter of human dignity to demonstrate one's disagreement with the dogmas of the church; inner freedom had to manifest itself openly; clergymen, like other individuals, must be free to

49. Thierbach, *Wislicenus,* pp. 18 ff.

express their beliefs and convictions—and they must speak out against the Pietists who wanted to degrade the church to the function of supporting the privileged classes in Prussia.[50]

Under the influence of Ruge and other Young Hegelians, Wislicenus decided to move to Halle in 1841. He considered the long years of his peaceful, quiet life in the country a period of preparation for future political activity, and was now ready to take a leading role in public affairs. He applied for the vacant position of pastor of the Laurentius Church in Neumarkt, on the outskirts of Halle. The congregation was impressed with his seriousness of mind, demonstrated devotion to public service, and feeling of responsibility, and requested the church authorities to have him transferred. Still convinced that the young pastor had given up his former nationalistic and liberal ideas, the Consistory authorized the transfer. Ironically, the official announcement of Wislicenus's appointment in the local paper stressed the fact that the authorities hoped that the "pious Pastor Wislicenus" would help to "stem the tide of disbelief" in Halle.[51] By now, however, Wislicenus was determined to join other like-minded clergymen in the struggle against what Dulon called "the barbarous Prussian state" (*der Barbarenstaat Preussen*), and he welcomed Uhlich's initiative in organizing the Friends of Light.

Uhlich was undoubtedly personally responsible for much of the agitation for freedom that the Friends of Light began in 1841. His skills as a popular speaker and organizer contributed to the amazing progress made by the movement in the following years. Uhlich craved popularity and was gratified by the fact that he was usually the main speaker, presiding officer, and general organizer at the biannual general meetings of the society which were inaugurated at Köthen in 1842 and also at innumerable branch meetings all over Germany. His popularity was reflected in the many songs and toasts praising him as "our O'Connell"—as in the following:

> Here's a health to our O'Connell too,
> Though he has ne'er been sued;
> He leads the heart of man and maid

50. Woeniger, *Wislicenus*, pp. 8–12.
51. *Kirchliche Monatsschrift*, March 1841, p. 2.

Where'er to him seems good
To parliament he is not sent,
Pömmelte's rights to guard;
In Köthen's hall he proves his claim
To woolsack and to sword.

The people flock to honor him,
The clergy own his reign;
The king [52] himself, from Anderbeck,
Has followed in his train.

The other leaders of the Friends of Light accepted Uhlich's preeminence because of his appeal to large segments of the population and his ability to reconcile differences of opinion. König and Sintenis were his close friends and co-workers, and the young men— Baltzer, Dulon, and Wislicenus—for some time considered it a distinction that the "Saxon O'Connell" had asked them to cooperate with him. Actually an even more talented orator than Uhlich, the highly excitable and passionate Dulon was unwilling to compromise on any issue that he considered important. Consequently he often alienated even his friends and further antagonized those who disagreed with him. His outspoken sermons in several churches at Magdeburg made him a well-known and controversial public figure long before his appointment as second preacher of the large Reformed congregation of that city in 1843.[53] Baltzer was also highly effective as a speaker, but was less famous than his colleagues Uhlich and Dulon because he was reluctant to appeal to mass meetings by stirring up emotions. In this respect Baltzer tended to favor Wislicenus's approach of appealing to the intelligence of his listeners. In an age saturated with oratory, such speakers as Uhlich and Dulon could always draw large crowds to their meetings. Uhlich in particular was considered a "man of the people": he did not pretend to be a theologian of deep learning, and he had a remarkable instinct for the feelings and wishes of the populace. The "Saxon

52. An allusion to Pastor König. The song is quoted in *The German Reformation of the 19th Century,* by "the German Correspondent of the *Continental Echo*" (London, 1846), p. 32.

53. Ralph Meyer, *Geschichte der Deutschreformierten Gemeinde in Magdeburg* (Magdeburg, 1914), II, 44 ff.

O'Connell" was a typical popular leader whose pragmatic ways of thinking, plain language, and casual and unpretentious behavior constituted his main assets. He was able to reduce every aspect of theological rationalism to simple and reasonable statements.[54]

On the other hand, the "naïve and sentimental rationalism" of Uhlich "bored and depressed" Haym, Karl Schwarz, Max Duncker, and other academic intellectuals supporting the cause of the Friends of Light.[55] For some time they failed to realize the tremendous potential of the popular and "folksy" Uhlich for political leadership of the increasingly restless population of the 1840's. The Hengstenberg faction was much more able to sense the significance of Uhlich's agitation, and was alarmed by the fact that he had become the spokesman of the discontented middle classes expressing the "ideas, opinions, aspirations, and hopes of the masses" and being "a man who knows exactly what people want." [56] To the conservative Pietists there was nothing more subversive than stirring up the masses and appealing to their "common sense." Firmly opposed to the notion that congregations and their clergymen were free to interpret the official creed, the *EKZ* attacked the increasingly democratic leanings of the leaders of the society and accused them of "flattering the mobs by telling them that the majority could decide what was right and what was wrong." [57]

Pastors König, Sintenis, and Wislicenus—in marked contrast to Uhlich, Dulon, and Baltzer—did not excel in public speaking. König's influence was due mainly to the innumerable pamphlets (often published anonymously) [58] in which he conducted a violent campaign against "the Pietists in the clergy and in other offices." He accused the "true believers" of always "turning their eyes to heaven and talking about the heavenly kingdom," pretending that they were "not much concerned with worldly things," and in reality

---

54. Haym, "Protestantische Freunde," pp. 812 ff., and Fubel, "Protestantische Freunde," p. 855.

55. Haym, *Erinnerungen*, p. 162.   57. *Ibid.*, 1847, p. 984.

56. *EKZ*, 1845, p. 834.

58. Occasionally König acknowledged the authorship of some of his anonymously published pamphlets. Several years after the publication of a bitter attack on General Superintendent and Bishop Dräseke in *Der Bischof Dräseke und sein achtjähriges Wirken im preussischen Staate* (Leipzig, 1840), König admitted that he wrote this pamphlet. *Der rechte Standpunkt*, V, 28.

"doing everything in their power to control all crucial positions" in the country.[59] König thus echoed the charges of the liberal journalist R. E. Prutz, who attacked the Pietists as:

> the actual opposing party (*die eigentliche Gegenpartei*) . . . because it is in fact not concerned with whether we shall eventually be punished for what it calls our disbelief . . . by eternal damnation in hell. . . . What they really want is to prevent us from getting hold of positions and from gaining economic security (*Amt und Brot*). . . . Nor should we have political influence, power, and positions! They would allow us to remain heretics without positions and influence, but do everything to prevent us from acquiring positions as professors, clergymen, councilors, and [cabinet] ministers! [60]

In his pamphlets König consistently defended the right and duty of clergymen to take an independent stand on public issues. But he was careful not to defy the Consistory whenever he was reprimanded for his outspoken views. To König politics was an activity similar to war; occasional retreats were part of the general strategy for winning the campaigns. He was so obsessed with military terminology that in his series of pamphlets *Der rechte Standpunkt* he gave regular accounts of "battles," "skirmishes," "retreats," "defeats," and "victories." The political arena was a "battlefield" where the "forces of light and darkness"—the Friends of Light and the Pietists—clashed. In his pamphlets König devoted a special section to "News from the War Theatre" (*Nachrichten vom Kriegschauplatze*), which informed his readers of the latest developments. The struggle between Pietists and Friends of Light was obviously not presented on the literary level of the talented writers of the Young Germany group. The leaders of the Friends of Light did not engage in abstract and sophisticated "battles of ideas"; they were actually participating in a popular movement fighting against the autocratic government associated with the Pietists.

Sintenis was also a prolific writer of usually anonymous pamphlets in which he demanded complete freedom for clergymen to interpret the Gospels. He strongly rejected the demands of the Hengstenberg faction that pastors who refused to accept certain official

59. König, *Der rechte Standpunkt*, VI, 16 f.
60. Prutz, "Theologie oder Politik?" p. 39.

dogmas should be dismissed from their positions.[61] Wislicenus—who was considered by Haym, an acute observer, to be the "cleverest and noblest" of the leaders of the Friends of Light—was not a popularizer as a speaker or as a writer. He was logical, consistent, and inflexible. His sharp intellect did not tolerate Uhlich's "naïve and sentimental rationalism." Wislicenus's precise and logical way of expressing his ideas in speeches appealed to the intellect of people and not to their emotions. He was respected for the apparent sincerity of his convictions, but he seemed to have difficulty in conveying the warmth and compassion which inspired him to appeal to his fellow men. Consequently Wislicenus lacked popular appeal.

The ideas, attitudes, and behavior of the two most significant leaders of the Friends of Light were in very sharp contrast. The rationalistic ideas of Uhlich reflected the general *Gemütlichkeit* and spirit of compromise of a man who was devout and deeply religious but who was also convinced that Christianity was both for the heart and for the mind. He equated rationalism with a tolerant reasonableness, not with logic and consistency. Warmth, sentiment, and feeling permeated the common-sense philosophy of Uhlich. Contemporaries credited him with presenting and explaining the complex and learned academic approach of theological rationalism in a way that actually transformed it into a modest, gentle, and reasonable popular creed.[62] Uhlich had been the original organizer and remained the central figure of the society. Wislicenus had joined the Friends of Light to fight against autocratic rule in church and state. He shared the concern of the other leading members with personal freedoms and with security of positions. He was willing to participate in the campaign carrying their cause to the people. But up until 1844—when he made a dramatic appearance at the convention of the Friends of Light—Wislicenus did not share the limelight of his popular colleagues. He seemed to be engaged in much serious thinking about the ideological and social aspects of the political struggle. He seldom discussed the deep and underlying philosophical foundations of his position, but he made it clear in his speeches that he envisaged much more radical attacks on the "barbarous Prussian

---

61. [W. F. Sintenis], *Möller und Uhlich* (Leipzig, 1847), p. 3. See also Sintenis's *Herr Prediger G. A. Kämpfe in Magdeburg und die Kirchenlehre in Briefen an Carl Bernhard König* (Leipzig, 1846), pp. 6–9.

62. Haym, "Protestantische Freunde," pp. 810–813, and *Erinnerungen,* pp. 161 f.

state" than Uhlich would ever dream of. While Uhlich reinterpreted and popularized rationalism by the infusion of a warm and understandable *Gemütlichkeit* and common-sense reasonableness, Wislicenus seemed to have gone beyond rationalism by shifting the focus to the consequences of rationalistic thinking. The dynamic nature of Hegelian philosophy promised new and limitless horizons to the speculative mind of Wislicenus. He had started out with the other leaders of the society to carry their cause to the masses. In the course of a few years, however, his colleagues realized that Wislicenus was actually in the process of setting a new course for those more radical Friends of Light who were no longer satisfied with the original goals of the movement.

Wislicenus and his friends Rudolf Haym, Max Duncker, Karl Schwarz, and some other academic liberals believed that it was their duty to "raise the masses" to their level and not to permit the popular forces to compel the intellectuals to be "reduced to the level of the masses." Haym saw the dangers of this intellectual snobbery and had to admit that, as far as effectiveness was concerned, the "generally intelligible *Gemütlichkeit*" of Uhlich and other popular leaders was certainly more powerful than their academic Protestantism. But Wislicenus, "whose mind demanded the truth and only the truth," was so convinced of the unfailing logic of the Hegelian dialectic that he was willing to face the consequences of his position —whether popularity or disgrace. Unlike the other leaders of the movement, Wislicenus seemed to derive little satisfaction from being a public figure, although the Friends of Light owed some of their most spectacular triumphs to him. What really united this small complex group of leaders was the Pietist threat to their freedom of creed and to their positions. They were convinced that because they "knew the problems and aspirations of the people" generally and of their rationalist colleagues in particular, they were qualified to take leading roles in public life. The unexpectedly strong reaction of clergymen and laymen to the Sintenis affair in 1841 provided an excellent opportunity for Uhlich and his ambitious colleagues. They immediately seized the initiative and shifted the scene of the political arena from theological disputes and controversies between scholars, philosophers, and men of letters, to the organization of popular meetings. The parliamentary proceedings of these gatherings proved to be highly attractive to increasing numbers of people from all walks of life, not only in Prussia but also in other German states.[63]

The biannual conventions of the movement took place in Köthen. This small city in the duchy of Sachsen-Köthen was at an important new railroad junction whose large restaurant could serve considerable crowds. The initial meeting in September 1842 attracted about 150 persons, and the meetings in June and September 1843 attracted about 300 and 400 respectively. Because of the increase in numbers, the meetings in 1843 had to be held outside the building.[64]

In 1838 Arnold Ruge and other Young Hegelians associated with the *Hallische Jahrbücher* had expressed contempt for the crude simplicity of theological rationalism and its naïve adherents.[65] But in a few years they were convinced by the success of the Friends of Light in attracting popular support that religious ideas still deeply permeated the thinking of the German people. Ruge then declared that the struggle of the Friends of Light for freedom of creed and for a "people's church" was a necessary stage for the realization of political and social reforms. So impressed was he by the popular appeal of the leaders of the Friends of Light that with a typical Rugean turn of the dialectic he called the formerly despised rationalist pastors the continuers and renewers of the German Reformation "whom our time requires and whom philosophy demands." [66] In an impassioned plea to the liberals he urged that they be realistic and not ignore the dynamic possibilities provided by the movement of the Friends of Light. Realizing that political and social problems were considered by most Germans from a religious-ethical viewpoint, he warned the liberals, "Without religion the centuries will pass over Germany without a trace," and added that all the wisdom of intellectuals would "not bring freedom." [67]

Rudolf Haym, Karl Schwarz, Max Duncker, and other academicians at the University of Halle cooperated with the movement of the Friends of Light. They were motivated by the common desire of many liberal intellectuals to establish contacts with the middle classes and their newly emerging popular leaders. Obviously there

63. Haym, *Erinnerungen*, p. 163, and König, *Der rechte Standpunkt*, III, vii.
64. *AKZ*, 1842, p. 1430, and 1843, pp. 797 and 1342; Wangemann, *Sieben Bücher*, III, 189 ff.
65. *Hallische Jahrbücher*, 1838, pp. 96–116.
66. Ruge, *op. cit.* (n. 2 above), p. 100.   67. *Ibid.*, p. 101.

was a world of difference between the deep philosophical, historical, and theological thinking of such intellectuals as Haym, Schwarz, and Duncker, and the simple, common-sense approach of Uhlich, Sintenis, and König. But the fact could not be denied that the leaders of the Friends of Light had succeeded in capturing the imagination of the masses and had become spokesmen for some of their demands, hopes, and aspirations. The historically oriented mind of Duncker in particular perceived the possibility of enlisting the religious consciousness of the German people for the purpose of developing their political awareness.[68]

Haym and his fellow academicians, who considered Wislicenus the cleverest and most profound of the leaders of the Friends of Light, persuaded the young pastor that it was his duty to formulate a "specific principle" to guide the actions of the new popular movement. For some time Wislicenus had been uneasy about the obvious efforts of his rationalist clerical colleagues to gain popularity by interpreting the original goals of the society so that they would have the widest possible appeal. Uhlich in particular was responsible for their attempt to attract as many people as possible; he also prevented the drawing of a definite line between friends and enemies. By nature a compromiser and conciliator, Uhlich represented those elements of the movement who wanted to avoid building up a strong opposition. Consequently he tried to persuade his colleagues that disagreements could always be reconciled in a parliamentary debate and discussion: common sense would eventually prevail when there was a spirit of cooperation and willingness to compromise. Uhlich seemed to believe that, except for the Hengstenberg faction, most Protestants in the German states would join the Friends of Light in their struggle for intellectual freedom and for an independent *Volkskirche*. Thus he continued to advocate free and open discussion of issues to resolve differences between conflicting viewpoints. He deliberately avoided the clarification of positions, and refused to formulate firm and unequivocal goals for the movement despite Wislicenus's urging.[69]

On May 29, 1844, Wislicenus delivered his famous speech entitled "Scripture or Spirit?" (*Ob Schrift? Ob Geist?*) at the general

68. Max Duncker, *Die Krisis der Reformation: Ein Vortrag in der Versammlung der protestantischen Freunde zu Halle am 6. August* (Leipzig, 1845), pp. xxv–xxvi.
69. Fubel, "Protestantische Freunde," pp. 856 ff.

convention in Köthen. In an unprecedented open defiance of the official creed he declared that for the Friends of Light the highest authority was the "living spirit of truth developing freely" in humanity and in themselves, and not the Scriptures.[70] Arguing that one could not bind the "eternally developing and changing spirit of the times" to rigid dogmas, Wislicenus flatly refused to be bound by any specific confession of faith. Thus he publicly denied the right of the government to compel clergymen to accept the Apostolicum as prescribed in the Agende of 1829. Probably the great majority of his listeners—several hundred in number—understood little of the long philosophical justification of Wislicenus's thesis, but the courageous defiance of the government by a Protestant minister electrified the crowd and started discussion, newspaper reports, and governmental reaction which put the leaders of the Friends of Light in the limelight of national attention. Uhlich, who up to this point had always avoided an open challenge to the government, suddenly realized that he and the other leaders of the movement would either have to support Wislicenus in his stand or disassociate themselves from him. In either case, the Friends of Light faced a serious crisis. Everyone who left the meeting knew that Wislicenus's bold statements would have serious consequences not only for him but for those who identified themselves with his views.[71]

The months after the May convention witnessed an unceasing barrage of attacks on the Friends of Light by the Hengstenberg faction, which declared that Wislicenus's denial of the authority of the Scriptures disqualified him and like-minded ministers for holding clerical positions in the state church.[72] Professor Guericke, of the University of Halle, who attended the meeting at Köthen, reported in the *EKZ* that only about a fourth of those present were clergymen, the majority being artisans, townsmen, and farmers. The Hengstenberg faction thereupon seized the opportunity to charge the leaders of the Friends of Light with organizing "mass meetings of all sorts of discontented elements," who had "raised the banner of revolt against authority."[73] The campaign of the Pietists against

70. The speech is printed with comments and explanations in Gustav Adolf Wislicenus, *Ob Schrift? Ob Geist? Verantwortung gegen meine Ankläger*, 2d ed. (Leipzig, 1845).

71. *EKZ*, 1844, pp. 364–366, and Uhlich, p. 30.   72. *EKZ*, 1844, p. 577.

73. F. Guericke, "Köthener Convent der 'protestantischen Freunde' am 29. Mai 1844," *EKZ*, 1844, pp. 364, 579.

the Friends of Light produced hundreds of declarations, especially from clergymen living in the Junker-dominated eastern rural parts of the country, demanding the dismissal of Wislicenus and his followers.[74] These expressions of support for the Hengstenberg faction were in sharp contrast to the overwhelming enthusiasm of clergymen and laymen among the urban and rural middle classes, including many artisans, supporting the cause of the Friends of Light.[75]

The publication of Wislicenus's speech in pamphlet form further infuriated the Hengstenberg faction. Wislicenus was ordered by the provincial Consistory to appear in Wittenberg on April 30, 1845, and explain his theological views before a special investigating committee headed by Tholuck and Heubner. Defying the order, he declared that his views had been clearly stated in writing and that, therefore, no explanation was needed. Having refused to appear, he was ordered to defend himself before the provincial Consistory in Magdeburg on May 8. There he firmly declined to repudiate the ideas expressed in his Köthen speech. Six days later, the committee in Wittenberg decided that the Halle pastor was clearly in disagreement with the official creed. Consequently the Consistory gave Wislicenus an indefinite leave of absence and urged him to hand in his resignation. He then ceased to perform clerical duties at his church in Neumarkt, but refused to resign from the post.[76]

In response to the attacks on the leaders of the Friends of Light, and particularly on Wislicenus, groups of citizens in all the German states rushed to the defense of the now popular heroes. In public letters, artisans and others (describing themselves as *Professionisten*) in Köthen warned "Guericke and other Pietist spies" to keep away from the town and threatened Guericke with a public execution if he dared come there again.[77] The printing of such letters in the *EKZ* apparently indicated that Hengstenberg wished to discredit the forces supporting the Friends of Light by showing them to be irresponsible, violent elements of society bent on subverting state and church. Following Wislicenus's open challenge to the government in his Köthen speech and his refusal to appear before the Pietist

74. "Erklärung wider P. Wislicenus und Genossen," *EKZ*, 1844, pp. 577 ff.
75. Woeniger, *Wislicenus*, pp. 18 ff.   76. Thierbach, *Wislicenus*, pp. 36 f.
77. *EKZ*, 1844, pp. 503 f. and 568. See also *AKZ*, 1844, pp. 1576 and 1845.

"inquisitionary tribunal" at Wittenberg, people streamed in masses to meetings conducted in all parts of Germany by the Friends of Light. König expressed the jubilant and defiant mood of his fellow leaders when he declared in a pamphlet:

> The struggle has now finally entered the third stage. . . . In the first stage scholars fought their battles in the universities [and] in the second stage pastors disseminated the principles of freedom, justice, and common sense from the pulpits. . . . Now, in the third stage, the people themselves appear in the political arena . . . to take an active part in the struggle for their rights. . . . I and my colleagues are convinced that the voice of the people . . . as everyone can hear it in our meetings . . . is in fact the voice of God. . . . This is my belief, for which I am fighting.[78]

König's pamphlet was a sign of the open admission by the leaders of the Friends of Light that they were carrying their struggle for individual rights and freedoms to the people. These popular pastors now considered themselves politicians whose cause was identified with the political and social aspirations of elements of German society who were denied freedom of religious and political activity. Uhlich, Wislicenus, and their colleagues had apparently succeeded in becoming the leading spokesmen of some frustrated and bitter sections of the public that were increasingly hostile to the existing order. Following the Halle denunciation in 1831, Hengstenberg had started the campaign to "carry the fight [of the Pietists] from the lecture halls [of universities] to the Protestant church" and "from the field of scholarship into public life."[79] By 1844 it could be said— and, indeed, was said by Hengstenberg—that such a struggle had been carried by the Friends of Light to some of the most aggrieved elements of the population, who now threatened the "true believers . . . not only with spiritual weapons but also with mob action and violence." In a series of bitter attacks, Hengstenberg accused Wislicenus and other, like-minded clergymen of not only posing the question "Scripture or Spirit?" but actually proclaiming the alternative, "Scripture or public opinion?"[80]

The leaders of the Friends of Light, König declared, were "de-

---

78. König, *Der rechte Standpunkt*, II, 8–10.
79. *EKZ*, 1831, p. 2.   80. For one of these attacks see *EKZ*, 1844, p. 756.

termined to rely on the power of public opinion," and to continue their struggle for "Protestant freedom of self-government" and "freedom of belief and expression," and for "transformation of the state church (*Consistorialkirche*) into a people's church."[81] Typical of the tremendous excitement and the impatient mood of the people at the mass meetings of the Friends of Light after the "Wislicenus affair" was the reaction to the remark by the journalist Franz von Florencourt that clergymen who did not want to be bound by dogmas of the Apostolicum should voluntarily resign their positions. Amid continuous interruptions and catcalls, Uhlich insisted on the right of the speaker to express his views. When finally Florencourt concluded, Uhlich turned to the audience and asked, "Shall I answer him?" To this came a roar, in unison, of "Yes! With the club!" ("Ja! Mit dem Knüttel!")[82]

The year following Wislicenus's speech witnessed a phenomenal increase in the attendance at the meetings of the Friends of Light.[83] New branches were founded, mass meetings and conferences held, petitions circulated, and protests organized in practically every part of the country. Uhlich and the other leaders of the Friends of Light traveled constantly and addressed huge mass rallies. Within a year the pastors from the province of Saxony became national figures and the "Saxon O'Connell" emerged as the "traveling hero of the German people," familiarly greeted by thousands at open-air meetings and by throngs gathered at railway stations to welcome him. No doubt the organization of these meetings would have been impossible without the recently built railroads which connected the Prussian provinces.[84]

Judging by the records of the meetings, the discussion of problems concerning "God, religion, creed, and the virtues of life" was rapidly pushed into the background by political demands for "complete freedom of the press, speech, and free association," "self-government based on representation," and "a governmental system

81. König, *Der rechte Standpunkt*, II, 24 f.

82. See *EKZ*, 1846, p. 29, and Pröhle, "Protestantische Freunde," p. 66.

83. The September 1844 convention was attended by 800 persons, and about 3,000 were present in May 1845. *AKZ*, 1844, p. 1576, and 1845, p. 268. See also the numerous other reports in the *AKZ* and the *EKZ* during these years.

84. Robert Blum, ed., *Die Fortschrittsmänner der Gegenwart: Eine Weihnachtsgabe für Deutschlands freisinnige Männer und Frauen* (Leipzig, 1847), pp. 14 ff., and Wangemann, *Sieben Bücher*, IV, 205 ff.

in which the Protestant Church is one of the free institutions in our country." [85] It was probably because of such demands that the *EKZ* accused the leaders of the Friends of Light of "following the base and contemptible passions of the rebellious and discontented mobs," who had "lost all respect for God and for worldly rulers" and "become slaves of the flesh." [86] Yet, besides the handful of "enlightened, dissatisfied literati," the meetings were attended mainly by "handicraftsmen, teachers, lower officials, and other townsmen, and farmers." [87] The fact that these protesting assemblies could hardly be described as mere "mobs" was confirmed by General Superintendent Möller in Magdeburg in a report to Minister Eichhorn in Berlin. Möller stated that teachers and clergymen, merchants, and well-to-do farmers gathered at the meetings of the Friends of Light, and added: "There are also many lower officials present whose enlightened ideas welcome opposition to caste-spirit and to the aristocracy, which is considered the main supporter of the institutional structure of the Protestant church." [88]

In March, 1845, Uhlich spoke in the Berlin Zoological Garden at an open-air meeting organized by the local association of artisans (*Handwerkerverein*). The popular clerical leader attacked "the hateful faction (*die hassenswerte Partei*) of the Pietists," and declared that the German people were "tired of words" and "determined to proceed to deeds." [89] Reporting the meeting to its readers, the *EKZ* hastened to point out that the crowd had consisted mainly of artisans, with "a few writers" and "several physicians of different confessions" present, but "no clergymen." Consequently, Hengstenberg concluded that Uhlich and the other leaders of the Friends of Light had abandoned the pretense of merely representing rationalist clerics. The *EKZ* was particularly disturbed by the fact that not only were the wives of the liberal journalist Dr. Theodor Mundt and some other literati there, but also dressmakers, embroiderers, and other female workers were among "the supporters of complete freedom of conscience [and] of progress." It was

---

85. See *Politische Beobachtungen: Über die protestantischen Freunde*, no. 3 (Berlin, 1845), pp. 3 ff., and *Erste Mitteilung der protestantischen Freunde in Breslau: Den Freunden zur Beherzigung, Den Gegnern zur Prüfung* (Breslau, 1845), pp. 4 f.
86. *EKZ*, 1845, pp. 32 ff.   87. Wangemann, *Sieben Bücher*, IV, 206.
88. The report is printed in Breywisch, *op. cit.* (n. 25 above), pp. 165 f.
89. *EKZ*, 1845, p. 647.

outraged that a pastor of the state church should actually welcome the "shameful spectacle of women entering the public scene (*Schauplatz der Öffentlichkeit*) for the first time in German lands." [90] The journal failed to point out that these female workers could have problems and grievances similar to those of male artisans and workers.

The political, social, and economic tensions of the 1840's burst forth with particular vigor in the meetings of the Friends of Light in 1844 and 1845. These mass gatherings provided the channels for expressing the frustration and resentment of the nonprivileged elements of German society and the determination to bring about changes for their benefit. The growing political pressures reflected the serious economic crises of the 1840's and the general dislocation accompanying the first initial stages of modern industrial development in Prussia and other German states. The desperate and tragic uprising of the Silesian weavers in 1844 was only a particularly dramatic event in a series of hunger riots and demonstrations. Concurrently with the serious birth pangs of industrialization came an unprecedented population increase and a number of crop failures—including a blight that ruined the potato harvest in much of Europe and produced one of the major famines of modern times. Business depression, high prices, and unemployment further aggravated the problems of the Hungry Forties. The meetings conducted by the leaders of the Friends of Light showed plainly that large segments of the population which were agitated by economic insecurity and political frustration could be mobilized to seek the realization of their demands. The 1840's saw the first active participation of the German masses in political life since the Peasants' War. Thus the "common man again entered German history," partly because of the "unprecedented transmission of the liberal movement to anonymous masses of the German people." [91]

In December, 1844, Johannes Ronge, an expelled Silesian Catholic priest, and Robert Blum, a radical democrat (executed in the 1848 Revolution), began organizing what became known as the German-Catholic movement. The leaders of the Friends of Light

90. *Ibid.,* p. 648.
91. Krieger, *The German Idea of Freedom,* p. 283. See also Jacques Droz, *Les révolutions allemandes de 1848* (Paris, 1957), pp. 61, 108–112, and Conze, *Staat und Gesellschaft,* pp. 236, 258–261, 263.

welcomed this development of a new dissident group.[92] Because the German-Catholics were also opposed to autocratic government and religious dogmas in church and state, the Friends of Light considered their organization "another manifestation of the public sentiment." Although Ronge started the movement in the predominantly Catholic parts of Silesia, for a brief period the German-Catholics were successful in attracting followers in other parts of Germany as well. Ronge, Blum, and other leaders of the movement did not hesitate to declare that they considered religious radicalism a transitional stage to democratic radicalism. Both Ronge and Blum were anxious to cooperate with radicals wherever possible.[93] Like their Protestant counterparts, the German-Catholics tended to favor in religious matters a "presbyterian form of government," the "election of ministers by individual congregations," and "freedom from dogma and from the arbitrary decisions by a hierarchy." Visitors to the meetings of the Friends of Light and the German-Catholics in 1845 noticed no difference in the social composition of the audiences or in the issues that were discussed by the speakers.[94]

Frustrated in their hopes for political and social reforms, the liberal intellectuals for many years had been painfully aware of their inability to attract a popular following. They were now greatly impressed by the tremendous popular response to the leaders of the Friends of Light and of the German Catholics. Arnold Ruge saw in their struggle the "beginning of a political and social liberation" and declared that they were actually translating the "philosophic and political ideas of freedom into popular reality." Uhlich and his colleagues openly acknowledged that "liberals and literati" who were "striving only for political goals" had joined their ranks, and the liberal writer Theodor Mundt assured them that only in

92. Holden, *op. cit.* (n. 32 above), pp. 102–169. See also the collection of articles in *The German Reformation of the 19th Century* (cited in n. 52 above) and the many contemporary pamphlets available in the Starr King School of Religion, Berkeley, California.

93. See Theodor Brand, *Fackelzug für Johannes Ronge* (Breslau, 1845), pp. 14–16.

94. See the letter of Baltzer to the first general meeting of the German-Catholics, at Leipzig in March 1845, in Robert Blum and Franz Wigand, eds., *Die erste allgemeine Kirchenversammlung der deutsch-katholischen Kirche abgehalten in Leipzig: Authentischer Bericht, Im Auftrage des Kirchenvereins* (Leipzig, 1845), pp. 17 f. The same observation is recorded in *Ronge's erste Rundreise zu den Christlichen-Catholischen Gemeinden Schlesiens, Sachsens und der Mark: Denkschrift für alle Christkatholiken bearbeitet von einem seiner Begleiter* (Breslau, 1845), p. 8.

the idea of political freedom could Christian love be realized. The historian Georg G. Gervinus was one of many intellectuals whose enthusiasm over the success of the Friends of Light and the German-Catholics led them to expect these popular movements to end the Catholic-Protestant split in Germany and thus prepare the way for national unification.[95]

On May 15, 1845, Wislicenus appeared before the general convention at Köthen and was greeted as a hero by some three thousand persons. Of course, Uhlich did not share the radical Hegelian views of Wislicenus. But there were several reasons why the more cautious Uhlich, in presiding over the meeting, could not explain his disagreement with the admired hero of the day. First of all, Uhlich and his followers were aware of the need for unity in the movement; especially in view of the increasing attacks of the Hengstenberg faction, they could not afford to antagonize possible friends and sympathizers of Wislicenus. Stating that the defense of the right of freedom of conscience and expression did not mean identification with the increasingly radical views of their Hegelian colleague could have resulted in an immediate crisis, and could have wrecked the precarious "united front" of the Friends of Light. Overwhelmed by the tremendous reception given the author of *Scripture or Spirit?* (whom the mass rally welcomed as "one of us"), Uhlich chose to demonstrate the unity of the movement by joining in the hero worship.[96] But it was obvious that a serious crisis could not be avoided in the long run, and that a showdown between the moderately inclined conciliatory elements and the irreconcilable radicals could not be postponed indefinitely.

The Hengstenberg faction was infuriated by the fact that the leaders of the Friends of Light not only welcomed but actually

95. Arnold Ruge, "Drei Briefe über die deutsche religiös-politische Bewegung von 1845," in his *Gesammelte Schriften* (Mannheim, 1847), IX, 340; L. Uhlich, *Die Throne im Himmel und auf Erden und die protestantischen Freunde: Eine Erörterung, Zunächst den Lenkern von Staat und Kirche* (Dessau, 1845), p. 7; Theodor Mundt, *Der heilige Geist und der Zeitgeist: Zwölf Capitel den Reformfreunden auf katholischem, protestantischem, und jüdischem Gebiet gewidmet* (Berlin, 1845), p. 45; Georg G. Gervinus, *Die Mission der Deutschkatholiken* (Heidelberg, 1845), pp. 1–3.

96. *Der freie Verein der protestantischen Freunde und seine Widersacher vor dem Richterstuhle des deutschen Volkes: Zur Erinnerung an die Versammlung protestantischer Freunde zu Cöthen am 15. Mai 1845* (Dessau, 1845), p. 4, and K. Zimmermann, "Rückblick und Vorblick," *AKZ*, 1846, pp. 1–9, 17–22.

organized popular mass support for their cause. Reporting the Köthen convention in the *EKZ,* the "true believers" charged that Uhlich and his colleagues were responsible for "exciting the masses to overthrow the Protestant Church," "challenging *every* divine and worldly authority," and trying to "intimidate the government agencies with masses of people (*Menschenhaufen*)." [97] The government was also alarmed when its officials reported from all over the kingdom that by 1845 the movement of the Friends of Light had become the meeting ground for all those forces that opposed the autocratic order and rejected the system of arbitrary government:

> Rationalists, followers of Schleiermacher, Young Hegelians, Young Germans, liberals of all shades; the discontented and those eager for action; brave, peaceful townsmen and revolutionary demagogues; theologians, scholars, literati, publicists, officials, landowners, and merchants.[98]

In the months after the convention there was a wave of meetings organized by the Friends of Light. Uhlich was invited to every part of the country. On July 30 he addressed a meeting of more than six thousand persons at Breslau. In this province where the German-Catholic movement was particularly strong, Uhlich declared that the terms "Protestant Friends" (or Friends of Light) and "German-Catholics" could be applied to "all those who believe in a free church based on a free constitution, and in freedom of conscience and expression." "Because we are free men who want no dogmas and no symbols, we want emancipation from the chains of authoritarian belief," he declared, and concluded with these words: "In short, we want freedom." [99]

97. "Über die Versammlung der soi-disant protestantischen Freunde zu Cöthen den 15. Mai 1845," *EKZ,* 1845, p. 550, and 1846, p. 28; emphasis in original.

98. Rosenberg, "Theologischer Rationalismus," p. 533. Karl Bernhard Hundeshagen, a moderately liberal theologian from Hesse, was greatly impressed with the success of the Friends of Light in attracting Germans from all walks of life to their meetings. See his anonymously published *Der deutsche Protestantismus: Seine Vergangenheit und seine heutigen Lebensfragen im Zusammenhang der gesammten Nationalentwicklung beleuchtet von einem deutschen Theologen,* 3d ed. (Frankfurt am Main, 1850), pp. 376 ff. (The first edition was published in 1846.)

99. L. Uhlich, *Vortrag bei der Versammlung protestantischer Freunde in Breslau am 30. Juli 1845* (Breslau, 1846), p. 4. See also C. H. Krause, *Die protestantischen Freunde und ihre erste Hauptversammlung in Breslau* (Breslau, 1845), p. 9, and *AKZ,* 1845, p. 1290.

Halle had been a center of agitation for the cause of the Friends of Light since the founding of the movement in 1841. Although Wislicenus, Haym, Max Duncker, Karl Schwarz, and other intellectuals connected with the liberal clerical group did not have the popular appeal of Uhlich or König, they were able to attract a small following of handicraftsmen and merchants. In comparison with other branches, however, the Halle Friends of Light remained an academically oriented group whose meetings and discussions were often conducted on a philosophical-theoretical plane.[100] Uhlich, an infrequent visitor to their gatherings, felt that many in the audience understood little of the arguments presented by the speakers, and apparently was himself rather uncomfortable with the Halle group. He was particularly disturbed by the suggestion of Baltzer and Wislicenus that the leaders of the Friends of Light should resign their positions in the state church and become leaders of "free congregations."

On August 10 the Prussian government banned any further meetings of the Friends of Light on the grounds that they had become mass gatherings (*Volksversammlungen*) subversive to the existing order.[101] Baltzer, Wislicenus, and other radically inclined clergymen were now further strengthened in their belief that the institutional framework of the state church was actually an impediment to the attainment of their political goals.[102] Uhlich, König, and Sintenis, on the other hand, continued to insist that their positions helped them to work for the realization of their goals in the church.[103] König, however, suffered a heart attack in the autumn of 1845 and was incapacitated until his death in 1847, and Sintenis became so concerned with maintaining his clerical position that he began to restrict his activities to the writing of anonymous pamphlets. Thus Uhlich found himself the main active representative of those rationalist pastors who still hoped that their aims could be realized within the state church.

In June, 1845, the large congregation of the St. Catherine Church at Magdeburg invited Uhlich to become their pastor and

---

100. Haym, "Protestantische Freunde," pp. 824 ff.
101. The order is printed in *AKZ*, 1845, p. 1248.
102. Wislicenus, "Vorwort," *Reform*, 1848, pp. 1 f.
103. Uhlich, p. 114; König, *Der rechte Standpunkt*, V, 3 f.; Nigg, *op. cit.* (n. 3 above), pp. 86 f.

requested the Consistory to permit his transfer. In order to obtain the consent of the Consistory, Uhlich promised to devote all his time to pastoral duties in the service of his congregation. Soon after his arrival in Magdeburg, Uhlich organized weekly devotional meetings in the spacious yard of the parish house. But when the meetings began attracting several hundred people, who gathered in the street facing Uhlich's house, the police instructed him to discontinue the practice and warned him to restrict his activities to pastoral work. The police order stated: "The devotional meetings have developed into popular mass meetings in which polemics, agitation, and excitement have replaced edification." [104]

Energetic and tireless, Uhlich was nevertheless determined to express his views and to exert his influence in every possible way. When Frederick William IV called the first General Synod of the Protestant state church, in 1846, Uhlich objected publicly to the fact that members of the assembly were not elected by the congregations but appointed by the government. In several pamphlets he also criticized the proposed new declaration of faith for clergymen because it did not recognize the principle of change and progress. He continued to omit the Apostolicum in the church services, or else simply read it after announcing: "The old confession of faith of the Christian church reads . . ." In response to the charges of the Hengstenberg faction that he and other rationalist pastors failed to adhere to their clerical oaths, Uhlich stated flatly that they had never subscribed to a literal interpretation of the oath.[105] Toward this problem the attitude of Uhlich and other rationalist pastors was in keeping with the opinion of the old Burschenschaftler, Wislicenus. According to their interpretation, oaths sworn before officials were not binding on men who refused to accept the legitimacy of the autocratic government. As young students, Wislicenus and other Burschenschaftler had not hesitated to deny under oath their membership in the subversive student unions. The teaching of Wegscheider at Halle also strengthened the rationalist belief that there was no contradiction in holding certain views and performing the official duties of an "ecclesiastical officer." Uhlich openly admitted that

104. H. Eltester, *Über die amtlichen Verhandlungen betreffend den Prediger Uhlich zu Magdeburg* (Berlin, 1847), p. 16.

105. *EKZ*, 1846, p. 831; L. Uhlich, *Über den Amtseid der Geistlichen* (Leipzig, 1847), p. 3.

he had always endeavored to realize a more comprehensive and liberal conception of his profession. At the same time, he rejected firmly the urging of Wislicenus, Baltzer, and other "radicals" that he give up his position in the state church and join them in organizing "free committees of free Protestants." [106]

Uhlich's differences with the radicals encouraged the Hengstenberg faction in its demand for the dismissal of clergymen who refused to abide by the regulations of the state church as prescribed in the Agende. The *EKZ*, in an open letter to Uhlich, announced:

> The time has come for the leader of the so-called Friends of Light to decide . . . whether he should repudiate the "dragon's seed" of rationalism and become a faithful official of the Protestant Church . . . or continue on the path of defiance to divine and temporal authority . . . and thus join [his] friends Baltzer, Wislicenus, and other subversive individuals.[107]

The faction was now determined to demonstrate its influence by bringing about the removal of Uhlich and other clergymen who continued in their refusal to comply with the Agende. Uhlich's call to the St. Catherine congregation had been approved because of the concern of the provincial governor, Karl von Wedel, over the threat of civic disturbances in Magdeburg. Incensed by the "soft" attitude of Wedel and foreseeing the results of the appointment, Hengstenberg and the Gerlachs within a month persuaded Minister Eichhorn to appoint K. F. Göschel, a Pietist jurist and friend of Ludwig von Gerlach in the Ministry of Justice at Berlin, as president of the provincial Consistory at Magdeburg. Göschel's position was strengthened by the fact that for the first time a president of a provincial Consistory was given power to appoint or to dismiss clergymen. This change, which was made applicable throughout the country, deprived provincial governors of their authority in matters affecting personnel of the state church and made the presidents of Consistories directly responsible to the central government in Berlin. Despite Uhlich's evidently enormous popularity in Magdeburg, in January, 1846, Göschel decided to conduct an official investigation

106. L. Uhlich, *Zehn Jahre in Magdeburg, 1845–1855* (Magdeburg, 1855), p. 17; *Mitteilungen in Sachen des Predigers Uhlich in Magdeburg: Zur Vervollständigung der vom Konsistorium herausgegebenen Verhandlungen* (Magdeburg, 1847), pp. 6 ff.
107. *EKZ*, 1846, p. 894.

of the man who was now one of the living symbols of open defiance to the government and a popular hero all over Germany.[108]

Encouraged by his great popularity and embittered by the vicious attacks of the Hengstenberg faction, the essentially conciliatory and cautious Uhlich was gradually transformed into a fighter who boldly challenged the authority of the Consistory and its Pietist president in matters of free conscience. In a dramatic Reformation Day sermon on October 31, 1846, before a capacity crowd in the St. Catherine Church, Uhlich announced his refusal to submit to an official investigation by repeating the words of Martin Luther: "Here I stand, I can do no other!" [109] Forced into awareness by the uncompromising attitude of the Pietists, he recognized that the issue of obedience to the government could not be evaded forever and that the time had finally come for him to stand up and face the consequences of his position.

For a year the Consistory pressed Uhlich to modify his views and in particular to include the Apostles' Creed in the Sunday liturgy and in the baptismal ceremony. On January 14, 1847, Uhlich wrote to his friend Ludwig Engelke in Halle:

> I am fighting and I will continue fighting. . . . I am told that I shall be dismissed by the government in this year. . . . The whole Consistory and Göschel in particular concentrate their attacks on me. . . . But what encourages me is the fact that *I am not alone in this struggle.* . . . The governing committee of my congregation, the city council, the whole city, public opinion, and my clear conscience . . . all help me in the fight. . . . I am prepared for everything. . . . Only God knows what will happen.[110]

Flatly refusing to cooperate in the official investigations, Uhlich denounced the *EKZ* for its biased and inaccurate reporting of the meetings of the Friends of Light and in a letter to Hengstenberg accused him of being directly responsible for the government's action

---

108. See *Realencyklopädie für protestantische Theologie und Kirche,* 1st ed. (Leipzig, 1854–1865), XIX, 567–572.

109. "Die Antireformation in Magdeburg," *EKZ,* 1846, p. 66.

110. Printed in *Das Ketzergericht zu Magdeburg: Nebst vollständiger Mitteilung aller der Stellen aus Uhlich's Schriften welche nach dem Urteil des Konsistoriums zu Magdeburg Ketzereien enthalten, Beleuchtet von einem Geistlichen* (Leipzig, 1847), p. 16; emphasis in original.

to prohibit the gatherings as "tumultuous assemblies of unruly and riotous mobs" that were creating a revolutionary situation. On the contrary, he insisted, the Friends of Light were conducting orderly conferences of responsible citizens interested in the welfare of their country.[111]

In the course of the year large segments of the population of Magdeburg repeatedly expressed their support for Uhlich and his cause.[112] Overwhelmed by so much loyalty, Uhlich seemed to forget his previous cautious and evasive tactics. Because he had also become a strong advocate of political rights for women, in February a rumor that he was to be dismissed resulted in a mass demonstration by hundreds of women in front of Göschel's office. One of the delegates reminded Göschel that the Consistory had no right to demand that Uhlich teach such dogmas as "eternal damnation, resurrection of the body, and other nonsense in which no peasant believes any more," and added: "Uhlich and we believe that God is a God of love who does not damn His children." [113]

The Consistory president told the women that as a clergyman of the state church Uhlich must adhere to the official creed or face the consequences of disobedience. When one of the women declared that most pastors in the province shared Uhlich's views, and asked why it was only Uhlich who was being investigated, Göschel refused to discuss the matter. He concluded by stating, quite correctly, that the government's instructions to him had emphasized the politically subversive influence of their pastor.[114] Except for the pious circle around Frederick William IV, Göschel's secular superiors in Berlin were not much concerned with the religious beliefs of rationalist clergymen, but were alarmed by the politically explosive implications of their views.

In September, Consistory councilor Hermann Wagener ordered Uhlich to defend himself against the charge of having violated his clerical oath before the investigating committee of the Magdeburg Consistory. Wagener was a close friend and associate of the Gerlachs and other Junker Pietists; in 1848 he became the editor of the

111. Uhlich to Hengstenberg, January 14, 1847, Hengstenberg papers, Box V.

112. "Protestation der Gemeindeglieder von St. Katharinen in Magdeburg," *AKZ*, 1847, pp. 1514–16.

113. *AKZ*, 1847, pp. 437 f.   114. *Ibid.*, p. 437.

Kreuz-Zeitung.[115] The indignant pastor, however, refused to appear before what he called a "court of inquisition." Consequently he was suspended from his office on September 13. Thus Uhlich was finally forced into a position where, if he was to continue his efforts, he would have to follow the advice of Wislicenus and Baltzer and try to form a separate "free congregation." Very few people believed the official announcement that the popular pastor had been suspended because of his creed. The *AKZ* pointed out that "countless clergymen" had the "same theological beliefs and convictions," and that Uhlich's expressing his views publicly in sermons and speeches was what many other clergymen were doing. The *AKZ* stated the general contemporary opinion by asserting: "Nobody can deny the political nature of Uhlich's open defiance of the government." [116] Apparently the real reason for suspending Uhlich was that he had propagandized his liberal views in such a dramatically effective way that his opposition and antagonism to the state institution of which he was an official could not be ignored.

König was no longer alive by the end of 1847, and Sintenis tended to withdraw from public life. Dulon had finally left the much-hated Prussian *Barbarenstaat* for the city republic of Bremen. Wislicenus, Baltzer, and other radicals were actively agitating for drastic changes in the political and social order. Uhlich, who had for years claimed intellectual freedom for clergymen in the state church, now faced the problem of how to organize an independent community of like-minded people under his leadership. Unlike Wislicenus, who was not interested in regaining his former position in the state church, Uhlich insisted on his right to be reinstated as a clergyman. In a final desperate effort to regain his clerical position, Uhlich sent a personal petition to Frederick William IV. When the king visited Magdeburg, in December, the city government produced more than 20,000 signatures supporting Uhlich's petition and urged that this most popular clergyman the city had ever had be returned to office. The pious head of state, however, refused to consider the case. In a long-winded lecture he reprimanded the city fathers for their recourse to popular pressure on the government

115. See Shanahan, pp. 196 ff.
116. "Die Suspension des Pfarrers Uhlich in Magdeburg," *AKZ*, 1847, pp. 1497–1504, and 1505–13.

and advised them to respect the authority and the decisions of their superiors.[117]

In November Uhlich had organized a separate congregation in Magdeburg, hoping that eventually he and his parishioners could rejoin the state church. Apparently most of his followers also hoped for a reconciliation between him and the Consistory, and were opposed to a permanent separation from the state church. Against that possibility there was the Hengstenberg faction's determination to impose its theological and political views on clergymen, and to prevent the reinstatement of Uhlich.[118]

In its report on Frederick William IV's visit to Magdeburg, the *EKZ* concluded that the king had acted correctly on the basis of divine authority—"which has more validity than twenty million signatures." Uhlich was portrayed as a slavish "follower" and not a "leader" of the people:

> The wishy-washy character of Uhlich's actions has determined his whole clerical career. . . . In his efforts to please the majority he has used the Apostolicum in Pömmelte (where people expected him to use it) . . . but when the mobs of Magdeburg insisted on a "rational" creed he contemptuously dismissed the officially prescribed creed because "enlightened people no longer believe in such nonsense." . . . He pretended to lead a movement . . . but in fact he became the mere mouthpiece of the ever-changing moods and wishes of majorities. . . . He relied on the influence of the masses and has openly challenged the government by declaring: "They will not dare to dismiss me." [119]

The *EKZ* was perfectly correct in its observation that Uhlich had become the spokesman for the aspirations and wishes of popular forces. But it was inconsistent in claiming that the liberal leader had "pretended to lead a movement." For years the Pietists had accused Uhlich of organizing meetings and inciting "ignorant mobs" to oppose autocratic government in church and state. Practically every issue of the *EKZ* since 1842 had recorded the untiring

117. *Ibid.*, p. 1607, and E. H. Sachse, *Erinnerungen an die Entstehung und Entwicklung der Magdeburger freien Gemeinde: Eine Festschrift zur Jubelfeier des 25-jährigen Bestehens derselben am 29. November 1872* (Magdeburg, 1872), pp. 6 ff.
118. *EKZ*, 1847, p. 986.   119. *Ibid.*, pp. 985 f.

efforts of Uhlich to increase the effectiveness of the Friends of Light by persuading people that the aspirations and interests of the movement were identical with those of the nonprivileged classes.

Threatened in their intellectual freedom and facing the possible loss of their positions as "ecclesiastical officers" of the state church, Uhlich and the other leaders of the Friends of Light started a movement that became a major rallying point for the various discontented elements in the German states. The historical significance of the Friends of Light was not only that they furthered and popularized theological liberalism in the Protestant church and among the religiously oriented elements in the urban populace.[120] Uhlich and his colleagues had awakened the formerly nonpolitical German middle classes to the fact that in order to realize their aspirations, interests, and hopes they would have to exert popular pressure on the government. The Friends of Light succeeded in establishing the channels through which they and also the formerly isolated liberal intellectuals could reach the broad segments of the population. From 1841 on, the rationalist pastors activated thousands of people in the German states and kept drawing their attention to public issues. The Friends of Light accustomed the population to mass meetings, demonstrations, and parliamentary discussions and proceedings, and thus made them conscious of their strength and indicated ways to make their will effective. These clerical leaders, in the guise of religious conviction, legitimized political expression.

Contemporaries were aware of the fact that with the coming of the railroad the conferences of the Friends of Light had tremendously promoted the development of German nationalism. People from practically all German areas and all walks of life—"Saxons, Prussians, Silesians, Franks, Swabians and other South Germans, Rhinelanders, people from Schleswig and Holstein, Protestants and Catholics, city people and farmers"—streamed to the meetings. They came together to "discuss common problems and make common decisions" not only as Prussians or Saxons but primarily as Germans. People felt that the mass gatherings organized by the leaders of the Friends of Light were essentially "German in their aims" and were "drawing people together as Germans." [121]

120. See Nigg, *op. cit.* (n. 3 above), pp. 176 ff.
121. *Die kirchlichen Bewegungen in Deutschland und die protestantische Conferenz zu Berlin: Eine Stimme aus Schleswig-Holstein* (Schleswig, 1846), pp. 30 ff.,

Through ceaseless agitation and appeals, clerical leaders like Uhlich contributed greatly to the development of an atmosphere of political unrest and of opposition to the governments of the autocratic German states and to the privileged elements of society on the eve of the Revolution of 1848. The leaders of the Friends of Light, as noted earlier, performed the historical function of transmitting the liberal movement of intellectuals to the "anonymous masses of the German people," thereby preparing the ground for the organization of a great liberal party in Germany. The split between the moderately liberal majority of the Friends of Light led by Uhlich and the radical, more democratically and socialistically oriented minority led by Wislicenus developed long before the revolution of March 1848. After the prohibition of their meetings in 1845, the Friends of Light became part of and merged with the general political movement agitating for the transformation of autocratic Prussia into a constitutional regime and for the abolishment of hereditary privileges.

and Carl Gottlieb Bretschneider, *Über die jetzigen Bewegungen in der ev. Kirche Deutschlands* (Leipzig, 1846), pp. 3–8.

Part Four
The Radicals

7

Disunity and Idealism
of the Leaders

The split that had been developing in the leadership of the Friends of Light since the Köthen convention in 1845 became an established fact during the first months of 1846. On January 16, Wislicenus published an open letter in the journal *Volksblatt für Stadt und Land* in which he explained his position. The occasion that prompted Wislicenus's action was the dismissal of Julius Rupp from his post as preacher to the troops—*Divisionsprediger*—at Königsberg in December 1845. As a career- and security-minded ecclesiastical candidate at the Wittenberg Seminary in 1831, Rupp had pretended to follow the Pietist "party line" in order to promote his chances for a clerical appointment.[1] When he was eventually appointed to the military position in his native city of Königsberg in 1842, he began to express his long-concealed opposition to the official creed of the state church and to cooperate with Jacoby and other local liberals in stirring up popular feeling for political and social changes in Prussia. In 1844 he led mass demonstrations in support of the

1. See above, p. 69. For Rupp's career as a religious and political leader see Carl Schieler, *Dr. Julius Rupp, ehem. Privatdozent, Oberlehrer, und Divisionsprediger zu Königsberg in Preussen und die freie religiöse Bewegung in der katholischen und evangelischen Kirche Deutschlands im 19. Jahrhundert: Ein Beitrag zur Kirchengeschichte des 19. Jahrhunderts* (Dresden, 1903), and Johannes Kissling, *Der deutsche Protestantismus, 1817–1917* (Münster i. W., 1917–1918), I, 206–211.

newly founded "Gustav Adolph Association," which he wished to develop into an "organization for the expression of the free spirit." [2] Isolated from the agitation of the Friends of Light in their main centers, Rupp's activities were confined to Königsberg. Late in 1845, apparently confident of wide public support for his criticism, Rupp openly challenged the authority of the government to enforce the official creed in a sermon delivered before hundreds of people. Because he persisted in omitting the Apostolicum from the religious services, Rupp was dismissed from his position in December 1845. The former preacher maintained, even so, that he still considered himself a minister of the Protestant church, which for him was a community of Christians and not an institution of the state.[3] Subsequently Rupp consented to his election as chief preacher of a free congregation (*freie Gemeinde*) organized by some of his liberal friends and supporters, who declared that people from all denominations and of various beliefs, including Jews and freethinkers, could take part. The announcement of the founding of the group in the local press made it obvious that the Königsberg liberals considered the venture an act of defiance against the government's dismissal of the popular clergyman.[4]

Although Rupp made it clear that he would continue performing the religious duties of a Protestant minister as he interpreted them, Wislicenus welcomed the opportunity to state publicly the views of the radicals on the nature of free congregations. In the open letter he explained that the radicals' ideology would not allow them to "work with a given existence and infiltrate the ideal into it." Rather, they wanted to "break with the past completely and

2. Haevernick to Hengstenberg, March 9, 1844, Bonwetsch, *Briefe an Hengstenberg*, p. 98. See also "Zur Charakteristic von Julius Rupp," *EKZ*, 1847, pp. 114–121, and Ferdinand Falkson, *Die liberale Bewegung in Königsberg, 1840–1848: Memoirenblätter* (Breslau, 1888), pp. 160 f. The "Gustav Adolph Association" was named after the Swedish king Gustavus Adolphus who in the Thirty Years' War was considered the main protector of the interests of German and other European Protestants fighting for religious freedom. The purpose of the association was to help German Protestants in predominantly Catholic areas who needed financial assistance to maintain their religious institutions. Money was regularly collected in the Protestant states for the purpose of assisting the Protestant Diaspora.

3. *Julius Rupp und das Königsberger Consistorium* (Königsberg, 1846), pp. 4 ff.; Julius Rupp, *Offenes Sendschreiben an Franz Schuselka* (Königsberg, 1846), p. 2.

4. *EKZ*, 1846, pp. 22–27, 846–848, and *Geschichte der Stiftung und Entwickelung der freien Gemeinde zu Königsberg in Preussen, in aktenmässiger Darstellung* (Königsberg, 1848), pp. 4 ff.

replace it with something new." Wislicenus—expressing a view shared by Baltzer, Dulon, and some other radicals—wanted to displace categorically the "given forms of existence at the behest of an uncompromising ideal and its requirement of an absolutely conformable reality." In other words, the free congregations must become new "islands of freedom for all like-minded individuals." The more such congregations could be organized, the faster would be the process of replacing the old institutions and ways of life with new ones.[5]

The dismissal of Rupp was taken by the radicals as clear proof that "independent minds" could not possibly remain in the state church. Hailing the establishment of Rupp's free congregation, Wislicenus set out to explain the radical view as to how such communities should function and what the role of their leaders should be. In the first place, stated Wislicenus, the free congregations would not be religious organizations at all, but rather political associations of like-minded persons. There would be no need for church buildings, because meetings would be conducted in large auditoriums and halls. Instead of enduring long, boring hymns and officially prescribed liturgical ceremonies, members of the groups would sing songs that inspired them to action and discuss contemporary problems that concerned their everyday lives and interests. Podiums, desks, tables, and chairs would replace the altars and pews of former times. The leadership of the free congregations was not to be formally concentrated in professional ministers forming a distinctive clerical status group (*Predigerstand*), set off from the "ordinary" membership. Professional clergymen with permanent tenure for life would be replaced with "speakers" (*Sprecher*). Like the other officeholders, speakers would be elected for specific terms only. Such moderate liberals as Uhlich and Sintenis insisted that clergymen who were dismissed from their clerical positions because they refused to accept the official creed still continued to be ministers of the "true church"—the invisible community of all Christian believers. But the radicals were not concerned at all with an "invisible

5. G. A. Wislicenus, "Offener Brief an den Herrn Subrector Wechsler in Königsberg," *Volksblatt für Stadt und Land,* January, 1846, no. 38, supplement. For a discussion of "moderate versus radical" see Krieger, *The German Idea of Freedom,* pp. 301 ff. For the contemporary appraisal of the "radical" approach see Fubel, "Protestantische Freunde," p. 861.

church" and were violently opposed to the officially established Protestant state church.[6] In the first issue of their journal, *Kirchliche Reform* (*KR*), Wislicenus as editor boldly announced, "Reform cannot come from above," and declared that only the people themselves, led by men of determination and firm convictions, could force the complete political and social reorganization of society. Proclaiming the radical view, "We live in an era of reform," Wislicenus called for drastic reforms in all institutions of the country.[7]

Wislicenus's radical ideas and proposals created a tremendous excitement in Prussia and the other German states. The popular hero of the Köthen convention, who had been acclaimed by thousands as "one of us," now shocked the great majority of the Friends of Light and their liberal supporters with his demands. It was soon apparent that except for a handful of like-minded rank-and-file pastors (such as the dismissed B. M. Giese of Arensnesta in the province of Saxony, who considered "speakers" of free communities the "democratically elected representatives of the majority,") [8] Wislicenus, Baltzer, and Dulon could not count on attracting a large following. In their impatience to introduce reforms in society the radicals seriously underestimated the religious, spiritual, and sentimental attachment of Germans to their historical development. Most people were shocked when the radical journal announced that the traditional old church services with their altars, liturgies, hymns, and ceremonies should be cast aside. While they might agree that "new battles require new flags whose signs and symbols must be evident to all the world, capturing the imagination of a new era," [9] they did not wish to repudiate their past completely.

After the dismissal of Rupp, Wislicenus was convinced that his own position as an "ecclesiastical officer" was not worth fighting for, and he no longer wished to remain a professional or lay member of the Protestant state church. He ignored the demands of the Consistory that he renounce his views, and did not even bother to announce his resignation from his position as pastor of the Lauren-

6. See the article by Friedrich Valtzer, "Die Stellung des Geistlichen in der Gemeine," *Kirchliche Reform*, 1846, pp. 1–7; hereafter cited as *KR*.

7. "Vorwort," *KR*, January, 1846, p. 1.

8. B. M. Giese, *Bekenntnisse eines Freigewordenen, mit besonderer Beziehung auf Kämpfes Beantwortung der Uhlich'schen Bekenntnisse* (Altenburg, 1846), p. 9.

9. Wislicenus, "Wiederherstellung der Augsburger Confession," *KR*, January, 1846, p. 23.

tius church in Halle. When, on May 28, 1846, Wislicenus was officially notified of his dismissal, he actually welcomed it. Unlike Uhlich, who tried desperately to retain his position in the state church, Wislicenus welcomed his freedom of action to organize the new communities that he wished to use as models for a new society of justice and equality.[10]

Less than a year after the dramatic public demonstration of the "united front" of the Friends of Light leadership at the general convention at Köthen, the radicals decided to separate themselves not only from the state church but also from their moderate colleagues, friends, and sympathizers. Such prominent members of the original Halle group supporting the cause of the Friends of Light as Haym, Duncker, and Karl Schwarz agreed with Uhlich and many other liberal clergymen that what the radicals proposed was no longer a liberal Protestant church but a democratic and even socialistic society based on majority rule. In April, shortly before Wislicenus's dismissal, the leading members of the Halle branch of the Friends of Light met. After a stormy discussion the moderates and the radicals finally separated, and "those who no longer belonged together" decided to go their separate ways. According to Haym, who was one of the main participants, only a small minority joined the "adventurer" Wislicenus to "make the leap into emptiness with their leaders." [11] The general liberal opinion seemed to be that Wislicenus could no longer claim to speak for the aspirations of the broad segments of the nonprivileged middle classes. Henceforth he could only hope to attract isolated and embittered radical intellectuals who claimed to represent the interests of the increasing numbers of that new element of society which Marx and other socialists called the proletariat and which was trying to make a place for itself in the changing society of the late 1840's.[12]

Wislicenus was aware of the difficulties that lay ahead of him and his supporters, but he was determined to continue along his chosen path. His ancestors had suffered because of their commitment

10. *Die Amtsentsetzung des Pfarrers Gustav Adolf Wislicenus in Halle durch das Konsistorium der Provinz Sachsen, Aktenmässig dargestellt* (Leipzig, 1846), pp. 3–5; hereafter cited as *Die Amtsentsetzung.*

11. *Erinnerungen,* pp. 165 f., and his "Protestantische Freunde," pp. 836 f.

12. See Conze, "Vom 'Pöbel' zum 'Proletariat,'" pp. 33 ff.; Hamerow, *Restoration,* pp. 75 ff.

to religious freedom; they had left their native Hungary as martyrs of the Habsburg persecution of Protestants. Their descendant Gustav Adolf Wislicenus now not only claimed religious and intellectual freedom, but also demanded the reorganization of society and the emancipation of man from economic deprivations. The fact that he was responsible for providing for a family with seven children and still had the courage to give up security as a clergyman of the state church earned the respect and even admiration of all who knew him. His former associates and friends as well as his most determined enemies had to admit that Wislicenus was a man of firm convictions and determination who could never compromise on basic issues. At the same time, his lack of willingness to accommodate his ideas to the ways of thinking of other persons resulted in the alienation of some of his most sincere friends and followers. He had not consulted anyone at the time of publishing his open letter in a journal. He stubbornly refused to listen to the advice of admirers and friends that he not take the final step of organizing "free congregations" and make any future reconciliation with the government impossible.[13]

At a meeting of sincerely devoted associates and friends from Halle, Magdeburg, and Berlin in the familiar railroad restaurant at Köthen, in June, Wislicenus refused to reconsider his position. When he was asked to remain faithful to his old liberal Friends of Light comrades, he declared that he could not be faithful to them without being unfaithful to himself and his convictions. He did not share their optimism that there was hope for gradual improvements in church and state in the near future. After the meeting Haym commented sadly that apparently Wislicenus had decided to sacrifice himself for a lost cause. Thus, at a time when the increasing poverty and desperation of the Hungry Forties were instilling in some segments of society a deep bitterness and hostility to all propertied classes, Haym expressed the reluctance of the liberals to force the government to take drastic actions against themselves. Having cooperated with Wislicenus for years, Haym and his fellow liberals hoped that their friend would soon rejoin them and repudiate his radical ideas. Haym suggested that perhaps it was due to the influence of Baltzer that Wislicenus had departed from their ranks. In

13. Haym, "Protestantische Freunde," pp. 837 ff.

their discussion the liberals considered the possibility that the government would put an end to the radical agitation of Baltzer and his followers in Nordhausen, and that Wislicenus would again have a "mighty following" and not aspire to lead tiny groups of radicals intent on a socialistic reorganization of society.[14]

In announcing the decision of the Consistory, the official statement declared that Wislicenus's dismissal was "strictly a legal question" concerning his failure to fulfill the duties of a government official.[15] Apparently the Consistory based its decision on the policy of the "Christian-German" regime of Frederick William IV to compel clergymen to accept the official creed. Wislicenus, in admitting openly that compliance with church and government regulations was impossible for him, charged that these regulations ignored the "development of modern science," and declared that he was determined to continue on the path of what he considered the "inevitable progress of humanity toward a just social order."[16] Although aware of his isolation from the main stream of the liberal opposition, he was confident that the new radical movement he was seeking to organize would develop into a strong and significant political force. To this end, he tried to enlist the support of like-minded radicals of various backgrounds. He particularly welcomed the cooperation of the Jewish freethinker and writer Rudolph Benfey, who urged Jews to unite with Christians in the new movement for the emancipation of man. Wislicenus joined Benfey in assuring Jews that the free community was not a "Christian society," in which the Jews would have to be baptized. On the contrary, these groups could provide the best organizational framework for enlightened individuals from all walks of life and from various religions and racial backgrounds who believed in the "gospel of humanity."[17]

Another enthusiastic supporter of the idea of building "islands

14. *Ibid.*, pp. 839 f.   15. The statement is printed in *Die Amtsentsetzung*, p. 90.

16. By "modern science" Wislicenus meant not only philological research on the Scriptures but also the theories of contemporary social thinkers. See his article "Meine Absetzung durch das Konsistorium der Provinz Sachsen," *KR*, September, 1846, pp. 20 ff.

17. *KR*, February, 1846, p. 31; Rudolf Benfey, *Die Stellung des fortgeschrittenen Juden zu der freien evangelischen Gemeinde* (Halle, 1846), pp. 2–4, and his *Die protestantischen Freunde und die Juden* (Leipzig, 1847), pp. 6–9. Also *EKZ*, 1847, pp. 62 f.

of freedom" through the organization of free congregations was Karl Theodor Bayrhoffer, professor of philosophy at the University of Marburg. A champion of the radical Left Hegelian position and a prolific writer on theological and political issues, Bayrhoffer was the leading organizer of the Marburg free congregation. He agreed with Wislicenus and other radical leaders that the officers of their new organization were "teachers and leaders," and that to them religion and prayer meant "searching and finding the true nature of things." Because some people tended to believe that the "free religious movement" of the Friends of Light was a "German Reformation of the nineteenth century," [18] Bayrhoffer set out to explain the essentials of the radical movement. Disassociating themselves from the liberal rationalist pastors of the Friends of Light, the radicals denied that the free congregations had any religious functions or aspirations. According to Bayrhoffer, the main goal of their movement was to "focus on worldly problems of this world." [19]

The writers Wilhelm Jordan and Robert Prutz were scolding Germans in the mid-1840's for their foolish absorption in religious problems when political and economic issues should demand their full attention. Prutz in particular was disgusted with what he considered the "religious masquerade":

> Our age offers no true homage to politics or literature, nor to trade or art. . . . The German is of more delicate stuff; he despises the common materialism of worldly interests, he turns his eyes upward to heaven, he abandons this world in order to reserve for himself in good time a secure and comfortable place in the next world. Theology—that is the true great concern of the day! The center of German life! The battle cry of parties! What of England and France? We have Uhlich and Hengstenberg! What of Russia and the closing of the Polish border? We have Ronge and the bishop Arnoldi of Treves! What of the Spanish marriage and the English customs tax? We have the Friends of Light and the German-Catholics. . . . The German constitutional question? We arrange for a General Synod. Commercial conferences? We go to Köthen. Interest in art and lit-

18. Very characteristic of this view of the Friends of Light movement are the reports printed in *The German Reformation of the 19th Century* (London, 1846).

19. See his *Das wahre Wesen der gegenwärtigen religiösen Reformation in Deutschland* (Mannheim, 1846), pp. 3–15, and *Das Verhältnis der Lichtfreunde zu der protestantischen Kirche: Eine Erklärung* (Offenbach a. M., 1846), p. 4. Also *KR*, February 1846, p. 32.

erature? We dispute the merits of the Trinity. . . . Here we have in sum the national interests of the German people in the years 1840 to 1845: the red thread which marks its way through the confusion of these years is spun of spiritual wool. Dogma is our *contrat social,* clergymen are our folk heroes, theological questions are the questions of the moment, the questions of the nation.[20]

Prutz also denied the contention of Ruge, Gervinus, Mundt, and other enthusiastic supporters of the Friends of Light that the kind of mass movement created by Uhlich and his clerical following contained the germ of a political and social revolution.[21] Prutz exclaimed: "We conduct politics as we hold Friends of Light, Pietist, and German-Catholic meetings—why not politics as politics? Why don't we stop this whole religious masquerade, cast off the theological cowls, and freely, with open minds, look the problems of the times in the eye?" [22]

The radical leaders did not need the encouragement of Jordan, Prutz, and other critics to abandon theology for politics. Wislicenus and his movement were deeply involved in plans to change drastically the political and social structure of German society. Rudolf Haym expressed the view of the Halle liberals who, because they were opposed to the socialistic ideas expressed in the *Kirchliche Reform,* were hostile to Wislicenus's organizing of "free congregations." But Haym and his colleagues had also arrived at the conclusion that clerical leaders should concentrate on the political

20. Prutz, "Theologie oder Politik?" pp. 13 f. By "English customs tax" the author apparently meant the protective tariff on imports of grain, which was repealed in England in 1846. The reference to Bishop Arnoldi is in connection with the display at Treves in 1846, of what he claimed was the "Holy Coat of Jesus." Many thousands of Catholics made the pilgrimage to see what the bishop claimed was the garment worn by Christ before his crucifixion. The controversy over the unauthenticated relic gave rise to the German-Catholic movement. The phrase "the red thread" is used to emphasize the conspicuous persistence of a particular attitude (in this case the spiritual tendency in German culture). See also Wilhelm Jordan, *Ihr träumt! Weckruf an das Ronge-berauschte Deutschland* (Leipzig, 1845), pp. 3 ff., chiding the Germans for their preoccupation with the religious aspects of the German-Catholic movement.

21. A. Ruge, "Drei Briefe, über die religiös-politische Bewegung von 1845," *Gesammelte Schriften* (Mannheim, 1847), IX, 336–340; G. G. Gervinus, *Die Mission der Deutschkatholiken* (Heidelberg, 1845), pp. 3 ff.; T. Mundt, *Der heilige Geist und der Zeitgeist* (Berlin, 1845), pp. 2 ff.; Gustav von Struve, *Briefe über die Kirche und Staat* (Mannheim, 1846), pp. 20 ff.

22. "Theologie oder Politik?" p. 50.

problems of the country; Haym thus voiced the opinion of many liberal intellectuals who had welcomed the Friends of Light but had grown tired of the religious terminology of the movement.[23]

Wislicenus and the other radical leaders were willing and most anxious to "look the problems of the times in the eye." In response to French reports in the *Revue Indepéndante* about the essentially political character of the Friends of Light, the *KR* tried to clarify the position of the radicals. Wislicenus agreed with the author of the article on "Les amis de la lumière"—Daniel Stern (probably a pseudonym)—that the "true essence of the struggle" in the German realms was the dissatisfaction of the people with autocratic government in both church and state. In short, the issues were "freedom versus arbitrary authority, free criticism versus blind belief." He warned, however, that such a statement as "the demand for religious freedom is merely a demand for political freedom" was an oversimplification and indicated ignorance of the religious traditions of the Germans. Not by direct revolutionary attacks upon the state, as suggested by the French writer, but by appeals to the religious-moral conscience of Germans would Prussia, and all Germany, be transformed into a free society. Thus Wislicenus made it clear that the strategy of his movement was to work for social and economic reforms and to assume that political reforms would inevitably follow. Hundreds, or possibly even thousands, of free congregations would have to be organized to serve as models for the transformation of the autocratic German states into a social republic of all Germans.[24] Baltzer, saying "This is what we want," agreed wholeheartedly with Wislicenus that only children should have a "fatherly government" (*väterliche Regierung*); adults must have a well-organized and responsible constitutional system of their own creation.[25] Baltzer and Wislicenus were united in their belief that the organization of free congregations was the best way to advance the cause of popular democracy and socialism.

Baltzer had been elected by the congregation and the city government of Nordhausen to become their chief preacher. The Consistory, however, would not confirm the appointment, because the radical minister stubbornly refused to abide by the official regu-

---

23. Rudolf Haym, *Die Krisis unserer religiösen Bewegung* (Halle, 1847), pp. 2 f.
24. *KR*, March, 1846, pp. 28 f.
25. "Der Kirchenstreit im Kanton Waadt," *KR*, May, 1846, p. 21.

lations of the state church. Baltzer decided not to wait until the government brought action against him, and on January 6, 1847, he resigned his position as assistant pastor in Halle. Simultaneously, he notified the newly founded free congregation of 160 persons at Nordhausen that he accepted the leadership of the group. He promised to make Nordhausen a model for democratic self-government.[26]

Rudolf Dulon had been stirring up popular sentiment for the cause of the Friends of Light in Magdeburg since moving to that city in 1843 as preacher of the German Reformed church there. He was no longer concerned with theological controversies. Under the influence of the Friends of Light, Dulon's attention was increasingly drawn to political issues. He became completely absorbed in a dedicated struggle for what he conceived to be the political and social rights of the common people,[27] and from January, 1846, to the end of 1847 he conducted an especially relentless campaign despite his poor health.

On February 18, 1846, German Protestants commemorated the three-hundredth anniversary of Martin Luther's death. In Saxony, the homeland of the Reformation, the occasion was a particularly important one and the citizens of Magdeburg turned out in large numbers to listen to the sermons of Dulon, Uhlich, and other clergymen who were known for their opposition to the increasing Pietist influence in the church.

Dulon's sermon, entitled "Luther's Heritage and Our Freedom," was based on the fifth chapter of Galatians, the first verse: "Stand fast therefore in the liberty wherewith Christ hath made us free, and be not entangled again with the yoke of bondage," and Second Corinthians, chapter three, the sixth verse: ". . . the letter killeth, but the spirit giveth life." So many people wanted to hear the fiery preacher that the doors of the church were kept open to enable the overflow crowd to listen. In this emotionally charged sermon Dulon demonstrated the talent for public speaking that in 1848 would make him the greatest popular orator of the revolutionary

26. *KR,* January, 1847, p. 40, and Eduard Baltzer, *Delitsch-Halle-Nordhausen: oder, Mein Weg aus der Landeskirche in die freie protestantische Gemeinde, Aktenmässig dargestellt* (Leipzig, 1847), pp. 12–14. Also *AKZ,* 1846, p. 806, and 1847, p. 112.

27. R. Dulon, *Gruss und Handschlag* (Hamburg, 1853), pp. 3 f.

movement in the free city of Bremen. No government, he declared, had the right to force "free Protestant clergymen to accept such doctrines as the sinful nature of man, the Trinity, and Redemption." Moreover, the government violated the old Protestant freedoms of conscience and belief when it supported the efforts of a particular faction to impose the Pietist creed. Denying emphatically the right of the government to decide theological disputes by fiat, Dulon advised clergymen: "If the authorities of the state church continue forcing you to accept theological dogmas in which you do not believe, [then] you cannot . . . and must not . . . remain the officials of the church, which *does not deserve your services.*" [28]

There could be no doubt in the minds of his listeners that Dulon was attacking not only the imposition of an officially sanctioned creed for clergymen but also the very basis of the traditional political and social order in Prussia: loyalty and obedience to government authorities. Anticipating the Pietists' response to his attacks, Dulon defended passionately every man's right to develop and to perfect the freedom that Luther had secured for Protestants when he broke the tyranny of Rome. "Is it possible," he asked his audience, "that the educated men and women of our enlightened nineteenth century have not progressed in three hundred years to the point where they can decide for themselves the *true meaning of freedom?* Do they not know that they have a right to a dignified and decent existence as human beings?" Dulon's questions expressed clearly the radical notion that every individual had a right to decide the nature of his freedom.[29]

Like Wislicenus, Baltzer, and other radicals, Dulon not only denied the validity for all time of certain theological dogmas but, by implication, also challenged the unchanging, traditional authority based on divine sanction that the "Christian-German" government of Frederick William IV claimed as the source of its political and

---

28. In his *Luthers Nachlass und unsere Freiheit: Predigt am 18. Februar 1846 gehalten und mit einem Vorworte vom Lehren gemäss den Bekenntnisschriften* (Altenburg, 1846), pp. 4 ff.; emphasis in original.

29. *Ibid.,* p. 7; emphasis in original. For Dulon's role in the 1848 Revolution see Heinrich Tidemann, "Pastor Rudolf Dulon: Ein Beitrag zur Geschichte der Märzrevolution in Bremen," *Bremisches Jahrbuch,* 34 (1934), 201–260, and Friedrich Iken, *Die Wirksamkeit von Pastor Dulon in Bremen, 1848–1852* (Bremen, 1894), pp. 4–18. Also Fritz Fischer, "Der deutsche Protestantismus und die Politik im 19. Jahrhundert," *HZ,* 171 (1951), 486.

social power. The Magdeburg Consistory—alarmed by Dulon's views, his public agitation for those views, and what it conceived to be his subversive influence—sent a report about his activities to Eichhorn, who as minister of ecclesiastical affairs and education immediately instructed General Superintendent Möller to begin an investigation of the case. But the majority of the council of his church strongly supported Dulon and requested that he be granted a special leave of absence to recover from a very bad cold whose symptoms raised fears of tuberculosis. The Consistory granted the leave in the hope that Dulon would consider his responsibility to his large family, reconsider his views, and on his return avoid inciting the population with inflammatory sermons. Although Dulon refused to be bound by any promises to the Consistory, poor health prevented the resumption of his clerical duties before the first months of 1847.[30]

Wislicenus and Baltzer shared with Dulon the conviction that not only dissident clerical leaders but also the enlightened members of their congregations should be urged to sever their ties with the state church. Because the radicals did not think that the journal of the Friends of Light, *Blätter für christliche Erbauung von protestantischen Freunden,* could be used for the propagation of their movement, Wislicenus decided to publish a new periodical, the *Kirchliche Reform,* which appeared in January, 1846. As chief editor, he invited persons of radical views to contribute articles that would clarify their political, social, and economic ideas. Wislicenus stated in the *KR* that while he had tried in the past to steer the Friends of Light movement toward clearly defined goals, Uhlich and other vacillating leaders had deliberately avoided commitment to a clear and unambiguous course of action.[31] He did not seem to realize that part of the phenomenal success of the Friends of Light was due to the fact that they tried to appeal to all dissatisfied segments of society. By avoiding identification with any single group, such as clergymen, farmers, handicraftsmen, teachers, or civil servants, the moderate leaders could claim to represent the aspirations of all nonprivileged elements in the German states.

In September, 1846, a group of thirty-two men joined Wislicenus

30. Tidemann, *op. cit.,* pp. 176 ff.
31. "Meine Absetzung durch das Konsistorium der Provinz Sachsen," *KR,* September, 1846, pp. 20–28.

in founding the free congregation of Halle. In the request for official recognition of the new group by the city government, Wislicenus described the organization as a free social association open to all interested people. He carefully emphasized that the congregation was not a religious group, and that members were completely at liberty to follow the dictates of their consciences in matters of religion.[32] The recognition was granted and Wislicenus became the first elected speaker of the Halle free congregation and started a vigorous campaign to recruit new members. At the meetings, held usually on Friday evenings and Sunday afternoons, Wislicenus or one of the more articulate members delivered speeches on such topics as history and ethics, and on political, social, and economic problems. These were followed by open discussion of the issues that had been raised.

Although from the very beginning the free congregations had difficulties in attracting members in any considerable number, Wislicenus and the other radical leaders were not discouraged. They expected eventually to succeed in gaining the support of the non-propertied and distressed working classes and bringing them into the movement. The membership of the Halle group grew from the original 32 in September, 1846, to 50 by November, and to about 70 by March, 1847. The Nordhausen free congregation also had difficulties in substantially increasing its original membership of about 160.[33] The radical leaders insisted, however, that they were spokesmen for untold thousands of "proud workers whose pride [was] based not on the inherited blood of an ancestor and the undeserved grace of a king but on the accomplishment of work." [34]

The aggressive campaign of the KR for the promotion of socialistic ideas soon produced charges by the Hengstenberg faction that the radicals were "agitators, communists, and revolutionaries." But the bitter attacks of the EKZ on Wislicenus, Baltzer, Dulon, and other leaders of the radical movement merely drove these men to propose increasingly extreme solutions for the political, social, and economic ills of the time. The KR became an outspoken advocate of socialistic reforms, not only incurring the hatred of the conservatives

32. KR, October, 1846, pp. 35 f.
33. Ibid.: November, 1846, pp. 28–29; February, 1847, pp. 30 f.; March, 1847, pp. 1–22. Also EKZ, 1846, pp. 903 f.
34. See the anonymous article "Warum die Gegner über uns unwillig sind?" KR, June, 1846, pp. 1–6.

but also alienating the liberals, who were horrified to see their former clerical colleagues turn to socialism.[35] Addressing themselves to the burning issue of unemployment, the radicals boldly asserted the right of each individual to gainful employment. An anonymous article entitled "A Contribution to Answering the Question: How Does One Produce Bread? How Does One Create Work?" flatly stated that it was the duty of society to provide work for all. If the existing organization of the economy was unable to perform this function, then the government should see to it that large-scale public works were initiated to solve the problem of full employment. True Christianity, the article asserted, required that each able and willing man maintain his human dignity as a respected, productive citizen of society. Proper education would serve the purpose of encouraging people to participate in the economic development of their country, and would ensure cooperation between the social classes, but ultimately it was the duty of the government to force the rich, if necessary, to contribute to the welfare of the poor.[36]

Although the Halle free congregation consisted of only about seventy persons (among whom were several women and four Jews,) it was far from being a united group. It included distinct factions with different motives and goals. Some members had joined because of personal loyalty to and admiration for Wislicenus. Some were former supporters of the Friends of Light (such as the publisher Gustav Schwetschke in Halle) who continued to hope that eventually the Protestant church would allow freedom of creed so that they could rejoin it.[37] A significant faction was composed of some non-residents of Halle who lived in various parts of Germany and joined for the purpose of demonstrating their extreme resentment against the ruling authorities in the German states. Obviously, these men could not take an active part in the meetings of the free congregation in Halle. But they wrote letters and expressed their views vigorously.

---

35. *EKZ*, 1846, pp. 903 f., and 1847, pp. 62–64, 111 f.; H. A. W. Hieronymi, *Die Hegelianer als Lichtfreunde: oder, Zwei Dokumente der neuesten Marburger Kirchenphilosophie, beleuchtet mit dem Lichte des praktischen Verstandes und aus der Hegelschen in die gewöhnliche Deutsche übersetzt* (Darmstadt, 1847), pp. 4 ff. The article "Die Taktik der Antiprotestanten," *KR*, June, 1846, p. 31, was aimed at both conservative and liberal critics of the radicals.

36. "Ein Beitrag zur Beantwortung der Frage: Wie schafft man Brot? Wie schafft man Arbeit?" *KR*, September, 1846, pp. 1–7.

37. Haym, *Erinnerungen*, p. 164, and Wislicenus's "Kurze Nachricht über die freie Gemeinde in Halle," *KR*, March, 1847, pp. 1–22.

The declaration of intention that was required for membership provided a dramatic and demonstrative means of proclaiming their hostility to the status quo and the whole system which it represented. It was in harmony with this attitude that the lawyer Gustav von Struve, the outstanding leader of the political radicals in the South German state of Baden, had joined the free congregation as a corresponding member. Struve was convinced that all radicals in Germany should unite their efforts to promote the cause of a "free and democratic society." He had supported the German-Catholic movement in 1845, but had become convinced that the development of "islands of freedom" through the organization of free congregations would prove more effective for the realization of his goals.[38] Similar considerations prompted Dr. Friedrich Möller, a relative of the pious General Superintendent Möller in Magdeburg, to declare his membership. Having completed his university studies, Möller had abandoned the prospective security of a teaching career because he did not want to be bound by the rules and regulations imposed on civil servants. Subsequently he began studying medicine in the hope that his new occupation would allow him more freedom to participate in the "struggle for the rights of the common people."[39]

The most forceful faction in the Halle group, and the one that actually dominated it, was led by the radical Left Hegelians: Wislicenus, the Jewish writer Rudolf Benfey, and the theological candidate Karl Kleinpaul, who looked to the free congregations as the institutional expressions of the historical consciousness of the age. Kleinpaul, unable to obtain a position in Prussia because of his radical views, was glad to accept a post as pastor of a small working-class parish on the outskirts of Hamburg in January, 1847. Soon he joined forces with a Jewish merchant, Georg Fischel, to organize a free congregation there similar to the one in Halle.[40] Kleinpaul became an active leader of the movement and continued to cooperate with Wislicenus for several years. Benfey was a prolific writer and was also well known for his Friday evening lectures, in which he consistently urged a sweeping reorganization of society, "based on reason and justice."[41] The intolerant and forceful domination of the free

38. *AKZ*, 1847, p. 437.
39. *KR*, December, 1846, pp. 31 f.
40. *KR*, November, 1846, pp. 28 f.
41. See his article "Schelling und Hegel: oder Über das Verhältnis von Natur und Geist," *KR*, July, 1847, pp. 13–29.

community by Wislicenus and his radical colleagues resulted in the withdrawal of Schwetschke and his supporters in October, 1847.[42]

Baltzer, the leader of the free congregation at Nordhausen, declared himself in full agreement with the aspirations of the Halle group and urged Wislicenus to call for a "united front" of all radicals. The German-Catholic leader Ronge, in a sensationally revealing conversation with Kleinpaul in Hamburg, announced that the supporters of his movement shared the aspirations of the free congregations and would soon join them. The two men met in December, 1846, and Kleinpaul published contents of the conversation in the February issue of the *KR*. According to the report, Ronge freely admitted that he had started the German-Catholic movement for purely political reasons, and denied having any religious motivation in promoting it. He urged his followers to join the free congregations. He agreed with Baltzer that the terms "Catholic" and "Protestant" were meaningless in connection with the German-Catholic and Friends of Light movements and, to avoid any identification with religious aims, should no longer be so used. Both movements had been essentially political in nature and had used religious terminology in order to enjoy more freedom to propagate their political ideas. The moment of truth had finally arrived, he suggested, when the real goals of the radical movement could be declared. These goals were:

> *Raising the lower classes* by improving their standard of living and by assuring their equality with the propertied classes; making the government responsible for the support of the poor, sick, unemployed, and unfortunate; *assuring the dignity and equality of women* by extending political and social rights to the fair sex; the right of *trial by jury;* and the conduct of all governmental proceedings in public sessions and other "inalienable" rights.[43]

Obviously the radicals were more concerned with the economic and social problems of the Hungry Forties than were the liberals, whose main goal was to break the political domination of church and state by the conservative aristocratic and bureaucratic elements and their allies. While the liberals were fighting for a constitutional parlia-

42. *AKZ*, 1847, pp. 1342 f.

43. Karl Kleinpaul, "Die Stellung des Herrn Ronge zum Deutschkatholizismus," *KR*, February, 1847, pp. 11–15; emphasis in original. See also the comments of Balzer, *ibid.*, pp. 30 f.

mentary regime and for basic political rights, the radicals went further and demanded a government responsible for the economic well-being of its citizens. To the radicals, economic and social reforms were even more basic and certainly more urgent than political changes.

Ronge and Wislicenus soon realized they had made a serious error in publicizing the conversation. Ronge's admission of having organized the German-Catholic movement for political purposes, without any religious motivation, created a scandal and offended many of his old supporters who had sincerely regarded their demands for religious and political freedoms as being inseparable. After talking over the matter, the two men decided that Wislicenus should try to explain the conversation between Ronge and Kleinpaul so that Ronge would not be exposed as a cynical politician who had tried to deceive the government as well as his followers regarding the true nature of his movement. Consequently, Wislicenus published a lengthy article in the KR to make clear that Ronge's political ideas had developed gradually and that he could not have held such "progressive" views when he founded the German-Catholic movement in 1845.[44] But the fact remained that Kleinpaul had hurt Ronge and the whole radical movement by publishing the article. Instead of attracting new followers to the radical cause, Ronge had antagonized many of his old German-Catholic supporters.

The radicals were determined to carry their struggle for the realization of a "free and just social order" to the masses. In January, 1847, in the Vorwort of the KR, Wislicenus promised to clarify the goals of his movement in the forthcoming issues of his journal. He also expressed his willingness to pay some attention to the problems of the church. But he hastened to declare that he and the other radical leaders were no longer members of that state institution and hence could not participate in the struggle for reforming it. In concluding his article, Wislicenus declared that he would concentrate all efforts on building more free congregations. He denied that they were isolated from the main stream of German life, and asserted that in addition to the comparatively small number of official members of free congregations there were thousands who considered themselves members at heart.[45]

44. "Der Kleinpaul'sche Brief über Ronge," KR, March, 1847, pp. 28–32.
45. "Vorwort zum neuen Jahrgange," p. 2.

Actually, it was very apparent that the radicals represented only small groups of individuals who could no longer reach the masses. Wislicenus and his colleagues who had parted with the Friends of Light were no longer popular heroes. They were determined fanatics who tried desperately to recruit a following from the ranks of the suffering victims of the Hungry Forties. Like other socialistic groups, including that of the young Karl Marx, the Wislicenus socialists were officers without armies. In sharp contrast to Marx, Wislicenus was totally ignorant of the economic and social forces operating in the 1840's. He was unable to fulfill the promise of providing firm guidelines for his followers. He relied on Benfey and Kleinpaul to borrow some of the general ideas of other socialistic individuals and groups. Two months after his assertion that thousands of persons favored the free congregations, Wislicenus had to admit that the radical movement consisted of small groups "sailing upon the wide sea without a compass, searching for the land." Those who were afraid of the unknown, suggested the bitter and frustrated radical leader, should stay anchored safely in the port; the courage of a Columbus was required of those who would embark on the trip. The only consolation Wislicenus could offer was the hope that like Columbus they would eventually reach the shores of a new world.[46]

Wislicenus had been propelled to national renown because of his association with the popular Friends of Light movement. But by nature he was not a man for the masses. As the keen observer Rudolf Haym had noticed at the height of the success of the Friends of Light, Wislicenus was an essentially lonely man, an introvert; his dogmatism was based on deterministic Hegelian concepts.[47] While the *KR* tried to create the impression that its editor and his fellow radicals were leaders of the oppressed lower classes, Wislicenus occasionally admitted that their movement was unable to attract a popular following such as the Friends of Light had enjoyed. In issue after issue the journal urged like-minded persons to sever their ties with the church and join the free congregations. But the campaign to gain more members and supporters for the cause of their particular brand of socialism was an evident failure, and this fact further deepened the rift between the radicals and their former Friends of Light colleagues. Uhlich and the other liberal leaders at

46. *KR,* March, 1847, pp. 5 ff.
47. Haym, "Protestantische Freunde," pp. 811–813.

first simply ignored the appeals of Wislicenus, but later expressed open hostility to his movement and charged the radicals with having "betrayed the cause of [popular] freedom to the cause of intellectualism." In direct reference to Wislicenus's unwillingness to modify his stand on the inevitability of a future socialist society, the liberals concluded that he and his colleagues had "escaped one form of dogmatic orthodoxy only to fabricate another." The Halle free congregation was considered by the liberals "just another of those socialistic clubs" which were motivated by an unrealistic enthusiasm for equality (*Gleichheitsschwärmerei*) that could never be realized.[48]

Just as the pious Tholuck was forced to side occasionally with his rationalist colleague Wegscheider in opposing the theological radicalism of Bruno Bauer and David Friedrich Strauss, so the liberal Uhlich now joined Hengstenberg's *EKZ* in condemning the Wislicenus radicals. Uhlich and his followers accused Wislicenus of having sacrificed his role as a popular leader for the sake of championing the socialistic ideas of a small group of philosophers. The liberals expressed the disillusionment of all those who, having looked forward to the "creation of a popular force led by Wislicenus and other heroes of yesterday," now considered the radicals to have abandoned the popular will in order to create a discussion hall for science (*Disputiersaal der Wissenschaft*). Faced with the increasingly extreme views of the radical leaders, the Hengstenberg Pietists and the liberals seemed also to agree as to the subversive nature of the activities of Wislicenus and his associates.[49]

On March 30, 1847, the Prussian government issued a decree which sought to regulate the legal position of the free congregations by recognizing the right of secession from the state church of all those who refused to accept the officially prescribed creed and liturgy.[50] The decree, also known as the Edict of Toleration (*Toleranzedikt*), was not the result of any genuine belief in toleration as an ideal. Rather it was designed to purge one of the most crucial institutions in Prussia of all dissident elements and to deprive them of their right to be elected to civic offices. Uhlich and the other

48. Hieronymi, *op. cit.* (n. 35 above), pp. 14 ff., 67.
49. *Ibid.*, p. 7, and C. Zschiesche, *Die protestantischen Freunde: Eine Selbstkritik, Sendschreiben an Uhlich* (Altenburg, 1847), pp. 3 ff.
50. The text of the decree was printed in the *EKZ*, 1847, pp. 545–549.

liberal Friends of Light leaders sharply opposed the provision of the decree which declared that those who seceded were no longer members of the Protestant church. The Friends of Light contended that they considered themselves "members of the eternal and invisible Protestant church" despite the fact that they had ceased to belong to an organizational framework controlled by the conservative Pietists as the agents of the government.[51] On the other hand, so great was the contempt of the radicals for the Prussian state and its state church that for them secession according to the provisions of the decree was meaningless. Unlike Uhlich, Rupp, Sintenis, and their liberal colleagues and followers, the radicals were not concerned with the controversy about the "visible versus invisible Protestant church," which to them was ridiculous. Dulon declared openly that he was unwilling to accept the authority of the Prussian government to restrict his political rights. Consequently, in November, 1847, he left the "barbarous" Prussian realm and accepted a position as a preacher in the city republic of Bremen.[52]

On February 3, 1847, Frederick William IV called for the convening of the representatives of the eight provincial diets to the United Diet (*Vereinigter Landtag*) in Berlin on April 11. The people of Prussia, who had been promised a constitution in 1810, 1811, 1814, 1815, and 1820, looked forward to the meeting with hopes for political reforms. The gathering, however, was to be diluted in its authority by the definition of its right. The United Diet was to consist of two curial assemblies of locally selected individuals from the provinces, a noble curia of 72 high-ranking nobles and a curia of the three estates, made up of 231 locally selected nobles, 182 urban representatives, and 120 peasant representatives. The powers of this body were to be extremely limited. It was to have only consultative powers; its taxing power was to be limited to the imposition of new or increased taxes; and its approval for governmental borrowing was to be required only in peacetime. Addresses to the king required a two-thirds vote; sessions were to be secret, but stenographic reports of the meetings were to be published.

51. Julius Rupp, *Die Symbole oder Gottes Wort? Ein Sendschreiben an die evangelische Kirche Deutschlands* (Königsberg, 1847), pp. 4–7. Also the anonymous *Der protestantischen Freunde Wollen, Wirken, und Glauben* (Magdeburg, 1847), pp. 11–15.

52. Tidemann, *op. cit.* (n. 29 above), pp. 162 ff.

In opening the United Diet, in April, 1847, the king immediately disappointed hopes for a constitution: he declared that no written piece of paper was ever to come between him and God in order to govern the country with "its paragraphs" and thus supplant the "old fealty." Yet the United Diet was highly significant in that it provided a national assembly in which political figures from all over Prussia held extensive discussions on some of the major problems facing the country. There were extensive debates concerning finances, the privileged position of the army, civil rights, and the necessity for a permanent national representative body meeting regularly. The majority of the assembly consisted of the liberal opposition, led by the Westphalian Baron Georg von Vincke and the Rhenish merchants David Hansemann, Ludolf Camphausen, and Hermann von Beckerath, among others. To the amazement of many Germans, several members of the nobility cooperated with the liberal opposition in its demands for political reforms. Beckerath and Hansemann were joined by 158 colleagues in the diet in expressing support for the principle of absolute separation of civil rights from any requirement of membership in the Protestant or Catholic churches. Although Beckerath, Hansemann, and most of their liberal colleagues were bitterly opposed to the ideas of the radicals, the fact that Jews, as well as Protestant and Catholic dissenters, were ineligible for election to the offices of the diet outraged their sense of justice. Beckerath introduced a resolution in which he urged his colleagues to prove that they wished to establish "the Christian state not on the basis of outward appearances or formal creeds, but rather on the foundations of the spirit of Christianity." He urged the annulment of the discriminatory articles in the Edict of Toleration, as well as the law of 1823 governing the composition of the provincial estates, which limited eligibility for office to members of the Protestant and Catholic churches. Supporting Beckerath's resolution, Hansemann stated flatly: "One will desert a state in which one cannot participate in political rights." [53] This was, in fact, what Dulon and some others did when they left Prussia.

Minister Eichhorn defended the position of the government. He reiterated once again the theory of the "Christian-German state" as expounded by Frederick William IV and the Junker Pietists, who

53. Karl Biedermann, *Geschichte des ersten preussischen Reichstags* (Leipzig, 1847), pp. 181–187, 191.

identified political competence with religious orthodoxy and made membership in one of the two Christian churches the primary qualification for the enjoyment of civil rights. Supporting the government Count von Finckenstein contended not only that the enfranchisement of Jews would endanger the vitality of the Prussian state, but that dissenters who had left the Catholic and Protestant churches should never be allowed to hold public office. Beckerath's motion was defeated by a majority of 319 votes. Triumphantly, Finckenstein expressed the position of the Junker Pietists after the voting when he stated that the discriminatory clauses in the law constituted the basic foundation of the Prussian state without which the entire structure would ultimately collapse in ruins. The *KR* savagely attacked Finckenstein and his fellow conservatives for their views, and Wislicenus concluded that only desperate men facing an abyss could act in such a foolish way as the Prussian Junkers and their allies.[54]

The chief political struggle hinged on the financial laws that the government presented to the United Diet and that actually had been a major reason for convening it. Foremost was the wish of the government to have the diet assist in financing the railroad that was to connect East Prussia with Berlin. The government had embarked on preparatory work, since private capital had not been forthcoming for building the expensive line. On the crucial question of backing governmental expenditures, the diet refused to underwrite a guarantee of state loans for the eastern railroad as long as it was not itself assured of a permanent existence. Since its demand for regular meetings was turned down, it rejected by a large majority any state loans.

The United Diet was dissolved by the king in July. It had discussed a great deal; the mere fact that uncensored reports of its deliberations were permitted to appear in the press considerably increased the tempo of political life. But nothing was solved. Frederick William IV was disappointed but not worried. He greatly underestimated the effect that the crystallization of an inimical public opinion through an organ like the United Diet was bound to have on the German nation. Prompted by the revolution in Paris, the king in early March of 1848 granted permission for the United

54. *Ibid.*, p. 189, and Wislicenus's "Der Vereinigte Landtag über Religionsfreiheit," *KR*, July, 1847, pp. 26–35.

Diet to meet periodically. But this concession fell far short of the popular demands that had grown in the meantime and that were no longer concerned exclusively with Prussia. The liberal movement that suddenly enveloped all of Germany aimed at a modern constitution and a national state.

The liberals continued to be hostile to the attempts of Wislicenus and the other radical leaders to transform the free congregations into organizations for socialist agitation on the model of the Halle group. On the other hand, impatience was expressed with the continuation of theological controversies among some leaders of the Friends of Light and the German-Catholic movement. In taking this position, Rudolf Haym was representative of most liberals. He had arrived at the conclusion that one should concentrate on the political problems of Germany. "Politics alone" corresponded to the "demands of the time," he declared, because the "will and logic of history" demanded that "Germany should now enter the political age." [55] Haym and many similarly inclined persons believed that a constitutionally limited parliamentary regime for Prussia should be the primary goal. In sharp contrast, the radicals were convinced that only dramatic social and economic changes could solve the problems of their turbulent age.

It was apparent that the radicals had considerable difficulty in attracting followers to their free congregations. Both the liberals and conservatives charged that the Wislicenus radicals were confused intellectual dreamers paying little attention to pragmatic politics. Answering these accusations, Wislicenus declared in the *KR* that the free congregation represented the peculiarly "German practice" of politics, adapted to the special needs of the "German genius." [56] Thus he tried to draw a sharp line between the "French ways" of Proudhon and other French and some German socialists, and the "German ways" of the radical movement. Lacking the philosophical insights of a Proudhon or Marx, Wislicenus found it extremely difficult to explain his position. Apparently his background as a member of the Halle Burschenschaft continued to influence his thinking along nationalistic and idealistic lines. His democratic socialism tended to emphasize the peculiarly "German" problems

55. *Op. cit.* (n. 23 above), pp. 2 f.
56. "Über Prutz 'Die gegenwärtige religiöse Bewegung in Deutschland,'" *KR*, May, 1847, pp. 21–27.

of the proletarians, and conflicted sharply with the "scientific" international socialism of Marx, Engels, and their followers. Impelled by his characteristic dedication to the noble ideal of a "free and just German society," Wislicenus continued to proclaim the seemingly unrealistic hopes of his small socialistic group. In a dramatic appeal to philosophers, politicians, nationalists, socialists, and proletarians, he presented the free congregation as the ideal organization for realizing radicals' aspirations:

> Join us, you *philosophers* who believe that German philosophy has reached the stage of realizing itself; in the free congregation you will find ideal and reality combined! Join us, you *politicians* who favor freedom of the press; you will find freedom of speech and press in the free congregation! Join us, you *nationalists* who demand a unified Germany; we acknowledge no difference between Germans! Join us, you *socialists* who demand the raising of the proletariat to human dignity; we in the free congregation not only speak of brotherly love but have made it actual practice.[57]

In a series of special appeals, the radicals also implored Jewish citizens not to "ask" but to "fight" for political rights—and to fight by "attacking" the system that discriminated against them. All Jews should join the free congregations, declared Kleinpaul, because in those islands of freedom there was no difference between Jew and Christian.[58] The *KR* boldly announced: "It is our task to oppose and to destroy whatever needs opposing and destroying, so that we can prepare for the future society."[59]

Wislicenus insisted that his movement sought not only to improve material conditions for the workers but also to liberate them from ignorance and raise their moral and spiritual standards. The "true" socialists Moses Hess and Karl Grün joined the "scientific" Marx and Engels in denouncing the Wislicenus radicals for their concern with spiritual and moral improvement. Although an article in the *Trier'sche Zeitung,* the organ that Hess and Grün published in Treves in the Rhineland, praised Wislicenus as a "pure and noble" leader whose courage all socialists admired, it accused the

---

57. *Ibid.,* p. 23; emphasis in original.
58. Karl Kleinpaul, "Die Juden und die freie Gemeinde," *KR,* April, 1847, pp. 1–7.
59. April, 1847, p. 24.

radicals of ways of thinking characteristic of clergymen. Neither religious nor philosophical "ideas," but only material "facts" determined society, asserted the anonymous "true socialist" writer. Moreover, it was ridiculous for the free congregations to claim that they would build a peculiarly "German" socialist society based on the "German genius." Also it was absurd, he concluded, to expect philosophers, politicians, nationalists, and socialists to cooperate in the building of socialism: "What cheap and showy spiritual quackery (*geistliche Marktschreierei*)! One thinks he is standing in front of a market stall where everything is for sale at the same price." To add insult to injury, he asserted that the unctuous style of Wislicenus's journal reminded the reader of Hengstenberg's *EKZ*.[60]

Late in 1847 the *KR*, in an article by Wislicenus, replied to the criticism of the Treves journal and summed up the general position of the radicals. The article utterly rejected the notion that their thinking was dominated by theological and spiritual ideas. It insisted, however, that their brand of socialism considered both material and ideological factors crucial in human affairs. It also opposed the contention of the "true socialists" that only by revolutionary means could a new social republic be established. Wislicenus's sense of justice and feeling of compassion for the suffering proletarians of the Hungry Forties had influenced him to embrace an idealistic socialism. He was convinced that it was of prime importance to improve the material conditions of the lower classes. But he also insisted that it was necessary to implant an ideology of humanism in society. He firmly believed that the "Reformation of the nineteenth century" would transform the German states into a unified social republic without force and violence. "Only the power of the *spirit without force*" could bring about such fundamental changes, he asserted.[61]

There was a tremendous difference between the idealistic socialism of the Wislicenus radicals on the one hand, and the "true" socialism of Grün and Hess, and the "scientific" socialism of Marx, on the other. The *Trier'sche Zeitung* constantly scorned the Wislicenus group for failing to realize that they lacked means to satisfy the material needs of their members: they could not "fill the empty

---

60. "Die religiöse Bewegung und der Sozialismus," *Trier'sche Zeitung*, May 21, 1847, p. 2; this newspaper is hereafter cited as *TZ*.
61. *KR*, September, 1847, pp. 20–24; emphasis in original.

stomachs of Catholics, Protestants, and Jews" by "warming up and dishing out the old soup of Schleiermacherian pathos." Thus it was utterly utopian to assume that it was possible to prepare for a socialist republic in the free congregations.[62] Obviously, the failure of the contemporary utopian communities in the far-off United States was influential in convincing the "true socialists" that such schemes, presupposing the withdrawal of select individuals to live by themselves, revealed their promoters' lack of understanding of the problems of society as a whole in the slowly developing industrial age. In a characteristic statement addressed to the Wislicenus radicals, the Treves journal—vastly oversimplifying the turbulence of the age— summed up the historical materialism of the "true socialists" in the flat assertion that lack of food was the sole basis for the agitation and various manifestations of discontent in the 1840's. Fully accepting the Feuerbachian proposition that "a man is what he eats," the journal chided the utopian idealism of the radicals. Bread—meaning food in the broad sense—was everything: "Bread means religion—even Christ has declared bread to be his body; bread means ideas because all knowledge is concentrated on the problem of how to maintain life; politics means bread because only he who can secure a living is really free."[63]

Wislicenus did not think that "bread is the beginning and the end, the first and the last consideration man has." He wanted more than the improvement of material conditions of the proletariat. True, Christ had referred to his body as bread, but he had also called his body the "true bread . . . the bread of life," and had declared that "man shall not live by bread alone"; and thereby Wislicenus tried to clarify the position of his small socialistic group. He ignored the charges that his movement was still rooted in bourgeois concepts of Christianity, and to illustrate his commitment to spiritual and idealistic values he further quoted the founder of Christianity: "I am the bread of life: he that cometh to me shall never hunger; and he that believeth on me shall never thirst. . . . Whoso eateth my flesh, and drinketh my blood, hath eternal life . . . For my flesh is meat indeed, and my blood is drink indeed."[64] There could have

62. *TZ*, June 8, 1847, p. 1. See also Karl Marx, *Die Frühschriften* (Stuttgart, 1953), pp. 14 ff., and *TZ*, May, 29, 1847, p. 2.

63. *TZ*, May 23, 1847, p. 3.

64. *KR*, October, 1847, pp. 12–16; quoting John 6:32, 35, 54–55; Matt. 4:4; Luke 4:4.

been no more effective demonstration of the belief of Wislicenus and his fellow radicals that to them economic security meant only partial freedom. Their democratic socialism had much more in common with the ideal of the ancient Christian communities than with the type of society that the "true" and "scientific" socialists demanded.

Even so, disappointment in their hopes of attracting a large following finally persuaded the radicals that they should not restrict their activities to the free congregations. They realized that it was impossible to have "islands of freedom" when they were surrounded by a sea of hostility. In its December, 1847, issue the *KR* notified its supporters that beginning in January, 1848, the journal would be published simply under the title *Reform* and would be dedicated to the struggle for a just society. In an editorial of the January issue Wislicenus announced that as the church of the Middle Ages had aimed at influencing every aspect of society, so the radical movement was now reaching out to shape the social republic that would soon emerge in a unified Germany. He noted, further, that the Friends of Light movement had provided the necessary transition from the nonpolitical age to the new age of democratic socialism.[65]

The radicals were aware that it would be extremely difficult for them to attract masses of followers. In this respect the leaders of the free congregations were like the "true" and "scientific" socialists, who were meeting with no better result in their efforts to enlist the unemployed and miserable proletarians. But to the charges of the Hengstenberg faction that he and his colleagues were leading isolated small groups of "agitators, communists, and revolutionaries," Wislicenus stated indignantly that the goal of "democratic socialism" had nothing to do with "communism." [66]

The radical leaders were undoubtedly influential in diverting some of the energies of their supporters from purely theological and religious problems to secular ones. Stressing the notion that "God has loved the world" and urging Germans to concern themselves with the material conditions of life on earth, Wislicenus and his colleagues suggested an alternative to the Pietist emphasis on the God-given nature of the existing society. The radicals implored people to build a society of justice and urged them to work for a secular heaven on earth. Undoubtedly they speeded up the process of "turn-

---

65. "Der Sozialismus und seine Zukunft," *Reform,* January, 1848, pp. 29 ff.
66. *Ibid.,* p. 31.

ing the eyes of Germans from heaven to earth" and creating belief that a "just republic" could be brought into being.

The leaders and supporters of the free congregations felt that they were fighting for spiritual independence, rational justice, and political liberty. In their eyes, these causes were one. They by no means shared common political and social creeds; but, as Jacques Droz has pointed out, the free congregations "played a forceful and directive part in the democratic movement" of the 1840's and the revolutionary actions of the year 1848.[67] Whatever the difference in their concepts, these free congregations were one of the few links between the middle class and the working class, which the free congregations desired to gain for their cause, and in this way contributed to the union of the revolutionary forces, brief and temporary as that union was.

67. Jacques Droz, "Religious Aspects of the Revolutions of 1848 in Europe," in Evelyn M. Acomb and Marvin L. Brown, eds., *French Society and Culture Since the Old Regime* (New York, 1966), p. 139.

Epílogue

During the Revolution of 1848, the Protestant state church was a fighting instrument of the conservative reaction against the political opposition. Under the leadership of the Hengstenberg faction and the "small but mighty" clique of Junker Pietists, the conservative elements of the clergy engaged in a massive campaign to convince the population that the political upheaval was not only against the God-given order but also against God and religion. The newly founded *Neue Preussische Zeitung* (or *Kreuz-Zeitung*) joined the *EKZ* in the common effort to identify the revolutionary upheavals with an overall attack on the religious foundations of church and state. The Hengstenberg faction declared that the demands of the political opposition were based on disrespect for the will of God, and blamed the pernicious influence of rationalistic and Hegelian thinking for stirring up the mobs against "throne and altar." [1]

When under the impact of the dramatic events of the March days "the army was demoralized, the aristocracy grumbled and sulked, the bureaucracy could only whine," and Frederick William

---

1. Practically every issue of the *EKZ* in 1848 attacked the revolutionaries as godless and immoral rebels against the God-given order. For discussions of the Protestant conservative influence see Shanahan, pp. 192 ff.; Jordan, pp. 146 ff.; Jacques Droz, *Les révolutions allemandes de 1848* (Paris, 1957), pp. 504 ff.; and Walter Delius, *Die evangelische Kirche und die Revolution 1848* (Berlin, 1948). Ernst Schubert's *Die evangelische Predigt im Revolutionsjahr 1848* (Giessen, 1913) has a good selection of sermons attacking the revolutionary movement as the work of Satan. Tholuck's sermons are printed in his *Predigten über die neuesten Zeitbewegungen* (Halle, 1848).

IV was a "frightened middle-aged figure on horseback," [2] pathetically eager to conciliate the revolutionaries, the leaders of the conservative Pietists decided to join and lead the forces of the counterrevolution. Hengstenberg, Tholuck, Hahn, Kahnis, the Gerlach brothers, Thadden, Kleist-Retzow, and their pious associates and supporters at the royal court and in the clergy, the army, and the bureaucracy were determined to defend their privileged positions in the Prussian state. The army and the Protestant church proved to be particularly crucial institutions in the struggle to defeat the revolution. The church considered the revolution against the "God-given" order sinful and rallied to the defense of the monarchy. The army, although not "religiously minded," identified its interests with those of the autocratic regime. Each institution had its own motives, but each identified itself with the defense of the state of Frederick William IV.

Boldly announcing that they would fight for their "rights from above" against the "revolution from below," the Pietist Junkers and their allies in the Protestant clergy became the vanguard of the conservative counterrevolution. By the end of September, General Leopold von Gerlach and the other noble Pietists of the "Camarilla" were actually conducting the business of the government in the name of the stunned head of state.[3] Crucially influencing Frederick William IV and the army, the most decisive instrument of power in the Prussian state, the East Elbian squirearchy was also successful in enlisting the support of the Protestant church for its cause. For more than two decades the small but highly influential group of "awakened" Junkers had supported the Hengstenberg faction that by 1848 was exercising effective control over the clergy. Greatly strengthened by the infusion of non-noble talent within their ranks,[4] the Old Prussian aristocrats demonstrated the vitality, adaptability, unity of purpose, and esprit de corps of their class in opposing the liberal and democratic aspirations of the nonpriviliged elements of society.

2. Hamerow, *Restoration,* p. 174.

3. In fairness to Frederick William IV, it should be noted that *during the period of reaction* and in some respects he showed more determination than his conservative advisers. See Rudolf Stadelmann, *Soziale und politische Geschichte der Revolution von 1848* (Munich, 1848), pp. 145–150.

4. See Nikolaus von Preradovich, *Die Führungsschichten in Österreich und Preussen, 1804–1918, mit einem Ausblick bis zum Jahre 1945* (Wiesbaden, 1955), pp. 161 f.

The furious struggles between conservatives, liberals, and radicals in the Protestant clergy after 1815 had constituted a dress rehearsal for the Revolution of 1848. The issue of constitutional government versus autocratic rule had already been fought out and decided in one of the most crucial institutions of the Prussian state. The liberally inclined clergymen had become alarmed at the increasing radicalization of the Friends of Light movement. The turn of the Wislicenus radicals to republicanism and socialism, and their complete disassociation from traditional religion and the Protestant church, convinced most of the church liberals that their interests were more closely tied to the maintenance of the status quo than they had realized. In the face of the radical threat, the majority of the liberals in the Protestant church found themselves acquiescing in the conservative domination of the Prussian state and church, while hoping to realize some of their goals in the course of time.

In contrast to the "united front" of the conservatives, the disunity of the liberals and radicals was demonstrated by the great diversity of their political ideas, doctrines, and slogans during the revolution. Every shade of opinion was represented—from the democratic-socialistic republicanism of Wislicenus, Baltzer, Dulon, and other radicals to the constitutional monarchism of such former Friends of Light leaders as Uhlich, Haym, Duncker, and Karl Schwarz.[5] Not even on the crucial question of the separation of church and state were the liberal and radical leaders united. Their economic preferences ranged from the confused democratic socialism of Dulon and Wislicenus to the laissez-faire of such moderates as Nitzsch, Uhlich, Haym, and Karl Schwarz. Basically the disunity of the radical and liberal leaders seemed to conform to the nature of their theological and philosophical differences, and to their backgrounds and personalities.

As one of the delegates to the Berlin constitutional assembly in 1848, Uhlich joined those liberal politicians who voted in favor of a constitutional monarchy with a government responsible to the national legislature. The "Saxon O'Connell" denied any republican sympathies and openly repudiated his former sympathy with Wislicenus and other radical republicans.[6] Wislicenus and his friend

---

5. Droz, *Les révolutions allemandes*, pp. 529 ff.
6. See Leberecht Uhlich, *Die Novembertage in Berlin und Brandenburg, Zugleich ein politisches Bekenntnis: Dokumente zur Revolution von 1848* (Magdeburg, 1848), pp. 3 ff.

Robert Blum were among the most active members of the Frankfurt Preparlament, and Wislicenus was elected chairman of the Halle "Democratic People's Association." In October, Wislicenus represented the association at the second "Democratic Congress" in Berlin, where he aligned himself with the socialist left wing. He was among the most violent republican opponents of the draft constitution worked out by the Frankfurt Parlament, in which Ruge and Blum joined the other radicals in opposition to the liberal majority of that assembly. Rudolf Dulon welcomed the Revolution of 1848 as the "work of God" and became the leader of the democratic government in Bremen that administered the city for several months.[7]

Having purged the Protestant clergy of its openly dissident leaders and having neutralized their followers and sympathizers by threats of dismissal, the Hengstenberg faction was successful in mobilizing the militantly conservative elements of the Protestant church for the counterrevolution. In opposition to the revolutionary demands for the separation of church and state to assure the autonomous and independent government of all "religious associations" in a united Germany, the conservatives declared unequivocally that "throne and altar" must remain united forever. To demonstrate the "united front" of the organized Protestant state church for the "Christian-German state" and to work out plans for Protestant unity in the German states, a general conference of clergymen and laymen met at Wittenberg in September. Organized and dominated by the conservative Pietists and their allies, the Wittenberg *Kirchentag* was an impressive demonstration of their successful struggle against the revolution.[8] Johann Hinrich Wichern, the founder of the "Inner Mission," made a dramatically eloquent reply to the Communist Manifesto on the social question. Blaming the socialists and communists rather than the liberals for the revolutionary upheavals,

7. See Friedrich Iken, *Die Wirksamkeit von Pastor Dulon in Bremen, 1848–1852* (Bremen, 1894), pp. 6 ff., and Richard Lempp, *Die Frage der Trennung von Kirche und Staat im Frankfurter Parlament* (Tübingen, 1913), pp. 127 ff.

Many "Forty-Eighters," including the young Carl Schurz, Dulon, and Wislicenus, left their native country after 1848 and went to the United States. Franz Sigel, the son-in-law of Dulon, became a general in the Union Army during the Civil War.

8. See *Die Verhandlungen der Wittenberger Versammlung für Gründung eines deutschen evangelischen Kirchenbundes im September 1848* (Berlin, 1848), pp. 3 ff., and Friedrich M. Schiele, *Die kirchliche Einigung des evangelischen Deutschlands im 19. Jahrhundert* (Tübingen, 1908), pp. 18–33. Also *EKZ*, 1848, pp. 270 ff., 404 ff., and 561 ff.

Wichern expressed the belief of the Protestant conservatives that poverty and suffering were moral issues requiring the cooperation and assistance of church and state. He thus voiced the general opinion of the Pietists that the "social problem" could be solved by means of traditional Christian charity rather than legislation. Under the influence of such men as Kleist-Retzow, Senfft-Pilsach, and Friedrich Julius Stahl, the Central Committee of the "Inner Mission" soon became a "Pietistic-aristocratic undertaking." [9]

The Kirchentag solemnly accepted the resolution proposed by Hengstenberg, that November 5 should be observed as a day of prayer in repentance for the sinful uprising against God and the God-given authorities. This action of the assembly was taken in the shadow of the events that liquidated the March revolution. The split of the political opposition into liberal and democratic factions after March resulted in a basic weakening of the revolutionary movement and thus prepared the way for the victory of the counter-revolution. The enormous disparity between the political aspirations of the divided revolutionists and the mass support and actual power and influence they commanded was clearly demonstrated in the Protestant church, where in a few decades an active conservative instrument of power had been developed. The 500 delegates at the Wittenberg Kirchentag listened with approval to Wichern's denunciation of the revolution. They enthusiastically supported his appeal for a continuation of the fight against those who had "corrupted and misled" the people. Dramatically agitated, Wichern warned the propertied classes of the danger of socialism and communism and thus reinforced their fears and anxieties that had been aroused by the demands of such former clergymen as Wislicenus, Dulon, and other revolutionary radicals. Thus Wichern echoed the horror of both Luther and the Pietists at the "wild and chaotic forces" unleashed by human passions that threatened the God-given order necessary for taming the animal nature of man.

On November 9, when General Wrangel's troops began their march to Berlin to assure the victory of the counterrevolution, Frederick William IV declared that he had "started the work in the name of the Lord and Saviour." The historical significance of this statement becomes evident in the light of the successful efforts

9. Shanahan, pp. 213 ff.

of the Hengstenberg faction and its allies to discredit the revolution as a "blasphemous violation of temporal and divine authority."

In the course of a few decades of severe factional struggles within the ranks of its clergy, the Protestant state church in Prussia had emerged as a powerful and highly active conservative institution, able to influence crucially the outcome of the Revolution of 1848. Its clergymen, most of whom identified themselves with the Hohenzollern regime before, were even more firm in their support after the revolution failed, and continued to uphold the monarchy's claim to rule by the "grace of God" until the collapse of the Second Reich in 1918. The inability of German Protestantism to side with the people during and after the Revolution of 1848 had the baneful consequence of alienating the German masses from the church and eventually driving many of them to embrace the secular religions of Marxism and National Socialism.

Select Bibliography

Unpublished materials consulted and cited consist of (*a*) the Hengstenberg papers in the Staatsbibliothek der Stiftung Preussischer Kulturbesitz, formerly the Preussische Staatsbibliothek, Berlin; (*b*) the Gerlach family archives at the University of Erlangen; (*c*) the Schleiermacher papers in the Literatur-Archiv des Instituts für deutsche Sprache und Literatur of the Deutsche Akademie der Wissenschaften, Berlin; and (*d*) the letters of Heinrich Leonhard Heubner, August Neander, and Richard Rothe, in the personal papers of the late Bishop Halfmann held by his widow, Mrs. Anna Halfmann, in Kiel.

Adam, Alfred. *Nationalkirche und Volkskirche im deutschen Protestantismus.* Göttingen, 1938.

Arnim, Bettina von. *Bettina von Arnim und Friedrich Wilhelm IV: Ungedruckte Briefe und Aktenstücke.* Edited by Ludwig Geiger. Frankfurt a. M., 1902.

Arnim, H. von, and Below, G. von, eds. *Deutscher Aufstieg: Bilder aus der Vergangenheit und Gegenwart der rechtsstehenden Parteien.* Berlin, n.d.

Arnold, Robert. "Aufzeichnungen des Grafen Carl von Voss-Buch über das Berliner Politische Wochenblatt." *Historische Zeitschrift,* 106 (1911).

Auer, Karl. "Friedrich Nicolai als Zeuge des kirchlichen Lebens in Berlin." *Jahrbuch für Brandenburgische Kirchengeschichte,* 10 (1913).

Augusti, J. C. W. *Über das Amt eines Generalsuperintendenten in der evangelischen Kirche, besonders in der preussischen Monarchie. Beiträge zur Geschichte und Statistik der evangelischen Kirche.* Leipzig, 1838.

Bachmann, Johannes, and Schmalenbach, Theodor. *Ernst Wilhelm Hengstenberg: Sein Leben und Wirken nach gedruckten und ungedruckten Quellen dargestellt.* 3 vols. Gütersloh, 1876–1892.

Baltzer, Eduard. *Delitsch-Halle-Nordhausen: oder, Mein Weg aus der Landeskirche in die freie protestantische Gemeinde, Aktenmässig dargestellt.* Leipzig, 1847.

———. *Erinnerungen: Bilder aus meinem Leben.* Frankfurt a. M., 1907.

Barth, Karl. *Die protestantische Theologie im 19. Jahrhundert: Ihre Vorgeschichte und Geschichte.* 2d ed. Zurich, 1952.

Bassewitz, Magnus, Freiherr von. *Die Kurmark Brandenburg im Zusammenhang mit den Schicksalen des Gesammtstaats Preussen während der Jahre 1809 und 1810.* Edited by Karl von Reinhard. Leipzig, 1906.

Bauer, Bruno. *Briefwechsel zwischen Bruno Bauer und Edgar Bauer während der Jahre 1839 bis 1842.* Leipzig, 1844.

———. *Die bürgerliche Revolution in Deutschland seit dem Anfang der deutsch-katholischen Bewegung bis zur Gegenwart.* Berlin, 1849.

———. *Herr Dr. Hengstenberg: Kritische Briefe über den Gegensatz des Gesetzes und des Evangeliums.* Berlin, 1839.

———. *Kritik der evangelischen Geschichte des Johannes.* Leipzig, 1840.

———. *Kritik der evangelischen Geschichte der Synoptiker.* Leipzig, 1841.

———. "Das Leben Jesu von D. F. Strauss." *Zeitschrift für spekulative Theologie,* 2 (1837).

———. *Die Posaune des jüngsten Gerichts über Hegel den Atheisten und Antichristen.* Leipzig, 1841.

———. "Die religiöse Bewegung." In *Vollständige Geschichte der Partheikämpfe in Deutschland während der Jahre 1842–1846.* 3 vols. Charlottenburg, 1847.

Bauer, Johannes, *Schleiermacher als patriotischer Prediger: Ein Beitrag zur Geschichte der nationalen Erhebung von hundert Jahren.* Giessen, 1908.

Bauer, Karl. *Adolf Hausrath und seine Zeit.* Heidelberg, 1933.

Bayrhoffer, Karl Theodor. "Die Lichtfreunde in Marburg: Nebst Bemerkungen über den Verein aller freien Gemeinden." *Kirchliche Reform,* January, 1847.

———. *Der praktische Verstand und die Marburger Lichtfreunde.* Darmstadt, 1847.

———. *Das Verhältnis der Lichtfreunde zu der protestantischen Kirche: Eine Erklärung.* Offenbach a. M., 1846.

———. *Das wahre Wesen der gegenwärtigen religiösen Reformation in Deutschland.* Mannheim, 1846.

Becker, Dr. Hermann. *Zur Geschichte des Geschlechtes der Hengstenberg. Beiträge zur Geschichte Dortmunds und der Grafschaft Mark,* edited by Karl Ruebel, Vol. VII. Dortmund, 1878.

Behnsch, Ottomar, ed. *Für Christkatholisches Leben: Materialien zur Geschichte der Christkatholischen Kirche.* 6 vols. Breslau, 1845–1848.

Benecke, Hermann. *Wilhelm Vatke in seinem Leben und Schriften.* Berlin, 1883.

Benfey Rudolf. *Die protestantischen Freunde und die Juden.* Leipzig, 1847.

———. *Die Stellung des fortgeschrittenen Juden zu der freien evangelischen Gemeinde.* Halle, 1846.

Benz, Ernst. *Bischofsamt und Apostolische Succession im deutschen Protestantismus.* Stuttgart, 1953.

Bergengrün, Alexander. *Staatsminister August Freiherr von der Heydt.* Leipzig, 1908.

[Berghaus, Heinrich.] *Statistik des preussischen Staats: Versuch einer Darstellung seiner Grundmacht und Kultur, seiner Verfassung, Regierung und Verwaltung im Lichte der Gegenwart.* Berlin, 1845.

Bergsträsser, Ludwig. *Geschichte der politischen Parteien in Deutschland.* 8th and 9th ed. Munich, 1955.

Bericht über die Umtriebe der Frömmler in Halle. Altenburg, 1830.

Bericht über die Verwaltung der Stadt Berlin in den Jahren 1829 bis inc. 1840 hg. v. den Städtischen Behörden. Berlin, 1842.

Bernstorff, Gräfin Elise von. *Erinnerungen: Ein Bild aus der Zeit von 1789–1835.* 2 vols. Berlin, 1896–1899.

Beyschlag, Willibald. *Aus meinem Leben: Erinnerungen und Erfahrungen der jüngeren Jahre.* 2d ed. 2 vols. Halle, 1896.

———. *Carl Immanuel Nitzsch: Eine Lichtgestalt der neueren deutsch-evangelischen Kirchengeschichte.* 2d ed. Berlin, 1882.

———. "Zum Andenken an D. Carl Immanuel Nitzsch." *Theologische Studien und Kritiken,* 1869, no. 4.

Bezold, Friedrich von. *Geschichte der rheinischen Friedrich-Wilhelm Universität von der Gründung bis zum Jahr 1870.* Bonn, 1920.

Bezzenberger, Adalbert. *Aktenstücke des Provinzial-Archivs in Königsberg aus den Jahren 1786–1820, betr. die Verwaltung und Verfassung Ostpreussens.* Königsberg, 1898.

Biedermann, Karl. *Die Aufgabe des ersten Vereinigten Landtages in Preussen.* Leipzig, 1847.

———. *Deutschland im Achtzehnten Jahrhundert.* 2d ed. 2 vols. Leipzig, 1880.

———. *Dreissig Jahre deutscher Geschichte.* Breslau, n.d.

———. *Geschichte des ersten preussischen Reichstages.* Leipzig, 1847.

Bigler, Robert. "The Rise of Political Protestantism in Nineteenth Century Germany: The Awakening of Political Consciousness and the Beginnings of Political Activity in the Protestant Clergy of Pre-march Prussia." *Church History,* 34 (1965).

Bippen, Wilhelm von. *Geschichte der Stadt Bremen.* Halle a. d. S. and Bremen, 1904.

Bismarck, Otto von. *Fürst Bismarcks Briefe an seine Braut und Gattin.* Edited by Herbert Bismarck, Stuttgart, 1900.

Blätter zur Erinnerung an das Stiftungsfest des Prediger-Seminars zu Wittenberg, gefeiert am 29. und 30. September 1842. Manuskript für Brüder und Freunde. N.p., n.d.

Blueher, Karl. *Neueste kirchliche Ereignisse: Geschichte der lutherischen Parochien Hoenigern und Kaulwitz in Schlesien.* Nuremberg, 1835.

Blum, Robert. *Der Kampf zwischen Licht und Finsternis.* Offenbach a. M., 1845.

————, ed. *Die Fortschrittsmänner der Gegenwart: Eine Weihnachtsgabe für Deutschlands freisinnige Männer und Frauen.* Leipzig, 1847.

————. *Volkstümliches Handbuch der Staatswissenschaften und Politik: Ein Staatslexicon für das Volk.* Leipzig, 1848.

————. and Wigand, Franz, eds. *Die erste allgemeine Kirchenversammlung der deutsch-katholischen Kirche abgehalten zu Leipzig, Ostern 1845: Authentischer Bericht, im Auftrage der Kirchenversammlung.* Leipzig, 1845.

————. *Die zweite allgemeine christ-katholische Kirchenversammlung abgehalten zu Berlin, Pfingsten, 1847: Authentischer Bericht, im Auftrage der Kirchenversammlung.* Leipzig, 1847.

Bocke, K. G. *Der Preussische legale evangelische Pfarrer.* 2d ed. Halle, 1836.

Böhme, Karl. *Gutsherrlich-bäuerliche Verhältnisse in Ostpreussen während der Reformzeit von 1770 bis 1830.* Leipzig, 1902.

Bollert, Martin. *Gottfried Kinkels Kämpfe um Beruf und Weltanschauung bis zur Revolution.* Bonn, 1913.

Bonwetsch, Georg Nathaniel. "Die Anfänge der Evangelischen Kirchenzeitung: Ein Beitrag zur Geschichte des religiösen und kirchlichen Lebens im 19. Jahrhundert." In *Geschichtliche Studien: A. Hauck zum 70. Geburtstag.* Leipzig, 1916.

————, ed. *Aus Tholucks Anfängen: Briefe an und von Tholuck.* Gütersloh, 1922.

————. *Aus 40 Jahren deutscher Kirchengeschichte: Briefe an Ernst Wilhelm Hengstenberg. Beiträge zur Förderung christlicher Theologie.* 2 vols. Gütersloh, 1917–1919.

————. *Briefe an Johann Heinrich Kurtz.* Leipzig, 1910.

————. *Gotthilf Heinrich Schubert in seinen Briefen.* Stuttgart, 1918.

————. *Der Historiker Heinrich Leo in seinen Briefen an Hengstenberg.* Berlin, 1918.

————. *Das religiöse Erlebnis führender Personlichkeiten in der Erweckungszeit des 19. Jahrhunderts.* Berlin-Lichterfelde, 1917.

Boost, J. A. *Was waren die Rheinländer als Menschen und Bürger und was ist aus ihnen geworden: Historisch-Praktisch dargestellt.* Mainz, 1819.

Bornkamm, Heinrich. *Mystik, Spiritualismus, und die Anfänge des Pietismus im Luthertum: Vorträge der theologischen Konferenz zu Giessen.* Giessen, 1926.

Borowski, Ludwig Ernst. *Ausgewählte Predigten und Reden.* Edited by K. L. Volkmann. Königsberg, 1833.

————. *Die Stimme Gottes vom Himmel herab, Es soll, es soll ja geholfen werden: Predigt zur vaterländischen Festfeier beim Beginn des Befreiungskrieges, den 11. April am Palmsonntag gehalten über Jerem. 30, 7–9.* Königsberg, 1813.

Botzenhardt, Erich, ed. *Freiherr vom Stein: Briefwechsel, Denkschrifte und Aufzeichnungen.* 7 vols. Berlin, 1930–1937.

Bramstedt, Ernest K. *Aristocracy and the Middle Classes in Germany: Social Types in German Literature, 1830–1900.* Rev. ed. Chicago, 1964.

Braubach, Max. *Die Universität Bonn und die deutsche Revolution von 1848–1849.* Bonn, 1948.

Bretschneider, Karl Gottlieb. *Aus meinem Leben: Eine Selbstbiographie.* Edited by Horst Bretschneider. Gotha, 1852.

————. *Über die jetzigen Bewegungen in der ev. Kirche Deutschlands.* Leipzig, 1846.

Breywisch, Walter. "Uhlich und die Bewegung der Lichtfreunde." In *Sachsen und Anhalt: Jahrbuch der Historischen Kommission für die Provinz Sachsen und für Anhalt,* Vol. II. Magdeburg, 1926.

Briefe aus und über Amerika. Dresden, 1845.

Bruford, W. H. *Germany in the Eighteenth Century: The Social Background of the Literary Revival.* Cambridge, England, 1959.

Brunner, Otto. *Land und Herrschaft.* 4th ed. Vienna and Wiesbaden, 1959.

————. *Neue Wege der Sozialgeschichte.* Göttingen, 1956.

Brunschwig, Henri. *La crise de l'état prussien à la fin du XVIIIe siècle et la genèse de la mentalité romantique.* Paris, 1947.

Buchheim, Karl. *Geschichte der christlichen Parteien in Deutschland.* Munich, 1953.

Bülow-Cummerow, Ernst von. *Preussen: Seine Verfassung, seine Verwaltung, sein Verhältnis zu Deutschland.* 3d ed. Berlin, 1842.

Burdach, Franz. *Rückblick auf mein Leben.* Leipzig, 1848.

Busch, Alexander. *Die Geschichte der Privatdozenten: Eine soziologische Studie zur grossbetrieblichen Entwicklung der deutschen Universitäten.* Stuttgart, 1959.

Chronik der St. Elisabeth Gemeinde zu Berlin. Berlin, 1857.

Clapham, J. H. *The Economic Development of France and Germany, 1815–1914.* Cambridge, England, 1951.

Coelln, Daniel von, and Schulz, David. *Über die theologische Lehrfreiheit auf den evangelischen Universitäten und deren Beschränkung durch symbolische Bücher.* Breslau, 1831.

Conze, Werner. "Vom 'Pöbel' zum 'Proletariat': Die Voraussetzungen für den Sozialismus in Deutschland." *Vierteljahrschrift für Sozial- und Wirtschaftsgeschichte,* 41 (1954).

————, ed. *Staat und Gesellschaft im deutschen Vormärz, 1815–1848.* Stuttgart, 1962.

Cousin, V. *De l'instruction publique dans quelques pays de l'Allemagne et particulièrement en Prusse.* 3d ed. 2 vols. Paris, 1840.

Craig, Gordon. *The Politics of the Prussian Army, 1640–1945.* New York, 1964.

Croon, Gustav. *Der rheinische Provinziallandtag bis zum Jahre 1874.* Düsseldorf, 1918.

Dawson, Jerry F. *Friedrich Schleiermacher: The Evolution of a Nationalist.* Austin, Texas, 1966.

Delius, Walter. *Die evangelische Kirche und die Revolution 1848.* Berlin, 1948.

Dibelius, Otto. *Das Königliche Predigerseminar zu Wittenberg, 1817–1917.* Berlin-Lichterfelde, 1917.

————. "Friedrich Wilhelm IV und die Idee des christlichen Staats." *Die Furche,* 22 (1936).

Diestel, Georg. *Wie das Evangelium entstellt wird in unserer Zeit.* Königsberg, 1830.

Dieterici, C. F. W. *Geschichtliche und statistische Nachrichten über die Universitäten im preussischen Staat.* Berlin, 1836.

Dilthey, Wilhelm. *Leben Schleiermachers.* Berlin, 1870.

————. "Schleiermachers politische Gesinnung." In his *Gesammelte Schriften,* Vol. XII, *Zur Preussischen Geschichte.* Leipzig and Berlin, 1936.

Doering, Heinrich. *Die deutschen Kanzelredner des 18. u. 19. Jahrhunderts, nach ihrem Leben und Wirken dargestellt.* Neustadt a. d. Orla, 1830.

————. *Die gelehrten Theologen Deutschlands im 18. und 19. Jahrhundert, nach ihrem Leben und Wirken dargestellt.* Neustadt a. d. Orla, 1831–1835.

Drews, Paul. *Der evangelische Geistliche in der deutschen Vergangenheit. Monographien zur deutschen Kulturgeschichte,* Vol. 12. Jena, 1905.

————. *Theologische Studien und Kritiken.* Leipzig, 1892.

Dreyhaus, Hermann. "Der preussische Correspondent von 1813–1814 und der Anteil seiner Gründer Niebuhr und Schleiermacher." *Forschungen zur brandenburgischen und preussischen Geschichte,* 22 (1909).

Droz, Jacques. *Le libéralisme rhénan, 1815–1848.* Paris, 1940.

————. *Les révolutions allemandes de 1848.* Paris, 1957.

————. "Religious Aspects of the Revolutions of 1848 in Europe." In *French Society and Culture since the Old Regime,* edited by Evelyn M. Acomb and Marvin L. Brown. New York, 1966.

Dru, Alexander. "The Reformation of the 19th Century: Christianity in Germany from 1800 to 1848." *Dublin Review,* 116 (1952).

Drummond, Andrew L. "Church and State in Protestant Germany before 1918." *Church History,* 13 (1944).

————. *German Protestantism since Luther.* London, 1951.

Dülong, Paul von. *Wanderungen und Heimkehr einer deutschen Familie: Geschichte der Familie von Dülong (d'Oulon, Doulon, Dulong).* Görlitz, 1915.

Dulon, Rudolf. *Gruss und Handschlag.* Hamburg, 1853.

————. *Luthers Nachlass und unsere Freiheit: Predigt am 18. Februar 1846 gehalten und mit einem Vorworte vom Lehren gemäss den Bekenntnisschriften.* Altenburg, 1846.

Dunkmann, Karl. *Die Nachwirkungen der theologischen Prinzipienlehre Schleiermachers.* Gütersloh, 1915.

Eggert, Oskar. *Stände und Staat in Pommern im Anfang des 19. Jahrhunderts.* Köln and Graz, 1964.

Eichhorn, Karl Friedrich. *Deutsche Staats- und Rechtsgeschichte.* 4th ed. Göttingen, 1834.

Engel, J. J. *Lobrede auf den König.* Berlin, 1781.

Epstein, Klaus. *The Genesis of German Conservatism.* Princeton, 1966.

[G. Eylers.] "Das evangelische Kirchenwesen." In his *Zur Beurtheilung des Ministeriums Eichhorn von einem Mitgliede desselben.* Berlin, 1849.

Eylert, R. F. *Charakter-Züge und historische Fragmente aus dem Leben des Königs von Preussen, Friedrich Wilhelm III.* 3 vols. Magdeburg, 1843–1846.

Fagerberg, Holsten, *Bekenntnis, Kirche, und Amt in der deutschen konfessionellen Theologie des 19. Jahrhunderts.* Uppsala, 1952.

[Failly, G. de.] *De la Prusse et de sa domination sous les rapports politique et religieux, spécialement dans les nouvelles provinces, par un inconnu.* Paris, 1842.

Falkson, Ferdinand. *Die liberale Bewegung in Königsberg, 1840–1848: Memoirenblätter.* Breslau, 1888.

Fischer, Fritz. "Die Auswirkungen der Reformation auf das deutsche und west-europäisch-amerikanische politische Leben." In *Europa in evangelischer Sicht,* edited by F. K. Schumann. Stuttgart, 1953.

———. *Moritz August von Bethmann-Hollweg und der Protestantismus.* Berlin, 1938.

———. "Der deutsche Protestantismus und die Politik im 19. Jahrhundert." *Historische Zeitschrift,* 171 (1951).

———. *Ludwig Nicolovius: Rokoko, Reform, Restauration.* Stuttgart, 1939.

Foellmer, Oskar. *Geschichte des Amtes der Generalsuperintendenten in den altpreussischen Provinzen.* Gütersloh, 1931.

Foerster, Erich. *Die Entstehung der Preussischen Landeskirche unter der Regierung König Friedrich Wilhelms des Dritten nach den Quellen erzählt: Ein Beitrag zur Geschichte der Kirchenbildung im deutschen Protestantismus.* 2 vols. Tübingen, 1905–1907.

Fontane, Theodor. *Gesammelte Werke.* 2d ser. Vol. III. Berlin, 1920.

———. *Wanderungen durch die Mark Brandenburg, II, Das Oberland.* 15th ed. Stuttgart, 1919.

Forell, George W., et al., eds. *Luther and Culture.* Decorah, Iowa, 1960.

[Frederick William III.] *Luther in Beziehung auf die preussische Kirchenagende.* Berlin, 1827.

[C. G. Fubel.] "Die protestantischen Freunde." *Jahrbücher der Gegenwart,* 3 (1845).

Gagern, Heinrich C. E., Freiherr von. *Mein Anteil an der Politik.* Stuttgart and Tübingen, 1833.

Gass, Johann Christian. *Wie sollen wir die jetzige Zeit beurtheilen?* Breslau, 1817.

Gass, Wilhelm, ed. *Friedrich Schleiermachers Briefwechsel mit Johann Christian Gass.* 4 vols. Berlin, 1852–1856.

Generalsynodalbuch: Die Akten der Generalsynoden von Jülich, Cleve, Berg, und Mark. Düsseldorf, 1846.

Gerlach, Ernst Ludwig von. *Aufzeichnungen aus seinem Leben und Wirken, 1795–1877.* Edited by Jakob von Gerlach. 2 vols. Schwerin in Meckl., 1903.

———. *Von der Revolution zum Norddeutschen Bund: Politik und Ideengut der Preussischen Hochkonservativen, 1848–1866.* Edited by Hellmut Diwald. 2 vols. Göttingen, 1970.

Gerlach, Leopold von. *Denkwürdigkeiten aus dem Leben Leopold von Gerlachs, Generals der Infanterie und General-Adjutanten König Friedrich Wilhelms IV*. 2 vols. Berlin, 1891–1892.

Gerlach, Otto von. *Die kirchliche Armenpflege nach dem Englischen des Dr. Chalmers*. Berlin, 1847.

———. *Otto von Gerlachs Predigten*. Edited by J. G. Seegemund. Berlin, 1850.

The German Reformation of the 19th Century. By the German correspondent of *The Continental Echo*. London, 1846.

Gervinus, Georg G. *Einleitung in die Geschichte des neunzehnten Jahrhunderts*. Leipzig, 1853.

———. *Hinterlassene Schriften*. Vienna, 1872.

———. *Die Mission der Deutschkatholiken*. Heidelberg, 1845.

Glossy, Karl, ed. *Literarische Geheimberichte aus dem Vormärz*. Vienna, 1912.

Goebel, Max. *Die evangelische Kirchenverfassungsfrage*. Bonn, 1848.

———. *Geschichte des christlichen Lebens in der Rheinisch-Westfälisch Evangelischen Kirche*. 3 vols. Coblenz, 1852–1860.

Goldschmidt, Friedrich and Paul. *Das Leben des Staatsraths Kunth*. 2d ed. Berlin, 1888.

Gollwitzer, Heinz. *Die Standesherren: Die politische und gesellschaftliche Stellung der Mediatisierten, 1815–1918*. 2d ed. Göttingen, 1964.

Granier, H., ed. *Berichte aus der Berliner Franzosenzeit, 1807–1809*. Publicationen aus den preussischen Staatsarchiven, no. 18. Leipzig, 1913.

Guericke, Ferdinand. *Abriss der Kirchengeschichte*. Halle, 1842.

———. *Geschichte der lutherischen Gemeinde in und um Halle*. Halle, 1835.

———. *Urkunden betreffend die lutherischen Gemeinden in und um Halle in ihrer Bedrängung*. Halle, 1835.

Haake, Paul. *J. P. F. Ancillon und Kronprinz Friedrich Wilhelm IV von Preussen*. Munich and Berlin, 1921.

Hahn, August. *Lehrbuch des christlichen Glaubens*. Breslau, 1844.

———. *Predigten und Reden unter den Bewegungen in Kirche und Staat seit dem Jahre 1830*. Breslau, 1852.

Hahnzog, C. L. *Patriotische Predigten*. Halle, 1785.

Hamerow, Theodore S. *Restoration, Revolution, Reaction: Economics and Politics in Germany, 1815–1871*. Princeton, 1958.

Hansen, Joseph. *Preussen und Rheinland von 1815 bis 1915*. Bonn, 1918.

———, ed. *Quellen zur Geschichte des Rheinlandes im Zeitalter der französischen Revolution*. 4 vols. Bonn, 1931–1938.

———, ed. *Rheinische Briefe und Akten zur Geschichte der Politischen Bewegung, 1830–1850*. 2 vols. Essen, 1919.

———, ed. *Die Rheinprovinz, 1815–1915: Hundert Jahre preussischer Herrschaft am Rhein*. 2 vols. Bonn, 1917.

Hanstein, Gottfried. *Predigten in den Jahren 1813 und 1814 gehalten*. Magdeburg, 1819.

Harnack, Adolf von. *Geschichte der Königlich Preussischen Akademie der Wissenschaften zu Berlin*. 3 vols. Berlin, 1900.

Hashagen, Justus. *Der rheinische Protestantismus und die Entwicklung der rheinischen Kultur.* Essen, 1924.

————. et al., eds. *Bergische Geschichte.* Burg an der Wupper, 1958.

Hausrath, Adolf. *Richard Rothe und seine Freunde.* 2 vols. Berlin, 1902–1906.

————. *David Friedrich Strauss und die Theologie seiner Zeit.* 2 vols. Heidelberg, 1876–1878.

Haym, Rudolf. *Ausgewählter Briefwechsel Rudolf Hayms.* Edited by Hans Rosenberg. Berlin and Leipzig, 1930.

————. *Aus meinem Leben: Erinnerungen.* Berlin, 1902.

————. "Ein modernes Glaubensbekenntnis." *Jahrbücher für speculative Philosophie,* 2 (1847).

————. *Die Krisis unserer religiösen Bewegung.* Halle, 1847.

————. *Das Leben Max Dunckers.* Berlin, 1891.

————. "Die protestantischen Freunde in Halle." *Jahrbücher der Gegenwart,* 4 (1846).

————. *Die romantische Schule.* Berlin, 1870.

Heffter, Heinrich. *Die deutsche Selbstverwaltung im 19. Jahrhundert: Geschichte der Ideen und Institutionen.* Stuttgart, 1950.

Heger, Adolf. *Evangelische Verkündigung und deutsches Nationalbewusstsein: Zur Geschichte der Predigt, 1806–1848.* Berlin, 1939.

Hengstenberg, Ernst Wilhelm. *Einige erläuternde Bemerkungen zu der Ministerialverfügung über Mysticismus, Pietismus, und Separatismus.* Berlin, 1826.

————. *Einige Worte über die Notwendigkeit der Überordnung des äusseren Wortes über das innere, Nebst Stellen aus Luthers Schriften.* Berlin, 1825.

"Hengstenberg (E. W.) und die Evangelische Kirchenzeitung." *Conversations-Lexikon der neuesten Literatur,* Vol. II. Leipzig, 1833.

Hermelink, Heinrich. *Das Christentum in der Menschheitsgeschichte von der Französischen Revolution bis zur Gegenwart.* 2 vols. Tübingen and Stuttgart, 1951–1953.

Heubner, Heinrich Leonhard. *Die christliche Freude über unsere Befreiung: Am zweiten Sonntag nach Epiphanias, den 16. Januar 1814.* Wittenberg, 1814.

————. *Die gegenwärtige Zeit der Not ein göttlicher Ruf zur Besserung: Am 19. Sonntag nach Trinitatis, 24. Oktober 1813.* N.p., n.d.

Hieronymi, H. A. Wilhelm. *Die Hegelianer als Lichtfreunde: oder Zwei Dokumente der neuesten Marburger Kirchenphilosophie, beleuchtet mit dem Lichte des praktischen Verstandes und aus der Hegelschen in die gewöhnliche Deutsche übersetzt.* Darmstadt, 1847.

————. *Was wollen wir? Rede gehalten nach seinem Übertritt zu der neuen allgemein-christlichen Kirche vor der Gemeinde zu Magdeburg.* 3d ed. Magdeburg, 1848.

Hinrichs, Carl. *Preussentum und Pietismus: Der Pietismus in Brandenburg-Preussen als religiös-soziale Reformbewegung.* Göttingen, 1971.

Hintze, Otto. "Die Epochen des evangelischen Kirchenregiments in Preussen." *Historische Zeitschrift*, 97 (1906).

——. *Gesammelte Abhandlungen.* Edited by Fritz Hartung. 3 vols. Leipzig, 1941–1943.

——. *Die Hohenzollern und ihr Werk.* 7th ed. Berlin, 1916.

Hirsch, Emanuel. *Geschichte der neueren evangelischen Theologie im Zusammenhang mit den allgemeinen Bewegungen des europäischen Denkens.* 5 vols. Gütersloh, 1949–1954.

——. *Staat und Kirche im 19. und 20. Jahrhundert.* Göttingen, 1929.

Hofferichter, Theodor. *Die kirchliche Bewegung: Briefe an seine Freunde.* Breslau and Steinau, 1847.

Hoffmann, J. G. *Die Bevölkerung des preussischen Staates.* Berlin, 1839.

Holborn, Hajo. "Der deutsche Idealismus in sozialgeschichtlicher Beleuchtung." *Historische Zeitschrift,* 174 (1952).

——. *A History of Modern Germany.* 3 vols. New York, 1959–1969.

——. "The Social Basis of the German Reformation." *Church History,* 5 (1936).

Holden, Catherine M. "A Decade of Dissent in Germany: An Historical Study of the Society of Protestant Friends and the German-Catholic Church, 1840–1848." Ph.D. dissertation, Yale University, 1954.

Holl, Karl. *Die Bedeutung der grossen Kriege für das religiöse und kirchliche Leben innerhalb des deutschen Protestantismus.* Tübingen, 1917.

Horn, Curt. "Die patriotische Predigt zur Zeit Friedrichs des Grossen." *Jahrbuch für Brandenburgische Kirchengeschichte,* 19 (1924).

Hubatsch, Walther. *Geschichte der evangelischen Kirche Ostpreussens.* 3 vols. Göttingen, 1968.

Huber, Ernst Rudolf. *Deutsche Verfassungsgeschichte seit 1789.* 4 vols. Stuttgart, 1957–1969.

Hundeshagen, Karl Bernhard. *Beiträge zur Kirchenverfassungsgeschichte und Kirchenpolitik insbesondere des Protestantismus.* Wiesbaden, 1864.

——. *Calvinismus und staatsbürgerliche Freiheit.* Zürich, 1846.

[——.] *Der deutsche Protestantismus: Seine Vergangenheit und seine heutigen Lebensfragen im Zusammenhang der ganzen Nationalentwicklung, Beleuchtet von einem deutschen Theologen.* 3d ed. Frankfurt a. M., 1850.

——. *Einige Hauptmomente in der geschichtlichen Entwicklung des Verhältnisses zwischen Staat und Kirche.* Heidelberg, 1860.

Iken, Friedrich. *Die Wirksamkeit von Pastor Dulon in Bremen, 1848–1852: Ein kirchliches Gedenkblatt aus der Revolutionszeit.* Bremen, 1894.

[Jacoby, Johann.] *Vier Fragen: Beantwortet von einem Ostpreussen.* Mannheim, 1841.

Jahrbuch für die amtliche Statistik des preussischen Staats. Berlin, 1863.

Johnson, Robert Clyde. *Authority in Protestant Theology.* Philadelphia, 1959.

Jordan, Erich. *Die Entstehung der konservativen Partei und die preussischen Agrarverhältnisse von 1848.* Munich and Leipzig, 1914.

Jordan, Erich. "Friedrich Wilhelm IV und der preussische Adel." Ph.D. diss., University of Berlin, 1909.

Jordan, Wilhelm. *Ihr träumt! Weckruf an das Ronge-berauschte Deutschland.* Leipzig, 1845.

Die Jubelfeier der Reformation zu Wittenberg im Jahre 1817: Beschreibung nebst Predigten und Reden die dabei gehalten worden sind. Wittenberg, 1817.

Kade, Franz. *Schleiermachers Anteil an der Entwicklung des Preussischen Bildungswesens, 1808–1818.* Leipzig, 1925.

Kaehler, Siegfried A. *Studien zur deutschen Geschichte des 19. und 20. Jahrhunderts.* Edited by W. Bussmann. Göttingen, 1961.

Kahnis, Karl Friedrich August. *Der innere Gang des deutschen Protestantismus.* 3d ed. 2 vols. Leipzig, 1856.

———. *Die Lehre vom Heiligen Geist.* Leipzig, 1846.

———. *Dr. Ruge und Hegel: Ein Beitrag zur Würdigung Hegel'scher Tendenzen.* Quedlinburg, 1838.

Kampe, Ferdinand. *Geschichte der religiösen Bewegung der neueren Zeit.* 4 vols. Leipzig, 1852–1860.

———. *Das Wesen des Deutschkatholizismus mit besonderer Rücksicht auf sein Verhältnis zur Politik.* Tübingen, 1850.

Kamptz, Karl Albert von. "Über das bischöfliche Recht in der evangelischen Kirche Deutschlands." *Jahrbücher für die preussische Gesetzgebung, Rechtswissenschaft, und Rechtsverwaltung,* Vol. 31. Berlin, 1828.

Kantzenbach, Friedrich Wilhelm, ed. *Baron H. E. von Kottwitz und die Erweckungsbewegung in Schlesien, Berlin, und Pommern.* Ulm, Donau, 1963.

———. *Die Erweckungsbewegung: Studien zur Geschichte ihrer Entstehung und ersten Ausbreitung in Deutschland.* Neuendettelsau, 1957.

Kaufmann, Georg. *Geschichte der Universität Breslau, 1811–1911.* Breslau, 1911.

———. "Ranke und die Beurteilung Friedrich Wilhelms IV." *Historische Zeitschrift,* 88 (1902).

———, ed. *Geschichte der Fächer, Institute, und Ämter der Universität Breslau, 1811–1911.* Breslau, 1911.

Keller, Suzanne. *Beyond the Ruling Class: Strategic Elites in Modern Society.* New York, 1963.

Kersken, Hermann. "Stadt und Universität Bonn in den Revolutionsjahren 1848–1849." Ph.D. diss., University of Bonn, 1931.

Keyserling, Leonie von. *Studien zu den Entwicklungsjahren der Brüder Gerlach, mit Briefen Leopolds von Gerlach und seinen Bruder an Karl Sieveking.* Heidelberg, 1913.

Kinkel, Gottfried. *Gottfried Kinkels Selbstbiographie, 1838–1848.* Edited by Rudolf Sander. Bonn, 1931.

Kissling, Johannes B. *Der deutsche Protestantismus, 1817–1917: Eine geschichtliche Darstellung.* 2 vols. Münster i. W., 1917–1918.

Knapp, Georg Friedrich. *Die Bauern-Befreiung und der Ursprung der Landarbeiter in den älteren Theilen Preussens.* 2 vols. Leipzig, 1887.

Knapp, J. G. Fr. *Oehler: Ein Lebensbild*. Tübingen, 1876.

Koch, *A. D. Heinrich Leonhard Heubner in Wittenberg: Züge und Zeugnisse aus und zu seinem Leben und Wirken*. Wittenberg, 1885.

Köhler, K. A. *1813–1814: Tagebuchblätter eines Feldgeistlichen*. Berlin, 1912.

Köhler, Walter. *Luther und das Lutherthum in ihrer weltgeschichtlichen Auswirkung*. Leipzig, 1933.

Köllmann, Wolfgang. *Sozialgeschichte der Stadt Barmen im 19. Jahrhundert*. Tübingen, 1960.

König, Carl Bernhard. *Bitterwasser: Verordnet dem nur zu treuen Hengstenberg*. N.p., 1846.

———. *Herr Hengstenberg, Anno 1845*. Braunschweig, 1845.

———. *Die neueste Zeit in der Evangelischen Kirche des Preussischen Staates*. Braunschweig, 1842.

———. *Der rechte Standpunkt*. No. 1. Magdeburg, n.d. Nos. 2–5. Magdeburg, 1841–1844. No. 6. Altenburg, 1845.

[———.] *Wanderung durch Vaterhaus, Schule, Kriegslager, und Akademie zur Kirche: Mitteilungen aus dem bewegten Leben eines evangelischen Geistlichen*. Magdeburg, 1832.

[Kohler, Hermann.] *Tagebuch des Kandidaten Hermann Kohler*. Leipzig, 1838.

Koselleck, Reinhart. *Preussen zwischen Reform und Revolution: Allgemeines Landrecht, Verwaltung, und soziale Bewegung von 1791 bis 1848*. Stuttgart, 1967.

———. "Staat und Gesellschaft in Preussen, 1815–1848." In *Staat und Gesellschaft im deutschen Vormärz, 1815–1848*, edited by Werner Conze. Stuttgart, 1962.

Kriege, Anneliese. "Geschichte der *Evangelischen Kirchenzeitung* unter der Redaktion Ernst Wilhelm Hengstenbergs, 1827–1869." Ph.D. diss., University of Bonn, 1958.

Krieger, Leonard. *The German Idea of Freedom: History of a Political Tradition*. Boston, 1957.

Krug, Leopold. *An meine deutschen Mitbürger*. Leipzig, 1830.

Krüger, M. Gustav, ed. *Berichte über die erste evangelische Generalsynode Preussens im Jahre 1846, mit einem Anhage der wichtigsten Aktensstücke*. Leipzig, 1846.

Krummacher, F. W. *Eine Selbstbiographie*. Berlin, 1869.

Krummacher, Friedrich Wilhelm. *Gottfried Daniel Krummacher und die niederrheinische Erweckungsbewegung zu Anfang des 19. Jahrhunderts*. Berlin, 1935.

Krummacher, G. D. *Predigt von der Wiederherstellung*. Düsseldorf, 1816.

Kulke, Michael. *Gnadenführungen Gottes in dem Leben des Schulvorstehers Friedrich Samuel Dreger*. Berlin, 1860.

Kupisch, Karl. *Das Jahrhundert des Sozialismus und die Kirche*. 2d ed. Göttingen, 1960.

———. *Vom Pietismus zum Kommunismus: Historische Gestalten, Szenen, und Probleme*. Berlin, 1953.

Kupisch, Karl. *Zwischen Idealismus und Massendemokratie: Eine Geschichte der evangelischen Kirche, 1815–1945.* Berlin, 1955.

Lebenslauf der sämtlichen Mittglieder des Königlichen Prediger-Seminars zu Wittenberg vom 1. Juli 1817 bis Ende Dezember 1866, hergestellt von den Mitgliedern des Prediger-Seminars. Stuttgart, 1868.

Legge, J. G. *Rhyme and Revolution in Germany.* London, 1918.

Lehmann, Hartmut. "Friedrich von Bodelschwingh und das Sedanfest: Ein Beitrag zum nationalen Denken der politisch aktiven Richtung im deutschen Pietismus des 19. Jahrhunderts." *Historische Zeitschrift,* 202 (1966).

Lehmann, Ludwig. *Bilder aus der Kirchengeschichte der Mark Brandenburg.* Berlin, 1924.

———. *Kirchengeschichte der Mark Brandenburg von 1818 bis 1932.* Berlin, 1936.

Lempp, Richard. *Die Frage der Trennung von Kirche und Staat im Frankfurter Parlament.* Tübingen, 1913.

Lenz, Max. *Geschichte der Königlichen Friedrich-Wilhelms Universität zu Berlin.* 5 vols. Halle, 1910–1918.

Leo, Heinrich. *Meine Jugendzeit.* Gotha, 1880.

Lewalter, Ernst. *Friedrich Wilhelm IV: Das Schicksal eines Geistes.* Berlin, 1938.

Lichtfreund, Freimund [pseud.]. *Berichte über die Umtriebe der Frömmler in Halle: Oder Welch' Zeit ist es im Preussischen Staate?* Altenburg, 1830.

Lilge, Frederick. *The Abuse of Learning: The Failure of the German University.* New York, 1948.

Lisco, Gustav. *Zur Kirchengeschichte Berlins: Ein geschichtlich-statistischer Beitrag.* Berlin, 1857.

Löwenstein, Julius. *Hegels Staatsidee: Ihr Doppelgesicht und ihr Einfluss im 19. Jahrhundert.* Berlin, 1927.

Ludolphi, Ingetraut. *Heinrich Steffens: Sein Verhältnis zu den Lutheranern.* Berlin, 1962.

Lütge, Friedrich. *Deutsche Sozial- und Wirtschaftsgeschichte.* Berlin, Göttingen, and Heidelberg, 1952.

Lütgert, Wilhelm. *Die Religion des deutschen Idealismus und ihr Ende.* 3d ed. 4 vols. Gütersloh, 1929–1930.

Manteuffel, Otto, Freiherr von. *Unter Friedrich Wilhelm IV: Denkwürdigkeiten des Ministerpräsidenten Otto Freiherrn v. Manteuffel.* Edited by Heinrich von Poschinger. 3 vols. Berlin, 1901.

Marheineke, Philip Konrad. *Einleitung in die öffentlichen Vorlesungen über die Bedeutung der Hegelschen Philosophie in der Christlichen Theologie.* Berlin, 1842.

———. *Zur Kritik der Schelling'schen Offenbarungs-Philosophie.* Berlin, 1845.

Martin, Alfred von. "Autorität und Freiheit in der Gedankenwelt Ludwig von Gerlachs: Ein Beitrag zur Geschichte der religiös-kirchlichen und politischen Ansichten des Altkonservatismus." *Archiv für Kulturgeschichte,* 20 (1930).

————. "Die politische Ideenwelt Adam Müllers." In *Festschrift für Walter Götz: Kultur- und Universalgeschichte.* Berlin, 1927.

————. "Der preussische Altkonservatismus und der politische Katholizismus in ihren gegenseitigen Beziehungen." *Deutsche Vierteljahrsschrift für Literaturwissenschaft und Geistesgeschichte,* 7 (1929).

————. "Weltanschauliche Motive im altkonservativen Denken." In *Deutscher Staat und deutsche Parteien: Beiträge zur Deutschen Partei- und Ideengeschichte,* edited by Paul Wentzge. Munich and Berlin, 1922.

Marwitz, Louise von der, ed. *Vom Leben am preussischen Hofe, 1815–1852: Aufzeichnungen von Caroline v. Rochow, geb. v. d. Marwitz und Marie de la Motte-Fouqué.* Berlin, 1908.

Marx, Karl. *Die Frühschriften.* Edited by S. Landshut. Stuttgart, 1953.

Mathilde Tholuck geb. Freiin von Gemmingen-Steinegg, heimgegangen am 1 Mai, bestattet am 10 Mai 1894. Privately printed. Halle a. S., 1894.

Mayer, Gustav. "Die Anfänge des politischen Radikalismus im vormärzlichen Preussen." *Zeitschrift für Politik,* 6 (1913).

————. *Friedrich Engels: Eine Biographie.* 2 vols. The Hague, 1934.

————. "Die Junghegelianer und der preussische Staat." *Historische Zeitschrift,* 121 (1920).

Mehnert, Gottfried. *Evangelische Kirche und Politik, 1917–1919: Die politischen Strömungen im deutschen Protestantismus von der Julikrise 1917 bis zum Herbst 1919.* Düsseldorf, 1959.

Meinecke, Friedrich. "Bismarcks Eintritt in den christlich-germanischen Kreis." *Historische Zeitschrift,* 90 (1903).

————. *Preussen und Deutschland im 19. und 20. Jahrhundert.* Munich and Berlin, 1918.

————. *Weltbürgertum und Nationalstaat: Studien zur Genesis des deutschen Nationalstaats.* 3d ed. Munich and Berlin, 1915.

————. *Das Leben des Generalfeldmarschalls Hermann von Boyen.* 2 vols. Stuttgart, 1895–1899.

————. *Das Zeitalter der deutschen Erhebung, 1795–1815.* 2d ed. Bielefeld, 1913.

Meisner, Heinrich, ed. *Friedrich Schleiermachers Briefwechsel mit seiner Braut.* 2d ed. Gotha, 1920.

————. *Schleiermacher als Mensch, II, Sein Werden und Wirken, Familien- und Freundesbriefe, 1786–1834.* 2 vols. Gotha, 1922–1923.

Menken, Gottfried. *Über Glück und Sieg der Gottlosen.* Frankfurt a. M., 1795.

Metger, Hermann. *Der Rationalismus und der Separatismus an der Ostsee.* Stolpe, 1833.

Meyer, Christian. "Aus dem Lebensgang eines evangelischen Geistlichen im 17. und 18. Jahrhundert." *Zeitschrift für Kulturgeschichte,* 3 (1893).

Meyer, Ralph. *Geschichte der Deutschreformierten Gemeinde in Magdeburg.* 2 vols. Magdeburg, 1914.

Mueller, Josef. *Die erste Generalsynode der evangelischen Landeskirche Preussens und die kirchlichen Bekenntnisse.* Breslau, 1847.

————. *Die evangelische Union: Ihr Wesen und göttliches Recht.* Berlin, 1854.

Müsebeck, Ernst. *Das preussische Kultusministerium vor hundert Jahren.* Stuttgart and Berlin, 1918.

Mundt, Theodor. *Der heilige Geist under der Zeitgeist: Zwölf Capitel den Reformfreunden auf katholischem, protestantischem, und jüdischem Gebiet gewidmet.* Berlin, 1845.

Nadler, Josef. *Die Berliner Romantik, 1800–1814. Ein Beitrag zur gemeinvölkischen Frage: Renaissance, Romantik, Restauration.* Berlin, 1921.

Neander, August. *Erklärung über meine Theilnahme an der Evangelischen Kirchen-Zeitung und die Gründe mich von derselben ganz loszusagen.* Berlin, 1830.

Neher, Walter. *Arnold Ruge als Politiker und politischer Schriftsteller.* Heidelberg, 1933.

Neumann, Sigmund. *Die Stufen des preussischen Konservatismus: Ein Beitrag zum Staats- und Gesellschaftsbild Deutschlands im 19. Jahrhundert.* Berlin, 1930.

Nicolovius, Alfred. *Die bischöfliche Würde in Preussens evangelischer Kirche.* Königsberg, 1834.

——. *Denkschrift auf Georg Heinrich Ludwig Nicolovius.* Bonn, 1841.

Niebuhr, Berthold G. *Geschichte des Zeitalters der Revolution.* Hamburg, 1845.

Niemeyer, Hermann Agathon. *Gedächtnispredigt auf den Hochseligen König.* N.p., n.d.

Nigg, Walter. *Die Geschichte des religiösen Liberalismus: Entstehung, Blütezeit, Ausklang.* Zurich and Leipzig, 1937.

Nitzsch, Carl Immanuel. "Otto von Gerlach." *Deutsche Zeitschrift für christliches Leben und christliche Wissenschaft,* 1850.

——. *Urkundenbuch der Evangelischen Union mit Erläuterungen.* Bonn, 1853.

Noyes, P. H. *Organization and Revolution: Working Class Associations in the German Revolutions of 1848–1849.* Princeton, 1966.

Olshausen, Hermann. *Was ist von den neuesten kirchlichen Ereignissen in Schlesien zu halten?* Königsberg, 1833.

Palmer, Robert R. *The Age of the Democratic Revolution: A Political History of Europe and America, 1760–1800.* 2 vols. Princeton, 1959–1964.

Paulsen, Friedrich. *Geschichte des gelehrten Unterrichts auf den deutschen Schulen und Universitäten vom Ausgang des Mittelalters bis zur Gegenwart.* 3d ed. 2 vols. Berlin and Leipzig, 1919-1921.

Perthes, Clemens Theodor, ed. *Friedrich Perthes Leben, nach dessen schriftlichen und mündlichen Mitteilungen aufgezogen.* 3 vols. Hamburg and Gotha, 1848–1855.

Petersdorf, Hermann von. *Kleist-Retzow: Ein Lebensbild.* Stuttgart and Berlin, 1907.

——. *König Friedrich Wilhelm der Vierte.* Stuttgart, 1901.

Pflanze, Otto. *Bismarck and the Development of Germany: The Period of Unification, 1815–1871.* Princeton, 1963.

Pinson, Koppel S. *Modern Germany: Its History and Civilization.* 2d ed. Edited and enlarged by Klaus Epstein. New York, 1966.

———. *Pietism as a Factor in the Rise of German Nationalism.* New York, 1934.

Preradovich, Nikolaus von. *Die Führungsschichten in Österreich und Preussen, 1804–1918, mit einem Ausblick bis zum Jahre 1945.* Wiesbaden, 1955.

Die Protokolle der von der Versammlung zu Vereinbarung der preussischen Staatsverwaltung ernannten Verfassungskommission. Edited by K. G. Bauer. Berlin, 1849.

Prutz, Hans. *Die königliche Albertus Universität zu Königsberg in Preussen im 19. Jahrhundert.* Königsberg, 1894.

Prutz, R. E. "Theologie oder Politik? Staat oder Kirche?" In his *Kleine Schriften zur Politik und Literatur,* Vol. II. Merseburg, 1847.

Raack, R. C. *The Fall of Stein.* Cambridge, Mass., 1965.

———. "A New Schleiermacher Letter on the Conspiracy of 1808." *Zeitschrift für Religions- und Geistesgeschichte,* 16 (1964).

———. "Schleiermacher's Political Thought and Activity, 1806–1813." *Church History,* 28 (1959).

Realencyklopädie für protestantische Theologie und Kirche. 1st ed. 19 vols. Leipzig, 1854–1865. 2d ed. 17 vols. 1877–1888. 3d ed. 24 vols. 1896–1913.

Reimer, Georg, ed. *Aus Schleiermachers Leben in Briefen.* 4 vols. Berlin, 1860–1863.

Die Religion in Geschichte und Gegenwart: Handwörterbuch für Theologie und Religionswissenschaft. 2d ed. Tübingen, 1927–1932. 3d ed. 6 vols. 1957–1962.

Reuss, Fürstin Eleonore. *A Pietist of the Napoleonic Wars and After: The Life of Countess von Reden.* London, 1905.

———. *Adolf von Thadden-Trieglaff: Ein Lebensbild gezeichnet nach Erinnerungen seiner Kinder und Freunde.* 2d ed. Berlin, 1894.

Ritschl, Otto. *Die evangelisch-theologische Fakultät zu Bonn in dem ersten Jahrhundert ihrer Geschichte.* Bonn, 1919.

Ritter, Gerhard. *Die preussischen Konservativen und Bismarcks deutsche Politik, 1858–1871.* Heidelberg, 1913.

———. "Das Problem einer evangelischen Volkskirche und das Erbe des 19. Jahrhunderts." *Die Wartburg,* 29 (1929).

———. *Staatskunst und Kriegshandwerk: Das Problem des "Militarismus" in Deutschland,* I, *Die altpreussische Tradition, 1740–1890.* 3d ed. Munich, 1965.

———. *Stein: Eine politische Biographie.* 3d ed. 2 vols. Stuttgart, 1958.

Rohr, Donald G. *Origins of Social Liberalism in Germany.* Chicago, 1963.

Rosenberg, Hans. "Arnold Ruge und die Hallischen Jahrbücher." *Archiv für Kulturgeschichte,* 20 (1930).

———. *Bureaucracy, Aristocracy, Autocracy: The Prussian Experience, 1600–1815.* Cambridge, Mass., 1958.

———. "Die 'Demokratisierung' der Rittergutsbesitzerklasse." In *Zur Geschichte und Problematik der Demokratie: Festgabe für Hans Herzfeld,* edited by Wilhelm Berges and Carl Hinrichs. Berlin, 1958. Reprinted in *Moderne deutsche Sozialgeschichte,* edited by Hans-Ulrich Wehler. Cologne, 1966.

Rosenberg, Hans. "Geistige und politische Strömungen an der Universität Halle in der ersten Hälfte des 19. Jahrhunderts." *Deutsche Vierteljahrschrift für Literaturwissenschaft und Geistesgeschichte*, 7 (1929).

———. *Probleme der Sozialgeschichte*. Berlin, 1969.

———. *Rudolf Haym und die Anfänge des klassischen Liberalismus*. Munich and Berlin, 1933.

———. "Theologischer Rationalismus und vormärzlicher Vulgärliberalismus." *Historische Zeitschrift*, 141 (1930).

———. "Zur Geschichte der Hegelauffassung." In Rudolf Haym, *Hegel und seine Zeit: Vorlesungen über Entstehung und Entwickelung, Wesen, und Wert der Hegel'schen Philosophie*, edited by Hans Rosenberg. 2d ed. Leipzig, 1927.

Rosenkranz, Karl. *Königsberger Skizzen*. Danzig, 1842.

Rothfels, Hans. *Theodor von Schön, Friedrich Wilhelm IV, und die Revolution von 1848*. Halle a. d. S., 1937.

Rotscheidt, Wilhelm. *Quellenkunde zur rheinischen evangelischen Kirchengeschichte*. Essen, 1910.

Ruge, Arnold. *Arnold Ruges Briefwechsel und Tagebuchblätter aus den Jahren 1825–1880*. Edited by Paul Nerrlich. 2 vols. Berlin, 1886.

———. "Drei Briefe über die religiös-politische Bewegung von 1845." In his *Gesammelte Schriften*, Vol. IX. Mannheim, 1847.

———. *Preussen und die Reaktion*. Leipzig, 1838.

———. "Selbstkritik des Liberalismus." In his *Gesammelte Schriften*, Vol. III. Mannheim, 1846.

Rupp, Julius. *Julius Rupp: Briefe, 1831–1884*. Edited by Lina Rupp. Heidelberg, 1907.

———. *Die Symbole oder Gottes Wort? Ein Sendschreiben an die evangelische Kirche Deutschlands*. Königsberg, 1847.

Schaff, Philip. *Germany: Its Universities, Theology, and Religion*. Philadelphia, 1857.

Schaper, Ewald. *Die geistespolitischen Voraussetzungen der Kirchenpolitik Friedrich Wilhelms IV von Preussen*. Stuttgart, 1938.

Scheibel, Johann Gottfried. *Actenmässige Geschichte der neuesten Unternehmung einer Union zwischen der reformierten und lutherischen Kirche vorzüglich durch gemeinschaftliche Agende in Deutschland und besonders in dem Preussischen Staate*. 2 vols. Leipzig, 1834.

———. *Geschichte der lutherischen Gemeinde in Breslau vom Nov. 1830 bis zum Februar 1832*. Nuremberg, 1832.

———. *Luthers Agende und die neue Preussische*. Leipzig, 1836.

———. *Mein Weg und mein Recht*. Nuremberg, 1834.

———. *Mitteilungen über die neueste Geschichte der Lutherischen Kirche*. 2 vols. Altona, 1837–1838.

[———.] *Das trennende Unionswerk: oder, Die neue preussische Agende, Beleuchtet von einem evangelischen-lutherischen Geistlichen*. Breslau, 1832.

Schellbach, Martin. *Tholucks Predigt: Ihre Grundlage und ihre Bedeutung für die heutige Praxis*. Berlin, 1956.

Schiele, Friedrich M. *Die kirchliche Einigung des evangelischen Deutschlands im 19. Jahrhundert.* Tübingen, 1908.

Schieler, Carl. *Dr. Julius Rupp, ehem. Privatdozent, Oberlehrer, und Divisionsprediger zu Königsberg in Preussen und die freie religiöse Bewegung in der katholischen und evangelischen Kirche Deutschlands im 19. Jahrhundert: Ein Beitrag zur Kirchengeschichte des 19. Jahrhunderts.* Dresden, 1903.

Schilfert, Gerhard. *Sieg und Niederlage des demokratischen Wahlrechts in der deutschen Revolution, 1848–1849.* Berlin, 1952.

Schleiermacher, Friedrich. *The Life of Friedrich Schleiermacher as Unfolded in his Autobiography and Letters.* Translated by Frederica Rowan. 2 vols. London, 1860.

———. *Sämmtliche Werke.* Edited by Georg Reimer. 30 vols. in 29. Berlin, 1835–1884.

———. *Schleiermachers Werke.* Edited by Otto Braun and Johannes Bauer. 4 vols. Leipzig, 1910–1913.

———. *Soliloquies.* Translated by H. L. Friess. Chicago, 1926.

———. *Über die Religion: Reden an die Gebildeten unter ihren Verächtern.* 3d ed. Berlin, 1821.

Schnabel, Franz. *Deutsche Geschichte im neunzehnten Jahrhundert.* 3d and 4th eds. 4 vols. Freiburg i. B., 1948–1955.

Schoeps, Hans Joachim. *Das andere Preussen: Konservative Gestalten und Probleme im Zeitalter Friedrich Wilhelms IV.* Stuttgart, 1952.

———. *Die Ehre Preussens.* Stuttgart, 1951.

———. "Die lutherische Hochorthodoxie Preussens und der Katholizismus: Friedrich Heiler zum 60. Geburtstag." *Zeitschrift für Religions- und Geistesgeschichte,* 4 (1952).

———. "Neues zur preussischen Geistesgeschichte des 19. Jahrhunderts." *Zeitschrift für Religions- und Geistesgeschichte,* 17 (1965).

———. "Ungedrucktes aus den Tagebüchern Ludwig von Gerlachs." *Zeitschrift für Religions- und Geistesgeschichte,* 16 (1964).

———, ed. *Aus den Jahren Preussischer Not und Erneuerung: Tagebücher und Briefe der Gebrüder Gerlach und ihres Kreises, 1805–1820.* Berlin, 1963.

Schrader, Wilhelm. *Geschichte der Friedrichs Universität zu Halle.* 2 vols. Berlin, 1894.

Schramm, Percy Ernst. *Hamburg, Deutschland, und die Welt: Leistung und Grenzen hanseatischen Bürgertums in der Zeit zwischen Napoleon I und Bismarck: Ein Kapitel deutscher Geschichte.* Munich, 1943.

Schubarth, Karl Friedrich. *Über die Unvereinbarkeit der Hegelschen Staatslehre mit dem obersten Lebens- und Entwicklungsprinzip des Preussischen Staats.* Leipzig, 1839.

Schubert, Ernst. *Die evangelische Predigt im Revolutionsjahr 1848: Ein Beitrag zur Geschichte der Predigt wie zum Problem der Zeitpredigt.* Giessen, 1913.

Schüddekopf, Otto Ernst. *Die deutsche Innenpolitik im letzten Jahrhundert und der konservative Gedanke.* Brunswick, 1951.

Schulte, F. von. *Karl Friedrich Eichhorn: Sein Leben und Wirken*. Stuttgart, 1884.

Schulte, Wilhelm. *Volk und Staat: Westfalen im Vormärz und in der Revolution 1848–49*. Münster, 1954.

Schulz, David. *Unfug an heiliger Stätte: oder, Entlarvung Dr. J. G. Scheibels*. Breslau, 1821.

———. *Das Wesen und Treiben der Berliner Evangelischen Kirchenzeitung*. Breslau, 1839.

Schuselka, Franz. *Deutsche Volkspolitik*. Hamburg, 1846.

———. *Deutsche Worte eines Österreichers*. Hamburg, 1843.

———. *Die Lösung der preussischen Verfassungsfrage*. Hamburg, 1847.

———. *Die neue Kirche und die alte Politik*. Leipzig, 1845.

Schwarz, Karl. *Zur Geschichte der neuesten Theologie*. 2d ed. Leipzig, 1856.

———. *Dr. Rupps Ausschliessung aus dem Gustav-Adolf-Verein: Eine Streitschrift*. Berlin, 1846.

———. *Das Wesen der Religion*. Halle, 1847.

Seeberg, Reinhold. *Die Kirche Deutschlands im neunzehnten Jahrhundert*. 2d ed. Leipzig, 1904.

Seegert, Reinhart. *Friedrich Engels: Die religiöse Entwicklung des Spätpietisten und Frühsozialisten*. Halle, 1935.

Selle, Götz von. *Geschichte der Albertus Universität zu Königsberg in Preussen*. Würzburg, 1956.

Shanahan, William O. *German Protestants Face the Social Question: The Conservative Phase, 1815–1871*. Notre Dame, Indiana, 1954.

———. *Prussian Military Reforms, 1786–1813*. New York, 1945.

Sie wissen was sie wollen! Eine Verteidigungsschrift in Sachen der protestantischen Freunde. Leipzig, 1846.

Siegfried, André, and Latreille, André. *Les forces religieuses et la vie politique: Le catholicisme et le protestantisme*. Paris, 1951.

Simon, Walter M. *The Failure of the Prussian Reform Movement, 1807–1819*. Ithaca, N.Y., 1955.

Stadelmann, Rudolf. *Soziale und politische Geschichte der Revolution von 1848*. Munich, 1948.

Stahl, Friedrich Julius. *Die gegenwärtigen Parteien in Staat und Kirche*. Berlin, 1863.

Steig, Rudolf. *Heinrich von Kleists Berliner Kämpfe*. Berlin, 1901.

Stern, Fritz. *The Politics of Cultural Despair: A Study in the Rise of the Germanic Ideology*. Berkeley and Los Angeles, 1961.

Stillich, Oscar. *Die politischen Parteien in Deutschland*. 2 vols. Leipzig, 1908–1911.

Strauss, David Friedrich. *Die Halben und die Ganzen: Eine Streitschrift gegen die HH. DD. Schenkel und Hengstenberg*. Leipzig, 1865.

———. *Das Leben Jesu kritisch bearbeitet*. 2 vols. Tübingen, 1835–1836.

Struve, Gustav von. *Briefe über die Kirche und Staat*. Mannheim, 1846.

———. *Diesseits und jenseits des Oceans*. 4 vols. Coburg, 1863–1864.

Thadden, Rudolf von. *Die Brandenburg-Preussischen Hofprediger im 17. und*

18. Jahrhundert: Ein Beitrag zur Geschichte der absolutistischen Staatsgesellschaft in Brandenburg-Preussen. Berlin, 1959.

Thadden-Trieglaff, Adolf von. *Der Schacher mit Rittergütern: Vorgetragen in der General-Versammlung der Pommerschen ökonomischen Gesellschaft am 10. Mai 1842, zu Coeslin, 1844.* N.p., n.d.

―――. *Über Menschenschau unter Landwirten: Rede gehalten am 21. April 1839 zu Regenwalde.* Berlin, 1842.

Thierbach, C. *Gustav Adolf Wislicenus: Ein Lebensbild aus der Geschichte der freien religiösen Bewegung, zu seinem 100 jährigen Geburtstag.* Leipzig, 1904.

Tholuck, F. A. G. *Die Glaubwürdigkeit der evangelischen Geschichte: Zugleich eine Kritik des Lebens Jesu von Strauss.* Halle, 1837.

[―――.] *Die Lehre von der Sünde und vom Versöhner: oder, Die wahre Weihe des Zweiflers.* Hamburg, 1823.

―――. *Predigten über die neuesten Zeitbewegungen.* Halle, 1848.

[―――.] *Eine Stimme wider die Theaterlust.* Berlin, 1827.

―――. *Vermischte Schriften.* Hamburg, 1839.

―――. *Vier Predigten über die Bewegungen der Zeit, gehalten im akademischen Gottesdienste der Universität Halle im Sommer 1845.* Halle, 1845.

Thomas, R. Hinton. *Liberalism, Nationalism, and the German Intellectuals, 1822-1847: An Analysis of the Academic and Scientific Conferences of the Period.* Cambridge, England, 1951.

Tidemann, Heinrich. "Pastor Rudolf Dulon: Ein Beitrag zur Geschichte der Märzrevolution in Bremen." *Bremisches Jahrbuch,* 33 (1931) and 34 (1934).

Tiesmeyer, Ludwig. *Die Erweckungsbewegung in Deutschland während des 19. Jahrhunderts.* 4 vols. Kassel, 1901-1912.

Tillich, Paul. *Perspectives on 19th and 20th Century Protestant Theology.* New York, 1967.

―――. "The Social Functions of the Churches in Europe and America." *Social Research,* 3 (1936).

Tischhauser, Christian. *Geschichte der evangelischen Kirche Deutschlands in der ersten Hälfte des 19. Jahrhunderts.* Basel, 1900.

Treitschke, Heinrich von. *Deutsche Geschichte im neunzehnten Jahrhundert.* 5 vols. Leipzig, 1874-1879.

Treue, Wilhelm. "Adam Smith in Deutschland: Zum Problem des 'politischen Professors' zwischen 1776 und 1810." In *Deutschland und Europa: Festschrift für Hans Rothfels,* edited by Werner Conze. Düsseldorf, 1951.

Troeltsch, Ernst. *Die Bedeutung des Protestantismus für die Entstehung der modernen Welt.* Munich and Berlin, 1911.

―――. *Gesammelte Schriften,* IV, *Aufsätze zur Geistesgeschichte und Religionssoziologie.* Edited by Hans Baron. Tübingen, 1925.

―――. *The Social Teachings of the Christian Churches.* 2 vols. London, 1949.

Tschirch, Otto. *Geschichte der öffentlichen Meinung in Preussen vom Baseler Frieden bis zum Zusammenbruch des Staates, 1795-1806.* Weimar, 1933.

Tschirn, Gustav. *Zur 60-jährigen Geschichte der frei-religiösen Bewegung.* Bamberg, 1904.

Tzschirner, Heinrich Gottlieb. *Die Gefahr einer deutschen Revolution.* Leipzig, 1823.

————. *Protestantismus und Katholizismus aus dem Standpunkte der Politik.* Leipzig, 1822.

Uhlich, Leberecht. *Leberecht Uhlich: Sein Leben von ihm selbst beschrieben.* Gera, 1872.

————. *Die Novembertage in Berlin und Brandenburg, Zugleich ein politisches Bekenntnis: Dokumente zur Revolution von 1848.* Magdeburg, 1848.

————. *Die protestantischen Freunde: Sendschreiben an die Christen des deutschen Volkes.* Dessau, 1843.

————. *Siebzehn Sätze in Bezug auf die Verpflichtungsformel protestantischer Geistlicher, ausgegangen von der Synode zu Berlin 1846.* Wolfenbüttel, 1846.

————. *Die Throne im Himmel und auf Erden und die protestantischen Freunde: Eine Erörterung zunächst den Lenkern von Staat und Kirche.* Dessau, 1845.

————. *Über den Amtseid der Geistlichen.* Leipzig, 1847.

————. *Zehn Jahre in Magdeburg, 1845–1855.* Magdeburg, 1855.

Urkunden betreffend die neuesten Ereignisse in der Kirche und auf dem Gebiete der Theologie zunächst in Halle und Berlin, Gesammelt und herausgegeben zur richtigen Beurtheilung und sorgfältigen Erwägung für alle wahre Freunde der evangelischen Kirche. Leipzig, 1830.

Urkunden über das Verfahren des Königlichen Consistorii zu Magdeburg gegen den Pastor Sintenis, mitgeteilt von einem Freunde der Wahrheit. Leipzig, 1840.

Valentin, Veit. *Geschichte der deutschen Revolution von 1848–1849.* 2 vols. Berlin, 1930–1931.

————. *The German People: Their History and Civilization from the Holy Roman Empire to the Third Reich.* New York, 1946.

Valjavec, Fritz. *Die Entstehung der politischen Strömungen in Deutschland, 1770–1815.* Munich, 1951.

Verhandlungen der Evangelischen General-Synode zu Berlin vom 2. Juni bis zum 29. August 1846: Amtlicher Abdruck. Berlin, 1846.

Verhandlungen der Provinzial-Versammlung des Hauptvereins der Gustav-Adolf-Stiftung in der Rheinprovinz. Elberfeld, 1847.

Verhandlungen der Vierten Rheinischen Provinzial-Synode: August–September 1844. Barmen, 1845.

Die Verhandlungen der Wittenberger Versammlung für Gründung eines deutschen evangelischen Kirchenbundes im September 1848. Berlin, 1848.

Verhandlungen des zum 2. April 1848 zusammenberufenen Vereinigten Landtages. Edited by E. Bleich. Berlin, 1848.

Vermeil, Edmond, Hahn, K. J., and Le Bras, Gabriel. *Les églises en Allemagne.* Paris, 1949.

Viebahn, Georg von. *Statistik des zollvereinten und nördlichen Deutschlands.* 3 vols. Berlin, 1858-1868.

Wagener, Hermann. *Die kleine aber mächtige Partei.* Berlin, 1885.

Wangemann, Hermann Theodor. *Drei preussische Dragonaden wider die lutherische Kirche.* Berlin, 1884.

————. *Geistiges Regen und Ringen am Ostseestrand: Ein kirchengeschichtliches Lebensbild der ersten Hälfte des 19. Jahrhunderts.* Berlin, 1861.

————. *Die kirchliche Cabinetts-Politik des Königs Friedrich Wilhelm III, insbesonderheit in Beziehung auf Kirchenverfassung, Agende, Union, Separatismus.* Berlin, 1884.

————. *Sieben Bücher preussischer Kirchengeschichte: Eine aktenmässige Darstellung des Kampfes um die lutherische Kirche im 19. Jahrhundert.* 4 vols. Berlin, 1859-1861.

Weidemann, Karl. *Die Pietisten in Halle in ihrer tiefsten Erniedrigung: oder, Was wollen die Pietisten in Preussen.* Merseburg, 1830.

Weigelt, Horst. "Interpretations of Pietism in the Research of Contemporary German Historians." *Church History,* 39 (1970).

Wendland, Walter. *Kirchengeschichte der Mark Brandenburg.* Berlin, 1929.

————. *Ludwig Ernst von Borowski, Erzbischof der Evangelischen Kirche in Preussen.* Königsberg, 1910.

————. "Die praktische Wirksamkeit Geistlicher im Zeitalter der Aufklärung, 1740-1806." *Jahrbuch für Brandenburgische Kirchengeschichte,* 9 (1913).

————. *Die Religiosität und die kirchenpolitischen Grundsätze Friedrich Wilhelms des Dritten in ihrer Bedeutung für die Geschichte der kirchlichen Restauration.* Giessen, 1909.

————. *Siebenhundert Jahre Kirchengeschichte Berlins.* Berlin and Leipzig, 1930.

————. "Studien zur Erweckungsbewegung in Berlin, 1810-1830." *Jahrbuch für Brandenburgische Kirchengeschichte,* 19 (1924).

————. "Zur reaktionären Gesinnung R. F. Eylerts." *Jahrbuch für Brandenburgische Kirchengeschichte,* 10 (1913).

Werdermann, Hermann. *Die deutsche evangelische Pfarrfrau: Ihre Geschichte in 4 Jahrhunderten.* Wittenberg, 1935.

————. *Der evangelische Pfarrer in Geschichte und Gegenwart: Im Rückblick auf 400 Jahre evangelisches Pfarrhaus.* Leipzig, 1925.

————. *Pfarrerstand und Pfarramt im Zeitalter der Orthodoxie in der Mark Brandenburg.* Berlin, 1929.

Wichern, Johann Hinrich. *Gesammelte Schriften.* Edited by Friedrich Mahling. 6 vols. Hamburg, 1901-1908.

Wiegand, Friedrich. "Eine Schwärmerbewegung in Hinterpommern." *Deutsche Rundschau,* 167 (1921).

————. "Der Verein der Maikäfer in Berlin." *Deutsche Rundschau,* 160 (1914).

Winter, Friedrich Julius. *August Kahnis: ein theologisches Lebens- und Charakterbild.* Leipzig, 1896.

Winter, Friedrich Julius, ed. *Geistliche Weckstimmen aus der Zeit der Erniedrigung und Erhebung unseres Volks.* Leipzig, 1913.

Wislicenus, Gustav Adolf. *Ob Schrift? Ob Geist? Verantwortung gegen meine Ankläger.* 2d ed. Leipzig, 1845.

Witte, Hermann. *Die pommerschen Konservativen: Männer und Ideen, 1810–1860.* Berlin and Leipzig, 1936.

Witte, Leopold. *Das Leben D. Friedrich August Gotttreu Tholucks.* 2 vols. Bielefeld and Leipzig, 1884–1886.

Wittram, Reinhard. *Das nationale als europäisches Problem.* Göttingen, 1954.

———. *Nationalismus und Säkularisation: Beiträge zur Geschichte und Problematik des Nationalgeistes.* Lüneburg, 1949.

Woelbling, F. *Der Gotteskämpfer: Leichenpredigt über Moses, 32, 28, vor der Beisetzung der Leiche Ernst Wilhelm Hengstenbergs.* Neu-Rupping, 1869.

Woeniger, A. T. *Wislicenus und seine Gegner.* Leipzig, 1845.

Ziegler, Theobald. *D. F. Strauss.* 2 vols. Strassburg, 1908.

———. *Die geistigen und sozialen Strömungen des neunzehnten Jahrhunderts.* Rev. ed. Berlin, 1916.

———. *Menschen und Probleme.* Berlin, 1914.

Zschiesche, Carl. *Die protestantischen Freunde, Eine Selbstkritik: Sendschreiben an Uhlich.* Altenburg, 1847.

Zum Gedächtnis Dr. Heinrich Leonhard Heubners, zum Besten der Heubnerstiftung, herausgegeben von den Mitgliedern des Königl. Prediger-Seminars. Wittenberg, 1853.

CONTEMPORARY PERIODICALS AND NEWSPAPERS

Allgemeine Kirchen-Zeitung. Darmstadt. 1822–1848.

Evangelische Kirchen-Zeitung. Berlin. 1827–1850.

Hallische Jahrbücher. Halle. 1837–1841.

Jahrbücher der Gegenwart. Halle. 1846–1847.

Kirchliche Reform: Monatsschrift für freie Protestanten aller Stände. Halle. 1846–1847.

Reform. Halle. 1848.

Trier'sche Zeitung. Treves. 1847.

Index

291